Queer in a Wee Place

Queer in a Wee Place

Small Nations, Sexuality and Scotland

Edited by
Yvette Taylor

BLOOMSBURY ACADEMIC
LONDON • NEW YORK • OXFORD • NEW DELHI • SYDNEY

BLOOMSBURY ACADEMIC
Bloomsbury Publishing Plc, 50 Bedford Square, London, WC1B 3DP, UK
Bloomsbury Publishing Inc, 1359 Broadway, New York, NY 10018, USA
Bloomsbury Publishing Ireland, 29 Earlsfort Terrace, Dublin 2, D02 AY28, Ireland

BLOOMSBURY, BLOOMSBURY ACADEMIC and the Diana logo are trademarks of
Bloomsbury Publishing Plc

First published in Great Britain 2026

Copyright © Yvette Taylor, 2026

Yvette Taylor has asserted her right under the Copyright, Designs and Patents Act, 1988, to be identified as Editor of this work.

For legal purposes the Acknowledgements on p. viii constitute an extension of this copyright page.

Cover design and illustration by Madeleine Leisk

This work is published open access subject to a Creative Commons Attribution-NonCommercial 4.0 International licence (CC BY-NC 4.0, https://creativecommons.org/licenses/by-nc/4.0/). You may re-use, distribute, reproduce, and adapt this work in any medium for non-commercial purposes, provided you give attribution to the copyright holder and the publishers, provide a link to the Creative Commons licence, and indicate if changes have been made.

No part of this publication may be used or reproduced in any way for the training, development or operation of artificial intelligence (AI) technologies, including generative AI technologies. The rights holders expressly reserve this publication from the text and data mining exception as per Article 4(3) of the Digital Single Market Directive (EU) 2019/790. Bloomsbury Publishing Plc does not have any control over, or responsibility for, any third-party websites referred to or in this book. All internet addresses given in this book were correct at the time of going to press. The author and publisher regret any inconvenience caused if addresses have changed or sites have ceased to exist, but can accept no responsibility for any such changes.

A catalogue record for this book is available from the British Library.

A catalog record for this book is available from the Library of Congress.

ISBN: HB: 978-1-3505-1303-7
PB: 978-1-3505-1302-0
ePDF: 978-1-3505-1305-1
eBook: 978-1-3505-1304-4

Typeset by Newgen KnowledgeWorks Pvt. Ltd., Chennai, India
Printed and bound in Great Britain

For product safety related questions contact productsafety@bloomsbury.com.

To find out more about our authors and books visit www.bloomsbury.com and sign up for our newsletters.

Contents

Acknowledgements viii
Notes on Contributors ix

Introduction

1   Big conversations in queer wee places: Small nations, sexuality and Scotland   3
    Yvette Taylor

Part 1 Queer Counts! Categories, Legalities and Challenges

2   Yes!   23
    Robyn O'Donnell

3   Hate crime in Scotland and the classification of queer lives: Doors, data and definitions   25
    Kevin Guyan

4   Queer hope and LGBTQ+ rights in a wee place   39
    Sharon Cowan

5   The construction of Scotland's LGBTQ+ population in the census   51
    Kirstie Ken English

6   The revolt and revolting   65
    Jj Fadaka

Part 2 Queer States: Legacies and Transformations

7   Queer provincialisms in (post-)Brexit Britain   79
    Yvette Taylor

8   Scotland's menstrual landscape, a red flag?   93
    Kate Molyneaux

9   Queer in Scotland: A wives' tale in conversation   105
    Aoife Christoffersen and Ashlee Christoffersen

10	Being queer in Scotland: Conversational snapshots *Dario Luis Banegas and Drew Bain*	117
11	Queer New Scots? On migration, queerness and Scottish exceptionalism *Francesca Stella*	129
12	Assemblages *Mae Diansangu*	141

Part 3 Queer Homelands: Myths, Migrations and Movements

13	Leaving is queer: Loving and leaving a wee place *Finn Mackay*	153
14	The aul' days: Ewan Forbes and the ghost in the machine *Zoë Playdon*	165
15	A queer poetics of belonging: From *dui Bangla* to Glasgow *Tanvir Alim and Rohit K. Dasgupta*	177
16	Lessons in geography: Learning from Maud Sulter *Natasha Thembiso Ruwona*	189
17	Unintended *poiesis* *Sindhu Rajasekaran*	199

Part 4 Queer Creations: Vibrations, Glitches and Curiosities

18	Queer wee filmic places: Creating a utopic gaze through queer film exhibition in Scotland *Leanne Dawson*	213
19	Queer curiosities: LGBTQ+ equity in Scotland's museums *Joe Setch*	225
20	After Morgan: On legacy and queer elders in poetry *Andrés N. Ordorica*	237
21	Brilliant vibrating interface: Queering the post-internet through poetry and practice *Kirsty Dunlop and Maria Sledmere*	247

22 International stories on a Scottish stage: A conversation on
    representation, recognition and activism through the *As Is* ethnodrama   261
    Harvey Humphrey, Slater Cain, Gina Gwenffrewi, Leni Daly,
    Odhran Thomson and Mathew Wilkie

Part 5 Queer Education: (Post-)Compulsory Classroom Contexts

23 Black Scottish writing and the fiction of diversity   275
    Churnjeet Mahn

24 Welcome home? Finding your (queer) place in Scotland and in STEM   291
    Marco Reggiani and Jessica Gagnon

25 Disabled queer student experiences of Scottish higher education   305
    Jack McKinlay

26 NOHOMO in the classroom: Queer ideas through and beyond Scottish
    classrooms   317
    Dan Brown

Index   329

Acknowledgements

Thanks to everyone who presented at and attended the 'Queer and the Cost of Living Crisis' seminar series, which ran from 2023 to 2025 as part of my Royal Society of Edinburgh (RSE) personal fellowship 'Queer Social Justice'. I am grateful to the RSE for funding received and to follow-up impact acceleration funds, which resulted in a series of 'Queer Social Justice Pop-Ups' throughout Scotland, also enabling conversations with key activists, organizations and authors represented in this book: LGBTQ+ student representatives at universities across Scotland; Rebecca Don Kennedy of the Equality Network; Vic Vallentine at the Scottish Trans Alliance; Patrick Harvie (MSP) and Emma Roddick (MSP); Jordan Daly from Time for Inclusive Education (TIE); Sue John and Adele Patrick from Glasgow Women's Library (GWL); and author Ely Percy. Thanks to Amanda Aitken for producing an accessible sound file for the longer GWL interview referenced in the introductory chapter to this volume: 'Conversations with Glasgow Women's Library Co-Directors Sue John & Adele Patrick: Queer in a Wee Place'.

Thanks to those involved in the 'Queer in a Wee Place: Small Nations, Sexuality and Scotland' conference at the University of Strathclyde, which far exceeded my expectations as a profoundly collegial, hopeful and passionate place – this was a stand-out conference and a reason for doing the work in and out of academia! Thanks to the Glasgow-based MLK social enterprise for the catering, and to Maddie Breeze and Churnjeet Mahn for emergency weekend delivery ensuring all were well-fed! Thanks to Madeleine Leisk for so carefully and beautifully producing an illustrated guide to the 'Queer and the Cost of Living Crisis' seminar series, available open access, and to Chloe Henderson of Coin-Operated Press CIC who facilitated a 'Queer Social Justice' zine workshop. Copies of these zines have been made available at Lighthouse Books, Category Is, the Glasgow Zine Library, the Highland Zine Bothy and are archived at the University of Strathclyde.

A version of Chapter 7 by Yvette Taylor appeared in Y. Taylor, *Working-Class Queers. Time, Place and Politics* (London: Pluto, 2023). A version of Chapter 24 by Churnjeet Mahn appeared in M. Breeze, Y. Taylor and C. Costa, *Time and Space in the Neoliberal University. Fractures and Futures in Higher Education.* (Switzerland AG: Springer Nature, 2019). Thanks are given to publishers for enabling reproduction here.

Thanks most of all to the contributors to this collection who have shared their sense of queer in (and beyond) Scotland, as misfit, practice, belonging, escape – and often as work still to do.

Notes on Contributors

Tanvir Alim completed their PhD at the School of Social and Political Sciences at the University of Glasgow and holds a masters in Social Work. Their research explores forms of collective action in South Asia, focusing on NGOization and digital culture. A self-taught interdisciplinary artist working with both textual and visual media, Tanvir combines a background in arts management and community organizing and is committed to community-based, multidisciplinary collaborations at the intersection of lived experiences and independent publishing. Tanvir has curated and facilitated workshops and exhibitions at various institutions, including the Refugee Festival Scotland, Schwules Museum Berlin and many others.

Drew Bain is Community and Engagements Coordinator at Duncan Place, Leith. He has worked with different charities in Scotland, including LGBT Health and Wellbeing. He is a strong advocate for the inclusion of all gender identities. Drew and Dario Luis Banegas have been together since January 2022.

Dario Luis Banegas is Senior Lecturer in Language Education at Moray House School of Education and Sport, University of Edinburgh. He is involved in community engagement, research and teaching projects connected to gender and sexuality in language teaching and intersectionality in language teacher education.

Dan Brown is a queer, working-class dance artist and practitioner from Blackburn, West Lothian, now based in Glasgow. His work exists in dance, contemporary performance and film and utilizes persona and popular iconography to contextualize meaning and mediate his own autobiography, opening up the micro to relate to the macro. Dan has made a variety of short films through primary school residencies with 21Common and Reconnect Regal, which places the young people at the heart of the creation of the film and allows them to become autonomous collaborators.

Slater Cain (they/them) is a director, producer and puppeteer based in Glasgow. Awarded a Bachelor of Fine Arts in Theatre Arts from Boston University, Slater spent six years making independent theatre in Brooklyn before relocating to Glasgow after the pandemic. Their work seeks to explore and celebrate the queer and trans experience while creating safe spaces for community to blossom. Their select directorial credits include *As Is* (world premiere), *The Obligatory Scene* (international – IDGTF '19 and Fresh Fruit '19), *WE ReMember*, *The Zero Hour* and *Passing* (world premiere).

Aoife Christoffersen (she/her) is a non-academic residing in Scotland from 1999 to 2022. She works as an instrumentation technician in the offshore oil and gas industry since 2002. She came out as queer and trans at age thirty-three, in 2018, going through medical and social transition since then, and navigating socially in her personal, college and professional life in an industry not renowned for queer acceptance. Aoife is a technically minded and practical person but also expresses her artistic side through various musical outlets, painting and drawing.

Ashlee Christoffersen (she/her) is an academic who lived and worked in Edinburgh from 2016 to 2022. Previously Ashlee worked in the LGBT sector in London. Ashlee is currently a Banting Postdoctoral Researcher at York University (Toronto) and an honorary fellow at the University of Edinburgh. She is the author of *The Politics of Intersectional Practice: Representation, Coalition and Solidarity in UK NGOs* (2024).

Sharon Cowan is Professor of Feminist and Queer Legal Studies at the School of Law, University of Edinburgh. Her research focuses on gender, sex and sexuality-related issues across a range of areas, including equality law, asylum law, and criminal law and criminal justice. Her recent research includes a comparative socio-legal project looking at the impact of law on transgender people; a project on trans-inclusive practices in museums and galleries; law and policy on sexual misconduct on campus; and a Scottish government-funded project examining the operation of 'rape shield' legislation and the use of complainers' sexual history evidence in Scottish sexual offences trials.

Leni Daly (they/them) is an actor and writer based in Fife. Graduating with a diploma in stage and screen performance in 2020, Leni aims to write for LGBTQ+ audiences and include trans and queer characters in their work. Writing these plays also means creating more jobs for queer people, extending to both cast and crew. Their first play, *Nightlight*, explores themes of mental health, working-class power struggles, disability and living outside the gender binary. Before delving into the arts, Leni obtained a degree in conservation biology from the University of Stirling, specializing in ecological bat work. They are a lover of comedy, oranges and trans joy.

Rohit K. Dasgupta is Associate Professor of Gender and Sexuality Studies, LSE and a visiting fellow at the University of Glasgow. Rohit co-authored *Desi Queers* (2025) with Churnjeet Mahn and DJ Ritu.

Leanne Dawson is Senior Lecturer in Film Studies and German Studies and an Equity, Diversity and Inclusion consultant. Her publications include *Queering German Culture* (2018), *Queer European Cinema* (2017), *Crisis–Connection–Culture: Alternative Responses to Covid-19* (2020), *Queer/ing Film Festivals* (2018), *Queer European Cinema* (2016) and *The Other: Gender, Sexuality and Ethnicity in European Cinema and Beyond* (2014). She was the first chair of the Scottish Queer International Film Festival, works with several other international film festivals and has teamed up with organizations such as the Independent Cinema Office, Inclusive Cinema and the British Film Institute to improve diversity and inclusion onscreen.

Mae Diansangu is a queer poet and spoken-word artist from Aberdeen. She has performed at literary festivals across Scotland and appeared on BBC Scotland's *Big Scottish Book Club* and BBC Radio 4's *Tongue and Talk*. Her series of poems 'black lives, heavy truths' is part of the National Library of Scotland's collection. You can read her work in the anthologies 'Tales fae the Doric Side' and 'Re creation – a queer poetry anthology'. Mae writes in both English and Doric, and her first collection *Bloodsongs* was published in autumn 2024.

Kirsty Dunlop is an interdisciplinary writer and new media researcher based in Glasgow. She is currently undertaking a doctorate in creative writing at the University of Glasgow, writing and coding interactive, electronic work on her practice-based concept 'Emergent Essaying', thinking through video gameplay design in collaboration with technology, language, experimentation and hybridity. They are editor-in-chief at SPAM Press, a tutor in creative writing and English literature at the University of Glasgow and regularly lead workshops and guest lectures on electronic literature, most recently with the Edinburgh Futures Institute. Their published research can be found here: Springer for ICIDS: Interactive Storytelling.

Kirstie Ken English is a mixed-methods social researcher and quantitative-methods tutor at the University of Glasgow. Their interests and expertise are in the production and use of equality, diversity and inclusion data, gender, sexuality and human rights. Their PhD in sociology was on 'How differences in terms of sex and gender should be represented by UK population surveys'. They strive to promote better data literacy and reflexive, transparent approaches to data production and application.

Jj Fadaka is a writer, facilitator and radical based in Edinburgh. Their writing explores the possibility of abolition, feminism and love to create change. Their work speaks to the political urgencies we face while centring community-making in our resistance. Jj's spaces, on and off the page, draw on Black feminist radical traditions to explore desire in a world without barriers. You can find them facilitating world-building workshops and juicy conversations. They find belonging in radical pedagogy, music, visual arts and performance.

Jessica Gagnon has worked in higher education in the United States and the UK for twenty years. She is a sociologist of higher education whose research is primarily focused on inequalities, particularly in STEM. Her recent projects include the Royal Society of Chemistry (RSC)-funded LGBTQual+ project, the Engineering and Physical Sciences Research Council (EPSRC)-funded IGNITE Network+ project, the Natural Environment Research Council (NERC)-funded E-DIAL project, and the EPSRC-funded STEM Equals project. She grew up in a working-class, single-mother family and is the first in her family to attend university.

Kevin Guyan is a writer and researcher whose work explores the intersection of data and identity. He is the author of *Rainbow Trap: Queer Lives, Classifications and the Dangers of Inclusion* (2025) and *Queer Data: Using Gender, Sex and Sexuality Data* *for Action* (2022). Kevin is a chancellor's fellow at the University of Edinburgh, and Director of the Gender + Sexuality Data Lab.

Gina Gwenffrewi (she/her) is an interdisciplinary researcher, tutor and lecturer in trans studies, queer studies and English literature at the University of Edinburgh. As well as being an academic manager at SUISS, she lectures and publishes on trans issues relating to trans cultural production, media studies and digital humanities.

Harvey Humphrey (he/they) is an activist-academic and occasional poet, works at the University of Glasgow as a lecturer in social research methods. They focus on co-production, creative methods, creative practice, ethics and representation. Their work cuts across queer disability studies and trans studies. They have published on queer, creative and co-produced methodologies. They also produce theoretical and creative work considering queer, trans and disabled lives.

Finn Mackay is Senior Lecturer in Sociology at the University of the West of England, Bristol, and the author of two books: *Radical Feminism: Activism in Movement* and *Female Masculinities and the Gender Wars*. After a background in domestic abuse prevention policy and the women's sector, Finn returned to academia and completed a PhD at the University of Bristol in the Centre for Gender and Violence Research. Finn is a proud ambassador for the Worker's Educational Association, an editor for the *Journal of Lesbian Studies* and a trustee of the Feminist Archive and the British Sociological Association.

Churnjeet Mahn is Professor of English and Deputy Associate Principal for Research and Knowledge Exchange at the University of Strathclyde. Churnjeet has conducted equalities-led research across several projects including working with a leading refugee and migrant collective to address structural homophobia in the organisation (PI, States of Desire, AHRC) and with heritage sector partners in Scotland to address structural racism (PI AHRC EDI Fellowship; PI White Thinking, AHRC). Alongside this, she served on the Steering Group of the Scottish Government–commissioned Empire, Slavery and Scotland's Museum project which conducted the largest national consultation on public attitudes to race and heritage. Churnjeet has also collaborated on several heritage projects including Curating Discomfort at the Hunterian Museum, where she was involved in the work around the Jamaican Galliwasp (which has been repatriated). Churnjeet is co-author of *Desi Queers: LGBTQ+ South Asians and Cultural Belonging in Britain*, with Rohit K. Dasgupta and DJ Ritu (2025).

Jack McKinlay is a PhD researcher at the Strathclyde Institute of Education, University of Strathclyde. His research explores disabled queer student experiences of Scottish higher education, exploring both institutional structures and everyday experiences of university. He explores how disability and queerness intersect and is experienced within academic and peer spaces, shaping students' place, fit and participation in university. Jack has presented his research at national events and has been a panel speaker at a 'Queer and the Cost of Living' seminar series.

Kate Molyneaux is a PhD graduate in the Strathclyde Institute of Education, University of Strathclyde. Her research experiences of menstruation in Scotland explore the (re)construction of gender and class through the lens of period products, as well as the social ordering of women and girls and their navigation of the social, political and environmental pressures surrounding menstruation. Kate has co-organized the University of Strathclyde's Feminist Research Network from 2020 to 2023. She has presented her work at events on an international level and recently worked on an evaluation of Scottish Ballet Safe to Be Me® programme.

Robyn O'Donnell is a poet and photographer from Edinburgh. Her work is about sex, falling in love too easily and the end of the world. She likes Lego, coffee shops and has had too many long walks on the Montrose beach to tolerate another. She's published in Dyke News, performed across various Edinburgh venues and taken photos of it all for over twenty years.

Andrés N. Ordorica is a queer Latinx writer based in Edinburgh, Scotland. Drawing on his family's immigrant history and his own third-culture upbringing, his writing maps the journey of diaspora and unpacks what it means to be from *ni de aquí, ni de allá* (neither here, nor there). He is the author of the poetry collection *At Least This I Know*. His writing has been shortlisted for the Morley Prize for Unpublished Writers of Colour, the Mo Siewcharran Prize and the Saltire Society's Poetry Book of the Year. *How We Named the Stars* is his first novel.

Zoë Playdon has thirty-five years of experience in front-line LGBTQI human rights. She is Emeritus Professor of Medical Humanities at the University of London and, prior to that, was Professor of Postgraduate Medical Education at both NHS Kent, Surrey, and Sussex Regional Postgraduate Medical Deanery. She is a former co-chair of the Gay and Lesbian Association of Doctors and Dentists (GLADD) and co-founder, with Dr Lynne Jones MP, of the Parliamentary Forum on Gender Identity in 1994. Zoë's recent book, *The Hidden Case of Ewan Forbes*, won a Stonewall US Honor Award and is currently being adapted for television.

Sindhu Rajasekaran has a PhD in creative writing from the University of Strathclyde, where she was a recipient of the Dean's Global Research Award. She is an author, academic and filmmaker. Her debut novel *Kaleidoscopic Reflections* was longlisted for the Crossword Book Award in 2011, while her book of non-fiction is the best-selling *Smashing the Patriarchy: A Guide for the 21st Century Indian Woman*. Sindhu's prose and poetry have appeared in internationally acclaimed literary magazines. She has also published a collection of short stories titled *So I Let It Be* released in 2019. Her PhD research has been published as *Forbidden Desire: How the British Stole India's Queer Pasts and Queer Futures*.

Marco Reggiani is an interdisciplinary researcher whose work straddles urban studies, sustainability, social justice and education. Using an intersectional lens, Marco's research explores the ways institutions reproduce inequalities and addresses issues of visibility and inclusion of marginalized individuals, particularly in STEM and higher education. His recent projects include the RSC-funded LGBTQual+ project and the Engineering and Physical Sciences Research Council (EPSRC)-funded IGNITE Network+ and STEM Equals projects. Marco was the recipient of a Japan Foundation Fellowship for the Revitalizing Shrinking Cities in Japan project, and he is the author of two books about Japanese cultures and everyday lives.

Joe Setch is an Edinburgh-based museum sector professional who works in the marketing team at Museums Galleries Scotland, the national development body for museums. His experience in a variety of voluntary, front-of-house and collections roles at Scottish museums has afforded him valuable insights into how these organizations communicate their aims, interpret their collections and engage with their audiences. In 2018, Joe graduated from the University of Glasgow with an MLitt in Early Modern History, where his studies centred on everyday emotions and experiences in seventeenth-century Scotland.

Maria Sledmere is an artist and writer based in Glasgow. She is Senior Lecturer in English and Creative Writing at the University of Strathclyde, researching and teaching on energy, environment and innovative poetry. Maria was recently included in the Saltire Society's '40 under 40' list celebrating 'outstanding Scottish creatives'. They are managing editor at SPAM Press, tutor at Beyond Form and the87press, and the author of over twenty creative publications including *An Aura of Plasma around the Sun* (2023), *Cocoa and Nothing* (2023, with Colin Herd) and *Visions & Feed* (2022). Her personal website is: www.mariasledmere.com.

Francesca Stella is Senior Lecturer in Sociology at the University of Glasgow, where she convenes the MSc in Global Migrations and Social Justice. Her research and teaching focus on sexuality, migration and gender. She has published widely on these topics. She is a long-standing member of GRAMNet, a network based at the University of Glasgow that brings together researchers, practitioners and activists working on migration and asylum. Her research includes work on lesbian lives in Soviet and post-Soviet Russia, queer migration from Eastern Europe to Scotland, and language learning and migrant 'integration'.

Yvette Taylor is a sociologist in the Strathclyde Institute of Education, who teaches on the interdisciplinary MSc in Applied Gender Studies. Yvette was a Scottish parliamentary fellow, researching LGBTQ+ lives in the pandemic, and has worked with Scottish Ballet exploring inclusive curriculum in schools. Yvette is the author and (co-)editor of numerous books on queer life and class inequality, including *Working-Class Queers: Time, Place and Politics* (2023), *Queer Precarities in and out of Higher Education* (2023) and *The Handbook of Imposter Syndrome* (2022). Yvette completed a Royal Society of Edinburgh Personal Fellowship on Queer Social Justice (2024–5) and organized the 'Queer and the Cost of Living Crisis' seminar series.

Natasha Thembiso Ruwona is a Scottish-Zimbabwean artist-writer, researcher and community events producer. Her work is rooted in place-making and collaboration, where she curates nurturing spaces for people to connect and gather. Her recent projects as an artist include a film commission for Middlesbrough Arts Week 2024 titled *Fugitive Sound Studies*, initially developed as part of the FLAMIN Fellowship 2023–4. In 2023, she was a finalist for the Michael O'Pray Moving-Image Writing Prize, with her writing published in *Art Monthly*. In addition, Natasha was commissioned to create a film for 'Resisting Toxic Climates: Gender, Colonialism, and Environment', a conference hosted by the British Academy and the University of Edinburgh.

Odhran Thomson (he/him) is an actor, writer, poet and habitual apple-cart upsetter. Commissioned by Vanishing Point in 2022, he works to place emphasis on trans and queer joy through his practice – creating the perfect balance of witty mischief and thought-provoking reflections on gender, identity and positivity. Drawing from his experience of transition in the UK, Odhran will bring you intricate rhymes, politics and heartfelt honesty, all with a sense of the optimism of youth. Odhran places a particular focus on creating room for celebration of the calm contentment that can and should accompany queer and trans life in 2023.

Mathew Wilkie (he/him) is a queer activist and researcher focusing on trans liberation and community power. He works across third sector and academic institutions to develop community-led research projects with underserved populations using an assets-based approach. He lectures on an ad-hoc basis on trans liberation within sport and the art of curating trans-inclusive spaces.

Introduction

1

Big conversations in queer wee places: Small nations, sexuality and Scotland

Yvette Taylor

I think because of where my politics sit like people assume I'm really optimistic and idealistic, and I'm actually really cynical ... I spend a lot of time kind of feeling completely defeated and going 'right, well if I can't get this one tiny thing changed how are we going to also change the world?' But it is possible ... Recognising economic, social, and cultural rights as well as civic and political rights in Scotland, it's huge. It's a huge step forward. (Emma Roddick, MSP for the Highlands and Islands[1])

A queer introduction

This collection *Queer in a Wee Place: Small Nations, Sexuality and Scotland* provides wide-ranging views on what it means to be queer in Scotland with a breadth of topics variously pitched as progressive, vibrating, poetic, curious, conversational and creative. Through a series of critical reflections, creative interventions and collaborative exchanges, it explores how sexuality and gender are shaped, counted and contested in the 'wee places' of a small nation with large aspirations. What emerges is not a single story of a queer Scotland, but one that resists simplification, insists on complexity and attends to the ways in which nation, space, identity and belonging are always in flux. Smallness – geographic, demographic or symbolic – can be both a site of erasure and one of imaginative possibility. The potential queering of life in Scotland is tempered or 'glitched' by authors' reluctance regarding reductive measures – whether as census data, hate crime counts or tokenistic classroom content – and an awareness of myth-making around home and nationhood which often reinscribes inequalities of class, gender and race (Strachan 2014; Mahn 2019; Sobande and hill 2022). So, what does it mean to have 'big conversations' about queerness in ostensibly peripheral places?

In between cynicism and desires to 'change the world', this book came about incrementally during many big talks, efforts and organizing, formalized in events, seminars, workshops and a conference: like all these events that precede it, this book continues to commit to being accessible as an open-access publication, and in wanting more from education, outputs and publics (Zaino 2023). To make something open does not automatically make it good or useful, but as a commitment to openness as a pedagogy and practice, this introduction aims to showcase some big conversations, efforts and voices throughout the practice and production of *Queer in a Wee Place* – with an extended invite to readers to decide what this work does and who it is for. Some key voices include not only the authors themselves but also attendees in related workshops, seminars, conferences and pop-up events, who hosted, participated and extended conversations. This introduction pulls in some of these conversations as reflective of a long process in getting to this page: this includes LGBTQ+ student representatives at universities across Scotland; Rebecca Don Kennedy of the Equality Network; Vic Vallentine at the Scottish Trans Alliance; Patrick Harvie (MSP) and Emma Roddick (MSP); Scottish writer Ely Perc; Liam Stevenson of Time for Inclusive Education (TIE); and Glasgow Women's co-directors, Sue John and Adele Patrick.

These conversations are also in dialogue with a range of long-term and newer contributions from LGBTQ+ authors who help diversify the reading list for academic and non-academic audiences, both inside and outside formal classroom spaces and across the shared terrain of wee places which produce significant content, feelings and meanings. In the Scottish context, there has been a proliferation of celebrated books with LGBTQ+ content and often by LGBTQ+ authors – for example, *Wain: LGBT Reimaginings of Scottish Folktales* (Plummer 2019), a stunning collection of LGBT-themed poems retelling Scottish myths like selkies and kelpies, or *Tonguit* (Giles 2015) which offers experimental queer poetry in a blend of English, Orcadian and Scots, with radical, intimate and local resonance. *Young Mungo* followed Booker Prize-winning (2020) *Shuggie Bain* (Stuart 2020, 2022) and echoes similar themes of love, identity and survival, focusing on a queer love story between two young men in sectarian Glasgow. Set in Edinburgh, Radcliffe's *The Old Haunts* (2023) explores grief and gay identity in the 1980s and 1990s, while Logan's *The Gloaming* (2018) tells a magical queer tale set on a Scottish island. There are many more rich literary contributions set in wee nations, such as *Queer Square Mile: Queer Short Stories from Wales* (Bohata et al. 2022) and *The Henna Wars* by Adiba Jaigirdar (2020) set in modern Dublin, following Nishat, a Bangladeshi-Irish teen who comes out as a lesbian; and in these, readers find the questions of identity, community and belonging stretch beyond the pages and beyond a singular place, instead providing queer possibilities.

Like this collection, *Decolonizing Sexualities: Transnational Perspectives, Critical Interventions* offers an interdisciplinary combination of essays, manifestos, poetry and creative work to explore how sexuality, race, gender and religion interweave in transnational settings (Bakshi et al. 2016). Specifically, it challenges colonial knowledge systems and recentres queer and trans people of colour voices globally. *Queer Diasporas* (Patton and Sánchez-Eppler 2000) investigates how queer identity shifts when diasporic peoples cross cultural and national borders, crucial for decentring US norms, as also reflected in *Queer Asia: Decolonising and Reimagining Sexuality and Gender* (Luther and Ung Loh 2024), which, like this collection, builds on conference contributions (the annual Queer Asia Conference). *Queer Sites in Global Contexts: Technologies, Spaces and Otherness* (Ramos and Mowlabocus 2021) offers twelve empirical case studies from Brazil, the Caribbean, the Middle East, Asia and more and highlights how LGBTQ+ people inhabit both digital and physical spaces in marginalized, underrepresented national settings. *Imperialism within the Margins: Queer Representation and the Politics of Culture in Southern Africa* (Spurlin 2006) focused on post-apartheid South Africa queer cultural productions as resisting and intersecting with Euro-American queer norms. In promoting a South–North dialogue which challenges the dominance in theorizing queer knowledge, *Queering Paradigms IV: South–North Dialogues on Queer Epistemologies, Embodiments and Activisms* (Lewis et al. 2014) enables global conversations that criss-cross those axes as pulled from the 'Queering Paradigms' conference held in Rio de Janeiro, Brazil. All these works, and many more important contributions, centre queer experiences in non-Western contexts and confront the limitations of dominant US and Eurocentric queer theory. Methodologically they often use interdisciplinary methods to rethink queer identity and place and highlight how local histories, languages and social systems shape queer lives differently from Western narratives. *Queer in a Wee Place: Small Nations, Sexuality and Scotland* benefits from these contributions and the long-term continued bridging between theory, creative practice and the attentiveness towards coming from *somewhere*, rather than speaking for *everywhere*.

Aware of such harms, this collection also thinks about provincializing the Global North and locating difference where it is often overlooked or not expected: within the North and its 'wee places' of marginality, difference and distinction (see Taylor; Stella; Banegas & Drew, this collection). This is a specific effort in implicating place, and the case of Scotland, while aiming for broader resonance in rescaling international cases, and via structures of, for example, race, ethnicity, class and gender (Fadaka; Mackay; Dawson, this collection), which are mobilized and materialized globally (Thembiso Ruwona; Rajasekaran, this collection). We join others who unpack national specificity while exercising a queer scepticism about nationality and the confines and violences of national boundaries, restricted citizenship status and the everyday infrastructures and intimacies which uphold these (Reggiani & Gagnon; McKinlay; Dan Brown; Setch, this collection): in this, Scotland is just 'another place' to be scaled and stretched through comparable questions of identity, difference and distinction (Christoffersen & Ashlee Christoffersen, this collection; Davidson et al. 2018; Taylor 2023). Several countries have a similar size or population to Scotland, and some examples include the Czech Republic, Ireland and Slovakia: other countries like Denmark, Norway and Finland are larger in area than Scotland but have similar population sizes, while the US state of South Carolina is comparable in size and Singapore is a closer match in terms of population. These scales are invoked not to simply render these relative but also to point to the productive scope of thinking in and across national spaces.

As a final output, this book came about approximately one decade after my own return to Scotland and working back through my own attachments to place, its organizations, institutions and people – many of whom are colleagues, collaborators, campaigners and friends, also represented here. But these attachments are never final and continue to be made in and across generative 'wee places'. Titling an event, or this book, as 'wee' holds a risk that it'll be overlooked, that it won't have 'world leading' impact, or general significance, or global reach. Sometimes being 'queer' or 'wee' can be felt as reductions and misfits – as not relevant or significant enough, as marginal, peripheral or an afterthought. Rather than being everywhere or everything, this collection tries to hold common space, weaving together recent and long-term conversations, including from those attending, supporting, returning to and extending the dialogue. Together we focus on the question of nationhood, identity, transformation and stagnation – whether queer belonging in nation states is something to be hopeful of or suspicious about – and what kinds of traces we leave as we roll the map out, archive or abandon it. This introduction aims to pay respect to the conversations in common that have shaped the collection – and to 'exit well' with a sense of what's to come, signposting chapter contents and future conversations.

Unequal inclusion and the fragility of progress

The opening excerpt from then minister for equalities, migration and refugees, Emma Roddick (MSP), situates big 'world' hopes through tiny changes – often continued and returned to over the long term, felt as exhaustion, as well as recognition. Framed within debates on nationhood and queerness which implicate and surpass Scotland, this book makes a case for looking inwards and outwards, as part of a queer-rescaling effort. To consider these dynamics in the wake of Scotland's independence referendum (2014), the UK's withdrawal from the EU (2020) and ongoing ramifications of crisis, austerity and the Covid-19 pandemic is to situate Scotland not only as a nation in transition but also as one nested within overlapping and contested global structures. The UK itself is increasingly unsettled, the EU remains fractured in key ways, and the broader international order is shaped by the growing assertiveness of hostile right-wing forces that challenge rights to citizenship, belonging and recognition across borders. In this context, left-leaning movements often struggle for visibility or viability within dominant political frameworks worldwide. These developments compel us to think across scales from the local to the global and about how place, identity and policy are made and unmade. Progressive initiatives may emerge as globally celebrated models – or claims – only to be swiftly dismantled (see Guyan; Cowan; English, this collection). Here we think about the scales of place and what comes to matter; where progressive policies may by celebrated, and then revoked; when the Global North remains normative; and where being 'world leading' can be read and felt as violent and ignorant with undertones of colonial continuity (see Fadaka; Dasgupta & Alim; Mahn, this collection).

Inclusion remains persistently under threat and chronically under-resourced. This is evident in the rise and fall of Equality, Diversity and Inclusion (EDI/DEI) initiatives – including those critiqued or dismantled in policy and practice (Zabrowskis 2023).[2] The abrupt withdrawal of equality policies under the US Trump administration, along with the dismissal of DEI advocates from key public bodies, underscores the fragility of progress and its global ramifications. Amid these reversals, the question emerges: how do we hold space for both the pessimism and optimism of what a queer nation might be (Humphrey et al., this collection)? What is, was or could be 'Scotland' and how should it function on the world stage: as an example, an exception, a site of celebration or a cautionary tale?

Across the UK, the Equality Act 2010 was once heralded as a transformative milestone, establishing legal entitlement to equal treatment for minoritized groups. Yet, paradoxically, the same legislation has been used to obstruct the Gender Recognition Reform (Scotland) Bill, with the Westminster government invoking a Section 35 order to block its implementation. The UK Supreme Court has since ruled that the terms 'man', 'woman' and 'sex' in the Equality Act refer solely to biological sex assigned at birth – even for those with Gender Recognition Certificates (GRCs) (see Playdon, this collection, for a historicization of trans presence vis-à-vis changing laws). This legal framing reinforces a hierarchy of 'protected characteristics', often casting them as mutually exclusive or even oppositional. And while some have called for social class to be added as a protected characteristic, such a move remains unlikely in a capitalist framework where class injury is depoliticized, reduced to interpersonal harm rather than addressed as a matter of structural redistribution.

This book builds on and extends several vital, ongoing queer conversations about class (Brim 2020; Dawson 2023; Taylor 2007, 2009, 2023; Alexopoulos et al. 2025), including as a barrier in accessing social and cultural institutions and in enjoying 'progress'. These themes were further explored in the long-term conversations over the course of writing this book, including in the 'Queer and the Cost of Living Crisis'³ seminar series. Although the series was primarily based at the University of Strathclyde (Glasgow), it also aimed to challenge the tendency to over-represent the central belt region *as* Scotland: I invited Scottish National Party MSP Emma Roddick and Green MSP Patrick Harvie – representing both newer and long-standing voices in Scottish politics – whose lived experiences have placed them at the forefront of LGBTQ+ activism. Their contributions have spanned from campaigning for trans rights to fighting for the repeal of Section 28/2A, as one of the early actions of the newly devolved Scottish Parliament. We were joined by Vic Valentine and Rebecca Don Kennedy from the Equality Network, who have taken up the mantle of leadership from the now-retired Tim Hopkins, another key figure in LGBTQ+ rights in Scotland whose advocacy I remember from earlier campaigns for civil partnership and same-sex marriage, now part of legislated mainstream recognition. Incorporation into the mainstream has its costs, and dominant culture often reasserts new margins, even as it absorbs previously excluded identities (see Molyneaux, this collection). Whether we feel hopeful, ambivalent or sceptical about inclusion in state structures and recognized family forms may depend on our own proximity to these emerging (and often familiar) norms (see Christoffersen & Christoffersen, this collection).

Younger LGBTQ+ people often sit outside the normative framing of citizenship, often realized through residency, consumption and employment (see Dan Brown, this collection). These key areas are increasingly precarious for youth, as the range of LGBTQ+ student representatives from across Scottish universities expressed:

> I'm actually the Black Asian minority ethnic representation of the LGBT+ Society – it is such a long name – LGBT+ Society. I often joke about being like the minority of minorities. My friends keep telling me like 'go on dating apps and stuff', and I'm like 'I can't. I'm Muslim, genderfluid, bisexual, potentially have autism, ADHD, disabled. I will get hate crimed'. But like living within all these like minorities it feels like I'm just like on the edge of everything. (LGBTQ+ student representative)

Discussion echoed the need to imagine inclusive content beyond classroom content, as a laudable aim of the TIE Scottish campaigning group. Post-school transitions, including to university, don't always ensure an equalized educational – or employment – experience or outcome (see Mahn; Reggaini & Gagnon, this collection). For many, the state and its social institutions can never be queered, and supporting infrastructures are more threatened than ever before. In our times, the welfare state is rendered more and more precarious, and as Vic Valentine made clear, navigating the system as a trans person often means being let down and falling out of the supposed safety net. Issues of queer unemployment, precarity, homelessness, educational and health inequalities endure, with evidence pointing to increased gaps in a supposedly progressive Scotland.

The promise of civic nationalism is threatened by an inattentiveness to multidimensional inequalities, despite the formalization and even popularized vocabulary of 'protected characteristics' and 'intersectionality'. Some are still 'on the edge of everything'. While editing incoming chapters, I listened to Patrick Harvie's sense of long-term gains alongside persistent and new inequalities, connecting with transphobic backlash familiar to the past times of Section 28/2a's pervasive homophobia. I sat with Emma Roddick's sense of optimism and cynicism in seeing a 'huge step forward' for Scotland, alongside a sense of things still to do. Prevailing anti-trans sentiment featured prominently in discussions and became something to manage in securing venues, audiences and safer spaces – rainbow lanyards were strategically deployed and at a time when the Scottish Parliament banned these. The once-self-declared 'world leading' LGBT-supportive and rainbow-tie-wearing parliament has witnessed and been complicit in many threats to LGBTQ+ rights, now banning rainbow lanyards at Holyrood. Jordan Daly of the TIE campaign expressed a sense of outstanding actions and crisis contexts:

> There are some recommendations from the LGBT Inclusive Education Working Group's Report to the Scottish Ministers (2018) that are still outstanding, particularly relating to review of Scotland's Curriculum, school inspections, qualifications and assessment ... we are also navigating a cultural climate where initiatives related to advancing equity and inclusion for minoritised groups are subject to misrepresentation and attack, while we collectively face a disinformation crisis. With Section 28, we have seen the damage that can be done when moral panic takes hold. It is therefore critical that the Scottish Government continues to uphold and enhance its educational programmes, including LGBT Inclusive Education, that are designed to counter prejudice and support all learners. This includes continuing the rollout of the 'Delivering LGBT Inclusive Education' national professional learning course and working with local authorities to support all teachers to complete it.[4]

Yet the conversations continued in this collection – there was talk of queer creativity, resilience, friendship and joy; of mutual aid, pragmatism and taking care of ourselves and each other (see O'Donnell; Ordorica, this collection). Some attendees got to practise queer yoga as a way of moving together while leaning into our sore points, with support. Which is to also make clear the inequalities within queer communities:

> But, you know, the LGBT+, the queer community, however we frame it, it does have many, many strengths about creating community ... But it's not universal ... And the experience of selfishness and of exclusion is part of the community as well ... it is certainly part of the anti-trans sentiment that's being deliberately cultivated at the moment. There are, you know, I'm really sorry to say, a small proportion of my generation who are pulling the ladder up. Like 'we got our rights. That's fine then isn't it?' ... But we need to talk about that tendency and why it happens and how we, you know, how we be better than that. (Patrick Harvie, MSP)

The events, conversations, pop-ups and workshops have involved poetry readings, letter writing, placard drawings and so on, with urges to repeat activities, to create and consolidate LGBTQ+ community (see also Humphreys et al., this collection). We have called on the Scottish, UK and other international legislators, governments and institutions to improve queer life and to think differently among and outside of community events – including beyond the LGBTQ+ calendar whether as Pride summer or History Months, or international Lesbian, Trans, Bi days. Participant feedback has struck me hard, including the response to the postcard prompt of writing to a colleague or friend and as a reminder of changing local, national and international climates, impacting everyday presences and still felt as exclusion:

> Dear colleagues,
> A 'gentle reminder', once again, that my pronouns are she/her.
> I understand 'nothing is meant' by it, that it's 'force of habit', muscle memory, the fingers just unconsciously hitting 'H-I-S' on the keyboard, the tongue slipping and my identity with it.
> But it has meaning, something *is* meant by it; the unconscious movement of those fingers is a reflection of that unconscious seeing, or not, of me.
> A mind's eye, yours, perceiving a man, fingers following: hand-eye coordination.
> Can you see me? I am right in front of you – see me.
> You don't need to (forget to) translate 'he' to 'she' if you don't fail to see her in the first place.
> Why could you not see her? (Workshop participant feedback)

The phrase 'gentle reminder' carries the weight of the work queer people are often required to do over and over again to be recognized, respected and seen. These are not isolated moments, they recur, and repetition can become erosion (see O'Donnell, this collection). And yet, within these reminding acts of protest and visibility, there is joy, community and sustenance. Can you see her now?

These questions became the sustenance of this book project, as well as the work still to do, reflected in feedback-conveying events as an 'inspiration' at the range and breadth of all the queer research and creativity occurring in this 'wee place' and reminding 'of the impetus behind research':

> Please continue these events! They really do bring communities together and each event has gotten bigger which really shows the need for spaces like this. (Workshop participant feedback)
>
> Interweaving poetry and short stories from queer voices with academic presenters provided a deeper level of meaning to the lived experience of queer people, reminding me of the impetus behind our research. (Workshop participant feedback)

Contributors in this collection convey the impetus and weight of carrying conversations across time and place.

A queer commonplace?

Belonging is often rooted in place as localities or homes that hold a distinct (queer) character, captured by Ely Percy during the December 2024 'Queer in a Wee Place' conference. Ely reflected on coming out in 2001, shortly after Section 28 was repealed in Scotland and the shifting nature of queer spaces, particularly gay bars in the early 2000s, which once felt like strong community hubs. They praised recent developments like the Scottish LGBTQ+ magazine *Somewhere for Us*, which offers a platform for queer arts, culture and storytelling and fills a gap left by older publications like *ScotsGay*. Scotland-based authors Zoe Strachan and Louise Welsh were among Ely's early inspirations starting the 'sort of hunt for other queer Scottish stories' via a dial-up internet search. They described some felt differences between writing, talking and moving across Scotland and England:

> What else is queer about Scotland? Oh, this is a huge one. This is a brilliant question actually ... I lived in England for a wee while and I really did feel like it was a bit backwards. Like being LGBT in England it seemed to carry a weight. I don't know if that was different in the rest of the UK, but from Scotland I felt like you could walk into Glasgow and folk would be like that, 'alright hen, son, whatever you are', you know? But in England it was really, I still felt like there was a sort of, I don't want to say it's a shame, but it was a kind of, a conservativeness. Even with people who would've described themselves as Left ... I thought that there was still that sort of weight. (Ely Percy, author of *Duck Feet*)

In a later conversation, I spoke to Ely about their use of Scots language in writing and work – or weight – as always collective. They weren't exposed to literature in Scots until later in life and recount a formative moment when a tutor introduced them to James Kelman's *How Late It Was, How Late* (1994). This book, written in Scots and featuring a working-class protagonist, showed that writing in one's own voice and dialect could be both valid and celebrated (Kelman won the Booker Prize). However, Ely's early attempts to emulate Kelman's style didn't work, as they were trying to replicate someone else's experience. Only later did their own voice begin to emerge, as joyful, silly, queer, Scottish and working class. Ely began working on writing a queer, localized project inspired by 1980s rom-coms, moving away from the 'tragic lesbian play' they had started (*Julia and Juliet*), favouring instead more celebratory storytelling.

Like Ely, I had lived and worked in various parts of England (York, Newcastle and London). Almost a decade ago, I retraced my steps north somewhat reluctantly, as more of a return-to-the-scene-of-the-crime scenario rather than an easy homecoming. Such movements in, out and beyond Scotland are echoed in other authors' experiences often shaped by longing, fear, hope or stigma – felt through racism, sexism, transphobia and homophobia. Belonging is rarely simple. It manifests as (not) being Scottish, and in desiring more expansive, plural and migratory forms of connection. In this collection, responses to the question 'where are you from?' are addressed with care, hesitance and a queer deliberation – as preferences, routes, trajectories that circulate beyond us. Our queer stories have weight, and the size of this book is testament to that. But in articulating queer potential – always becoming, always vulnerable – authors are also cautious. They aim to hold ground lightly, seeking commonality while also making and giving up space.

Ely expressed a hopeful yet realistic view of the future for queer Scottish literature, emphasizing the urgent need for more diverse voices to be published, especially from New Scots – a term used to include people who have recently moved to Scotland, but which may miss out those who have long been here and are still excluded or not imagined to be 'New Scots', such as Glasgow's long-term South Asian community. Ely acknowledged the persistent challenges in the cultural sector, particularly due to funding cuts and limited publishing opportunities, which often results in talented writers struggling to continue. Ely was fortunate to receive support from Creative Scotland for their next novel, but stressed how many others lack such resources and how the industry frequently neglects writers whose first books don't become commercial hits. High-profile successes, such as *Shuggie Bain* winning the Booker Prize (2020), are rare and hinge on a combination of quality and luck, with major awards providing essential visibility and marketing power. Without such recognition, many deserving works struggle to reach a wider audience, and Ely cautioned that bad representation can be worse than no representation. The desire to see the queer Scottish literary landscape become richer, more inclusive and less constrained by commercial or cultural gatekeeping is a desire to complicate claims to space:

> But for me, a white person, I don't want to write from the first-person point of view of somebody that's, you know, that's a new Scot or whatever, because I don't have that experience. And somebody that's a new Scot, or, you know, a Black, brown writer isn't getting their work published. Why should I be taking that space up? (Ely Percy)

My own return to Glasgow implicates and entwines home and elsewhere – taking up space as travel, mobility, escape and homecoming (Taylor 2023). In London, I was broadly 'Scottish'; back in Glasgow, I became 'from *there*', specifically. My accent has changed again, and I'm often asked where I'm from: answering can feel like disconnection, revelation and confirmation. I can usually sense where the conversation is going, as I know the usual patterns and embodiments that are traced as go-to stories. In negotiating these distances, we can be careful about the question 'where are you from?' and how to address it when postcodes become predictive data, imbued with meaning and value. Often mistakes, category errors and hostilities are enacted, and 'gentle reminders' become painful repetitions: the term 'New Scots' may seek to welcome, but it's also a demarcation (Dasgupta & Alim; Stella, this collection).

In many ways Scotland is a changed place. Devolution and the independence movement allowed constituent UK nations to imagine divergent futures: more or less European, more or less left- or right-leaning, more or less capable of managing public health and economic justice. Much can be claimed through imagining difference as a turning point, with increased claims around a supposed Scottish transformation, through politics, culture, character or even competitiveness ('People Make Glasgow!'). But the Scotland I remembered, and realized again on return, was and is often still a place of sexism, racism, homophobia and transphobia, and of escalating poverty and inequality. The council estate where I grew up continues to rank poorly on measures of health, housing, employment and life expectancy – just as it did in the 1980s. These conditions persist, even as we move through them. My accent, like my sense of self, changes again: legible and located in Scotland, but vaguer in England, where it's simply 'Scottish'. Whether that's felt as comfort or constraint, visibility or erasure often depends on other intersectional inequalities. These are politicized and embodied forms of movement, identity and belonging – always contingent, always in negotiation.

I chatted with Ely about inhabiting a distinctly Scottish queer archive, or back lane, or lesbian library in visiting Glasgow Women's Library (GWL):

Ely: Did you ever go to the GWL?
Yvette: Yeah, I've been there, yeah.
Ely: And you know how that clatty, dirty lane bit they were up …
Yvette: Yes, I remember that!
Ely: …lovely organizations that are up this smelly, dirty lane!
Yvette: Yeah, yeah.
Ely: I'm writing about my fictional version of the GWL, because I wanted to be able to see both positive, negative, made up, all different kinds of things about it. I wanted to change the wallpaper. I didn't want to offend anybody. I wanted people to think, I wanted people to know like this is inspired by, but it's not the same place. I wanted to write a description of that lane… I couldn't go back to Glasgow and see that, because not only has that lane been tidied up, they've taken away the dirty cobbles and all the rest of it, and they've taken away the whole, they've cemented over it. They've got a nice wee car park bit there. So all the condoms and the take-away boxes and…
Yvette: That's right.
Ely: …the bit that said 'lesbian library' scrawled outside has all gone away.
Yvette: Yeah. That's right, I remember walking down that lane and being terrified.
Ely: Aye, yeah. And the lift. But I've made up a description, and I think I've just kept it very, very short. And I showed it to my pal and she was just like 'ah that, yeah that's it, nailed it'.

I recall being in GWL in the 1990s and, like Ely, navigating the back lane and often broken elevator. In returning to the relocated archive, as an academic, I think about the space I'd once inhabited in my teens and twenties located in the dimly lit backstreet lane. The work of this book is to attend to those moments of erasure and emergence. To notice the dirt and delight of a back lane marked 'lesbian library', before it was paved over. To remember what was scrawled on the wall before it was scrubbed clean.

Queer entrances and exits

During the 'Queer in a Wee Place' events, co-directors – and national treasures – Sue John and Adele Patrick spoke about the history and future of GWL and the challenges of claiming local, national and international inclusive presences.[5] Sue explained that GWL grew out of Women in Profile, an initiative launched in response to Glasgow being named European City of Culture in 1990. From the start, it sought to challenge masculinist narratives:

> There was this strong focus on Glasgow as a masculine city – shipbuilding, the Glasgow Boys artists from the early 20th century, and later the New Glasgow Boys in the 1980s from Glasgow School of Art. So many women were saying, 'What about us?' This whole year will pass and women won't even be acknowledged.

The founding of GWL was, and continues to be, a radical act of reclaiming cultural spaces embedding inclusivity intersections of gender, sexuality, class, race and community. Yet, as Sue acknowledged, public understanding still lags behind the library's expansive mission. Although GWL emerged to remedy that absence, Sue noted that misconceptions persist:

> People still think we're only for women. We're open to everyone. Yes, some events are women-only, but we use an inclusive definition that welcomes trans and non-binary people too.

GWL's work, like that of many feminist and queer-led cultural organizations across Scotland (Sledmere and Dunlop, this collection), underscores the transformative power of creative spaces that do more than reflect society they reimagine (Dan Brown, this collection). These institutions are not only about representation but also about reconfiguring who holds cultural power, whose stories are told and how inclusive futures are imagined (Fadaka, this collection).

In our conversation, Adele and Sue also reflected on the language and boundaries of identity itself – questioning the very terms 'Glasgow', 'Women's' and 'Library'. At GWL – and throughout this collection – queer-feminist politics are not confined to tick-box inclusivity. The insistence is on more than just space for cis, white, middle-class women and moving beyond superficial EDI efforts:

> I think it's incredible how little the F word is used within EDI ... I do see quite a lot of EDI work where the feminism's been rinsed out and there has been an

appropriation of methods or approaches to working or tools… that were forged in the white heat of feminist activism. (Adele Patrick, GWL)

As part of our discussion, Sue reflected on GWL's long-standing commitment to anti-racist practice and the complexities of public accountability. She described how, especially during pivotal moments such as the Covid-19 pandemic and the resurgence of Black Lives Matter, the Library recognized the importance of making public statements but not for the sake of optics. Instead, GWL has sought to amplifying the voices of Black women and women of colour both in literature and the visual arts (see Dasgupta & Alim; Diansangu; Fadaka; Rajasekaran & Thembiso Ruwona, this collection). Sue emphasized that this work is not new for the organization but that it's been a central theme throughout its thirty-year history. At the same time, she acknowledged the pitfalls of statements that serve only as self-congratulatory or performative gestures especially when issued by institutions failing to demonstrate genuine commitment (see Mahn; Reggiani & Gagnon, this collection). Even while recognizing the risks of being associated with 'virtue-signalling', co-opted by the right and anti-woke rhetoric, GWL remains committed to meaningful and ongoing anti-racist, anti-sexist and trans and non-binary inclusive work.

There is an appetite for EDI examples in practice across sectors and beyond handwringing or virtue-signalling. Many chapters in the collection attend to third sector, creative and public EDI initiatives (see Harvey Humphrey et al.; Joe Setch; Maria Sledmere & Kirsty Dunlop, this collection). In the UK, STEM initiatives are both driving and being driven by EDI policy (Marco Reggiani & Jessica Gagnon, this collection), yet there are still tensions in imagining inclusive and specifically anti-racist (Churnjeet Mahn, this collection), anti-sexist (Dan Brown, this collection) and anti-ableist (Jack McKinlay, this collection) classrooms. The disconnect between national agendas and lived realities endures, with EDI policy and practice becoming business opportunities, as well as grounds for mistrust and cynicism (e.g. Kirstie Ken English; Jj Fadaka; Kevin Guyan; Kate Molyneaux, this collection). In operating within marginalized and mainstreamed spaces, queer practitioners and authors can find themselves having to tick all the boxes (Leanne Dawson, this collection). In this 'niche', places and vocabularies, of writing in Scots, for example, can still achieve meaning and reach beyond 'wee places' (see Andrés N. Ordorica, this collection):

In England I couldn't find anybody to publish my work because I was writing in Scots, and I was getting a lot of folk coming back saying 'this is in slang', and I was just, after a while I got quite annoyed, because I was just like 'no it isn't' … I've got an audience. I was reading stuff aloud … folk would come up to me afterwards and … they would be really engaged with the characters … But did I think it was going to have as many readers as it, no. Did I think it was going to win a big prize? No. I just thought at least the people that, you know, that I went to school with, and people that went to school with my sister, I still thought, I kind of wrote it for them and for myself … And there's been people that have been from Wales, America, and different places that've said 'that was just like my school, but Scottish'. So I never, I guess I didn't really try that hard to make it accessible, and I think I just had to write it the way that I heard it. (Ely Percy)

The themes of groundedness and rootedness, as well as mobility and precarity, echo in the conversations between myself, Ely Percy, Sue John, Adele Patrick and others mentioned here as 'Queer in a Wee Place' conversationalists, including MSPs, the Equality Network, the TIE campaign and LGBTQ+ students. These themes continue to echo in this collection, particularly prominent in the range of creative contributions by Robyn O'Donnel, Mae Diansangu and Sindhu Rajasekaran. Auto-ethnographic accounts also echo these themes, reflected in chapters by Tanvir Alim and Rohit K. Dasgupta, Dario Luis Banegas and Drew Bain, and Aoife Christoffersen and Ashlee Christoffersen. These contributions help lay the groundwork for thoughtful departures, aiming to 'exit well' by leaving space for others to continue the dialogue. They foster communication across a diverse range of researchers, academics, creatives, practitioners and publics. In this spirit, I return to the reflections of GWL co-directors on what it means to 'exit well'.

> I'm not keen on the term resilience, but that sort of sense of endurance that has built up in the organization gives that real sense of grounding and rootedness. But I think the future is very, very exciting from a leadership perspective for me, because I am in the sort of steady but definite gracefully exiting, or as gracefully as I possibly can ... So my priority over the next wee while, or the priority of the organization, is how do we ensure that there's a real confidence in the critical conversations, in handling discomfort, in managing precarity, as Sue and I leave the organization? That there's a sort of blooming and blossoming rather than any type of sense of that change being an unsettling one ... So I'm really hoping that I can exit well, and with that sort of sense of laying things down. (Adele Patrick)

This book contributes to laying things down. It is an interdisciplinary and cross-sector effort, combining academic and non-academic voices, and across the career-course. It hopes to democratize and decentre ideals of expertise or authority, which conflict with queerer imaginations of knowledge and usefulness, in entering and exiting gracefully. Space is made for the interviews, ethnographies, surveys, histories and futures of LGBTQ+ people, with representation across the age range. Many of the contributions focus on a 'modern' Scotland, but several are also historically situated (e.g. Zoë Playdon) where the idea of the 'modern' nation – as dependent on racism and (neo)colonialism – is queried, as with ideas of homonationalism and pink-washing (Jj Fadaka, Natasha Thembiso Ruwona). Engagement with policy (e.g. Sharon Cowan, Kevin Guyan) and with lived, intersectional experiences (as explored by Finn Mackay, Francesca Stella and Yvette Taylor) draws attention to the specific historical, legal, religious and social contexts that have shaped modern Scotland – contexts that have left a complex and often difficult legacy for generations of queer people.

Part 1, 'Queer Counts! Categories, Legalities and Challenges', takes stock of how queer lives are made legible through policy, data, law, and activism and the dangers and possibilities that accompany such legibility. We hear from authors, organizers, researchers and activists on the themes of belonging, inclusion, visibility, hope, revolution and abolition, held against the hostilities of hate crime, transphobia, sexism and pervasive heteronormativity. Robyn O'Donnell's 'Yes' explores consent and queer relationality in Scottish contexts, offering a counterpoint to more institutionally focused chapters. Kevin Guyan dissects the categorization of hate crime, asking whose lives are protected and how. Sharon Cowan pushes further, queering the very hope that underpins rights-based progress, while Kirstie Ken English interrogates the census as both a tool of recognition and a mechanism of control. Jj Fadaka's 'The Revolt and Revolting' rounds off the section with a more radical critique, disrupting sanitized representations and insisting on the unruly, defiant aspects of queer life. Together, these chapters wrestle with the double-edged nature of inclusion – what is gained by being counted, and what is lost?

While Part 1 is concerned with official narratives and state recognition, Part 2, 'Queer States: Legacies and Transformations', turns towards the affective and material legacies that shape queer life in and beyond the state. We hear about the changing figurations of Scottish identity, imagined as an 'assemblage' of different parts, reduced (or expanded) as 'provincial' or provisional. Yvette Taylor's 'Queer Provincialisms' positions post-Brexit Scotland within wider geopolitical shifts, calling attention to the fragility of national progress. Kate Molyneaux queers menstrual policy to highlight the gendered assumptions within (feminist) nation-building. Through conversational snapshots, Aoife Christoffersen and Ashlee Christoffersen, and Dario Luis Banegas and Drew Bain, centre lived queer experience in and beyond Scotland. Francesca Stella brings in migrant voices, probing at the intersection of queerness and the 'New Scot' label, while Mae Diansangu's 'Assemblages' refracts identity through art, performance and the refusal to be fixed. This part stretches the notion of what it means to be in a nation, questioning who gets to belong and under what terms.

In Part 3, 'Queer Homelands: Myths, Migrations and Movements', the collection turns explicitly to history, movement and memory, where we think about leaving, escaping or being cast out of places, communities and families. These form the 'lessons in geography' we learn, as sometimes unintended and often as enforced. Finn Mackay's essay on leaving as a queer act powerfully critiques the romanticization of rural Scotland, while Zoë Playdon unearths the buried history of Ewan Forbes, challenging dominant medical and legal histories of trans identity. Rohit K. Dasgupta and Tanvir Alim offer a queer diasporic poetics rooted in Glasgow, while Natasha Thembiso Ruwona learns from Maud Sulter, a Black Scottish artist whose work challenges both racial and sexual normativity. Sindu Rajasekaran closes the part with 'Unintended Poiesis', a meditation on the accidental creativity of queer life. These pieces trouble static ideas of homeland, highlighting instead movement across time, borders and forms of kinship.

Part 4, 'Queer Creations: Vibrations, Glitches and Curiosities', is where creative practice becomes central and we hear about creative interventions and DIY cultures, where institutions have failed queer practices, or when failure is embraced as a queer glitch or interruption. We see how these manifest and even vibrate on the Scottish stage, with a focus, too, on museums, films, poetry, ethnographies and letter writing. Both stylistically and substantively, contributors offer an array of ways into thinking about small nations, sexuality and Scotland. From Leanne Dawson's exploration of queer film exhibition as a utopic gesture to Joe Setch's critique of museum curation, the focus shifts to how queer stories are curated, told and displayed. Andrés N. Ordorica explores legacy and lineage in poetry, while Maria Sledmere and Kirsty Dunlop bring queerness into contact with digital life, queering the post-internet landscape. The 'As Is' ethnodrama is a collective act of queer storytelling by Harvey Humphrey, Slater Clain, Gina Gwenffrewi, Mathew Wilkie, Leni Daly and Odhran Thomson and explores trans and non-binary experiences in particular through collective conversations. The speaker navigates the everyday realities of queer life – silenced truths, hidden emotions and social constraints – through intimate moments and emotional truths. Like other poems in the collection, these query and celebrate love as a transformative force that defies binaries and categorization. This section affirms that queer creativity is not just aesthetic but also political, offering new forms of expression, community and resistance.

Part 5, 'Queer Education: (Post-)Compulsory Classroom Contexts', turns to education as both site and struggle. Authors think about what else is learned in education, besides the formal – if changing – curriculum: how do we learn to undo inequalities of race, class, gender, disability and sexuality, for example. How do queers learn to be otherwise and what might others learn from queers? Churnjeet Mahn critiques the tokenism of including Black Scottish writing in educational curricular contexts, while Marco Reggiani and Jessica Gagnon explore the challenges of queer belonging in STEM. Jack McKinlay documents the often-erased experiences of disabled queer students, and Dan Brown closes with a pedagogical call to arms, imagining classrooms where queerness is not an add-on but a foundation. These chapters ask what queer education could be not just in content but as practice, and not just as tolerance but as transformation.

What this collection contributes is a diversity of experience and meaning of being queer in Scotland, and how this is conceptualized and expressed by queer people and by social agencies, institutions and wider society. It moves between critical analysis and poetic expression, lived experience and legal critique, showing how queerness exceeds categorization even as it contends with it. It insists that even in 'wee places' big conversations are not only possible but also necessary – and that the periphery is often where the most urgent thinking happens:

> Today was:
> Insightful, different, challenging, engagement was high
> Exercises were interesting and outside of the box
> I felt a sense of pride in every queer individual who came here today: who engaged, shared and laughed. ('Queer in a Wee Place' conference participant feedback)

Above all, this collection invites readers to imagine Scotland not as a fixed homeland but as an evolving, contested and queerly possible place. It hopes to be a useful, engaged and shared entry point that 'exits well' by inviting further conversations and actions.

Notes

1. 'Queer and the Cost of Living Crisis' was held at the University of Strathclyde 2023–5 as part of the RSE-funded Personal Research fellowship on Queer Social Justice. Series themes have been published as an illustrated booklet, thanks to the creative efforts of designer Madeleine Leisk, and series transcripts are available open-access. I followed this with a series of 'Queer Social Justice Pop-Ups' and worked in collaboration with Coin-Operated Press to produce a Queer Social Justice zine, donating to regional groups and venues including the Highland Zine Library.
2. The UK Supreme Court unanimously held that, within the Equality Act 2010, the terms 'woman', 'man' and 'sex' refer exclusively to biological sex at birth, not gender identity – even for individuals with GRCs. This interpretation was applied to single-sex services and public spaces, meaning organizations may lawfully restrict access based on birth sex. However, the court affirmed that GRCs remain valid for most other legal purposes. Many LGBTQ+ groups have condemned this, and the Human Rights Watch describes the ruling as severely regressive, warning that it creates legal avenues for excluding trans people in public services and facilities.
3. See note 1 above.
4. Personal e-mail correspondence partially reproduced with permission.
5. See 'Conversations with Glasgow Women's Library Co-Directors Sue John & Adele Patrick: Queer in a Wee Place', https://pureportal.strath.ac.uk/en/publications/conversations-with-glasgow-womens-library-co-directors-sue-john-a. Accessed 27 March 2025.

References

Alexopoulos, M., Basiuk, T., Hochreiter, S. and Ristić-Kern, T. (eds). *Reading Literature and Theory at the Intersections of Queer and Class*. Abingdon: Routledge, 2025.

Bakshi, S., Jivraj, S. and Posocco, S. (eds). *Decolonizing Sexualities: Transnational Perspectives, Critical Interventions*. Oxford: Counterpress, 2016.

Bohata, K., Morgan, M. and Osborne, H. (eds). *Queer Square Mile: Queer Short Stories from Wales*. Wales: Parthian, 2022.

Brim, M. *Poor Queers. Confronting Elitism in Universities*. Durham, NC: Duke University Press, 2020.

Davidson, N., Liinpää, M., McBride, M. and Virdee, S. (eds). *No Problem Here: Understanding Racism in Scotland*. Edinburgh: Luath Press, 2018.

Dawson, L. 'Beyond Box Ticking and Buzzwords: A Queer, Working-Class, Anti-Racist, Anti-Ableist Sharing in UK Academic'. In Y. Taylor, M. Brim and C. Mahn (eds), *Queer Precarities in and out of Higher Education*, pp. 97–116. London: Bloomsbury, 2023.

Giles, H. J. *Tonguit*. Glasgow: Freight Books, 2015.

Jaigirdar, A. *The Henna Wars*. London: Hachette, 2020.

Kelman, J. *How Late It Was, How Late*. London: Penguin, 1994.

Lewis, S. E., Borba, R., Fabrício, B. F. and de Souza Pinto, D (eds). *Queering Paradigms IV: South–North Dialogues on Queer Epistemologies, Embodiments and Activisms*. Oxford: Peter Lang, 2014.

Logan, K. *The Gloaming*. London: Penguin, 2018.

Luther, J. D. and Ung Loh, J. (eds). *Queer Asia Decolonising and Reimagining Sexuality and Gender*. London: Bloomsbury, 2024.

Mahn, M. 'Black Scottish Writing and the Fiction of Diversity'. In M. Breeze, Y. Taylor and C. Costa (eds), *Time and Space in the Neoliberal University. Fractures and Futures in Higher Education*, pp. 119–41. Switzerland AG: Springer Nature, 2019.

Patton, C. and Sánchez-Eppler (eds). *Queer Diasporas*. Durham, NC: Duke University Press, 2000.

Plummer, R. *Wain: LGBT Reimaginings of Scottish Folktales*. Birmingham: Emma Press, 2019.

Radcliffe, A. *The Old Haunts*. Oxford: Fairlight Moderns, 2023.

Ramos, R. and Mowlabocus, S. (eds). *Queer Sites in Global Contexts Technologies, Spaces, and Otherness*. London: Routledge, 2021.

Sobande, F. and hill, l.-r. *Black Oot Here. Black Lives in Scotland*. London: Bloomsbury, 2022.

Spurlin, W. *Imperialism within the Margins: Queer Representation and the Politics of Culture in Southern Africa*. London: Palgrave, 2006.

Strachan, Z. (ed.). *Out There: An Anthology of Scottish LGBT Writing*. Glasgow: Freight Books, 2014.

Stuart, D. *Shuggie Bain*. London: Picador, 2020.

Stuart, D. *Young Mungo*. London: Picador, 2022.

Taylor, Y. *Working-Class Lesbian Life: Classed Outsiders*. London: Palgrave, 2007.

Taylor, Y. *Lesbian and Gay Parenting: Securing Social and Educational Capitals*. London: Palgrave, 2009.

Taylor, Y. *Working-Class Queers. Time, Place and Politics*. London: Pluto, 2023.

Zabrowskis, M. 'Exploiting Shared Queer Knowledge'. In C. Mahn, M. Brim and Y. Taylor (eds), *Queer Sharing in the Marketized University*, pp. 81–95. London: Routledge, 2023.

Zaino, K. 'Wanting More from OER: Enacting a Queer of Color Commitment to Open'. In C. Mahn, M. Brim and Y. Taylor (eds), *Queer Sharing in the Marketized University*, pp. 135–49. London: Routledge, 2023.

Part 1

Queer Counts! Categories, Legalities and Challenges

2

Yes!

Robyn O'Donnell

It's early September 2024, our minibus bumbles over beautiful, barren highland hills. Low morning light streams through the windows, catching the hair of the girl asleep on my shoulder. A couple of rows over, a tear falls down the face of another new friend, we watch the view in silence, sad to leave, happy to have been here, a turbulent joy. We're returning home from Camp Trans Scotland, a weekend spend on and around an old scout camp, with a cohort of beautiful transexuals, slightly misorganized and perfectly imperfect. The only cis people we saw were a gardener and distant shapes of waving hillwalkers.

This was the quiet moment I started writing this poem in. Thinking about its future lines and things that I will edit out, what to include and what hoard selfishly for myself, of better titles and folded meaning. The poem will annoy me for a week or so, stuck in my brain, refusing to leave me alone until I put finger to key. I'll keep writing it in the shower, while walking to the shop, in all the moments where I'm trapped with my thoughts. By the time I sit at a keyboard, it will be my enemy, an annoying companion.

We make queer spaces for ourselves, drawing little circles around pubs, classrooms, stages, cafes. Workshops, swimming pools and glens. Sometimes we take away trinkets, sometimes we take away lovers, friends. The most important thing we take are memories, the shared energy of other queers, to borrow those moments for my work, it is a privilege. To stand in the long shadow of queer work and make it ever so slightly larger. It's an incomparable feeling. I am happy I am queer, I am overjoyed to be trans.

The boy's tear is wiped away, the girl slips off my shoulder and wakes up, hills give way to suburban Glasgow. I go home with my poem, to read it in bars and bookshops, to see it in print in this book and for a moment, I get to be back in that morning light.

Yes

Yes Yes Yes
Yes.

Yes swimming, Yes dancing Yes,
yes baptism, water, stone, bare skin
Yes Yes
Yes to faggots, to dyke, trannies, the rest and in between

yes yes and yes,

Yes spinning t-boys, yes, gayest of gordens, yes
yes Charlie and Kit, dancing bottoms, turned leaders turned switch.

Yes dyke bar, f for phalloplasty, yes wonder wall, mermen
and yes.
yes mushrooms, always mushrooms, mycelium growing up though the souls of
our feet, Transition goals, flat chested fungi yes

Yes tits on men, girls, boys, and dicks the same, yes pussies hitting cold water and
genital solidarity. yes.

yes, me too bestie and calling each other gay, yes
Yes tick plucked off flashed ankle by experienced hand, yes, yes

Yes she, YES he, Fae? Yes! and yes, Yes Zafira
yes Riot, name and nature, yes.

Yes
Yes fire, poem, song, moment, fiddle, rap.
yes? aye! Scots, explanation stretching lang, vocabularies
chaste vulgarities
yes, so so so yes.

Yes weaving, spells, stories, baskets
Yes to purple thread on wrist, tied tight by love
Yes, to the last of the magic, spell woven, warm, soft hands, hard touch

Yes,
to saying yes

Yes
Yes Yes Yes
and yes to no
just for the craic

3

Hate crime in Scotland and the classification of queer lives: Doors, data and definitions

Kevin Guyan

A razor-thin line exists between safety and danger for LGBTQ people in Scotland. One misstep – a glance at the wrong person, a flamboyant hand gesture, a lilt in your speech – can mark the moment when everything changes for the worse. Smiles turn to tears, blood and bruises. When the switch happens, as it so often does, the response of the police and courts depends on who you are or are perceived to be. The process of classifying you as 'something' reflects societal assumptions about categories of gender, sex and sexuality: the lifestyles that count as lives, the practices deemed possible and where these decisions locate you on a hierarchical ladder stretching between protection and harm.

Hate crime is a term used to describe behaviour that is both criminal and rooted in prejudice. The Scottish government explains that when a hate crime occurs, 'the law has been broken, and the offender's actions were driven by hatred towards a particular group'.[1] In Scotland, the groups protected by hate crime law relate to race, religion, disability, age, transgender identity and sexual orientation. A hate crime is not a stand-alone offence, but a type of marker added to different incidents – for example, an assault, act of vandalism or murder can take the form of a hate crime. The introduction and expansion of hate crime law sits among other legislative developments intended to improve the experiences of LGBTQ communities in Scotland, including the introduction of civil partnerships and same-sex marriage, being counted in the national census, the Gender Recognition Reform Bill and the proposal to end conversion practices. Many of these legislative ambitions were premised on the uncomplicatedness of love. Commenting on the UK government's 2018 National LGBT Survey and LGBT Action Plan, sociologists Yvette Taylor and Matson Lawrence highlight how Penny Mordaunt MP (Member of Parliament) – in her role as minister for women and equalities – articulated LGBTQ equalities as 'driven by love'. As a driving force for action, 'love' has served as a deft strategy for advancing *some* equalities but also has the effect of 'positioning normative partnering as the way in which LGBTQI+ lives can be validated, accepted and made intelligible'.[2] The concept of love is thrust into an elevated enclosure where its matter-of-fact simplicity safeguards it from critical interrogation. 'Love is love', after all.

In this chapter, I focus on love's monstrous sibling: hate.³ In April 2024, the Hate Crime and Public Order (Scotland) Act 2021 came into effect, which consolidated existing protections against offences aggravated by characteristics, including sexual orientation and transgender identity, and introduced the offence of 'stirring up hatred', which criminalizes threatening or abusive behaviour against a group of people with a shared characteristic (e.g. lesbian women, trans men). Scotland's refreshed hate crime coverage has invited praise from LGBTQ equalities groups such as Equality Network, Stonewall Scotland and LGBT Youth Scotland and outrage from figures including tech mogul Elon Musk, podcast host Joe Rogan and – most infamously – author J. K. Rowling. This chapter uses the topic of hate crime to initiate a broader discussion of cracks in Scotland's liberal and inclusive imaginary as a queer, wee place. I highlight what happens at intersections where state classification practices – codified in legislation – meet the hard-to-define complexity of queer bodies, desires and identities, all overlaid by the choppy contours of where things happen. I describe how hate crime law beckons the police into the intimate nooks of queer lives and affirms state agencies as arbiters for what lives count, who is worthy of protection and which types of hate matter. I also discuss the role of data in translating messy queer experiences into palatable problems that are understood as easier for the state to resolve. This datafication of hate crime – executed via reporting apps, surveys, graphs and statistical tables – is prescribed for queer communities as something good for us. As a tonic, hate crime law plays to a gut emotion to get back at someone who wrongs us. I understand and recognize these feelings – I really do – but I am unsure if they are quenched by hate crime legislation. The introduction of more LGBTQ hate crime laws does not necessarily mean that LGBTQ people are less likely to encounter anti-LGBTQ hate. I conclude by questioning the merits of expanding hate crime law and whether Scotland provides a blueprint for other nations to adopt or reject.

The Hate Crime Act and Police Scotland

The passing of the Hate Crime Act in 2021 and its implementation in 2024 followed a long process of deliberation. In 2017, former judge Lord Bracadale was appointed by the Scottish Parliament to review and provide recommendations for reform of hate crime legislation. Following the publication of Lord Bracadale's report, the Scottish Parliament conducted a public consultation with evidence then scrutinized by the parliament's Justice Committee. During the eight-year incubation period between proposal and implementation, the issue of 'hate crime' attracted the attention of a disparate band of campaigners, writers, faith groups, secularists, comedians and academics. The issue became a magnet for catch-all fears and anxieties related to free speech and identity. What happened next is best explained using the concept of heteroactivism, a term coined by the scholars Catherine Nash and Kath Browne to describe opposition to LGBTQ equalities not necessarily premised on religious or conservative values.⁴ For heteroactivists, the expansion of LGBTQ equalities has gone too far and now jeopardizes the existing rights and freedoms of the 'normal' (cisgender, heterosexual) population. As Nash and Browne argue, freedom-of-speech claims have become 'a central and necessary tenet of contemporary heteroactivism' and are routinely 'used to attack LGBT legislative and political equalities' in countries including the UK, Ireland and Canada.[5] Particularly vocal among critics in Scotland was a cluster of anti-gender activists who feared that hate crime law would put at risk their freedom to publicly describe trans women as 'biologically male'.[6] For example, 'gender critical' former SNP (Scottish National Party) MP Joanna Cherry told the BBC the law would 'be weaponised by trans rights activists to try to silence, and worse still, criminalise women who do not share their beliefs'.[7] In this topsy-turvy imagining of the world, the idea of 'hate crime law' creates opportunities for heteroactivists to promote themselves as speaking a common-sense 'truth' and any opposition to their viewpoint, even from the people targeted by their 'truth' claims, represent an effort to 'silence' them.[8]

In April 2025, one year after the implementation of the Hate Crime Act, the UK Supreme Court heard the case *For Women Scotland v. The Scottish Ministers*, in which For Women Scotland (an anti-trans campaign group) challenged the definition of 'woman', 'man' and 'sex' used in Scottish legislation to increase the number of women on public boards.[9] The Court unexpectedly decided in favour of For Women Scotland, ruling that 'sex' in the 2010 Equality Act – a key piece of equalities legislation in England, Wales and Scotland – meant 'biological sex' or sex at birth. Although the full effects of the ruling remain unclear at the time of writing, an exclusively biology-first account of 'sex' risks nullifying the effects of trans people in possession of a Gender Recognition Certificate and excluding many trans people from legal protections.

Reviewing parliamentary debates and media comments from critics of Scotland's Hate Crime Act, I kept encountering the same image: the rat-a-tat-tat of a knock on someone's front door, their domestic bliss upended by the arrival of a police officer to share the solemn news that they are accused of a hate crime. In the bill's final debate, for example, former Labour MSP (Member of the Scottish Parliament) Elaine Smith queried whether 'in debating the hate crime bill, I am now being accused of hate crime and could expect to have the police at my door'.[10] Conservative MSP Russell Findlay also highlighted a situation 'where contentious discussions and disagreements in your home can result in a knock on the door from police'.[11] And, writing for *The Spectator* in March 2023, campaigner Lucy Hunter-Blackburn warned 'we can expect a deluge of complaints and many people will be subjected to varying levels of disruptive police attention for their legitimate and legal thoughts and arguments' before adding 'many more will have thought twice about what they say to avoid a knock on the door'.[12] The repeated image of a police officer intruding upon the privacy of the domestic realm has a history: the home has long presented a space where 'rules of society need not apply', to the historical detriment of women and/or queer people who suffer under the abusive control of husbands, fathers and other family members.

To accompany the law's implementation, Police Scotland organized bespoke training for its officers and launched a public information campaign. The campaign featured a character called the Hate Monster and highlighted that hate crime involves more than bad people making bad decisions. Using the slogan 'hurt people, hurt people', the campaign drew a link between hate crime and the socio-economic factors that often lie behind people's actions (e.g. economic deprivation, adverse childhood experiences, substance abuse and under-employment).[13] In April 2024, during the first week of the Hate Crime Act's implementation, Police Scotland received 7,152 online complaints.[14] Among these reports, 240 were recorded as hate crimes and 30 were recorded as non-crime hate incidents – around 3.8 per cent of all reports received that week. The following week, the number of complaints received dropped to 1,832, with 213 recorded as hate crimes and 25 recorded as non-crime hate incidents.

This frenzy of hate crime-related activities forges a closer relationship between the police and LGBTQ communities – as the documentation and reporting of hate encounters become an omnipresent feature of queer people's everyday lives. For some LGBTQ people, the involvement of the police in making people accountable for their actions and facilitating the retribution of those who break the law is a good thing. For others, the closer proximity between the police and LGBTQ communities moves us in a potentially harmful direction – particularly, for the most minoritized among LGBTQ people. Across the UK, evidence exists of institutional misogyny, racism and homophobia within the police and queer people are often at the frontline of calls to reduce (rather than increase) the powers of the police.[15] The role of the police in responding to past and ongoing harms has also encountered tensions within the #MeToo movement and the enthusiasm – among some prominent voices – to deploy the powers of the police to counter-attack the problems of misogyny and sexual harassment.[16] As philosopher Amia Srinivasan admits, 'It is hard to blame them. For centuries men haven't only assaulted and degraded women, but have used the state's coercive apparatus to enforce their right to do so. Is it not time women got to wield some of that same power to express their outrage and to take revenge?'[17]

Although this day of queer reckoning for past harms has not yet happened (nor, do I imagine, most LGBTQ individuals favour this vengeful rejoinder to history), it sometimes seems like the language used to describe LGBTQ–police relations is shifting. In May 2024, the chief constable of Police Scotland, Jo Farrell, apologized 'for the recent and historical injustices and discrimination that members of LGBTQI+ communities in Scotland have faced'.[18] Farrell explained:

> At times policing has not only failed to protect you but has contributed to the mistreatment and prejudice many have endured.
>
> Laws which criminalised love and identity were wrong, and policing must recognise and reflect upon our role in enforcing them. I am truly sorry for the serious and long-lasting physical and mental pain and harm caused, both to my internal colleagues, and to our communities.

While the apology signalled an effort to address the past and build a better relationship in the future, for opponents of LGBTQ equalities, Farrell's statement confirmed an alternate reality where equalities have gone too far and the police are now subservient to the whims of an LGBTQ minority. In this heteroactivist account of the world, hate crime law represented a wielding of LGBTQ power, the expression of outrage and hunger for revenge.

Having established the context for LGBTQ hate crime law in Scotland and potential risks that accompany the co-opting of the police into more facets of queer lives,

I now want to plunge deeper and examine four themes related to the socio-technical construction of LGBTQ hate crime. While this proposal might sound overly scientific, what I want to do – very simply – is counter the assumed objectivity and merits of using the law to address LGBTQ hate.

1. The construction of classifications

The classifications used in Scotland's hate crime law are not a carbon copy of the world 'out there' but are mediated through the design and implementation of legislation, reporting tools, training materials and public information campaigns. A myriad of quirks, nuances and life histories distinguish who we are as individuals. Classifying involves establishing what markers of difference – among these many possibilities – are worth counting. The Hate Crime Act identifies 'sexual orientation' and 'transgender identity' as protected characteristics and describes the categories recognized within these groups. For example, the legislation defines 'sexual orientation' as a:
Sexual orientation towards:

(a) persons of the same sex,
(b) persons of a different sex, or
(c) both persons of the same sex and persons of a different sex.

And 'transgender identity' is defined as a person who is:

(a) a female-to-male transgender person,
(b) a male-to-female transgender person,
(c) a non-binary person,
(d) a person who cross-dresses.

The law's wording is not chance. For example, use of the term 'a person who cross-dresses' followed evidence from the LGBTI human rights charity Equality Network, where they noted: 'The inclusion of cross-dressing also covers a potential loophole. Without it, any person charged with a crime against a trans woman, for example, which included the use of transphobic language, would be able to claim that they presumed the victim was a cross-dressing man.'[19] Likewise, for sexual orientation, the Hate Crime Act uses the term 'different sex' rather than 'opposite sex' to ensure the law covers individuals in relationships where someone identifies as non-binary. This decision enflamed the anti-gender campaign group LGB Alliance as they claimed the term 'different sex' had the effect of erasing 'lesbians and gay men as a category', an argument also made in their written submission in the *For Women Scotland v. The Scottish Ministers Supreme Court* case.[20] For LGB Alliance, 'if the law then redefines "sex" to mean a spectrum, then it is essentially redefining gay and lesbian to mean attracted to any sex, or to anyone who calls themselves the same sex'. As a magnet for catch-all fears and anxieties, LGB Alliance presented the Hate Crime Act as having the potential to not only negatively impact lesbians and gay men but also bring about their extinction!

Unlike the task of classifying phenomena in the natural world, like insects or plants, attaching categories to queer lives is like trying to pin jelly to the wall. Everything is moving: the person being classified, the person tasked with classifying them and the labels available to the classified and the classifier. Humans also have the habit of talking back: disputing or refuting the box assigned to them, dipping their limbs into adjacent boxes, stacking boxes on top of another or collapsing them to the floor and building something new on top. Hate crime law relies on drawing a distinction between 'X' and 'Y'. However, as these examples from the Hate Crime Act attest, creating classifications that everyone agrees upon is an impossible task.

2. Queer quantification

The socio-technical construction of hate crime classifications involves making design decisions that distribute protection unevenly. Why does the Hate Crime Act only name six protected groups? What about other minoritized communities such as unhoused people, poor people and women? Is it possible to devise an approach to hate crime that offers blanket protection for everyone? And how do we design systems capable of collecting, analysing and using data about hate crime? This final point features prominently in wider, ongoing efforts to address hate crime in Scotland. The use of the law – the Hate Crime Act – is one ingredient in a broader hate crime strategy and delivery plan, which runs from 2023 to 2026. Data-related actions include an overhaul of Police Scotland's crime and case management system, which will enable the collection of more detailed data about hate crime such as 'the groups targeted and the nature of the prejudice involved, including intersecting characteristics'.[21] A person's experience of a hate crime is not a flurry of ones and zeros so – using the legal classifications discussed in the previous section – qualitative experiences are translated into quantitative data that is comprehensible to counting machines. This data is then used to populate the graphs and tables in hate crime reports, the headline figures in statistical outputs and the tabloid column inches where commentators deliberate as to whether the number of LGBTQ hate incidents is going up or down.

Hate crime data becomes interoperable – in other words, events that occur at different times and in different places are made comparable, facilitating practices of analysis and prediction. Numerical information no longer serves the simple purpose of telling us what happened in the past – it also becomes possible to predict what will happen in the future and pre-emptively take action to control and manage the situation. Yet, as legal scholar and activist Dean Spade has argued, the collection of standardized data 'makes certain populations inconceivable or impossible, and establish modes of distribution that make some people more secure at the expense of others'.[22] Data matters in its context and the construction of two tiers of queers is nothing new. The splintering of communities and piecemeal delivery of 'inclusion' have been a feature of modern LGBTQ rights movements since their formation. While the social, cultural, political and economic standing of *some* queers has improved, others remain on the edge or – even worse – outside the dictionary for what counts as a community in need of protection.

3. Hate crime in a wee place

Further muddying the classifications associated with hate crime are the spaces and places where they occur. The Scottish Parliament's Justice Committee explored whether incidents within a private dwelling could count as a hate crime and agreed unanimously that just because an incident took place within someone's home should not offer an absolute defence against prosecution.[23] The committee's convener, former Conservative MSP Adam Tomkins, shared the example of a family gathering for Friday night dinner 'at which my unreconstructed and somewhat embarrassing elderly uncle makes disparaging remarks about a same-sex couple and my somewhat oversensitive fifteen-year-old daughter, offended at what she has heard, tells her best friend about what has been discussed at my family dinner table. Her friend's father is a police officer, and the next thing we know is that there is a knock at the door and my elderly uncle is under criminal investigation.'[24] In Tomkins's example, the uncle (what is it about outdated uncles …?) might have expressed abhorrent views but his actions were unlikely to meet the threshold for criminal investigation. During the bill's final debate in parliament, Conservative MSP Liam Kerr expressed concern that because the legislation failed to include any defence regarding private conversations in private dwellings, 'The police could come to someone's home, having received a report of their having stirred up hate around the dinner table, and could take witness statements from those present, which, presumably, could include their children.'[25] In Kerr's nightmarish vision of a future Scotland, the police are not simply knocking on the door but entering your home and taking witness statements around the family dining table.

The geographies of hate crime underscore assumptions about the separation of public and private spaces, which have historically helped facilitate the inclusion of *some* queer people (who conform with dominant categories of gender, race, disability and social class) but kept them at a distance. For example, the 1981 decriminalization of sex acts between men in Scotland over the age of twenty-one was premised on access to a private space of one's own – a luxury not available to everyone. As historian Matt Houlbrook has documented, writing on the decriminalization of private same-sex activities in England and Wales in 1967, the policing of same-sex activities in public or semi-public spaces continued at pace after the change in law.[26] Today, this type of inclusion-at-a-distance explains why certain issues, such as teaching primary school children about the existence of LGBTQ people, continue to evoke outrage among some opponents of LGBTQ equalities. The neat divide between public and private is understood to have been breached. The spaces where things happen can also offer a cruel justification if (or when) something goes wrong: the queer person who locates themselves in a space not designed for them becomes partly at fault for whatever happens next. The trans women using the *wrong* toilet. The gay man drinking at the *wrong* bar. The queer non-binary person commuting on the *wrong* bus. The razor-thin line between safety and danger becomes even thinner when LGBTQ people find themselves in the *wrong* place at the *wrong* time. Which reminds us that exposure to harm and access to protection are not distributed equitably among all LGBTQ people but vary according to intersectional privilege and the spatial contexts we navigate.

4. The demand for definability

In political chatter about LGBTQ equalities in Scotland, the motto 'love is love' no longer seems to possess the same currency. The demoted status of a life defined by love is perhaps no bad thing: for many LGBTQ people, love – in whatever shape or form – is not stitched into the DNA of everything they do as lives are also defined by pleasure, politics, desire, culture, care and community. While the language of love might have passed its political peak, the topic of hate continues to linger in the spotlight. The Scottish government had promised to introduce a bill to tackle misogyny before the end of the parliamentary term in 2026, based on recommendations from a review conducted by the human rights lawyer Baroness Helena Kennedy KC.[27] The legislation would have addressed the omission of 'women' as a protected characteristic in the Hate Crime Act but would have likely met hostility from anti-gender campaigners because of how lawmakers classify 'women'. Speaking with the BBC radio programme *Good Morning Scotland*, the former first minister Humza Yousaf confirmed that 'women and girls will be protected, and trans women will be protected as well'.[28] Describing the rationale behind this decision, Yousaf explained, 'When a trans woman is walking down the street and a threat of rape is made against them, the man making the threat doesn't know if they are a trans woman or a cis woman. They will make that threat because the perception of that person [is] as a woman'.

The borders of categories become a sticking point. Writing on the Hate Crime Act for *The National* newspaper in October 2023, former Alba MP Neal Hanvey made the claim: 'You can't protect what you fail to define.'[29] Like the image of a police officer knocking on your door, the assertion that you cannot protect what you cannot easily define regularly appeared across political and media commentary. For example, during parliamentary scrutiny of the bill, former Labour MSP Johann Lamont proposed an amendment to include a definition of 'sex'. Similarly, Elaine Smith MSP argued that parliamentarians 'have a responsibility to be very clear on what this parliament means when defining men and women as two sexes'. In many respects, these demands for clarity were answered by the unexpected April 2025 Supreme Court ruling on 'sex' in the Equality Act. However, even with the intervention of the courts, common-sense categories for sex, gender and sexuality are alluring but not universal – and when everyone is not included we create gaps, exceptions, outliers and rule breakers. Hanvey, Lamont and Smith's call for definitional clarity takes us down a narrow path. Protection cannot become the preserve of the definable. We *can* and *should* protect the lives of those whom the state is unable to define. Particularly, when definability reflects the knowledge and experiences of the mainstream (cisgender, heterosexual) majority. The demand that someone is 'definable' erases the undocumented – without passports, ID cards or birth certificates – or the wrongly documented, who need to navigate the markers of F and M. The unsure, who do not know who they are or do not wish to know. The bodies that exist along different axes of gender, sex and sexuality – products of cultures, races, religions or beliefs that are antithetical to the classification demands of the white, Global North. Efforts to fine-tune classifications (e.g. 'cross-dressers' and people of a 'different sex') are not enough to ensure the equal and universal distribution of protection under the law. There will always be identities, actions, lives and desires that are incomprehensible to the demands of classification regimes and related data practices. Society is premised on systems that fail to project the undefinable.

***

Thinking critically about the topic of hate crime allows us to ask what type of relationships should exist between the individual, wider society and the state, and how these relationships vary across and within LGBTQ communities. Do we prioritize a social contract where one party protects the other from harm? A bond that relies on the goodwill of the powerful and their classifications for who counts as worthy of protection? Or something more equitable and interactive, where all parties possess agency? The promise of an LGBTQ-inclusive Scotland is currently conditioned on queer people's willingness to engage in classification practices that imperfectly define their experiences. Of course, none of the politicians or campaigners who predicted a visit from a police officer following the introduction of the Hate Crime Act have had their fears realized. Their concerns were always hyperbolic hot air. As legal scholar Andrew Tickell noted, the law 'has yet again emboldened the many folk in Scottish political life who are having a rare old time peddling fiction about what's actually in the Hate Crime Act and painting dystopian pictures about the new and terrifying world of repression it will create'.[30]

Scotland offers a test case that problematizes any assumption that more LGBTQ hate crime laws means LGBTQ people are better protected from hate. As a blueprint for other nations to adopt or reject, Scotland demonstrates how demands for definability coerce LGBTQ people into explaining their hopes, desires and identities using a vocabulary that is sensical to the state. You are included – as part of this queer, wee nation – as long as you align with the categories and classifications expected of you. Let's instead imagine alternate futures, which exist outside of the need to establish hate crime classifications or quantify the hurt and harm directed towards LGBTQ communities. I hesitate when picturing a queer future where the police play a more prominent role. It is a future that does not welcome everyone. Non-participation is one of several possibilities, where LGBTQ people complicate the smooth running of classification systems as an active decision to reconfigure – from the bottom up – how these systems make sense of LGBTQ lives. We become a jagged spanner in the machine. But taking on the identity of classification killjoy can require you to reject the piecemeal protections available to you, which exposes you to further risk of harm. By refusing to participate and play by the rules, it becomes more likely you will hear the rat-a-tat-tat of a police officer knocking at your door.

Notes

1. Scottish Government, 'Hate Crime Strategy for Scotland', March 2023, 5, www.gov.scot/binaries/content/documents/govscot/publications/strategy-plan/2023/03/hate-crime-strategy-scotland2/documents/hate-crime-strategy-scotland-march-2023/hate-crime-strategy-scotland-march-2023/govscot%3Adocument/hate-crime-strategy-scotland-march-2023.pdf.

2. M. Lawrence and Y. Taylor, 'The UK Government LGBT Action Plan: Discourses of Progress, Enduring Stasis, and LGBTQI+ Lives "Getting Better"', *Critical Social Policy* 40, no. 4 (2020): 592, https://doi.org/10.1177/0261018319877284.
3. A pairing also discussed in Jin Haritaworn, *Queer Lovers and Hateful Others: Regenerating Violent Times and Places* (London: Pluto Press, 2015).
4. C. J. Nash and K. Browne, *Heteroactivism: Resisting Lesbian, Gay, Bisexual and Trans Rights and Equalities* (London: Zed Books, 2020), 10.
5. Nash and Browne, *Heteroactivism*, 148.
6. The most high-profile example is J. K. Rowling, who tried to goad Police Scotland into arresting her for publishing a list of ten trans women on social media platform X – which included a community activist, TV personality, model, rapist and child abductor – and stating they are not 'women at all, but men, every last one of them'; see https://x.com/jk_rowling/status/1774749954629652873 (1 April 2024).
7. J. Cook, 'Hate Crime Law: Force for Good or Recipe for Disaster?' *BBC News*, 14 March 2024, www.bbc.com/news/uk-scotland-68570614.
8. Nash and Browne, *Heteroactivism*, 47, 157.
9. Home Affairs Section, 'Supreme Court Judgment on the Meaning of "Sex" in the Equality Act 2010: For Women Scotland', Research Briefing, UK Parliament, 2025, https://commonslibrary.parliament.uk/research-briefings/cbp-10259/.
10. Scottish Parliament, 'Final Debate on the Bill', 11 March 2021, www.parliament.scot/bills-and-laws/bills/hate-crime-and-public-order-scotland-bill.
11. Scottish Parliament, 'Meeting of the Parliament', 17 April 2024, www.parliament.scot/api/sitecore/CustomMedia/OfficialReport?meetingId=15801.
12. L. H. Blackburn, 'Scotland's New Hate Crime Act Is Fraught with Danger', *The Spectator*, 23 March 2024, www.spectator.co.uk/article/scotlands-new-hate-crime-act-is-fraught-with-danger/.
13. Police Scotland, 'Hate Crime Campaigns', March 2024, www.scotland.police.uk/what-s-happening/campaigns/2023/hate-crime/.
14. Amy Cassidy, 'A Hate Crime Law Was Meant to Protect against Prejudice. It Ended Up Sowing Further Division', *CNN*, 10 April 2024, www.cnn.com/2024/04/10/uk/scotland-hate-crime-law-intl/index.html.
15. For example, see Baroness Casey, *An Independent Review into the Standards of Behaviour and Internal Culture of the Metropolitan Police Service* (London: Metropolitan Police, 2023), www.met.police.uk/SysSiteAssets/media/downloads/met/about-us/baroness-casey-review/update-march-2023/baroness-casey-review-march-2023a.pdf; His Majesty's Inspector of Constabulary, 'An Inspection of the Metropolitan Police Service's Response to Lessons from the Stephen Port Murders', HMICFRS, April 2023, https://assets-hmicfrs.justiceinspectorates.gov.uk/uploads/inspection-of-the-metropolitan-police-services-response-to-lessons-from-the-stephen-port-murders.pdf.
16. The role of the police in addressing problems brought to light during the #MeToo movement has also, in turn, inspired critical work on police abolition; see A. Phipps, *Me, Not You: The Trouble with Mainstream Feminism* (Manchester: Manchester University Press, 2020).
17. A. Srinivasan, *The Right to Sex* (London: Bloomsbury, 2021), 170.
18. Police Scotland, 'Apology to the LGBTQI+ Communities of Scotland', 29 May 2024, www.scotland.police.uk/what-s-happening/news/2024/may/apology-to-the-lgbtqi-communities-of-scotland/.
19. Equality Network, 'Submission to the Justice Committee on the Hate Crime and Public Order (Scotland) Bill', Scottish Parliament, 20 November 2020.

20. LGB Alliance, 'Submission to the Justice Committee on the Hate Crime and Public Order (Scotland) Bill', Scottish Parliament, 21 July 2020, 3, https://archive2021.parliament.scot/S5_JusticeCommittee/Inquiries/JS520HC295_LGB_Alliance.pdf. For further discussion of LGB Alliance's written submission in the Supreme Court case, see UK Supreme Court, 'For Women Scotland v The Scottish Ministers', No. UKSC/2024/0042, 16 April 2025, https://supremecourt.uk/cases/uksc-2024-0042.
21. Scottish Government, 'Hate Crime Strategy for Scotland', 11.
22. D. Spade, *Normal Life: Administrative Violence, Critical Trans Politics, and the Limits of Law* (Durham, NC: Duke University Press, 2015), 113.
23. Scottish Parliament, 'Meeting of the Parliament', 10 March 2021, 71, www.parliament.scot/api/sitecore/CustomMedia/OfficialReport?meetingId=13188.
24. Scottish Parliament, 'Meeting of the Parliament', 71.
25. Scottish Parliament, 'Meeting of the Parliament', 11 March 2021, 31, www.parliament.scot/api/sitecore/CustomMedia/OfficialReport?meetingId=1319.
26. M. Houlbrook, *Queer London: Perils and Pleasures in the Sexual Metropolis, 1918–1957* (Chicago: University of Chicago Press, 2006), 243.
27. In May 2025, the Scottish government confirmed that it would not bring forward a bill to criminalize misogyny and instead – in a bizarre decision that went against their previously stated approach and expert opinion – amend existing hate crime legislation to provide protections on the basis of sex; see BBC News, 'Scottish Government Drops Plans for New Misogyny Law', *BBC News*, 2 May 2025, www.bbc.com/news/articles/crkx31my24ro.
28. BBC News, 'Yousaf: Trans Women Will Be Protected under Misogyny Law', *BBC News*, 16 April 2024, www.bbc.com/news/articles/cw59e7dg2nlo.
29. N. Hanvey, 'The Hate Crime Act Seeks to Silence Women and LGB People', *The National*, 2 October 2023, www.thenational.scot/politics/23826297.neale-hanvey-hate-crime-act-seeks-silence-women-lgb-people/.
30. A. Tickell, 'Scotland's Hate Crime Act Has Plenty of Safeguards', *The Herald*, 19 March 2024, www.heraldscotland.com/politics/viewpoint/24190927.scotlands-hate-crime-act-plenty-safeguards/.

References

Baroness Casey. *An Independent Review into the Standards of Behaviour and Internal Culture of the Metropolitan Police Service*. London: Metropolitan Police, 2023. www.met.police.uk/SysSiteAssets/media/downloads/met/about-us/baroness-casey-review/update-march-2023/baroness-casey-review-march-2023a.pdf.

BBC News. 'Yousaf: Trans Women Will Be Protected under Misogyny Law'. *BBC News*, 16 April 2024. www.bbc.com/news/articles/cw59e7dg2nlo.

BBC News. 'Scottish Government Drops Plans for New Misogyny Law'. *BBC News*, 2 May 2025. www.bbc.com/news/articles/crkx31my24ro.

Blackburn, L. H. 'Scotland's New Hate Crime Act Is Fraught with Danger'. *The Spectator*, 23 March 2024. www.spectator.co.uk/article/scotlands-new-hate-crime-act-is-fraught-with-danger/.

Cassidy, A. 'A Hate Crime Law Was Meant to Protect against Prejudice. It Ended up Sowing Further Division'. *CNN*, 10 April 2024. www.cnn.com/2024/04/10/uk/scotland-hate-crime-law-intl/index.html.

Cook, J. 'Hate Crime Law: Force for Good or Recipe for Disaster?' *BBC News*, 14 March 2024. www.bbc.com/news/uk-scotland-68570614.

Equality Network. 'Submission to the Justice Committee on the Hate Crime and Public Order (Scotland) Bill'. Scottish Parliament, 20 November 2020.

Hanvey, N. 'The Hate Crime Act Seeks to Silence Women and LGB People'. *The National*, 2 October 2023. www.thenational.scot/politics/23826297.neale-hanvey-hate-crime-act-seeks-silence-women-lgb-people/.

Haritaworn, J. *Queer Lovers and Hateful Others: Regenerating Violent Times and Places*. London: Pluto Press, 2015.

His Majesty's Inspector of Constabulary. 'An Inspection of the Metropolitan Police Service's Response to Lessons from the Stephen Port Murders'. HMICFRS, April 2023. https://assets-hmicfrs.justiceinspectorates.gov.uk/uploads/inspection-of-the-metropolitan-police-services-response-to-lessons-from-the-stephen-port-murders.pdf.

Home Affairs Section. 'Supreme Court Judgment on the Meaning of "Sex" in the Equality Act 2010: For Women Scotland'. Research Briefing, UK Parliament, 2025. https://commonslibrary.parliament.uk/research-briefings/cbp-10259/.

Houlbrook, M. *Queer London: Perils and Pleasures in the Sexual Metropolis, 1918–1957*. Chicago: University of Chicago Press, 2006.

Lawrence, M. and Taylor, Y. 'The UK Government LGBT Action Plan: Discourses of Progress, Enduring Stasis, and LGBTQI+ Lives "Getting Better"'. *Critical Social Policy* 40, no. 4 (2020): 586–607. https://doi.org/10.1177/0261018319877284.

LGB Alliance. 'Submission to the Justice Committee on the Hate Crime and Public Order (Scotland) Bill'. Scottish Parliament, 21 July 2020. https://archive2021.parliament.scot/S5_JusticeCommittee/Inquiries/JS520HC295_LGB_Alliance.pdf.

Nash, C. J. and Browne, K. *Heteroactivism: Resisting Lesbian, Gay, Bisexual and Trans Rights and Equalities*. London: Zed Books, 2020.

Phipps, A. *Me, Not You: The Trouble with Mainstream Feminism*. Manchester: Manchester University Press, 2020.

Police Scotland. 'Apology to the LGBTQI+ Communities of Scotland', 29 May 2024a. www.scotland.police.uk/what-s-happening/news/2024/may/apology-to-the-lgbtqi-communities-of-scotland/.

Police Scotland. 'Hate Crime Campaigns', March 2024b. www.scotland.police.uk/what-s-happening/campaigns/2023/hate-crime/.

Scottish Government. 'Hate Crime Strategy for Scotland', 2023. www.gov.scot/binaries/content/documents/govscot/publications/strategy-plan/2023/03/hate-crime-strategy-scotland2/documents/hate-crime-strategy-scotland-march-2023/hate-crime-strategy-scotland-march-2023/govscot%3Adocument/hate-crime-strategy-scotland-march-2023.pdf.

Scottish Parliament. 'Final Debate on the Bill', 11 March 2021a. www.parliament.scot/bills-and-laws/bills/hate-crime-and-public-order-scotland-bill.

Scottish Parliament. 'Meeting of the Parliament', 10 March 2021b. www.parliament.scot/api/sitecore/CustomMedia/OfficialReport?meetingId=13188.

Scottish Parliament. 'Meeting of the Parliament', 11 March 2021c. www.parliament.scot/api/sitecore/CustomMedia/OfficialReport?meetingId=1319.

Scottish Parliament. 'Meeting of the Parliament', 17 April 2024. www.parliament.scot/api/sitecore/CustomMedia/OfficialReport?meetingId=15801.

Spade, D. *Normal Life: Administrative Violence, Critical Trans Politics, and the Limits of Law*. Durham, NC: Duke University Press, 2015.

Srinivasan, A. *The Right to Sex*. London: Bloomsbury, 2021.

Tickell, A. 'Scotland's Hate Crime Act Has Plenty of Safeguards'. *The Herald*, 19 March 2024. www.heraldscotland.com/politics/viewpoint/24190927.scotlands-hate-crime-act-plenty-safeguards/.
UK Supreme Court. 'For Women Scotland v The Scottish Ministers', No. UKSC/2024/0042, April 16 2025. https://supremecourt.uk/cases/uksc-2024-0042.

4

Queer hope and LGBTQ+ rights in a wee place

Sharon Cowan

Introduction

Almost ten years ago, in 2015, I became the professor of feminist and queer legal studies at the University of Edinburgh. The university principal at the time nervously called my head of school, asking for reassurance that it was appropriate to include the word 'queer' in my title, given its historical use as a denigratory slur. I confirmed that activists and academics had redeployed the term, and that 'queer studies' was a bona fide multidisciplinary field. One of the reasons for choosing my professorial title was to prise open spaces within mainstream university for feminist-queer concerns and contestations and the sorts of questions asked by the principal. My title also reflects a commitment to feminist and queer scholarship, to critically engage with the way that law has shaped and structured sexed and gendered identities, relationships and bodies in the UK.

Over the court of my academic career, my work has focused on the ways that sex, gender and sexuality have been given meaning within, and regulated by, law. In 2005, I published my first full-length article on these issues, entitled 'Gender Is No Substitute for Sex', where I aimed to explore the terms 'sex' and 'gender', 'in order to demonstrate that the development of discourses of sex and gender has had a direct impact on the legal regulation of the sexed body' (Cowan 2005). The context was the then new Gender Recognition Act in 2004 (GRA). The GRA was passed following a long consultation period, including with trans individuals and groups, and in response to the 2002 European Court of Human Rights (ECtHR) decision in *Goodwin v. UK* (2002) 35 EHRR 18. This case held that the UK law relating to transgender people breached Articles 8 and 12 of the European Convention on Human Rights (ECHR), on the right to private and family life, and the right to marry and found a family, respectively. The GRA was progressive in many respects: it had input from an expert group of trans people; trans people were not required to undergo sterilization or other intrusive surgeries; it allowed trans people to change the sex designated on their birth certificate if they met the GRA criteria, allowing them to marry in their 'acquired' gender; and it was met with largely positive responses from many in the trans community. The Act is still in force today.

However, along with other academics and activists, I have highlighted reasons to be critical of the GRA. The process of gender recognition was initially dependent on a pathologizing mental health diagnosis of 'gender identity disorder', which shifted to the less stigmatizing yet still medicalized term 'gender dysphoria' in 2013. Also, the GRA leaves the underlying binary male/female, fixed framework of sex and gender intact, even though it allows trans people to legally 'cross over' from one side of the binary to the other. And to be granted legal recognition, trans people must sign a legal declaration that they will stay in that 'acquired' gender for life. Still, the GRA represented a significant moment of formal state recognition for some trans people, and it was praised at the time as being transformative, bringing a 'new hope' that life would get easier for (at least some) trans and gender queer people in the UK.

In this chapter, I examine some of the shifts in law, policy and cultural politics surrounding the issue of LGBTQ+ equality, particularly relating to trans people. The question of what sex a person is has never been more relevant than in today's frenzied 'moral panic' over trans people's rights. I begin by revisiting the political turn in the UK towards rights-based protections for queer and trans people in the early 2000s before exploring the various ways that those rights claims have succeeded, and yet also been undermined through a mixture of (benign?) neglect and concerted resistance, particularly regarding the rights of trans people. I conclude that there is a place for queer hope, but currently perhaps only a 'wee place', and perhaps not created purely by legal means.

The great leap forward

In Scotland, by the turn of the twenty-first century, optimism that our 'wee place' was on a progressive march towards LGBTQ+ equality began to grow: in 2000, one of the first actions of the Scottish Executive, as it was then, was to repeal 'Clause 28' – that is, Section 28 of the Local Government Act 1988, which prohibited local authorities from promoting homosexuality; and in 2001, they equalized the age of consent for same-sex sexual activity. Across the whole of the UK, the GRA brought the first formal legal recognition of trans people's acquired gender for all purposes, providing they passed the Gender Recognition Panel assessment, and the Civil Partnership Act of 2004 allowed same-sex couples to formally register their partnerships. Same-sex adoption was permitted from 2009, and in 2010 the Equality Act consolidated and updated statutory protection across the UK against discrimination and harassment, including that based on sexual orientation and gender reassignment. Same-sex marriage was legalized in England and Wales in 2013, in Scotland in 2014 and in Northern Ireland in 2020. By 2016, the Westminster cross-party Women and Equalities Committee recommended that the GRA be reformed to make it simpler for trans people to gain formal legal recognition, by replacing the lengthy medicalized process with one of self-identification.

These positive changes were reflected in the rankings formulated by international human rights organizations. In 2015, the UK was rated first in Europe by ILGA-Europe (the European region of the International Lesbian, Gay, Bisexual, Trans and Intersex

Association) for progressing LGBTI rights. Although Scotland is not marked separately from the rest of the UK, ILGA-Europe said that, if it were, in 2015 Scotland would have ranked highest in Europe (above the UK), as the most inclusive for LGBTI equality and human rights legislation, meeting 92 per cent of ILGA-Europe's forty-eight-point criteria. Scotland retained that ranking in 2016. I remember sitting, in 2016, at an LGBTQ+ hustings in Edinburgh, attended by the leaders of the main parties in Scotland. Each one stood in turn to announce a manifesto commitment to making the process of gender recognition easier and less medicalizing and humiliating for trans people. Several of those leaders were themselves LGBTQ+ community members, and I recall suggesting to my friends that night that a similar event in Westminster was unthinkable. Nevertheless, Theresa May's Conservative government did announce in 2017 that they would consult on reforming the GRA. And in 2018, due to the unrelenting efforts of the Time for Inclusive Education (TIE) campaign, Scotland became the first country in Europe to introduce mandatory education about LGBTI equality in schools.

I discussed some of these positive shifts in another project (Cowan 2022), in which I interviewed trans people about their experiences of equality in Scotland between 2014 and 2016. Interviewees spoke about their participation in civic life and their sense that the law on equality, as well as the cultural context in Scotland, gave them more protections than elsewhere. In fact, one of my interviewees said that Scotland was 'the best place on the planet to be trans'. In her intersectional research on working-class queers, Taylor notes that participants had a similar reaction and highlights the (homo) nationalism evident in how Scotland has, particularly post-Brexit, held itself up as providing 'more space as a better place'. This is despite Scotland's ongoing rising rates of poverty and inequality and the continued prevalence of classist, racist, misogynistic and anti-LGBTQ and anti-immigrant beliefs and behaviours (2023, 63–4). Like Taylor's participants, who expressed optimism, pessimism and a feeling of stasis, most of the trans people I spoke to were simultaneously hopeful and deeply sceptical about law's ability to deliver social justice. I called this attitude, 'optimistic legal realism' – 'a complex interwoven blend of cautious, equivocal but also passionate acceptance and/or rejection of the power of law to achieve true equality' (Cowan 2021: 210–11). This optimistic legal realism manifested in people's commitments to 'keep trying', notwithstanding a lack of faith in law's ability to provide real and lasting protection of their rights. It was also reflected in their attachment to the idea of a distinctly Scottish approach to progressive legal reform, particularly to trans people's rights, and particularly when compared with England. Now as I write, in Edinburgh in 2025, I question whether things have gotten better, worse or both, for queer, trans, non-binary and gender-non-conforming people and what the immediate and more long-term future holds.

Six inches forward and five inches back?

Having been ranked by ILGA-Europe as first in Europe for LGBTI rights advancement in 2015, the UK has now declined to seventeenth position, according to the 2023 figures. This is widely thought to be the result of anti-trans rhetoric, as reported by the United

Nations Independent Expert on Protection against Violence and Discrimination Based on Sexual Orientation and Gender Identity (OUNHCR 2023). The precarity of these twenty-first-century progressive shifts can be seen across the UK, both for trans and non-binary people specifically, and for LGBTQ+ people more broadly. Here I present two examples to demonstrate the now seemingly entrenched toxicity and deep-seated resistance to what are often very basic LGBTQ+ claims to equality, dignity and recognition, raising the question of the role law *does* or *should* play in queer social justice. These are, first, freedom of speech and, second, gender recognition.

a. Freedom of speech in a culture of hostility

Even during the period when Scotland was ranked in first place by ILGA-Europe, hate crime perpetrated against trans people is widely documented to have been on the rise. In Scotland, figures from the Crown Office and Procurator Fiscal Service show that in 2023–4, police reported to them eighty-four charges of transgender hate crime (i.e. where an offence was said to be aggravated by prejudice relating to transgender identity). This was seventeen (or 25 per cent) more than the previous year. COPFS figures show that this number has been rising steadily since the relevant legislation was introduced in 2010. In the same year, 1,818 charges were reported to COPFS with an aggravation of prejudice relating to sexual orientation. Although this was 5.7 per cent fewer than in 2022–3, it is the first year the number of charges reported has decreased since 2014–15, and it is still 12 per cent higher than the number in 2020–1. Of course, this only reveals the incidence of hate crime reported by the police to COPFS for prosecution, which will likely be a significant underestimation of the prevalence of hate crimes.

In 2023, new legislation passed in 2021 but not yet in force, which reformed hate crime laws in Scotland, was fiercely debated in the parliament and in the press. The new law proposed extending the stirring-up racial hatred offence to stirring-up LGBTQ+ hatred. Opponents of this extension argued it would stifle freedom of speech or expression and would criminalize perfectly legitimate speech such as gender-critical beliefs (that is, belief that sex is only ever biological, binary and immutable). In this way, the Scottish government's attempt to explicitly signal increased criminal law punishment for violence motivated by hostility against LGBTQ+ individuals and communities was itself was met with hostility and vociferous objection. While these freedom-of-expression arguments failed to prevent the Hate Crime and Public Order (Scotland) Act 2021 coming into force in 2024, in the first few days of it becoming law, Police Scotland reported that they had received a substantial number of vexatious complaints, as well as being 'dared' by J. K. Rowling to arrest her for publicly referring to trans women as men (Cook 2024). Widespread fear-mongering that misgendering a trans person would become a hate crime and lead to those with gender-critical views being arrested, ensued, but was unwarranted – as shown by previous cases of misgendering. Freedom of speech is, in fact, specifically protected in the 2021 Act. However, while by themselves hateful attitudes towards trans and LGBTQ+ people do not meet the threshold of a criminal offence, they are part of a currently thriving culture of hostility and resistance to LGBTQ+ rights.

The argument for the primacy of freedom of speech over the dignity of and hostility towards trans people has had success in other areas of law. This is illustrated by recent employment discrimination cases, such as *Forstater v. CGD Europe and Others* UKEAT/0105/20/JOJ, where the Employment Appeal Tribunal (EAT) decided that gender-critical beliefs, and in fact *all* beliefs short of Nazism and totalitarianism are protected under the Equality Act 2010 characteristic of 'religion or belief'. The later EAT case – *MacKereth* [2022] EAT 99 – concerned a doctor who had applied to work as a health and disabilities assessor for Department of Work and Pensions (DWP) who said he would not use the preferred pronouns of service users. The EAT held that although his religious and gender-critical views were protected, the DWP had not discriminated against him because of those beliefs, but because of how they were manifested; the DWP had clear guidelines that the use of preferred pronouns was necessary and proportionate to meet the needs of vulnerable service users. And in *Higgs v. Farmor's School* [2023] EAT 89, the EAT re-emphasized that in assessing whether the expression or manifestation of the belief is problematic, a test of proportionality must be applied, to assess whether any restriction is justified. All three cases state clearly that every case is dependent on its own facts; therefore, although the *manifestation* of gender-critical beliefs *can* amount to harassment under the 2010 Act, it is not clear what degree of expression of such beliefs will meet that threshold, despite some guidance in *Higgs* about what sorts of considerations need to be balanced.

What *is* clear is that publicly expressing hostility towards LGBTQ+ and particularly trans people, while not in and of itself criminal, or even necessarily discriminatory, is becoming normalized. And law has a significant role to play in this process of normalization, as it can help to create an environment in which hateful views and beliefs can flourish openly and are perceived as being of equal standing to progressive equality-promoting beliefs, even where they cause humiliation and distress. Legislation such as the Equality Act should not adopt a neutral position here because its purpose is to advance equality by making discrimination, including harassment, unlawful, protecting those vulnerable to less favourable treatment because of a protected characteristic. But freedom-of-speech arguments have been used to obviate those aims.

As Cammaerts (2022, 738) puts it:

> The invocation of democratic civic rights, namely freedom of speech and open democratic debate, goes hand in hand here with anti-democratic aims and values; that is, claiming the oxymoronic democratic right to fuel hate, and express racist, sexist and LGBTQ-phobic discourses by considering these as equivalent to other views, opinions and political positions out there, and thus up for 'open' debate.

Hate crimes and legislation such as the Equality Act were first introduced *because* people were expressing harassing, threatening and discriminatory behaviour or attitudes towards people of a different race, gender or nationality to them. Over time we have extended these legal protections to people in other groups who have been vilified because of a characteristic they have, or has been attributed to them, such as being (or being perceived as) LGBTQ+ or disabled, for example. But these antagonistic or discriminatory attitudes and behaviours often cannot be tackled through law, and the argument for protection of freedom of speech and expression rights can distract from, and/or deliberately ignore, the insidious creep of underlying hate and hostility.

And so alongside these legal debates about 'balancing rights', we must also acknowledge the worrying indications of public support – at a level that is hard to gauge – for rolling back LGBTQ+ rights. For instance, the 2023 British Social Attitudes (BSA) survey found that 'attitudes towards people who are transgender have become markedly less liberal over the past three years' and that '64% describe themselves as not prejudiced at all against people who are transgender, a decline of 18 percentage points since 2019 (82%)' (Clery 2023). Evidently public attitudes can change relatively rapidly in either direction. Some of the participants in my trans equality project (Cowan 2021) were all too aware of this. One told me, presciently, in 2016:

> I'm very aware that things could change again, I don't take anything for granted and you know things are really wonderful now and getting more wonderful and that's, obviously we all love that, and if you're a young person now you've no idea how bad things could be, but … I think gosh, this could all change again and I feel very strongly, this is why, I read loads of history so I know what people are like and how things can change for good and ill, very easily.

Of course, another key shift in the last decade is Brexit. The UK's exit from the EU was not supported in Scotland, and as Taylor points out, some queers in our 'wee place' felt the loss of the generous protection afforded by 'Rainbow Europe' equality laws, even although others – those most marginalized – had never felt the benefit of these legislative shields (2023, 70). Campaign and lobbying groups, such as the 'Campaign for Real Education' and 'Citizen Go', are capitalizing on some of these legislative and cultural shifts. For instance, Citizen Go have organized events protesting the use of 'extreme' LGBTI+ educational materials in classrooms and – with others – have also campaigned against the use of puberty blockers for under-eighteen and against the continuation of Scottish government and other funding for the charity LGBT Youth Scotland. This has been supported by some media outlets, with the *Daily Mail* describing LGBT Youth Scotland as 'controversial' and 'toxic', stating that children are being 'brainwashed' by teachers who encourage them to celebrate the LGBTQ+ movement by decorating schools with rainbow flags.

This language calls to mind the hyperbolic nature of the protracted debates over whether to introduce – and later whether to abolish – Section 28 of the Local Government Act 1988. Like Citizen Go, those in favour of Section 28 often relied on religious or C/conservative ideals, for example, about family values, as well as parental control over what children are taught in schools, and similarly to current anti-trans campaigns, they relied on the vast wealth of extremely wealthy supporters – in this case Brian Souter, who funded the 'Keep the Clause' campaign. Such visceral and venomous attack on non-normative, marginalized communities are sometimes made by what might be considered 'fringe' individuals or groups, but Citizen Go claims to have the support of over 18 million people across a broad range of jurisdictions. And while Section 28 proponents used the term 'political correctness', to dismiss equality agendas, the current anti-LGBTQ+ (hetero)activism uses the language of 'woke'[1] to describe and dismiss those who are presented variously as oversensitive, out of touch elites, radical extremists, gender/race ideologues, irrational cranks or agitators (Cammaerts 2022, 736–8). Both periods of deep division in public opinion have been termed 'culture wars' (Duffy 2025; Cammaerts 2022). Both have been treated as crises or panics over children being brainwashed, either into being gay or being transed (Hines 2020). This kind of discourse undermines the legal and socio-political attempts to prioritize social inclusion and social justice for the most marginalized, such as the apparent legal protections provided by the Equality Act, as we will now explore.

b. Legal (mis)recognition of gender and the meaning of 'sex'

The question I posed in 2005, about the relevance of what sex someone is, appears more central than ever in the UK, and perhaps particularly so in Scotland, given the failed attempt by the SNP-led Scottish government in 2023 to reform the 2004 GRA to permit gender transition without a pathologizing medical diagnosis. The Gender Recognition Reform Act (GRR) passed in the Scottish Parliament in December 2022 by 86-to-39 votes. But the Westminster Conservative government blocked the Act in 2023 by the unprecedented means of a 'Section 35 order', preventing it from receiving Royal Assent. Section 35 of the Scotland Act 1998 gives the UK government the power to intervene on bills 'which the Secretary of State has reasonable grounds to believe would be incompatible with any international obligations or the interest of defence or national security; or where the legislation would have "an adverse effect" on reserved (not-devolved) matters'.

The argument made by the UK government was that the GRR would have an adverse effect on matters reserved to Westminster, namely the operation of the Equality Act 2010's protected characteristic of 'sex'. It was also argued that having a different legal recognition regime in each jurisdiction would be unworkable. These objections provoked heated disagreement. Regarding the first objection, it was suggested by the Scottish government that the definition of 'sex' in the 2010 Act remains the same irrespective of any changes introduced by the GRR. Regarding the second, the Scottish government stated that the UK currently recognizes the gender of those who have achieved recognition in a significant number of other countries, including EU states. At the time of writing this chapter, the current prime minister Keir Starmer has publicly stated his objections to the GRR, but has also expressed support for modernizing the GRA. Meanwhile, the Act remains in limbo, and it seems that neither the Scottish nor Westminster governments are willing to take up the matter in the foreseeable future. However, the definition of 'sex' in the Equality Act continues to be the subject of legal controversy.

Notably, there is no single legal definition of either sex or gender in the UK. The case that is often cited as defining sex as 'biological' is *Corbett v. Corbett* in 1970. However, this case does not provide a generalizable definition of sex, since it was decided fifty-five years ago in the narrow context of twentieth-century English marriage law. Justice Ormrod, the judge in the case, stated, 'The question then becomes what is meant by the word "woman" in the context of a marriage, for I am not concerned to determine the "legal sex" of the respondent at large' ([1970] 2 All E.R., at 48). Also, the ECtHR in *Goodwin v. UK* (2002) stated that a purely biological definition of sex was out of step with thinking across Europe and beyond because social roles and psychological traits also had to be considered. Moreover, Section 7 of the Equality Act 2010 refers to 'physiological *or other attributes of sex*' (emphasis added). In other words, the concepts of sex and gender are not legally fixed, or inevitably biological, and nor should they be in a society responsive to evolving human needs and interests. However, proactive campaigning and strategic litigation have been deployed in the last few years, to try to force, across several key policy and legal areas, such as the census, the Equality Act 2010 and the criminal law, a single legal definition of sex that *is* biological. Criminologist Ben Collier and I have argued (2022) that these various attempts to instil a binary, biological notion of sex in as many legal and administrative categories as possible in Scotland (and elsewhere) demonstrate a deliberate programme of *concept capture* through *category co-option* – that is, the slow takeover of administrative categories of sex/gender ultimately provides a mechanism through which a rigid and regressive binary and biological concept of sex is (re)produced and reiterated, largely through an appeal to 'common sense', freedom of speech and women's safety.

For instance, gender-critical campaigners have argued that the correct interpretation of the protected characteristic of sex in the Equality Act is the sex someone is attributed at birth. This would mean that a trans person with a gender recognition certificate affirming and registering their 'acquired' gender could only be protected under the Equality Act in their 'birth' sex. Even the Equality and Human Rights Commission (EHRC), the supposed watchdog and champion of human rights, who, according to their website, has an 'independent role enforcing equality law and protecting the rights of everyone in Britain', have supported these efforts to 'clarify' that sex means biological sex. In their April 2023 letter responding to then Conservative government's Equalities Minister Kemi Badenoch's question about the meaning of sex in the Equality Act 2010, the EHRC suggested that ensuring the definition of sex is 'biological' 'would bring greater legal clarity in eight areas', including giving maternity and pregnancy protections to trans men, protecting gay men and lesbians' rights to freedom of association (without trans people) and protections for men and women more generally.

These arguments have been taken up by lobbying and campaign groups who challenge inclusion of trans people, particularly trans women, in civic life. For example, For Women Scotland (FWS) challenged the Scottish government's Gender Representation on Public Boards (Scotland) Act 2018 (GRPB), Section 2 of which defined women as including all trans women, whether they had a GRC or not. This was contested by FWS in 2022 as interfering with the definition of women in the Equality Act 2010, a UK-wide statute, which can only be amended by the UK parliament. Although the initial court (the Outer House of the Court of Session) dismissed the case, FWS were successful on appeal to the more senior court – the Inner House of the Court of Session – which also upheld FWS's argument that the Scottish government had gone beyond their competence in defining woman in this way and had conflated two different protected characteristics – that of sex and gender reassignment.

Consequently the Scottish government then published revised guidance, stating that for the purposes of the GRPB, trans women with a GRC were to be treated as women. This was further challenged by FWS, who argued that the Scottish government had again conflated two different protected characteristics. The grant of a GRC did not, FWS said, alter one's sex under the Equality Act, because sex is biological. The Outer House dismissed the case again, and this time the Inner House agreed, stating:

> It would be anomalous ... to suggest that a person with a GRC in the male sex ... should be able to assert protection against sex discrimination as a woman, and vice versa. Such an approach would seriously undermine the intention behind the GRA. It cannot be viewed as mandated by or an intended consequence of the EA. (Para 50)

They concluded: 'A person with a GRC in the female gender comes within the definition of "woman" for the purposes of section 11 of the [Equality Act], and the guidance issued in respect of the 2018 Act is lawful' (para 65). The court also stated that sex, gender and associated terms can have narrow biological definitions or broader definitions, and that these definitions are not fixed across legal contexts (para 44).

FWS appealed this decision to the higher court – in this context, the UK Supreme Court. FWS made their written arguments public in advance of the hearing, and while they bear a striking resemblance to those made by the ECHR in their letter, mentioned earlier, they have been critiqued by legal experts as convoluted and hypothetical. Yet, in April 2025, the Supreme Court upheld FWS's challenge and unanimously decided that 'sex' in the Equality Act 2010, as a matter of 'ordinary language', had a biological meaning. The Inner House of the Court of Session had found a way to interpret the Act that protects pregnancy and maternity as sex-based characteristics grounded in biological functions, while still accepting that the Act in general protects trans people with a GRC in their 'acquired' gender and certified sex. But the Supreme Court said that the term 'sex' in the Act required a consistent reading across the board: to protect maternity and pregnancy, and to allow lesbian-only spaces to operate and exclude trans women, only a biological reading of sex makes sense. What the court intended the decision to mean for intersex or non-binary people is unclear as the judgment makes no mention of either group. Nonetheless, the court in paragraph 2 of its judgment said that this ruling only has effect with respect to the interpretation of 'sex' in the Equality Act. That aspect of the judgment appears to have been largely ignored by those media outlets who are proclaiming that trans women are not women in any respect (King 2025).

On 25 April 2025 the EHRC released an 'interim update' stating not only that they would revise the Statutory Code of Practice that guides employers and service providers on how to implement the Equality Act, but that, from this point onwards, 'trans women (biological men) should not be permitted to use the women's facilities and trans men (biological women) should not be permitted to use the men's facilities, as this will mean that they are no longer single-sex facilities and must be open to all users of the opposite sex'. This 'interim update' has no legal force and is, of course, extremely distressing for trans people who will be afraid to use the bathrooms and changing rooms that accord with their lived sex-gender, and confusing and concerning for service providers who are understandably unsure about how to implement such a blanket prohibition. Not only is the EHRC's 'update' unnecessarily hasty and crude, operationalizing it would entail extremely intrusive requests or inquiries based on normative assumptions about people's appearances.

In summary, in the relation to both gender recognition and equality-based protections, arguments about freedom of speech, freedom from discrimination and freedom of association have been used to exclude trans people and deprive them from their own basic freedoms to expression and equality-based rights. In addition, attempts by the Scottish government to signal state support for increasing trans inclusion have been met with public and media hostility and have ultimately been undercut by the UK's highest court and executive branch, raising serious questions about self-governance and cultural dissonance around LGBTQ+ inclusion and equality across UK jurisdictions. Although the legal rights of trans people were apparently formalized and celebrated through the GRA in 2004 and the Equality Act in 2010, their legal recognition and inclusion is under concerted attack by those who wish birth sex – defined as biological (though biological is not clearly defined) – to be the determinative basis of legal rights and protections. These are not the only barriers to inclusion and justice for trans people. For instance, as a result of the recent Cass report (2023), puberty blockers for under eighteen-year-olds have been banned indefinitely across the UK. The consequences for young trans and non-binary people will be long-lasting, the extent of which is as yet unknown. Trans people also face challenges in accessing healthcare across the UK, with waiting lists for an initial appointment with a gender clinic being said to now reach four years or longer.

Queer hope? Some concluding thoughts

The framework of *legal rights*, often based on fixed, rigid *identity categories*, has been seen as the most promising route to protect LGBTQ+ people from harm and to ensure their participation in civic life. While this has resulted in some successes, the question of whether and how to balance supposedly 'competing rights' remains. In the UK, we are currently experiencing a convergence of multipronged attacks based on three main grounds: the prioritization of rights of freedom of speech, expression and association; the primacy of women's 'sex-based' rights; and the rights of innocent children who we are told are at risk of harm or corruption by queer or gender 'ideology'. Although themselves grounded in claims to rights, these attacks are aimed at 'abnormalizing social justice' by positioning LGBTQ+ rights campaigns – and particularly efforts to secure trans rights – as extreme 'wokery' (Cammaerts 2022). This resistance to embedding trans rights in law and policy is part of 'a contextual expression of a wider trans-exclusionary political climate that has international dimensions' beyond the UK (Pearce et al. 2020, 680). We are also seeing the consequences of repeatedly delaying consideration of gender recognition reform. As the saying goes, nature abhors a vacuum, and such a vacuum was left by the Scottish and Westminster governments in the period between 2016 when the Women and Equalities Committee recommended reform and the multiple public consultations leading to an eventual bill in 2022 in Scotland. That void has been filled with loud and vehement voices shouting about the risks that trans people – and LGBTQ+ people more generally – pose to the community at large.

In this short chapter, I have not told you anything about what it feels for me to be queer in a 'wee place': the emotionally draining yet mundanely routine task of daily navigating a world that is often unwelcoming or flat out resistant to queers (and other minorities). Engaging with the tidal comings and goings of equality and diversity initiatives, legal and policy reform and public discourses, some of which is explicitly homophobic, biphobic and transphobic, is so exhausting that I sometimes wonder why I do this work, particularly when my efforts to learn and educate myself and others about the systemic nature of inequality are ignored, dismissed or misleadingly portrayed. This year has been an especially difficult one, and I no longer have a professional presence on any social media platform. And yet – is there still space for hope? Is hope the privilege of the privileged? In her dialogue with Jose Muñoz, Lisa Duggan has written:

> As a queer feminist anti-imperialist and utterly contrary and cranky leftist, I have my doubts about the political valences of hope ... I associate it with ... coercive groupthink, with compulsory cheerfulness, with subtly coercive blandness. (Duggan and Muñoz 2009, 276)

I am also suspicious of hope. It seems incongruous for a feminist, queer scholar who spends much of her time writing against law or professing to have lost hope in the face of adversity. And I have thought deeply about Duggan's insight that hope comes with baggage – hubris, privilege, cheerful conformity. However, ultimately, my commitment to social justice requires me to radically embrace hope. And I have tried to do this in some of my work on how spaces outside of law can and do offer hope for change. For example, I and others have looked elsewhere than the legislature or the courtroom for sources of inspiration and tools to tackle inequality, harm and violence (see, for example, the artistic works in the Scottish Feminist Judgments Project). Artistic and political communities provide at least some space for speaking, not only of what has been, but of 'the story of the world as we might desire it to be ... which is yet to be written but which insists that ... [it] is possible, desirable and necessary' (Serisier 2018, 215). This is not a hope that law will be at the core of our future, as the prime catalyst for social change (even though sometimes for some things law *can* 'work'). My hope is a political mode of critique that centres an imagined place of what *could* be. It is a queer refusal and an urgent, energetic resistance. But it is also an acknowledgement of the necessity of the pain and joy – and the pain and joy of the necessity – of doing queer, feminist, political work in a wee place.

Note

1. Woke is a term originally used during the twentieth century by African Americans to describe being aware of the racism and social inequalities they faced. It became used more widely in the twenty-first century, particularly as Black Lives Matter movement gathered momentum in the 2010s. It is now used as a denigratory label by those opposed to LGBTQ+ and other social justice and equality agendas.

References

Cammaerts, B. 'The Abnormalisation of Social Justice: The "Anti-Woke Culture War" Discourse in the UK'. *Discourse & Society* 33, no. 6 (2022): 730–43.

Clery, E. *A Liberalisation in Attitudes?* British Social Attitudes, 2023. https://natcen.ac.uk/sites/default/files/2023-09/BSA%2040%20Moral%20issues.pdf. Accessed 22 July 2025.

Collier, B. and Cowan, S. 'Queer Conflicts, Concept Capture and Category Co-option: The Importance of Context in the State Collection and Recording of Sex/Gender Data'. *Social and Legal Studies* 31, no. 5 (2022): 746–72.

Cook, J. 'How Is Scotland's New Hate Crime Law Going?' *BBC*, 2024. www.bbc.co.uk/news/uk-scotland-68746512. Accessed 22 July 2025.

Cowan, S. '"Gender Is No Substitute for Sex": A Comparative Human Rights Analysis of the Legal Regulation of Sexual Identity'. *Feminist Legal Studies* 13 (2005): 67–96.

Cowan, S. '"The Best Place in the World to be Trans"? Transgender Equality and Legal Consciousness in Scotland'. In P. Dunne and S. Raj (eds), *The Queer Outside in UK Law*, pp. 187–232. Bristol: Palgrave Macmillan, 2021.

Duffy, S. 'Moral Panics and Legal Projects: Echoes of Section 28 in United Kingdom Transgender Discourse and Law Reform'. *Gender and Justice* 1, no. 1 (2025): 78–99.

Duggan, L. and Muñoz, J. E. 'Hope and Hopelessness: A Dialogue'. *Women & Performance: A Journal of Feminist Theory* 19, no. 2 (2009): 275–83.

Hines, S. 'Sex Wars and (Trans) Gender Panics: Identity and Body Politics in Contemporary UK Feminism'. *Sociological Review* 68, no. 4 (2020): 699–717.

King, J. 'What the Supreme Court's Decision in for Women Scotland's Appeal Means'. *Journal of the Law Society of Scotland*, April 2025. www.lawscot.org.uk/members/journal-hub/articles/what-the-supreme-courts-decision-in-for-women-scotlands-appeal-means/.

OHCHR. 'United Nations Independent Expert on Protection against Violence and Discrimination Based on Sexual Orientation and Gender Identity'. www.ohchr.org/sites/default/files/documents/issues/sexualorientation/statements/eom-statement-UK-IE-SOGI-2023-05-10.pdf. Accessed 22 July 2025.

Pearce, R., Erikainen, S. and Vincent, B. 'TERF Wars: An Introduction'. *Sociological Review* 68, no. 4 (2020): 677–98.

Rainbow Europe Map and Index, 2023. www.ilga-europe.org/report/rainbow-europe-2023. Accessed 22 July 2025.

Serisier, T. *Speaking Out! Feminism, Rape and Narrative Politics*. Bristol: Palgrave Macmillan, 2018.

Taylor, Y. *Working Class Queers: Time, Place and Politics*. London: Pluto Press, 2023.

5

The construction of Scotland's LGBTQ+ population in the census

Kirstie Ken English

The 2022 Scottish census featured two new questions on trans status (gender modality) and sexual orientation, opening new possibilities for understanding Scotland's LGBTQ+ population.[1] The census sparked significant debate, particularly around the sex question and how trans people should be guided in answering it. This chapter delves into these debates, exploring the underlying assumptions about sex, gender and sexual orientation that shaped the census. Normative assumptions shape boundaries on how people are expected to exist and construct our understanding of Scotland's LGBTQ+ community. In 2021 England, Wales and Northern Ireland were the first countries in the world to include a sexual orientation question in their census. However, the responses to the 'sex question' undermined trans people's autonomy over their own identities. The 2022 Scottish census led in not only producing data on LGBTQ+ people but doing so in a way that respected autonomy. I highlighted this while recognizing ways that Scotland's LGBTQ+ people could be better represented.

I approached the topic of census representation as a queer trans person who is rarely represented by population surveys: LGBTI+ people are often talked about rather than integral to the survey design processes. My research featured focus groups with populations whose relationships to sex, gender and sexuality were overlooked by previous UK population surveys and an online survey of 347 LGBTQ+ people aged sixteen and over from across the UK. I adopted a queer-feminist stance on survey representation due to the critical perspective it provides on acts of categorization and quantification. And I lean towards other queer writing and learning on the role that governmental statistics play, in not merely collecting data, but producing knowledge by dictating the categories people are expected to exist within. Intersectional queer-feminist perspectives can help destabilize assumptions of objectivity in quantitative data production and promote more reflexive and transparent approaches.

This chapter begins by summarizing some of the reasons why the census matters, with a focus on intersectionality as an important policy term, albeit with different usages. Here it is used to denote how the census can provide insights into how demographic characteristic intersect and relate to different, overlapping experiences of privilege and oppression. From there, the design of the new census questions, the sex question guidance and the assumptions surrounding them will be discussed.

Throughout this chapter I refer to the trans status question as producing data on gender modality, which refers to the relationship between someone's sex assigned at birth and their gender, it is about if someone identifies with the gender assumed of their sex (cis) or does not (trans) (Ashley 2021). In spring 2024, data from the new census questions was published and here data will be compared with the other two UK censuses (the Northern Ireland census and the England and Wales census), which featured slightly different designs. I approach the topic of survey representation as both potentially beneficial and risky for LGBTQ+ people (English 2024). My key message is that data users should view LGBTQ+ population estimates with caution: merely counting us does nothing. What matters now is how the census data is applied to meet the needs of LGBTQ+ people across Scotland. Although the Scottish census's inclusion of LGBTQ+ people is 'world leading', it has limitations, and failing to recognize these risks misrepresenting or rendering invisible parts of our community.

What is a census and why does it matter?

The Scottish census is a massive survey conducted approximately every ten years, aiming to gather information on everyone in the country. Unlike other surveys, participating in the census is mandatory – if you don't fill it out, you could face a £1,000 fine. The 2022 census marked a shift by prioritizing online responses, though paper forms were still available if needed. Most of the census questions were mandatory, but there were three optional ones: faith/religion, trans status (gender modality) and sexual orientation. These last two were only for respondents aged sixteen and older.

A census seeks to produce data on the entire population, and this comprehensive approach reduces the risk of sample bias, which is a common issue in LGBTQ+ research, where certain groups, particularly white, middle-class men from urban areas, tend to be overrepresented. The response rate for UK censuses tends to be over 90 per cent, while the 2022 census had a slightly lower response rate of only 89.8 per cent (Scotland Census 2024). Despite this it remains the largest recent survey sample in Scotland. Thus, sample bias may be less of an issue for the census compared with other surveys, making it a good source of information about the LGBTQ+ population.

Beyond creating population estimates in terms of gender modality and sexual orientation, a key benefit of censuses is the range of questions they ask. The Scottish census of 2022 asked about many demographic variables, giving us an estimate of the size of the LGBTQ+ population and its characteristics when paired with the new questions. This enables intersectional analysis, with gender modality and sexual orientation intersecting with other factors of oppression and privilege, such as ethnicity, disability and economic class.

Yet, the power behind the census has both positive and negative ramifications for LGBTQ+ representation from it. On the one hand, the census indicates who and what matters to government inclusion, as an important form of recognition, which may translate to our needs being met. On the other, for census representation to be beneficial, three things must be true: First, the government must be representing sexual orientation and gender modality with the desire to use the data to meet our needs.

Second, their conceptualizations of sex, gender, gender modality and sexual orientation and the questions based on them must be inclusive and produced in collaboration with our community. If this second requirement is not met, some LGBTQ+ people may benefit from data representation while others end up worse off as they are delegitimized by their lack of inclusion. Finally, asking questions and producing data does nothing to promote our rights in and of itself. Positive change must be *enacted* based on the data.

Question design: Setting the limits for the LGBTQ+ population

The sex question has been in every UK census and has always featured a male/female binary, while the gender modality and sexual orientation questions are new to the 2021/2 census. Although the questions and options for the sex question have remained the same, the respondent guidance has not, which has been a major area of contention across the UK. The Scottish census retained the guidance promoted by trans people and our allies, which recommends that trans people respond based on how we live. The English, Welsh and Northern Irish censuses deviated from this producing guidance that stated respondents should answer in terms of the sex on their birth certificate. If this guidance was followed, only trans people with a Gender Recognition Certificate (GRC) would be represented based on how they live.

All three UK censuses represented sexual orientation in the same way but differed in responses. Only Scotland and England and Wales produced data on gender modality (trans status) but utilizing different question designs. Comparing Scotland's census data to the rest of the UK's helps highlight the impact of different approaches. There are issues with all three UK censuses, but Scotland's was more respectful of trans people's autonomy over our own identities, which is why I present it as world leading in terms of LGBTQ+ representation.

In the 2022 Scottish census data, 0.44 per cent of respondents indicated they were trans and 4 per cent stated they were lesbian, gay or bisexual, or used the text box to specify another identity, such as asexual or queer (LGB+) (NRS 2024). Across both the gender modality and sexual orientation questions, the non-response rate is much higher than the rate of people who indicated they were LGBTQ+ (Table 5.1).

Table 5.1 Non-response Rate for Gender Modality and Sexual Orientation UK Census Questions.

Question	Census	Non-response rate (%)
Gender modality	Scotland	5.9
	England and Wales	6
Sexual orientation	Scotland	8.2
	England and Wales	7.5
	Northern Ireland	7.9

Source: NISRA (2023), NRS (2024), ONS (2023a, 2023b).

When engaging with data, particularly on LGBTQ+ and other populations who face persecution, it's important to know that population estimates are always minimum counts. The scale of non-response to these questions further emphasizes that we don't know the true size of the LGBTQ+ population in Scotland or across the UK as there is no way to know how the non-respondents identify.

The sex question and its guidance

Census bodies have been considering how trans people respond to the census for over two decades. In 2001 informal guidance was implemented for those who contacted UK census bodies to enquire about the sex question. The guidance is now known as 'lived sex guidance', which states that respondents should answer the sex question based on how they live, meaning trans men select 'male' and trans women select 'female' (this means there's no option for those outside the gender binary). In 2011 this was formalized on the census websites, which could be consulted by those needing advice on answering questions. For the latest UK censuses, Scotland continued to use lived sex guidance, whereas England, Wales and Northern Ireland employed what I will refer to here as documented sex guidance.

Documented sex, as opposed to lived sex, refers to the sex markers on official documentation, specifically birth certificates. Documented sex guidance recommends that only trans people with GRCs, which allow them to change their birth certificates, should respond to the sex question based on how they live. Therefore, it recommends that most trans women select 'male' and most trans men select 'female'. Documented sex guidance is more commonly referred to as legal sex guidance, but given that there is no legal definition of sex within Scottish or UK law, this is a misleading and value-laden title. It is also the case that a person's official documentation, such as their birth certificate, passport and driving licence, could all have different sex markers on them. Birth certificates are focused on here not because they relate to any material difference in someone's sex/gender or experiences of them, but because they are the only documentation that requires formal approval to be changed. The focus on birth certificates was made particularly apparent when the sex-based rights group Fair Play for Women legally challenged the Office for National Statics (ONS), which is responsible for the English and Welsh census. ONS's sex question guidance already recommended that respondents answer in terms of 'legal documents such as a birth certificate, Gender Recognition Certificate, or passport'. However, after Fair Play for Women were given permission to pursue a judicial review this was changed to: 'If you are considering how to answer, use the sex recorded on your birth certificate or Gender Recognition Certificate' (ONS 2021).

This change was also implemented by the Northern Ireland Statistics and Research Agency (NISRA). For both the Northern Irish and English and Welsh censuses, this change came into effect after the censuses had already been made available to respond to but before the official census day (31 March 2021), meaning some early responders would have had different guidance. National Records of Scotland (NRS) was also taken to court over their sex question guidance but won, therefore retaining lived sex guidance.

On paper this means that the boundaries of sex set in the census differ depending on where in the UK you reside. In Scotland, how someone lives (if they are a man or a woman) is how they are understood. In the rest of the UK, how they are understood in the census is dictated by their successful engagement with the gender recognition process. Reform of the Gender Recognition Act (2004) has been one of the key trans rights battlefields in recent years. Collier and Cowan (2022) refer to the debate and subsequent legal cases over sex question guidance as a form of concept capture, in which gender-critical groups are attempting to build the boundaries surrounding who is considered male or female. This is part of a larger legal context in the UK beyond the census, in which attempts are made to create firmer conceptualizations of sex that disregard trans people's autonomy over their identity. The only reason the autonomy of trans people with GRCs is respected in documented sex guidance is the privacy protections within the Gender Recognition Act (2004) preventing the census from requiring them to disclose their sex assigned at birth.

The principle behind the guidance is to help participants answer questions and promote consistency so researchers know what data the question provides, yet the guidance fails to do that in two key ways. First, for guidance to be effective, respondents must read and follow it. At the time of writing, Scottish census data comparing responses to the sex and gender modality questions is not available. However, in England and Wales, despite the use of documented sex guidance, 67.5 per cent of trans men and 66.16 per cent of trans women responded based on how they live (ONS 2023a). Given that, as of December 2021, only 6,010 people had GRCs, at least 90.6 per cent of the respondents who indicated they were trans men or women did not read or disregarded the census guidance (Ministry of Justice 2021). This clearly indicates that the documented sex guidance in England and Wales was ineffective. This does not inherently mean that lived sex guidance is useful though. When researching how to implement sex question guidance, it was found that among trans respondents, who the guidance is aimed at, only 25 per cent even read the guidance (ScotCen 2019). It remains the case that we cannot tell on what basis many trans people responded to the sex question despite the use of guidance.

The second issue with sex question guidance, be it lived or documented, is that it is an inadequate solution to the issue of poor question design. It has been clear since 2001 that the sex question lacks clarity but, rather than redesign it, guidance has been implemented to clarify it. NRS (2018) found empirical evidence that supported a redesign of the census to better reflect non-binary people. Given that the census aims to represent the entire population of Scotland, minimizing non-response rate is a key goal for NRS when designing the census. They found that, alongside having stakeholder support, non-binary-inclusive questions led to a lower item non-response rate (0.55 per cent) compared with binary sex questions (0.8 per cent). However, the Culture, Tourism, Europe and External Affairs Committee, which oversaw the census, resisted non-binary-inclusive question designs, so this was ruled out relatively early in the design process (NRS 2019).

The sex question in the census presents the population of Scotland as being either male or female. The guidance recommended that trans men and women respond based on how they live but failed to represent non-binary people. In the next subsection

I discuss the alternative route to non-binary representation in the census. However, it is important to note that, regardless of this option, the sex question is mandatory, meaning that everyone was forced within binary boxes. The sex question is also the basis on which most data is disaggregated. This means that when discussing other variables such as employment, ethnicity, health and disability populations are discussed as being male and female, with no regard to those outside the binary.

The trans status (gender modality) question

I have used the term 'gender modality' to describe the subject matter of the new trans status question. This framing draws attention to the relationship between sex assigned at birth and gender as an important axis of privilege and oppression. Although referring to these questions as 'trans' is more familiar and accessible, it isn't dissimilar to referring to 'sexual orientation' questions as 'queer'. This places emphasis on those outside the norm, re-enforcing normative cisgender and heterosexual assumptions. Here I outline the gender modality question in the 2022 Scottish census and compare it with the one employed in the 2021 English and Welsh census, to critically engage with the gender modality data.

Scotland's gender modality question has two key elements. First it asks if someone is trans or has a trans history, and second it provides a text box for those that are to state a specific gender, as shown here:

> Do you consider yourself to be trans, or have a trans history?
> This question is voluntary
> Answer only if you are aged sixteen or over
> Trans is a term used to describe people whose gender is not the same as the sex they were registered at birth
> Tick one box only
>
> - No
> - Yes, please describe your trans status (for example, non-binary, trans man, trans woman): [text box]. (NRS 2024)

The term 'trans history' is used to denote people who perceive transition as a process they went through rather than an identity they currently hold. As shown above, the question included a summary of how trans is understood. This definition, paired with the fact that non-binary was included as an example 'trans status', indicates a non-binary-inclusive understanding of trans to denote anyone whose gender is not that assumed of their sex assigned at birth.

The text box featured in the gender modality question is a useful tool in some sense as it allows for respondents to state their gender in their own words. Given this is an optional question and the binary sex question is mandatory, all respondents are categorized in terms of the binary regardless of how they respond to the gender modality question. There is the risk of classifying gender as this secondary trait that only trans people possess. The harm of this links to the sex not gender-critical perspectives discussed by queer scholars, which can lead to the rights of trans people being undermined in the face of a binary biological essentialism.

The English and Welsh census also featured a gender modality question with two options and a text box, but the similarities end there as they opted to ask about gender modality descriptively rather than utilizing the term trans as shown here:

Is the gender you identify with the same as your sex registered at birth?
This question is voluntary

- Yes
- No, write in gender identity: [text box]. (ONS 2023a)

Table 5.2 depicts the data provided by the text box in both Scotland's and England and Wales's gender modality questions. In Scotland, 84.4 per cent of respondents who indicated they were trans used the text box (NRS 2024). In England and Wales only 55 per cent of respondents that indicated they were trans used it (ONS 2023a). Table 5.2 shows the rate of different text box responses for both census gender modality questions. The gender breakdown in the Scottish census data was as follows: 9,030 non-binary people, 3,310 men, 3,090 women and 1,450 indicated another gender identity (NRS 2024). The most common other identities listed were agender, gender-fluid and genderqueer (NRS 2024).

The data for Scotland differs from that for England and Wales particularly regarding the rate of respondents who stated they were non-binary. There are three possible reasons for this difference. First, the data represents a real difference in the genders of the trans populations in Scotland and England and Wales. Second, the differences in question design led to non-binary respondents in England and Wales being less inclined to use the text box. Third, the text data was coded differently between the

Table 5.2 Gender Identities of Trans Sample from the Scottish and English and Welsh Censuses 2021/2

Gender	Census	Percentage of overall trans sample
Men	Scotland	16.6
	England and Wales	18.3
Non-binary	Scotland	45.2
	England and Wales	11.4
Women	Scotland	15.5
	England and Wales	18.30
Other	Scotland	7.3
	England and Wales	6.8
No ID	Scotland	16.6
	England and Wales	45

Note: The trans sample size for Scotland is 19,900 and for England and Wales it is 262,000.
Source: ONS (2023a), NRS (2024).

two censuses. For example, it is unclear how the census bodies handled respondents who wrote more than one gender in the text box. If someone wrote that they were a 'non-binary trans man', would they be counted as non-binary or a trans man or placed within the 'other' category? A mix of all three of these reasons could have been present. In my research focus group and survey respondents alike argued for a move away from questions that force respondents to select one category, emphasizing they are not always mutually exclusive. This was further emphasized by the fact that when surveying 347 LGBTQ+ people across the UK, 53.3 per cent of them selected more than one gender label to describe themselves when given the opportunity. Therefore, over half of that sample would have had at least part of their gender overlooked by the gender modality questions utilized in the censuses.

The gender modality question in Scotland presents a non-binary-inclusive understanding of what it means to be trans. This is important as some non-binary people may not represent themselves as trans without this specification and it recognizes that issues impacting non-binary people are part of a larger trans struggle. The Scottish census data suggested that the largest proportion of Scotland's trans population are non-binary. However, lack of clarity around how the text data was coded or specific rates of other gender identities, such as agender, limits the value of this question somewhat.

The sexual orientation question

The 2022 Scottish census was one of the first to directly ask for sexual orientation data (after the English and Welsh and Northern Irish censuses). The implementation was a long time in the making with such a question being proposed for the previous census in 2011. Compared with the debate over the sex question guidance, the implementation of the sexual orientation question was smooth. However, here I will briefly note the debate over the predictive text function for the online sexual orientation question and how it relates to essential notions of sex, gender and sexual orientation.

Like the gender modality question, this was an optional question for people ages sixteen and over and featured a text box. Alongside the 'other' option, there were three sexual orientations to choose from as shown here:

Which of the following best describes your sexual orientation?
This question is voluntary
Answer only if you are aged sixteen or over
Tick one box only

- Straight/Heterosexual
- Gay or Lesbian
- Bisexual
- Other sexual orientation, please write in: [text box]. (NRS 2024)

Originally, taking advantage of the census primarily being conducted online, the text box had a predictive text feature which would provide suggestions of common sexual orientation options as respondents typed them in. However, the media created a moral panic surrounding this with headlines reading that there would be twenty-one options for the sexual orientation question. This was misleading as the twenty-one options spoken of were simply a list of commonly used sexual identities that the predictive text function was based on. This functionality would have reduced the amount of typing differences in the 'other' responses to make the data more uniform and easier to analyse. It would have also saved some time for respondents. However, due to the controversy this functionality was removed. This doesn't mean that respondents could not type in one of those twenty-one identity labels or any others. It just means that the data wouldn't be as uniform. It was also the case that predictive text wasn't removed from other questions with text boxes.

The basis for this controversy was in essentialist understandings of sexual orientation and how it relates to sex/gender. In a letter to the Culture, Tourism, Europe and External Affairs Committee, the sex-based rights group LGB Alliance took issue with the notion of the 'other' option entirely due to its ability to produce data not specifically on the sex people are attracted to (Culture, Tourism, Europe and External Affairs Committee 2020). This understanding of sexual orientation excludes and limits a vast array of people who don't identify as heterosexual, gay, lesbian or bisexual, and also makes assumptions about how trans people use these labels. The convenor of the committee shared this perspective as she cited the letter and stated that the predictive text function 'undermined and trivialised' sexual orientation based on the Equality Act (2010) (Culture, Tourism, Europe and External Affairs Committee 2020).

The way that LGBTQ+ lives are designed out and simplified for a heteronormative majority becomes more apparent in considering issues with the analysis of text data. Table 5.3 depicts the sexual orientations of everyone who stated they were lesbian, gay or bisexual or used the 'other' text box (LGB+) across the three UK censuses. In Scotland bisexuals made up the largest proportion of the LGB+ population with 80,256 respondents being bi, while 80,104 were gay or lesbian (NRS 2024). The most common text responses were asexual, pansexual and queer, which made up more than half of the text responses (NRS 2024).

Table 5.3 Sexual Orientations of the LGB+ Sample from the Scottish, English and Welsh and Northern Irish Censuses 2021/2

LGB+ sexual orientation	Census	Percentage of overall LGB+
Gay/lesbian	Scotland	43.5
	England and Wales	48.6
	Northern Ireland	56
Bisexual	Scotland	83.6
	England and Wales	40.5
	Northern Ireland	35.7
Other	Scotland	12.7
	England and Wales	10.7
	Northern Ireland	8.2

Note: The LGB+ sample size for Scotland is 183,860; for England and Wales 1,537,000; and for Northern Ireland 31,600.
Source: ONS (2023b), NISRA (2023) and NRS (2024)

Despite employing the same sexual orientation question design, the data produced by the UK censuses differs quite a bit.[2] The proportion of bisexuals in England and Wales and Northern Ireland was much smaller with gay or lesbian being the most common LGB+ option for both censuses (NISRA 2023; ONS 2023b). As was the case with the differences in the gender modality data, this could be due to a real-world difference in the populations, due to the geographic spread of queer people or differences in how the text data was coded. For example, it is unclear how the census bodies coded data in which respondents wrote one of the listed options and another identity: for example, if someone wrote 'bisexual and queer' how was that handled? Were they included in the overall bisexual count or were they classified as other? As was the case with gender data, my respondents emphasized the importance of recognizing that many people utilize more than one sexual identity label. When provided the opportunity to select more than one label at least 51 per cent of the 347 LGBTQ+ people I surveyed can be seen as falling into more than one category.[3] The sexual orientation question in the 2022 Scottish census recognized that people could have a range of sexual orientations but required that participants select one. As was the case with the gender modality question, there is a lack of clarity surrounding how text responses were coded by NRS.

Representation without consent or intersectionality

This chapter has considered ways that the census conceptualized Scotland's LGBTQ+ population, highlighting how assumptions surrounding sex, gender and sexual orientation manifested in its design and the way the data was presented. Here I consider the data through the lenses of feminist conceptualizations of consent and intersectionality. The census in its essence is not a consensual piece of data production due to it being mandatory for all citizens to fill in. However, its lack of consent goes further than that. For feminists, consent isn't simply a lack of coercion but rather the ability for all parties to have equal power to make choices. What this means for the census is that everyone should have the same capacity to be represented or not represented based on how they see themselves. This is not the case for anyone who does not fit within the required male/female binary or anyone who identifies with more than one gender or sexual orientation. Queer lives are simplified to fit normative understandings in the census. When surveying LGBTQ+ people across the UK I found that, in regards to both gender and sexuality, over half of my sample would not be fully represented when asked to describe themselves using one gender or sexuality label. This means that even with the included text boxes in the Scottish census sexual orientation and gender modality questions much of the nuance of LGBTQ+ identities is being lost.

Intersectional analysis using census data is something that may develop over time. Currently, NRS (2024) only provides disaggregated data on gender modality in terms of age and location, and sexual orientation in terms of age, location and sex. Therefore, an intersectional analysis that considers how gender modality, sexual orientation, ethnicity, faith, disability and other variables intersect to create differing experiences is currently not possible, never mind a more in-depth analysis of how these intersections relate to different experiences of forms of oppression such as homophobia, transphobia, racisms and ablism. While it's possible that more detailed data will be released in the future, my concern is that NRS may mirror the limited way that ONS provides disaggregated data on sexual orientation and gender modality in England and Wales. Currently, analysis on the English and Welsh census data can only be conducted on either gender modality and location or sexual orientation and location and one other variable at a time. This limitation likely exists due to the risk of identifying participants if too much detailed data is shared. However, this could be avoided by either providing disaggregated data without including geographic data, or rather than sharing the data itself, census bodies could produce intersectional analysis of the LGBTQ+ populations themselves for researchers to reference. A key benefit of census data is that it produces a lot of information on a range of variables, which can be utilized to inform intersectional analysis. However, this benefit is currently not being recognized due to the limited way that census data is shared.

Here I have presented the Scottish census as world leading in terms of LGBTQ+ population data. Its 'world leading' status is due to it being one of the only censuses to produce data on gender modality and sexual orientation while also respecting trans people's ability to know themselves. Its approach to conceptualizing sex is more respectful of trans identities compared with other UK censuses, and its data on gender modality could offers a deeper understanding of the trans population than that of the English and Welsh census, if the text data is fully shared. However, it still features design issues, and what potential it does have is also yet to be realized to be limitations in the way the data has been shared. The first major design issue is its mandatory binary sex question. This question was found to be confusing, but rather than redesigning it to make it clearer, census bodies instead provided guidance to the question that very few participants read. This question means that, regardless of non-binary people's representation in the gender modality question, census data will be primarily discussed in terms of males and females, re-enforcing binary norms. The second design issue is that by only counting people in terms of one gender and sexual orientation respectively the complexity of queer lives is overlooked. Moreover, the handling of text data lacks transparency and detail, and without access to fully disaggregated data or intersectional reports, any value the census has is yet to be realized. The Scottish census may be setting the bar for LGBTQ+ population representation, but that bar is yet to fully account for the realities of queer identities.

Notes

1. Gender modality is a term promoted by Florence Ashley (2021) to denote the relationship between a person's sex assigned at birth and their gender. Transgender (trans) and cisgender (cis) are both terms that denote gender modality.
2. In the Northern Irish census there was a dedicated 'prefer not to say' option in the sexual orientation question, which was the only difference between the way the three censuses approached this topic.

3. The count of those who selected more than one sexuality label excluded people who stated they were gay and lesbian as they are often utilized interchangeably. The same was true for those who selected queer, and another category as queer is sometimes utilized as an umbrella term capturing many identities. If these respondents were included in the count, then as much as 72 per cent of the survey respondents selected more than one sexuality label.

References

Ashley, F. 'Trans Is My Gender Modality: A Modest Terminological Proposal'. In *Trans Bodies, Trans Selves*, pp. 3–29. New York: Oxford University Press, 2021.

Collier, B. and Cowan, S. 'Queer Conflicts, Concept Capture and Category Co-option: The Importance of Context in the State Collection and Recording of Sex/Gender Data'. *Social & Legal Studies* 31, no. 5 (2022): 746–72.

Culture, Tourism, Europe and External Affairs Committee. *Session 5: Official Report of Meeting*. Scottish Parliament, 2020. www.parliament.scot/chamber-and-committees/committees/current-and-previous-committees/session-5-culture-tourism-europe-and-external-affairs-committee. Accessed 27 February 2024.

English, K. 'An Overview of the Risks and Benefits of Data Representation for LGBTI+ People'. In L. Webster (ed.), *Sage Research Methods: Diversifying and Decolonizing Research*. London: Sage Publications, 2024. https://doi.org/10.4135/9781529690767.

Ministry of Justice. 'Tribunal Statistics Quarterly: October to December 2021', 2021. https://assets.publishing.service.gov.uk/government/uploads/system/uploads/attachment_data/file/1059817/Main_Tables_Q3_2021_22.ods. Accessed 27 February 2024.

NISRA. 'Main Statistics for Northern Ireland Statistical Bulletin: Sexual Orientation', 2023. www.nisra.gov.uk/system/files/statistics/census-2021-main-statistics-for-northern-ireland-phase-3-statistical-bulletin-sexual-orientation.pdf. Accessed 27 February 2024.

NRS. 'Scotland's Census 2021: Sex and Gender Identity Topic Report', 2018. www.scotlandscensus.gov.uk/documents/census2021/Sex_and_Gender_Identity_Topic_Report.pdf. Accessed 19 March 2021.

NRS. 'Scotland's Census 2022: Sexual Orientation and Trans Status or History', 2024. www.scotlandscensus.gov.uk/2022-results/scotland-s-census-2022-sexual-orientation-and-trans-status-or-history/#:~:text=There%20were%20183%2C860%20LGB%2B%20people%20in%20Scotland.,16%20and%20over%20were%20LGB%2B. Accessed 27 February 2024.

ONS. 'Census 2021: Qualitative Research on the Guidance for the Question "What Is Your Sex?"', 2021. www.ons.gov.uk/census/censustransformationprogramme/questiondevelopment/genderidentity/census2021qualitativeresearchontheguidanceforthequestionwhatisyoursex. Accessed 27 February 2024.

ONS. 'Gender Identity: Age and Sex, England and Wales: Census 2021', 2023a. www.ons.gov.uk/peoplepopulationandcommunity/culturalidentity/genderidentity/articles/genderidentityageandsexenglandandwalescensus2021/2023-01-25#:~:text=The%20question%20on%20gender%20identity,aged%2016%20years%20and%20over. Accessed 27 February 2024.

ONS. 'Sexual Orientation, England and Wales: Census 2021', 2023b. www.ons.gov.uk/peoplepopulationandcommunity/culturalidentity/sexuality/bulletins/sexualorientationenglandandwales/census2021. Accessed 27 February 2024.

ScotCen. 'Testing Guidance for the Sex Question: Scotland's Census 2021', 2019. www.scot landscensus.gov.uk/media/h24ncabw/scotcen-testing-guidance-for-the-sex-question-december-2019-108p.pdf. Accessed 27 February 2024.

Scotland's Census. 'Quality of Small Area Statistics', 2024. www.scotlandscensus.gov.uk/census-blog/quality-of-small-area-statistics/. Accessed 27 February 2024.

6

The revolt and revolting

Jj Fadaka

The mainstream image of life in Scotland fears the voice of the revolt and revolting. Nearly a decade out from the 'we are a well-intentioned, liberal haven stuck to the rest of UK' rhetoric Scotland presented during the 2014 independence campaign, what has queer life uncovered about the reality of this place? When I speak of the revolt I mean the demands that directly address the political and social struggles minimized by the Scottish media and government class: the cost of living crisis, Israel's genocide in Palestine, climate catastrophe, capitalism, imperialism in the Global South, unnecessary homelessness alongside the rise of second, third, fourth and fifth homes. These are the concerns of movements for justice that live on from their twentieth-century roots into the social media age. In Scotland they centre around a rejection of liberalism and austerity as we see before our very eyes the work we care about sucked away from us to line someone else's pockets.

Telling and acting on the truth of how we live is queer methodology. The direction of wealth and decision-making only flows upwards and stays tightly controlled. That is the reality of the Scotland we live in, and until this changes there can be no safety, no haven, no respite for queer people whose lives are more likely to intersect with poverty, precarious work and food insecurity than upward mobility. Queer methodology asks for more than representation and class aspirations. We shouldn't need a promotion to continue living in the same accommodation and seeing 'one of our own' make it to a billboard does not necessarily translate to better access to work for the rest of us. A queer revolt asks for material change for all of us, whether you identify as queer or not because our politics understands that the tools to silence one marginalized community will surely be used on another. In this way, we create a queer meaning of family that fights for anyone who wants to live free.

When I speak of the revolting, I don't mean to offend anyone but our oppressors. The revolting are the people deemed unworthy of citizenship, whether they have papers or not. They live as second-class citizens. They can be questioned by anyone who identifies with authority. Have you ever been followed by a security guard in a store? Or accused of breaking into your home when fumbling with your keys? The underclass, the revolting, are seen as born to be sidelined, extra hands for the economy and then disappeared at will. This is where queer methodology learns from the Black Radical Tradition and incorporates long-felt knowledge that capitalism and white supremacy create immovable groups of race, gender and social class that no amount of money, success or social standing will scrub away. If you fall foul of these classes, that is, you are not born a white, cisgender male and in the governing class, you must spend your life atoning and conforming even to be considered for a normal, non-punishing life. And so few people make it there. Reclaiming a word is not as easy as using it in a new context, it takes true belief in yourself that you are more than the life that has been dictated to you, and overcoming the subtle and overt criminalization and punishment of a white supremacist heteronormative world, for me, will be a lifelong task. I invite you to use the word for yourself if you wish, or cross it out and write something else you identify with. Let this be the last time someone gives you a name.

Queer methodology

Queer methodology gives us two arenas for change, in the world and in ourselves. It carries the conversation of what it means to be queer beyond just your own circumstance or whether there are more queer people on TV or whether queer people can get married, but forces us to reckon with a total reimagining of the world. Yes, I want to live in a world where I can explore my sexuality without judgement but I want that for you too. Yes, I want queer cinema and stories and parties, but I want queer people to eat well, travel safely and have access to housing too. And I want that for everyone. Queer methodology asks if we can take more and more and more, until there is no barricade between them and us, have and have not. It is binary breaking down to the soil we stand on now.

Queer methodology is a lens to understand the structures and tools institutions of authority have to curtail the lives of a non-conforming, silenced population. Heteronormativity tells us that the 'average' person is straight, white, cisgendered, works a 9–5 office job, is happy with capitalism and is unquestioning of day-to-day politics when the election is four years out. They can afford their groceries easily, are concerned about climate change but leave the solutions to policymakers and when they want to feel good they can call a friend and do one of their many free or paid-for hobbies. Every Holy Sunday they have dinner with their close family. The way we work, the social support offered to us and the national imagination are based on everyone aspiring to meet this average and an acceptance that when we do, only then will we be deemed worthy of citizenship. Until such a time we are expected to work to prove ourselves and wait to unlock the ease of life this 'average', 'normal' person feels.

But queer methodology questions who decides on this average and helps us understand that actually; no one can or really wants to live the same ready-made life. Anyone who has lived in a small-town, tight-knit community or has even gotten to know their neighbours will tell you people are weird and very different to the ideals we are compared to. They have secrets, do bad things, fight with their family, lose their jobs, go hungry, have extensive families that cram in their house every holiday or see no one for months on end. Anyone who has ever had a place to themselves has cried after a hard day, dressed up in an outfit they don't feel confident wearing outdoors, had a long conversation with their pet as if they could speak back, had sex on the living room floor with the lights on in full view of the street opposite, danced naked while they cooked or some other thing you are being reminded of now. The way we are told to present and the curation of our public image usually don't align with our true selves or what we need to feel like ourselves. Queer methodology provides the opportunity to 'queer', that is, actions that release perfection, interrogate this expectation as punishing and isolating and use tools from intersecting movements to create a society based on belonging, understanding, curiosity and an acceptance that life is fundamentally about change, not control.

Abolition versus reform

The person I am now is born from seeking refuge in abolition. I understand I cannot separate my queerness from my blackness, from my gender identity, and this has brandished me as an object to be owned and redressed in a white heteronormative gaze. I live in a body that rebels against correction. To campaign for independence and craft its own image, Scotland has become obsessed with a uniform liberal myth of itself. The reality of queer working-class life has to be brushed over and muted in the national vision for change, to maintain the perfect dichotomy of good and evil between Scotland and its southern, dominant neighbour. By resting on their laurels in liberalism, Scottish institutions implicitly tell us that we should settle for a life where active harm is not eradicated but just slightly less rampant than homophobia and racism in England. The view that non-citizens, or people outside the 'norm', should be grateful to be tolerated is a paternalistic tradition of government, whereas abolition offers a vision of solidarity; not one of us is free until we are all free. In a collective jeopardy, we can find a fulfilling meaning behind the idea of what it means to be Scottish. Scotland would like to be innovative, open-minded and welcoming, at the forefront of advancing the image of the West as no longer interested in imperialism and world policing. However, the experience of living between intersecting marginalizations exposes that the foundations of belonging in Scotland still align more with white heteronormative (aka supremacist, racist, sexist) fundamentals of citizenship than the radical binary-breaking world being imagined and built by the global majority. Scotland is inviting these historically marginalized groups to meet them halfway when these groups have waited long enough, are using their efforts to create something new, and their desires have matured past compromise. Assimilation in a country with so much potential for real change, doesn't interest me either. It requires a bending towards an ideal of Western citizenship and ideology that will ultimately punish and shame every human and non-human being who does not serve its survival.

The struggle of who leads the future of Scotland relates to a key debate on the benefits of abolition versus institutional reform. Institutional reform concedes that the system and structure in place have a legitimate ultimate authority, and people within the system must appease their oppressors, prove their humanity and receive compassion on a case-by-case basis. There is no long-term strategy to free the person who will present the same argument next time, it is a draining, dehumanizing and redundant strategy. Abolition, when looking at the prison industrial complex, punitive policies in schools or the psychiatric model, takes power back into the hands of people affected by a punishing structure. It redistributes the power that the structure held and brings people affected into the decision-making process of how to rebuild. There are no assumptions, 'this is the way it's always been' or 'there's nothing we can really do about it'. Abolition challenges each of us to act on the world, rather than to just be enacted on. It reminds us that rather than being objects, peered at, toyed with and disposed of at will, we can be subjects, in control of our own destinies.

Scotland has only offered reform in the belonging of queer people here. The ruling parties, the Scottish National Party and to a lesser extent the Green Party and Scottish Labour have been sure to compare themselves against the politics of the 2010–24 UK Conservative government. The Scottish Parliament were the first British Parliament to introduce legislation to legalize gay marriage but despite rhetoric, have generally followed the UK government's lead in enshrining LGBTQ rights in law since, despite health and social care policy and the Gender Recognition Act being devolved matters. Nation states try to quell marginalized groups by encouraging them to seek change through parliamentary activism, rather than radical action. But these 'legitimate' routes only serve a class educated in the back channels of power. So while we wait for manifesto promises of more protections for LGBTQ people to materialize and tolerate Scottish politicians marching alongside us at Pride, those tight spaces in intersections continue to squeeze. A group that have found a listening ear in government, money and institutional influence to back their right to be seen and heard are 'gender critics', people who want to exclude transgender people from what they assess should be cisgender women-only spaces. Groups with the privilege of institutional acceptance find quicker routes to enacting change in white supremacist heteronormative systems. They speak a language of exclusion, perfect victimhood and maintenance of the status quo, which the system understands, so they are heard and their requests granted more quickly. Their demands are not a threat to heteronormativity but a continuation of the alienation of queer people. Gender critics have found advocates in the ruling political parties, written articles in the country's national papers and thereby shifted the national conversation to see their 'concerns' for women and children as worthy of legitimate debate and legal consideration. The underlying image they employ confirms those fundamentals of Western supremacy, keeping physical space and citizenship centred on our relationship to being cisgender, straight and white. Their dog whistles have followed us from the twentieth century also; queer people are a threat to national identity and the upbringing of Scottish boys and girls (rhetoric steeped in racism, xenophobia and eugenics); queer ideology is corrupting and must be policed. They are lobbying for a country in which any marginalized group must be legitimized and filtered through a white straight norm before they can be allowed to exist. As such, in reality, Scotland has become a site of fear and danger for transgender, gender non-conforming and non-binary people. Their access to health and social care, in line with their gender expression, has been interrupted by (gender) policing, not just from the government, healthcare workers or Police Scotland but also from any 'gender critic' who feels emboldened by the superiority of heteronormativity to question queer gender non-conforming and transgender people, in the street, the waiting room or national paper. Scotland's genderqueer, transgender and gender-non-conforming populations survive despite their lack of rights. Their and anyone else's right to live free and safely rely not on further reform but the abolition of heteronormativity in this country.

Abolition and queer methodology go hand in hand to make me question what other possibilities, apart from the routine directly in front of me, there are in living. I could live a queer life, be my authentic self and enable the same for others or reject curiosity in the hope of being accepted by a structure that works to limit everything that makes me, me. I ask myself, what does the world as is want to curtail in us? Queerness, fluid gender expression, a rejection of Western beauty standards, a will to never look the other way, anti-capitalism, desire, communism, deep affinity with anyone touched by injustice, compassion that turns to protest that turns to change, a need for more and more radical imagination. It is a life totally incompatible with any success from reform or assimilation into heteronormativity, and the only people who can bring it to life are those around us, rather than the people in Holyrood. With our revolting comrades, half a mind on the beauty of queer life and half on the revolt, what do we do with our time on the margins?

Queer theory on the dancefloor

A new wave of queer nation-building is crystallizing in Scotland. After a nine-hour retail shift, I walk home for a quick dinner, change and jump on the bus to the location. I don't have to reveal its name for you to know if you've been there before. A bouncer checks my ID. We're still trying to move past 'legal' documents giving us a name and a standardized face. Tonight I have (barely any) femme clothes on and light make-up and so look very different anyway. He squints, holds the plastic card up to my face and lets me in. Next barrier. This one a little more welcoming. Someone with a shaved head and oversized silver piercings takes my coat and gives me a stamp on the wrist. And when I open the double doors beyond them, my senses erupt. Hot tufts of air, a hundred sweaty bodies, bass slapping wall to wall, the smell of alcohol and a trail of weed immediately hook onto me. One of my favourite DJs is about to play, so I buy a drink (an energy drink since I gave up vodka and because of the aforementioned work shift) and navigate to the centre of the room. Two hours later, a friend arrives, their thoughts almost didn't let them make it, but I give them a reassuring squeeze and introduce them to the people I've just met. The crowd tightens around the DJ as a sign of approval and encouragement. Closer in means 'I like this', 'hold my drink' means your dancing is about to go in, or you're running away for an adventure, the brisk outside is just up the stairs if you need to recalibrate. I've had so many nights like this, scored by thunderous dance music so good it makes the next day a silent movie. It's where I go to clear my mind, feel my muscles, show myself off and be in queer community. Sometimes I think about political theory on the dancefloor and, a few days later, write poems about my analysis and how good the night felt. Sometimes I want to laugh and be silly so I do things that mean I can't remember the details but the scenes show up later in my dreams.

Dancing, enjoyment and excess play a central role in my vision of 'queering'. Not everyone wants to go partying, but everyone has desire. The way they want to be seen and express their vision of what the world could be without judgement. World-building is a practice of materializing your desires, for yourself and society. You'll need a canvas, the site you'll map these ideas onto. Central questions are 'Who is my community', 'What tools do I have', 'What would we do about this or that', 'Who will take responsibility for this?' 'What will we do when conflict arises?' In queer nightlife, I see an experiment in world-building. In the club lights, you get the chance to reinvent yourself over and over. Without words, you rise above the English language and find a new way to communicate. You read body language, you practise consent, and you make sure your friends are okay. You make sure you're okay. You understand and enact what makes you feel safe. You are the active ingredient in a world of your own making.

Queer people have historically used nightlife spaces to build solidarity, find safety, family and belonging. Scottish collectives like Mojxmma, Ponyboy, GullyGullyGully (Glasgow), Saffron Cherry, Femmergy, Porty Pride Ball (Edinburgh) and more have pioneered a new age of nightlife that provides welfare support for harassment, questions and advocacy and inbuilt access for disabled and neuro-divergent people. Experiencing their events and my desire for community has led me to start my own club night, RAVE4GOOD. Our existence is directly tied to the history of haven queer nightlife spaces. Fire Island, still the largest queer nightclub seen in Edinburgh, opened in 1978 and welcomed queer icons such as Eartha Kitt and the Village People. The club was renowned for its high-energy dance music, earning it comparisons to New York's Studio 54. It made music history as one of the first Scottish clubs where you could hear a DJ mixing records rather than just announcing songs, but the club shut its doors in 1989 when the venue was sold to Waterstones. A regular attendee of Fire Island, Derek Ogg would later tell the BBC he set up Scottish Aids Monitor after attending a disco one night and speaking to his friends about how many peers were travelling between New York and Scotland and bringing back news of a new virus affecting gay people. The twenty-first-century Scottish queer nightlife scene has organized rapidly to raise money for medical aid for Palestine, fund gender-affirming surgeries and start hardship funds for regulars. Queer nights have brought intersecting grief together under one roof of compassion, anger and action. Parties are thrown to remember our ancestors, anarchist punks, 1970s and 1980s trailblazers as well as tongue-in-cheek dedications to pop culture icons that give a hard life humour and camp.

In my home country, Nigeria, queer people dance in clubs that are queer in everything but name, underground raves erected and vacated overnight or rely on house parties with carefully vetted lists of 'I know this person, let them in'. Vincent Desmond, a Nigerian reporter, writes widely on the country's surviving LGBTQ+ network despite the criminalization of any queer relationships or advocacy since 2014. I've been planning a trip back and trying to map where to find my community outside my family ties. Although Scotland and other Western countries measure LGBTQ+ rights against countries like Nigeria to position themselves as morally progressive (despite homophobia in the Global South having direct ties to colonialism), permanent queer nightlife spaces are still hard to come by here and I still plan carefully in advance where I can go to feel safe and celebrated. Bonjour opened its doors on Saltmarket in Glasgow in 2021 and closed in 2023. As a lighthouse for centrally located queer people,

Bonjour ran as a worker-owned cooperative and prioritized the nightlife experience of people who were queer, transgender and non-binary, sex workers, disabled, neurodivergent and categorized by colour. Faced with the limited funding available for queer spaces in Scotland and financial pressures after the onset of the Covid-19 pandemic, the club was forced to close and no queer-first club has been able to open to fill this gap. In my current base in Edinburgh, queer people settle for singular 'queer nights' much like we wait and settle for other one-off events where we can gather for free or at a low cost. The struggle for property, land and the rights you are entitled to, even when you occupy that land, keeps the queer community isolated and unable to effectively organize or live with one another. How can I know what you need or check in with you if I cannot see you? And so I feel the struggle for space both here in Scotland and abroad, constantly meeting people on one faithful day and then parting ways, hoping we can meet in a space of our making again, outside of a heteronormative gaze or work or other burdens.

Queer nightlife spaces acknowledge that we move through life with mental and physical pain, we are hungry and in need, we are worried and anxious, but we can still be together, among it all. You don't have to leave anything at the door and present yourself as 'well'. In this way, queer methodology learns from disability justice as it learns to reject ableism, which is, in this context, the assumption of ability, energy and access. Inviting everyone in broadens the framing of who is allowed to desire and have those desires met. World-making on the dancefloor is a collective act of making safety, even if just for one night, even if we get it wrong tonight. Take this glimpse of the future and carry it with you. Here you can let go, take care of others and receive the same. There are no qualifiers for dreaming. You is enough.

There is usually a lump in my throat as the bouncer checks my ID. I'm reminded in that moment of the world I was born into and every way it has classified me. Borders and barriers exist to make us feel small and feeble against the authority of the land within it. I have the privilege of a British passport, but feel the pain and injustice of colonial land grabs and arbitrary border lines when I pass through an airport and see the crowd splinter at immigration control. I feel tired and disheartened when I think about the possibility of changing my name, and I feel the weight of holding someone who sighs in exhaustion as they think about the bureaucracy of legally changing their gender. I want to go to a club my undocumented friend can attend. I want my queer Nigerian community to have never been touched by white supremacist, homophobic colonizers. I want to betray the nation state that demands I am everything someone else said I was before I could speak for myself. I wonder sometimes what it would be like to introduce myself in dance, or facial expression, or decline an introduction. To change faces every day, like I change clothes and move through the many lives swirling within me. I wrap my coat tightly around my body as I wait in queues for Scottish clubs, waiting to unleash my interior, the warmest, softest place I keep my queerness and its possibilities until it is safe to announce. And when I arrive, that is, I know we are welcome and feel that sticky feeling of belonging keeping me in place, I see so many smiling, crying, laughing, grumpy queer faces, blinking back at me, a hall of mirrors of people living their lives in truth, even if the rest of the world isn't ready.

Free, free …

I also expected a big queer party at Edinburgh's 2024 Official Pride March. What could be more radical than hundreds of queer people walking through the city, chanting, singing and dancing? But on the soft green of the Meadows, after the procession was done, I felt something lacking, in a way I did not feel at the nightlife spaces I had started to call home. Compared to the rest of the country, Edinburgh is a rich, comfortable city. Meaning it also attracts people who need better proximity to their country's wealth and safety. People migrate to where the wealth is because that is where the work is, and the price of concentrating wealth so tightly means it is the city's responsibility to sustain the people who power its core. In an economy that relies on service work, zero-hour contracts and gig-based work, workers need to be within travel-at-the-drop-of-a-hat distance to their employer. Edinburgh is much the same as any city, its streets line poverty and riches side by side, and everyone from the local council to the top level of government works to ensure this does not affect the peace and usual day-to-day of the wealthy. At Pride marches, the enforced gap between classes, whether it is found in the distance between our bodies or the streets we live on, is physically filled as people from all classes come to enjoy the celebration and walk shoulder to shoulder. There is an air of joy and revelry, but that doesn't mean we are all celebrating the same thing.

Pride started as a protest, but today those roots are choked by corporate intervention and an ignorance or deliberate obscuring of the need for that protest to continue. I marched with the Radical Bloc, a cowpoke with a megaphone chanted 'FREE, FREE', and the bloc responded 'PALESTINE' 'CONGO' 'SUDAN'. Half a mile ahead, past the signs for trans solidarity, renters unions and the local radical political parties; a cinema chain's workers danced and played Billie Eilish. Further ahead, a bloc for a supermarket chain similarly didn't have much of their own words to say. Their 'celebration' of queerness consisted of rainbow lanyards and official company merch with a Pride pin attached. I wondered if they were paying their workers for the free advertisement.

The corporate blocs split with us and funnelled into a heaving Bristo Square, hosting the Official Pride stage, which would later feature Atomic Kitten and other pop acts. The performance was free, but the drinks (which you needed in the heat) and food were marked up. The Pink Economy, the spending power of the queer population, is a lucrative target market for the city's industry. Queer people with disposable income can see a cinema chain at Pride, feel warmth at this sign of allyship and elect to buy a ticket pass for the year. This transaction is the sole motivation for companies to sticker their queer employees, give them the afternoon off and send them out as silent advocates for businesses. Turning the queer community into a predictable consumer group to be researched and marketed to can be the only reason a company would care to advocate for morality that they do not show in any other area of our lives. Otherwise, these same chains would employ queer and feminist policies such as matching paternity leave to fostering, adoption and maternity leave. And we wouldn't have to wait until a white, silent picture of a queer person has become an accepted face in civil society, before they are recognized as safe to appear on advertising or merchandise. The image of a white, gender-conforming queer person or couple, who are always portrayed as silently content or repeating lines provided by the corporation, has been co-opted by business and is now safe to be seen as a legitimate customer (the business's version of a citizen).

In the UK, queer people marched on 1 July 1972, in honour of the Stonewall riots two years before. In the 1980s, they marched to protest the UK government's criminalization of same-sex relationships and Section 28 (the banning of LGBTQ+ 'promotion' in schools). More than fifty years on, we marched for Just Stop Oil activists, arrested at Heathrow Airport for protesting against climate extinction. In August 2024, five activists were arrested in Glasgow for protesting at a weapons factory producing drones used by the Israeli government. In March 2024, just a few metres off the route of the Edinburgh Pride march, five activists were arrested by Police Scotland for targeting a UK government building with red paint in protest of the state's support of the Israeli government. In July 2025, the group targeting weapon manufacturers and government agencies arming the Israel Defense Force, Palestine Action, were proscribed as a terrorist group. Anyone showing support for them can and have been arrested *en masse* by police forces across the UK.

In those tight processions, queer people across class, race, sexuality and gender expression stand side by side. The lives of the hundreds of people I passed that afternoon paint a mosaic of a disparate social group where the oppression of sexuality and gender expression can be selectively muted to better assimilate into other more comfortable categories, that is, middle-classness, whiteness and so on. But the degradation of the roots of our existence, that purposeful looking away from the other beings we share a bonded life with, cannot be maintained indefinitely. The lives of queer people living in occupation, fleeing hostile states by any means necessary, in prisons across our country or on the outskirts of the mine where they are indentured to work for our gadgets, put an asterisk on the so-called safety LGBTQ+ people have here. Queer methodology learns from our understanding of imperialism and colonialism's boomerang effect. An oppressive state tests the limits of its power and violence on a group of people the national imagination deems as less than human. At first, they usually live abroad, they are not named or given a collective dehumanized name (rebels, terrorists, migrants), and when the state has perfected its dark art, it calls it home, to experiment on disappearing and breaking people on its own soil.

Whether we face them or look away, the needs of queer people at home and far away still impact each of us in the community, and the lives we lead impact them. Queerness has put us in an interconnected web, which will take more than money or lack thereof to untie. Queer methodology employs the language of solidarity to help us understand 'community' is not just based on proximity, or likeness, or shared characteristics, but is built on a shared vision for the world, the tools we want to use to build it or at least a willingness to see each other as living beings worthy of love and compassion. Or we can more simply borrow a phrase from Black Americans, 'not all skin folk are kinfolk'. The world becomes so alienating in that way, you feel your community becoming smaller as you call out for solidarity and hear only half the people that are supposed to be your people respond. Or you stand shoulder to shoulder with a stranger so different from you, both screaming at the police to free a person you've never met, you lock eyes and realize you are all you've got against a world so united in its efforts to destroy you. That makes us family. Queering our lives, queering Scotland requires an implementation of revolt to topsy-turvy the heteronormative order of doing things. Ideologies of white domination – like 'only these are my people', 'as long as I'm alright', 'what have they ever done for me?' – rob us of the opportunity of sharing crucial life-sustaining work. And if queer people are to advance anything in this country, we need to live, identify our community and sustain the revolt of the revolting. The concerns of queer politics in Scotland should be the concerns of everybody, rising homelessness, affordable living, food scarcity, the ability to live and love well and the genocides and violent imperialism I have mentioned. In the two inches around you at the Pride march, you can make a life-long friend and the world gets a bit bigger, with more human faces, or you get to chatting and realize they don't care much about others, and the earth shrinks again, your face disappeared of its humanity with the shrug of their shoulders.

It is a necessary and urgent call to ask us to queer our lives again. Witnessing how humanization, understanding, curiosity and radical acceptance of desire and change splits open our understanding of what queer community is and can do. It can make your day worth living, teach you to be compassionate to yourself and orchestrate your own brave space to organize from. It gives us more people to love and be loved by. Queering comes with discernment, demands, advocacy, grief and growth. It is a cycle of abolition, tearing down to redistribute to retry again. It takes a lot of bravery and honesty. It is possible this wee country could become a queer place. Imagine a Scotland with equal safety for all gender expressions and sexualities, expanding that right for every being that steps on its soil, documented or undocumented. Imagine a total rejection of the Westminster machine and political power and decision-making encouraged and enabled at every level of society. Imagine having a day off for Pride! Less and less back-breaking work. A job market that can accommodate the creative, energized, innovative people it is supposed to champion. Look at the country as is. It's not a hopeless picture but a determined one. Queerness comes with protest, demands and actions. Family isn't given to people who just yesterday oppressed us so easily. Queer methodology is an open door to step in, but it requires you to then move from that comfortable 'normal' position. The full spectrum of who we are and the things we need to live can only be grasped when no one lives on the margins. Come into the light, revolting! Bring the struggles you carry within you and your right to a queer life.

Explore more on how to 'queer'

Read: Sadiya Hartman's *Wayward Lives and Beautiful Experiments*, Lola Olufemi's *Experiments in Imagining Otherwise*, Nat Raha and Mijke van der Drift's *Trans Femme Futures*

Listen: To conversations you hear on the street, to music, with and without lyrics, write to sounds that make you feel joyful and energized.

Dance: At RAVE4GOOD (see you there!).

Go to: Your local Pride, your community funded pride and queer events.

Feed: Yourself and your friends, someone new. Organize a potluck, food is a great equalizer, don't assume that everyone has access or energy to make a hot meal.

Initiate: Creative activities for yourself and people you care about, speak through drawings, charades, napping together, let people express in ways that make them feel seen and confident and you will be surprised what you will learn about each other. Initiate a protest, a zine drive, a discussion group.

Disrupt: The voice that tells you 'this is the way it is', give yourself a day to live in the future you are fighting for, how would you dress? What would you do with your day?

Withdraw: Your labour, your money, your attention, your energy, your presence from people and places that aren't in solidarity with you and your community.

Part 2

Queer States: Legacies and Transformations

7

Queer provincialisms in (post-)Brexit Britain

Yvette Taylor

Five years ago I would've called myself British, because I was against Scottish independence ... I would always say 'I'm from Britain, I'm Great British', and that was my right. Scotland is more progressive than England and the UK as a whole ... I have been slowly pulled more towards 'I'm Scottish, not British', and I still couldn't honestly answer you whether I'd vote 'yes' or 'no' [to independence] if I got the chance again. But I'm certainly now Scottish not British, and that is because I'd rather be European than be British. (Lachlan, twenty-four, white, gay cis man)

If someone LGBT lived in Scotland from the beginning of his life they can see some problems with LGBT, but I lived in a country where there's oppression. So when I came here I found all the equalities and all the freedom. There are some problems. But I see that the government's still working on it. But in Morocco the government, it's still oppressing for LGBT communities and society is against it. (Farj, twenty-six, mixed-race, bisexual trans person)

Introduction: Rainbow Europe, (post-)Brexit Britain and other states

What's at stake in state transformations, in the breaking up and reconstitution of nation states and how does this matter to queers? Is there hope in queer reconstitutions within and across the borders of the nation state? Many suggest a reorientation towards the Global South and local queer spaces as a provincial move away from Global North – and US-centric – research (Mahn et al. 2025). Such a redirection might also work to differentiate and challenge state-centrism, rather than seeking solution or solace from the state. Forms of provincialism, enacted in 'wee places', might productively position against big nationalism, including methodological nationalism, which assumes a fixed state rather than sites, subjects and borders in flux. Scotland – seemingly out of sync with the wider UK in voting against Brexit – pitches itself as part of a 'Rainbow Europe' while distancing from Britain (and England specifically). However, 'Europeanizing queer', for mobile 'world citizens' who can traverse borders, acts simply to replace US-centrism with Euro-centrism and heightens a binary between 'leading' and 'other' states. Here I explore the claims of citizens – and non-citizens – in (post-)Brexit Britain as 'queer provincialisms' are navigated.

Nation states are differentiated as guarantors and protectors of LGBTQ+ rights, and homonationalism extends into small spaces. The 'small space' I invoke here is Scotland as a devolved nation and constituent part of the UK. I do so as Scotland claims to be a different kind of nation, casting citizenship as civic, rather than ethnic and as closer to Europe in its pro-remain outcome than it is to England/Britain. This transitional moment – between a failed state represented by the UK Westminster government – and a different state which the Scottish government was often seen to embody – allows for an interrogation of nation states. There is queer potential in these transitions: some queers can enact their social and legal entitlements as full citizens and the impact of Brexit might be limited to, for example, frustrations around potential travel delays or longer-term relocation retirement plans. There are important differences in the experience of mobility as intersecting inequalities are mapped onto new–old bordering practices, regimes and institutions. Lachlan, for example, has the choice to move between Scottish-British identity categories, as politicized preferences, while others simply cannot choose.

Like Lachlan, some interviewees felt that space would be made in 'Rainbow Europe' to include the Saltire flag, even as a 'leading light'. Here Scotland takes up more space as a better place. While Lachlan refuses recognition, as not-British, he does so as a British passport holder, while for Farj, Britishness was aspirant as well as ambivalent, bound up in a migrating middle-class status not easily capitalized upon in the context of a new country. Claims about Scottish difference gloss over interviewees' lived experiences, wherein accounts of racism highlight the whiteness already at the centre of (homo)nationalist agendas, ever enacted in Scottish-British-European nation states. Racism, sexism, homophobia and transphobia were specifically mentioned as enduring realities curtailing a sense of state transformation, including an imagining of civic or queer citizenship. Farj's case – outlined in this chapter in some detail – challenges an additive or static view of inequality and identity.

The (post-)Brexit period stretches backwards from the 23 June 2016 referendum and forwards beyond the 31 January 2020 exit, as the regressive-progressive potential of states exceeds the Brexit timeline. In taking part in research between 2018 and 2021, interviewees expressed a sense of pessimism and optimism, as well as a sense of stasis. I interviewed queer workers, residents and parents, as well as those without employment, those unable to gain work, those with pending asylum claims and those with families and communities in and beyond the new EU–UK borders (Taylor 2023). Some interviewees expressed a generalized nervousness around (post-)Brexit Britain, fearing a potential lack of recourse to leading progressive 'Rainbow Europe' equality law. However, less privileged participants had never felt included or protected by those same laws. Highlighting intersecting inequalities in the (post-)Brexit context means being sceptical about the descriptive listing of 'protected characteristics' and equalities legislation more generally. Such scepticism and uncertainty becomes a problem with respect to empirical measures and categories, including the ones adopted in, and accountable to, EU funding programmes. The first section of this chapter thinks through how definitions of race, and other demographic characteristics, such as sexuality and gender, are included in, as and beyond a project count of 'sample size'. The second section discusses citizenship navigations in the (post-)Brexit context, including the case of Farj, a twenty-six-year-old asylum-seeker originally from Morocco, who describes themselves as mixed-race, bisexual, trans and middle class. Secondly, it situates Farj's optimism about Scotland alongside other interviewees' celebratory accounts. The third section considers interviewees' senses of sameness and difference, pessimism and optimism, as state and social structures are lived through continued crisis times.

Projecting whiteness: Working with (white) Europe

They think people in working-class council estates are Brexit crazy unionists, racist, homophobic, there's no place for us there, there's no LGBTQ there. Which is just a lie, which is just not true. (Dan, thirty-six, white, gay cis man)

The accounts in this chapter come from the 'Comparing Intersectional Lifecourse Inequalities amongst LGBTQI+ Citizens in Four European Countries' (CILIA) project (2018–21). Over the course of this project the number of EU partner countries (England, Germany, Portugal and Scotland) decreased by two as Scotland and England left the EU. The project was imagined in part to surpass the 'methodological nationalism' of using national frames, references and places to locate and include populations. Methodological nationalism means the Global North becomes both the starting and the end point – a heroic measure of progression now arrived at and via LGBTQ+ rights. Country context might be variously depicted as 'diverse' or 'homogenous', as central or periphery, and as (not) having a place or contribution in the context of research and researchers going 'everywhere'. The research partnerships in the grant were – and are – a long time in the making. So too are the very conditions and categories – intersectional inequalities in the context of LGBTQI+ citizenship across and within borders – that the project worked through.

In comparing distinctive nation states, the intention was to think about the stories and experiences of progress and the ways in which nations, communities and individuals claimed citizenship or were rendered unentitled to it. The point wasn't just to produce a simplistic count of good/bad nations or to plot a linear path which moved queers from the 'other' category to a full social and political count. In moving from being EU citizens to no longer being so, even if they felt and expressed themselves to still be 'European', interviewees in Scotland and England highlighted both the promise of and threat to citizenship and to 'Rainbow Europe'. EU participants often found themselves entangled in the bureaucracy of renavigating citizenship rights, including welfare, employment and residency. Within the research, Scotland was often collapsed into England, as England was conflated with Britain. On such occasions I found myself issuing an objective corrective, which was also imbued with subjective affects, as I too cast Scotland as *not just* a 'wee place' and as 'big enough'. I too navigated the questions of internationalisms and provincialisms scaled to questions of who and what counts in the (post-)Brexit moment. As Dan's opening quote implies, much can be at stake in the reduction of people and place, as council estates became represented as pro-Brexit concentrations, and the problem of Brexit became located as a problem of the white working classes. As Dan's indignation suggests, this often was, and is, simply not true, misreading working classes as homogeneously white and disguising the reality of more powerful middle-class Brexit voters.

In researching queer communities I've used and omitted class terms on project information and in recruitment processes, finding that flyers – when unmarked as projects recruiting from LGBTQ+ populations generally – typically recruit white, middle-class and gay cis male interviewees first. Aware of this, I decided to hold back in recruiting, to allow others time and space to come forward, and in particular to actively recruit across working-class and minoritized ethnic groups. I used a screening survey to balance those who'd rushed forward as eager LGBTQ+ citizens and those who held back. Gauging reasons for participating can also be an important factor to balance – with lots of enthusiasm among certain groups ('As an LGBTQ+ person …') sitting alongside a responsibility, reluctance and ambivalence. Still most participants were of white ethnic backgrounds, including participants from Scotland and the rest of the UK, Western, Central and Eastern Europe, the United States, Canada and New Zealand. Six participants were Black, South Asian, South East Asian and of mixed ethnic backgrounds, including participants from Scotland, the rest of the UK and Morocco. This lack of ethnic diversity is a project failure, but a failure that has a history as an embedded disciplinary practice so rooted that queer research projects may first be recognized as white projects, also imagining and projecting whiteness onto queer populations. This necessitates thinking outside the rainbow, and outside the normative markers even within queer populations, with whiteness constructed as central to LGBTQ+ identities.

Most participants described themselves as Scottish or as being from Scotland: years spent in Scotland impacted upon a sense of and claim to 'being Scottish' when not 'born in Scotland'. For some, dual citizenship meant a material hyphenation of British-Scottish-and … In constructing a recruitment survey, I paused on the 'list of ethnic groups' in official surveys, including expanded categories of whiteness. Whiteness as a category may be neutralized in the seemingly benign list of tick-boxes from which to select and vary – while the dominant effect of whiteness prevails. In responding to the categories used by the 2011 census the 'awkward etc.' box of 'Other, please state' was used. White participants used varied descriptors, to include, for example, 'White Scottish, Dutch, French-Canadian', 'Eastern European, Scottish', 'White European/Mediterranean'.

White[1]

- English, Welsh, Scottish, Northern Irish or British
- Irish
- Gypsy or Irish Traveller
- Any other white background

Participants of colour also modified and inserted Scottish descriptors (e.g. 'Scottish South Asian', 'Mixed Scottish'). British and Scottish national identity is racialized as white and the limited participation people of colour is not just a result of category failures, such as in the 2011 census list of ethnic groups, but of cultural exclusion, misrecognition and racism. Disclosures can happen without whiteness being disclosed: in talking about the lack of people of colour in the sample, the user group and its (non-)academic members (including myself) explained and excused, framing Scotland as 'not very diverse', as 96 per cent white. But a lack of ethnic diversity cannot be excused because of a supposedly low percentage of 'ethnic population', just as queer researchers would not likely be content with a simplistic LGBTQ+ count as then not amounting to enough or as not mattering. In describing herself, Jess uses 'pakeha' as a Māori-language term for white New Zealanders primarily of European descent – although the term and usage is not without controversy. Jess repeats the common-sense view of whiteness as just how-it-is, making 'quite white' difficult to refute:

> And then coming to Scotland that was quite interesting because Scotland's quite white, and so I maybe don't see as much of what goes on as I had a glimpse into like race and gender relations in New Zealand. I haven't seen as much of it here because I think Scotland's 97 per cent white. (Jess, thirty-three, pakeha, lesbian, cis woman)

The CILIA sample was diverse in terms of sexual and gender identifications: respondents variously described themselves as lesbian, gay, bisexual, pansexual, queer and asexual. Around a third of participants described themselves as trans, non-binary, intersex, genderqueer or gender-diverse; while the assumption might be that two-thirds were cis gender, not all remaining respondents self-selected this. This is suggestive of potential hesitancy around the category of 'cis', which may reflect its typically neutral or unmarked status, as with whiteness, middle-classness or heterosexuality. Yet it may also reflect a deeper ambiguity too – a pause and uncertainty on behalf of interviewees, as well as assumptions from researchers that there is nothing to explore or unpack around cis gender as a category or lived experience (Zabrowskis 2023). Lesbian, gay and bisexual interviewees did express varied experiences of inhabiting gender and sexuality queerly, of questioning normative assumptions of gender essentialism, of not inhabiting 'proper' femininity and masculinity, and many had been misgendered. This is not to conflate these expressions and experiences into trans and non-binary experiences – particularly in the context of increased transphobia – but rather to continue to queer sexual-gender categories.

Naming, coding and categorizing advantage and disadvantage in the context of queer lives can be difficult, where ideas of 'Rainbow Europe' act as homo-nationalist gloss, as queer metrics, which citizens move into as included. Dan's (thirty-six, white, gay cis man) opening quote resituates everyday, provincial progress *within* rather than *outside* of working-class communities, often assumed to be regressive as 'Brexit crazy unionists', with 'racist, homophobic' feelings. He does so as a named carer to his partner who has disabilities, living in an adapted council house on benefits, and supported by their rural community, refusing the go-to 'left behind' homogenized and racialized narrative projected onto white working-class communities. Dan does this without explicitly naming the whiteness implicit in shaping community, progress and protection. The below section highlights how different 'world citizens' navigate a threatened or secured 'Rainbow Europe', including as anxious, entitled and ambivalent citizens. I then turn to Farj's case; their status as a non-citizen troubles ideas of middle-class privilege, exemplified in the loss of migrating classed capitals, including material and linguistic capitals. Like others, Farj invokes a racialized global hierarchy of LGBTQ+ livability – yet it is one they are also judged by and implicated in rather than removed from. The objective census lists and codes are, for Farj, subjectively felt as not belonging, as non-citizenship. Farj's longer-term plan of seeking US citizenship, while positively assessing Scotland as *the place* to be LGBTQ+, sat alongside multiple visa and residency applications. In interviewees' accounts the underlying anxiety lurking in queer community is exposed; accepted borders and boundaries are not necessarily straightforward realities for queers.

World citizens in 'Rainbow Europe'

The loss of EU membership brings different fears for different queers. While some lamented the loss of a protective 'Rainbow Europe' others had never felt included within its realm. The very imagining of a 'Rainbow Europe' involves pink-washing nation states, while displacing homo- and transphobia onto other classed and racialized places and people inside (the 'council estate') and outside of Europe – Muslims, migrants and refugees are repeatedly depicted as stalling and draining the progressive liberal state. Europe's reinvention as LGBTQ+-friendly effaces the political struggles and slippages around this; and in reimagining nation states as places of loss or gain post-Brexit, forms of homonationalism emerge. Puar defines homonationalism as 'an analytical category deployed to understand and historicize how and why a nation's "gay-friendly" status has become desirable as a marker of progress, modernity and civilisation' (2013, 336). Nation-making in the UK has long exceeded its own borders, and its colonial past remains present, including in its imagining itself as a global leader.

In interview accounts a generalized sense of anxiety in losing the protective capacity of 'Rainbow Europe' was pitted against the UK 'hostile environment':

> It's the European Union that's given a lot of rights to the gay community and the people who are in charge of Brexit don't seem to be prioritizing that. So I do worry what would happen. At the same time I also feel like the LGBT community is confident in their own voice now, that if, you know, whatever were to happen we would campaign to stop, you know, our rights from being taken away. (Grace, thirty-two, white, bisexual, cis woman)

There were evident queer articulations of still remaining, being and feeling European, where turning to Europe in the face of hostile national policies and events could offer other identifications and possibilities. Yet these feelings and choices were not uncomplicated or unrelated to material realities – claims of, for and by 'world citizens' became statements and sites of privilege, where the 'wee place' of the local is extended globally. More privileged interviewees spoke of their travel plans being curtailed, where they had, for example, looked to relocate post-retirement to continental Europe. Often this ended up recirculating a hierarchy of places to *be* LGBTQ+, with even positive notions of progression ending up in this same framing loop ('So it's great to see how things have changed over time and how gay marriage has sort of spread like an excellent virus around the world and gone to more countries than I ever imagined' (Jess, thirty-three, pakeha, lesbian, cis woman)).

> My partner and I both have, her in particular, she has quite a global outreach in her career, so there's the possibility we'll live somewhere else next after Scotland, and certainly it being a gay-friendly place is like top of the agenda, especially with us hoping to have a family. (Jess, thirty-three, pakeha, lesbian, cis woman)

Others expressed concerns about the availability of health care and spoke of the possibility of seeking out new markets, in effect as mobile citizens. Some were awkwardly charged with self-managing their own health care, as also a way to manage being and identity in the world. Quinn (twenty-three, white, gay, non-binary), for example, was anxious that Brexit could mean 'I won't be able to access like HRT' (hormone replacement therapy), producing a 'kind of constant fear'. Such anxiety was related to a series of articulated costs and consequences and the challenges of moving to another country – in this case North America with a private health system – as compared with the challenges of remaining in Scotland. While Quinn does on balance have a degree of privilege in being able to move with their partner who is a dual citizen, their desire is simply to find a 'pocket of safety', to continue to access gender-affirming hormone replacement therapy and to lead a more liveable life.

Within the articulation of chosen mobilities, and constraints, of imagining futures 'here' and 'there', existed real and important questions of basic citizenship entitlements and rights. Clio was actively navigating legal entitlements between countries and between different legalized versions of what, who and where constitutes a relationship or a family. Clio had 'come out' five or six years before our interview and expressed a sense of progress and of 'standing on the shoulders of giants, right, and not letting the [LGBTQ+] flag down' yet felt that the 'fights start again'. As a dual British and Greek citizen Clio was now actively pursuing a French passport as part of this fight:

> When Brexit happened I was like 'What are we going to do? Because Greece won't recognize our marriage'. They will now, because basically the EU rapped them on the knuckle and said 'alright you don't have to do gay marriages, but you have to recognize marriages'. So, but at that time I was like 'I need to go and get my French passport so that should we need to leave you can come with me as my spouse', you know? (Clio, thirty-five, white European/Mediterranean, bisexual, cis woman)

Interviewees sought to navigate (post-)Brexit realities, with the sense of 'Rainbow Europe' rendered more complicated in comparing and contrasting across place. This became even more acute when faced with institutional, legal and medical barriers, as forces ever navigated through queerness, race and class. These ever-present intersecting inequalities surpass a count of 'protected characteristics' for (some) 'world citizens', with Farj's account highlighting many of these tensions.

Farj

Farj moved to Scotland in 2018 as a twenty-sex-year-old middle-class, mixed-race, bisexual, trans person. They were helped by the Free Church of Scotland and, as an asylum-seeker, they were not permitted to work and were living on a minimum income, while undertaking voluntary employment. Farj grew up in Morocco and speaks Arabic, French and English. Discussing their youth and schooling in Morocco, Farj described life as being very difficult for LGBTQ+ people, meaning 'years and years' of childhood traumas, which they had tried to 'just survive', experiencing depression and anxiety in trying to 'find myself' and 'my identities'. In many ways mirroring go-to social stories about the location of homophobia and transphobia, Farj then attributed this to the specific Moroccan and Muslim culture they'd lived in, where LGBTQ+ life 'didn't exist'. From a middle-class background, Farj went to university in Morocco and in France. While in France they converted to Christianity and established distance from the Muslim communities they'd previously been part of ('I've been converted to Christianity in France, so I could feel safe from our communities, from Moroccan communities'). Farj described their conversion to Christianity as following a chosen, individualized path, free from 'culture' or 'tradition', as opposed to 'following like sheep', a disposition which they projected onto contemporary Pakistani communities in Scotland.

Farj described how they couldn't 'find myself there', in France, deciding to move to Scotland. They expressed a sense of contentment in arriving in a 'safe place' where accessing legal support and healthcare was 'easy' ('very easy to get access to the health, I've got my GP and she's very, very friendly … and especially when we talk about the trans process'). They were not 'out' to their broader 'church family' but were to the (white, Christian, Scottish) family they lived with. Scotland was described as the 'most friendly country for LGBT', attributed to a 'neutral culture', variously described as Christian and specifically not Islamic. At the time of their interview in 2019, they were seeking asylum in Scotland. In recounting their journey through legal processes, Farj spoke of not 'coming out', nor using, let alone embracing or identifying through, the categories of LGBTQ+, conscious of how people might judge them. Farj had to navigate fear and shame, later coming to understand this as a 'normal' part of claiming asylum, with an updated and official statement about their LGBTQ+ status then made to the Home Office via their lawyer.

Farj's attribution of 'No problem here', in positioning Scotland as the best place to be LGBTQ+, didn't always measure up to relative comparisons (Davidson et al. 2018). Yet Farj seemed to have settled into a fit that was 'good enough', positively investing in a place and community which they could not afford to badmouth or spoil. Incidents of transphobia or homophobia were pushed to other people and other places ('I know that there are transphobic, LGBT-phobic persons, but I heard many stories in England, not in Scotland'). Hate crime was attributed to hateful others, to foreigners and outsiders, with 'the village' or 'somewhere' signalling an otherness, as uneducated or unsophisticated:

> It can be from foreigners that they came from other countries, that they are anti-LGBT communities, but not for the local people … it's just words from someone who lived in a village or somewhere.

Farj's account – negotiated as someone often on the outside and navigating ways in – complicates the story of LGBTQ+ progression and its alignment with 'best countries' – even as this is also repeated. The story of 'Rainbow Europe' is already fractured in Farj's experience of movement, including via France, and where their arrival in Scotland may not be the end destination. Farj expressed a desire to live in the United States, specifically in San Francisco, where things would, they felt, be 'much better'. Significantly, their move was also seen as an opportunity to connect back to Morocco, albeit from a distance:

> I'm still working on it [asylum claim] and at the same time if things don't go well, because I have an opportunity for United States, and if I go to United States I will go directly to San Francisco, it's the best city there … So I got an opportunity, it's Green Card lottery, the United States, they do it every year … And if I get a lot of protection there in United States I will fight for the rights in Morocco, and even I can go to Morocco with safety.

In many ways Farj's account is understandably pragmatic, with Morocco, as their birthplace, lingering as a comparative backdrop. Local political protest around the insufficiencies of the UK state, manifested through Pride presences and placards, for example, are placed within this ever-present comparative context:

> I saw someone has a banner and he said the government doesn't care about trans people … And when I compare it to Morocco it's, it's a big thing. Complaining about it, I found it, I don't find my place to complain about it. If I was in Morocco I would complain about everything there for LGBT rights, but here in Scotland as a trans person I get access to the healthcare, I get access to, I get appointment for the transition, medical transition. I know that in the education there can be some discriminations, but it's in the society not the government. And some services can be hard to change their laws. Here it can be the government that needs to do their job.

In such claims and contestations of governments (not) doing their job, the very purpose of the nation state comes into question. The Scotland which Farj arguably ambivalently settled into, while still awaiting settlement via their asylum claim, is a place which will judge and categorize them as a non-citizen. Navigating this, while seeking another 'best place', perhaps highlights the impossibility of finding home or of ever fully being in place when deemed not from a place. Accounts such as Farj's illuminate who and what is at stake in rebordering nations and citizens, even in the story of the good nation. Following Farj's complicated appraisal of Scotland as the place to be, the next section asks if the possibility of Scottish independence in the wake of Brexit can breathe new life into queer transformations, or if being 'queer in a wee place' still means living through rather than departing from the usual counts of class, race, gender and sexuality, as 'Big Scotland' takes on 'Little Britain'.

Queer in a wee place: From Little Britain to Big Scotland?

> I think Scotland's a leading light ... Why do we not want to connect across the world and use our knowledge of what we're doing in Scotland and spread the love a bit about what we're doing in Scotland? (Ian, forty-four, white, gay cis man)

Contemporary (re)imaginings of Scotland as a different place stretch across centuries, animated in the present through devolution and independence debates. Brexit re-exposed national myths, leading to increased distinction and division between 'us' and 'them', as well as 'then' and 'now'. Many interviewees spoke of the Brexit process as entangled with new and old feelings around Scottish independence, and some 'no' voters who wanted to remain part of the UK spoke of voting for independence if that meant staying in Europe. For those who had voted for Scottish independence, Brexit became an affirmation that Scotland should have left the UK and sought out other allegiances (even if this wasn't offered then or now).

Claims of difference, or Scottish exceptionalism, can function to gloss over inequalities, including shared legacies of and benefits from UK colonialism. The prevailing 'hostile environment' across constituent UK nations persists, with increased hate crimes reported across race, gender, sexuality and disability.[2] Yet despite evidence to the contrary, both Westminster and Holyrood Parliaments now make bold claims of being 'world leading' on LGBT inclusion (Lawrence and Taylor 2019). Claims appear in country counts of being the 'best place for LGBT rights', the 'friendliest gay city' or 'world leading' in LGBT+-inclusive education. Such border narratives are a fundamental part of the problem of states, as actively constituting a deeply racialized global hierarchy of (in)tolerance and (un)acceptable others and elsewheres.

Scotland has been long misplaced as provincial, as small, regional and rural, particularly via a Scotland–England comparative count of population sizes, big cities and so on. It has come to embrace this comparison as a sign of difference, with the diminutive 'wee' of Scots arguably symbolizing a linguistic, cultural and broader socio-economic departure, from England specifically, and Britain more generally. The prevailing political context of Scotland also questions the purchase and potential of 'queer provincialisms' in post-Brexit Britain. Scotland is arguably dismissive of long-standing similarities in terms of racist, sexist, trans and homophobic pasts and presents shared across constituent UK terrain, while also capitalizing upon a sense of its own world-leading status. Within imaginings of Scotland as a subjugated place, exploited or under-represented through Westminster rule, claims for Scottish independence re-emerge, especially around the flashpoints of Brexit, austerity regimes and the Covid-19 pandemic. Sally (fifty-six, white, lesbian) and originally from England, but had called Glasgow home for nearly thirty years, explaining that she was 'trying to get as many friends as possible to kind of move up here', contrasting the pessimism of Brexit with the optimism of Scotland as a 'pulse point' of change. This was reflected in other statements of Scottish difference as a 'leading light':

> I do think there are cultural differences that aren't expressed terribly well through Westminster. There are cultural nuances that I think in Scotland, in terms of LGBT

rights I think we're a bit further forward than perhaps other parts of the UK, or we'd like to think we are. (Amy, thirty-four, white, bisexual, cis woman)

Our problem always is that at the end of the day all major rules are made down in England, and I don't think England is quite as progressive as Scottish people tend to be. Scottish people always tend to be a bit more to the left and a bit more kind of open, politically at least. (Rose, forty-five, white, lesbian, cis woman)

Within some interviewee accounts, a simple 'better than England' approach became the measure through which to recognize and celebrate Scottish difference, often stated as self-evident rather than something to explain or work towards. The positioning away from a 'toxic England', to quote one interviewee, may be part of a Scottish exceptionalism, which exempts itself from the weight of the (UK) 'past', while continued sexual nationalism remagnifies the borders around states, citizens and others:

I think we're lucky in Scotland because I think it's better up here than it is in England. And it [same-sex marriage] kind of passed with no fanfare, everyone was like 'well obviously we're going to vote for it' ... Whereas in England there was all these massive debates ... So, you know, I kind of feel as if this is better than most places to stay. And I think it's been proven actually, it's better to stay in Scotland than anywhere else for LGBT rights. (Lorna, thirty-eight, white, lesbian, cis woman)

I think it's far and away better here than England. I think like England is a hellscape (laughs) and, yeah, just everything is worse there. (Lexi, thirty-two, white, lesbian, trans woman)

While my intentions are not to misplace interviewees' investments in a nation that might be becoming 'for them', feelings of ambivalence and disappointment also circulate in these claims. Scottish 'difference' wasn't always straightforwardly articulated, and others felt let down by continued uncertainty, including the retraction of support and resources for LGBTQI+ equalities initiatives and policies in a supposed moment of Scottish difference. Lexi qualified her above statement with a warning not to take the 'foot off the gas', with Scottish progression marked by more conservative flashpoints but still comparing favourably:

Scotland was, at one point, like right at the forefront of kind of moving, especially LGBT, equalities legislation forward, and then like took our foot off the gas ... I don't think this is like the best place in the world to be LGBT, but like I think it's pretty good. Definitely I would compare it favourably with the majority of the world, I guess. (Lexi, thirty-two, white, lesbian, trans woman)

Claims to difference were also viewed with suspicion, as a repeated policy gloss meaning that 'all forms of discrimination just evolve around legislation' (Alisha, thirty-nine, South Asian, lesbian). Alisha noted the stereotypes around Scotland and Scottishness 'which has a very benign series of cuddly and cosy stereotypes associated with it' as bypassing some of the negative associations with Britain and/or England.

National distinction in the idea that 'Scottish gays are better than any other' was similarly questioned by Dan:

> I don't believe in like, like 'Scottish gays are better than any other gays' and all that rubbish ... and I'd like our community to do so much more in, and challenge its own like internal homophobia, racism, transphobia, all this jazz. (Dan, thirty-six, white, gay, cis man)

Both Dan and Alisha's accounts expose the discrepancy between Scotland as a new civic nation and its enduring ethnic nationalism, embodied and embedded in the histories and presences of homophobia, transphobia and racism:

> It's hard not to have a really deep cynicism about Scotland because of the volume of racism I experienced growing up and all these other things, like and the history of the SNP being a relatively right-wing party. I'm like, we're only, we're always just a few steps away from that history and that legacy ... I've said I'm Scottish as a way of distinguishing myself, or distancing myself, from what feels like a particularly toxic brand of politics operating in the country right now. But my passport and the rights I have to be in the country belong to this weird union. And I'm like, the larger and more diffuse the unit I can belong to the better, or more specific. Like I'd rather be European or Glaswegian (laughs). Like I either want to be super-specific or super-general. And I feel comfortable saying that I'm Glaswegian. I'm a product of its institutions. Or I want to be European, because it doesn't really mean anything. Whereas right now British really feels like it's a negative term. But I still find Scottish an unsatisfactory term, and as it becomes more political and less just a factual designation of something the less likely I am to associate with it. (Alisha, thirty-nine, South Asian, lesbian)

Alisha's account is multiple and intersecting, moving across times, yet bypassing the supposed 'arrived at' LGBT state as leading showcase or 'white light'. Whiteness is fundamental to Britishness and Scottishness, and that the incorporation of Black and brown bodies has not significantly altered the white 'face of the nation' even as it has been obscured by claims of the all-inclusive state.

State transformation has different consequences for different queers as witnessed in the replacing of nation states via the Brexit process as 'big', 'wee', 'provincial' or 'world-leading'. Many interviewees' accounts echo contemporary assessments of exhausting and exhausted state processes, with some more subject to social and institutional regulation than others, including through persisting and pernicious asylum seeking processes, as in Farj's case. Brexit has increased racism: Boris Johnson's 'Vote Leave' campaign was built on racist, xenophobic rhetoric that blamed immigrants for 'burdening Britain' and supposedly stretching educational, social and healthcare systems. Such recent rhetoric and policy is in fact a long time in the making and the rhetoric of difference – as inclusive, civic and specifically Scottish – does not necessarily step away from these historical presences. Farj's experiences – like others who are actively holding, pursing and/or lamenting citizenship access and entitlements – can be understood as ever emergent from state sanctioned racism, homophobia and transphobia. Lived experiences in provincial, local, everyday places often collide with and surpass the rhetorics of reimagined states, which typically instrumentalize LGBTQ+ rights for the consolidation of nationalism. Queer left agendas need to be concerned with the hopeful and pragmatic possibilities in queer reconstitutions within and across the borders of the nation state, in looking backwards and forwards. This was demonstrated in Farj's articulated hopes in relocating to the United States via Scotland so that they can look – and go – back to Morocco. But these reorientations are represented in everyday 'provincial' as well as in 'exceptional' or even 'cosmopolitan' travels, as articulated by Dan in placing a working-class rural Scottish community at the centre of queer provincialisms.

Notes

1. The 2011 Census data used a standardized list of eighteen ethnic groups: www.ethnicity-facts-figures.service.gov.uk/style-guide/ethnic-groups#list-of-ethnic-groups.
2. Scotland – and the Scottish National Party in particular – has seen a resurgence in transphobic rhetoric, made mainstream in politicians' public comments in the wake of the 2019 public consultation on the GRA (2004). See, e.g., 'SNP Transphobia Row: Why Has Nicola Sturgeon's Party Been Accused of "Transphobic Views"?', www.scotsman.com/news/people/snp-transphobia-row-why-has-nicola-sturgeons-party-been-accused-transphobic-views-and-who-teddy-hope-3117850. Accessed 1 April 2022.

References

Davidson, N., Liinpää, M., McBride, M. and Virdee, S. (eds). *No Problem Here. Understanding Racism in Scotland*. Edinburgh: Luath Press, 2018.
Lawrence, M. and Taylor, Y. 'The UK Government LGBT Action Plan: Discourses of Progress, Enduring Stasis, and LGBTQI+ Lives "Getting Better"'. *Critical Social Policy* 40, no. 4 (2019): 586–607. https://doi.org/10.1177/0261018319877284.
Mahn, C., Dasgupta, R. and Ritu, D. J. *Desi Queers. LGBTQ+ South Asians and Cultural Belonging in Britain*. London: Hurst, 2025.
Puar, J. K. 'Rethinking Homonationalism', *International Journal of Middle East Studies* 45 (2013): 336–9.
Taylor, Y. *Working-Class Queers. Time, Place and Politics*. London: Pluto, 2023.
Zabrowskis, M. 'Exploiting Shared Queer Knowledge'. In C. Mahn, M. Brim and Y. Taylor (eds), *Queer Sharing in the Marketized University*, pp. 81–95. London: Routledge, 2023.

8

Scotland's menstrual landscape, a red flag?

Kate Molyneaux

Periods of change: Scotland's journey to free menstrual products

The 2020 Period Products (Free Provision) (Scotland) Bill has been covered in national and international headlines, as a celebration of more equalized and inclusive times – if not specifically feminist or queer times. The then first minister, Nicola Sturgeon, and Scottish Labour MSP Monia Lennon, who put forward the initial proposal for such a Bill in 2017, were subsequently listed as one of '12 women leaders who changed the world for better in 2020' by *Vouge India* (Peri 2020). Beyond these 'exceptional' women politicians, the wide spanning coverage framed the Period Poverty Bill as a marker of national progress, a place where periods had finally gone public, with period product provisions to be available in all educational institutions and local authority buildings such as libraries and community spaces.

While a new provision, feminist researchers have long highlighted how menstruation shapes everyday inequalities, and these conversations continue in academia and activism, which delves into cultural norms, gender roles and the policing of menstruation across spaces and places. Over the past seven years, the conversation has reached new heights, gaining momentum in both popular and political spheres. In 2017, Plan International UK conducted research on period poverty and found one in four users reported wearing menstrual products longer than recommended because they couldn't afford enough products, while one in ten could not afford menstrual products at all (Tingle and Vora 2017). This came on the heels of the UK government's pledge to scrap the tampon tax, a levy that had classified menstrual products as luxury items and renewed public and political interest.

This push for change was built upon the work of international grassroots movements, whose tireless work was crucial in merging third sector activism with political action. The momentum that began in 2017 marked a pivotal transforming, reimagining menstruation from a private 'women's issue', into one of public concern. Scotland had made strides in 2018 by funding free menstrual products in schools, universities and some charities supporting vulnerable populations. Policymakers cemented attention in Scotland, passing the Period Products Bill (2020), *mandating* the provision of free period products across local authorities, educational institutions and certain public service bodies. Importantly, the Bill promises to tackle period poverty but also the deeply ingrained stigmas surrounding menstruation and its impact on education.

Over the past seven years, discussions about menstruation have broadened in significant ways to encompass the entire spectrum of experiences menstruation as an embodied experience. These conversations have gained space across public and political discourse, where 'new' provisions become exemplars of national equality, diversity and inclusion policy, and indeed extended as indicative of national political climates, including of 'Scottish exceptionalism' (Hassan and Gunson 2018). Such an exceptionalism can fail to acknowledge local, national and international differences, where much of the current research on menstrual health, especially in places like Scotland and the rest of the UK, centres on Western cultural understandings of menstruation. Access to period products should be a given, not a cause for celebration. Thus, the boundaries of normative mainstreamed policy progress, whether framed as celebratory or transformational, are worthy of interrogation.

The stories I've encountered in my research reflect and challenge the Western framing of periods, including as something to self-manage. I've spoken to women and non-binary people, who grew up in Scotland and the rest of the UK, Ireland, Pakistan, China, South Africa and Dubai. Interviewees' experiences with menstruation are deeply shaped by local, national and international contexts, including an embodied sense of prevailing cultural and social norms. Menstruation is political, cultural and deeply personal. It shapes how we move through, in and against the world. While the conversation is expanding, we need to be mindful of whose voices are centred – and whose are left on the margins – and that policy progress in Scotland is not devoid of social or political weight. A continued normativity shapes Scotland's menstrual landscape, and this chapter interrogates this in relation to 'compulsory heterosexuality', where expectations of and from feminine bodies, is not simply over-ridden by providing 'period products'. I argue that queering periods offers an opportunity to rethink what we know about bodies, gender and identity. Queer experiences of menstruation don't fit neatly into these categories. Queer periods resist the binary structures that shape our identities and our relationships with our bodies. Menstruation, often framed as a cisgender woman's experience, is in reality an intersectional and complex one.

Stuck between one wee place and another

My exploration into menstrual research and politics also happen around the same time, 2018, during my third year of sociology and psychology undergraduation. I had moved from Ireland to Scotland to start my undergraduate degree, navigating a similarly wee country to my own and a new academic environment. In 2014 Ireland held a referendum on same-sex marriage, and at the time I lived in Vancouver and so found it unaffordable to fly home and very difficult to not cast my vote. Later, in 2018, Ireland held its historic #RepealThe8th[1] referendum to overturn the country's near-total ban on abortion, resulting in very divisive and passionate debates. I ensured I flew home from Scotland to vote with the hopes and eventful success of seeing the repeal of the eighth amendment. Growing up in the 2000s, I always knew that if I became pregnant, I'd have to fly to Great Britain to access an abortion, which in our imagining meant getting the cheapest possible flight to England. This wasn't some abstract fear but a practical reality that my friends and I discussed openly. We trusted that we would pool our resources to support each other in case one of us needed to make that journey. We knew girls who had travelled to England for abortions, and others who took matters into their own hands. This was a fear we all shared, despite using condoms and the contraceptive pill to mitigate against it.

The trauma of reproductive control and forced birth runs deep in Ireland's recent history. My parents' generation, during the 1980s, talked about the illegality of divorce, the reality of smuggled condoms from Northern Ireland and forced births at the hands of institutions like the Magdalene Laundries. Divorce was only made legal with conditions in 1996, with the repeal of the fifteenth amendment, passing only by a slight majority. These atrocities, many of which are only now coming to light, contributed to a deep intergenerational trauma. In the 1960s, my grandmother, who married a much older politician, adopted my mother in rural Kerry. All I know about this adoption is that my grandfather 'knew the local bishop', implying without *saying*, that my mother came from a mother and baby institution. This intergenerational pain and inequality created a backdrop that shaped my new perspective on menstruation and reproductive justice more generally, as queer issues that surpass national or legislative 'progress'. The RepealThe8th referendum felt like a turning point, not just for reproductive rights but for the broader resistance of Ireland as a wee place.

Queering menstruation has been central to my approach and politics from the very beginning of my political and academic menstrual engagement. In 2019 I took sexuality and gender as an elective module, I didn't know it then, but the lecturer and subject shaped the next few years of my academic life, inspiring me to explore menstruation through a queer lens. One assignment for this class was to produce a video. I can't remember the exact requirements, but what I created is something that my social circle remembers to this day.

The video starred my partner, a cis man, wheeling his bike into our flat and suddenly a look of surprise and worry passed over his face – suggesting, 'Uh oh, I just got my period, but I wasn't expecting it.' The rest of the video was a montage of my cis male and non-binary friends, all posing with artistically bloodied underwear around their ankles. Each photo purposefully included their hairy legs and whatever socks they were wearing, which at the time I used as shorthand to indicate 'maleness'. I went flat to flat across Edinburgh, asking them to participate in this somewhat jarring, but politically charged, project. I layered my voice over the visuals, explaining the complexities trans men face regarding menstruation and the barriers they may encounter in a world that still overwhelmingly equates periods with cis gender women. This project was my first deep dive into what would become a passion: queer menstruation. Through this assignment, I expanded my menstrual politics, researching and learning about how periods intersect with queer identities. I turned to zines and social media, where I found voices depicting queer periods.

In 2018, the Scottish government launched the consultation to reform the Gender Recognition Act (GRA), aiming to simplify the legal process for transgender people to legally change their gender – sparking debate across the country. At this time, Scotland also gained international attention by embedding LGBTQ+-inclusive education into its national curriculum, thanks to long-term efforts and more recent activism from groups such as Time for Inclusive Education (TIE) campaign. This dual promise of educating the next generation about LGBTQ+ identities and making their lived experiences procedurally smoother. Alongside these initiatives, introducing free period products in Scottish schools reflects a vision of exceptionalism – one complicated by the lived experiences of my interviewees.

Ireland and Scotland share similar stories of progress and constraint, each grappling with the weight of their respective histories while striving to define themselves through progressive legislation. These successes remain entangled with their pasts and the enduring power of traditional structures. In this mix of political conversations across two wee places and my discovery of feminist sociology, I began to trace the intersections between these movements and the normative power structures at play. I've spent years thinking through how menstruation is not just about bodies, but also deeply connected to societal structures and expectations – norms that go unnoticed until you fall outside them. For me, a bisexual woman living in Scotland and deeply embedded in the social constructs of menstruation, the Period Products Bill has both its triumphs and its blind spots. It claims to be inclusive, but when we look closely, we see who gets written into this narrative of inclusion – and, more tellingly, who gets left out.

Queerying menstrual experiences

While interviewing people who menstruate across Scotland, I found myself immersed in stories that were both deeply personal and strikingly similar. These stories reveal how people from across Scotland identify with and feel comfortable within their bodies, gender norms and the tangled expectations of heterosexuality. Over the course of a year, I met with twenty-seven women, queer and non-binary people who menstruate across Scotland asking questions about period products, their experiences and choices that determined product selection. Interestingly, not all period products are the same and usage typically has a progressive rout, starting with pads, moving on to tampons and for some participants, to menstrual cups and reusable underwear. The question gnawed at me: why is there a distinct pattern of period product use? Why is the tampon, specifically, seen as a 'grown-up' option? What lies beneath this assumption, and how does it reflect the way we construct and (hetero)sexualize bodies and norms? In thinking about the mainstreamed provision of period products in Scotland, questions can still be asked out what products are provided and chosen and what norms are reflected in this. Menstruation has been co-opted into a narrative of compulsory heterosexuality and Scotland's admirable focus on free product provision is undoubtedly important, but provision is not enough.

In telling people I research menstruation, they're often eager to share experiences with me. I've heard about many menstrual experiences outside my participant sample, from friends in social spaces and work colleagues, to my hairdresser and people I only know because we walk our dogs in the same park. It became clear very early in my research that people not only have a lot to say, but they are eager to say it, to have it heard. They have stories, opinions and experiences to share. Telling people what I research typically garners two responses – detailed shared of, at times, deeply personal experience or confusion and silence (to put it politely).

Hearing and receiving so many experiences took me back to my first period, my thirteenth birthday – a fact that seems laughable, symbolic of teen hood. I remember I asked my dad to come to talk with me. I had something I had to tell him. Shyly I said, 'you know, that thing that happens to girls when they get older'. He informed me this was normal and that I had two options: pads or tampons. He added my mom had used tampons and that both were in his bathroom for me to access. That's where my memory of that day ends. Reflecting on this, I realize I can't remember seeing the blood or how I felt – just having to tell my dad and his response. I remember over the next year or two popping into this bathroom to access theses tampons, the little mental box of self-insert tampons. In my later teens I remember the shock of my friends when I asked him to buy me period products, I brushed it off – how else was I meant to get period products?

I am not oblivious to the importance and impact of parental input and response, which is shaped by personal experience and reinforced by research on menstruation. While listening to my interviewees, the positioning of mother as the central figure in menstrual experiences struck me. Whether through direct guidance or, as many described, a sense of failure when that guidance was absent, the mother–daughter relationship around menstruation was powerfully ubiquitous. Fathers, it seemed, were largely absent from these stories. This dynamic underscores a broader social script about bodies, gender and (hetero)sexuality, engrained and expected in the mother–daughter relationship. Yet, my experience disrupts this traditional model. This, of course, points to the expected gender roles within a typical two-parent heterosexual household; the explanation and experience of menstruation within the mother–daughter relationship speaks to a larger societal script about bodies, gender and (hetero)sexuality, running alongside and within gendered roles.

The shift from girlhood to womanhood somehow mirrored the shift from pads to tampons and was a prominently shared experience. Many participants recalled how they began with pads in their younger years, then moved on to tampons, and later, some experimented with menstrual cups or reusable products. As adults, most used a combination of these options. But what stood out in their memories was the distinct moment of transitioning to tampons. For some, it symbolized a kind of freedom – a way to embody an older, more agentic self. However, the feedback from mothers around this shift was often fraught with some with discomfort towards girls' bodies, age, gender and sexualization.

One of my interviewees, Jo (twenty-five, white Scottish, bisexual cis women), depicts her mother's 'horror' that she had started using tampons, 'she was horrified. She was like, that's terrible, like, why would you want to do that? I don't even want to talk about it!' Robin's (twenty-five, white Scottish, straight cis women) experience was similar, as her mother questions her ability to use tampons: 'Why do you want those? Are you even able to shove them up there?' Using an emphatically repulsed tone, Robin ensured I understood her mother's disgust and shock. Again, this was mirrored by Leigh's (forty-one, white Irish, heterosexual cis women) mother, who 'freaked out' concerned as she was that tampons would 'make your hole really big'. These memories reveal a shared perceived discomfort among mothers regarding tampons, as distinct from disposable pads.

These reactions all revolved around one shared concern: the tampon's insertion into the body. It was as if the tampon symbolized a crossing of a line, a bodily intrusion that was inappropriate, sexualizing the bodies of interviewees during girlhood. Yet though their reactions to tampons, mothers were themselves sexualizing their daughters' bodies. Again and again, there is an underlying assumption that tampons especially, as well as other period products, carry with them the idea of sexual readiness or maturity. These concerns revolve around the idea that a girl's vulva might not be big enough for a tampon or that using one would make it too big. This reaction seemingly deals with the fact that a girl's vulva is changeable, and yet deems the changeability as inappropriate to a particular age or life stage, suggesting a fear of premature sexualization, while at the same time (hetero)sexualizing girls' bodies.

Emma (twenty-four, white South African, straight cis woman) remembered the moment everything shifted. The day she got her first period wasn't just about learning about pads or tampons. It felt like stepping into a new world – one filled with responsibilities and risks she hadn't known applied to her before. The burden didn't come from the period itself, but from the unspoken weight that came with it – the vulnerability of pregnancy, the sudden awareness of how men might perceive her differently. Her mother told her she had more responsibilities now. As Emma reflected on those early days, she remembered the fear, the idea that her body was a potential liability. Feminists have long discussed how gender roles shape the way girls connect with their bodies, negotiating worth and identity tied to this process of menstruation. For Emma, that connection became even more complicated when she developed an eating disorder, like many girls and young women. During that time, she stopped menstruating altogether, and with that loss came a sense of disconnection from her gender, 'when I didn't have my period, I felt like I wasn't really a woman'.

The onset, presence or absence of menstruation can be gender-affirming or negating. In a society that constructs menstruation as an essential part of womanhood, Emma's story ambivalently echoes that sentiment, of not wanting to or needing to feel like or be 'a woman'. Such a force seemed to dictate, confine and shape participants' sense of self. Being 'ready' to use a tampon wasn't just about physical maturity, but became about something more – sex, boys and an unspoken assumption that a girl's body, once menstruating, was now somehow prepared for adult experiences that she might not have even thought about. In a moment of period product provision, what makes a body 'ready' for a tampon? Social and cultural norms still circulate to ensure bodies enter the normative heterosexual matrix (Butler 1990), while pushing queer and non-binary experiences to outline the lines.

Bleeding outside the lines

Menstruation is deeply entangled with heteronormative assumptions, but there can be fractures within those rigid structures. The way we currently understand gender, bodies, and power is largely shaped by a heteronormative framework – one that reinforces traditional gender roles and compulsory heterosexuality. But as many experiences show, breaking free from these assumptions opens space for more inclusive and affirming ways of understanding menstruation. Erin and Emma describe their periods reinforce their sense of womanhood, although it comes with the risk of vulnerability and a loss of gender identity. Erin (twenty-five, white British, heterosexual) recalls a heighten connection to womanhood because of menstrual cramps induced by an IUD,[2] 'I felt more connected to Gaia and Mother Earth. I was like "Ah this is the pain that women bare".' But for others, like Stevie (twenty-six, white Scottish, queer non-binary), the connection between menstruation and gender caused 'slightly like dysphoric. Yeah, a bit of dysphoria.' It was only when Stevie separated menstruation from the idea of gender and womanhood – and by extension, from heteronormativity – that they found comfort with their menstrual body: 'My ex was, they were trans, like trans man. Like it is really hard. The way that they dealt with it, that changed in my mind to not something really associated with being like, female or gender.' Stevie's experience highlights the importance of breaking down the links between menstruation and rigid gender expectations.

When we deconstruct the assumption that menstruation is inherently tied to womanhood, we create more room for diverse, non-normative experiences of the body. This separation is crucial for challenging the gender binary and creating space for queer and trans experiences that don't fit neatly into these restrictive norms. Compulsory heterosexuality, which is woven into societal ideas about menstruation, plays a significant role in how we understand womanhood. By treating menstruation as tied to femininity, not only reinforces gender norms but also excludes anyone who doesn't fit the traditional mould. This essentialist view of menstruation as a 'feminine' experience marginalizes trans men, non-binary people and cis women who don't feel aligned with the traditional ideas of womanhood. Policies like the Period Products Bill (2021) risk (un)intentionally reinforcing reductive frameworks around menstruation often limited to 'tick-box' approaches to inclusion and lacking intersectional consideration.

Heteronormative thinking seeps into every part of our lives, shaping our experiences in ways we might not even realize, from everyday to institutional contexts. Niamh's (thirty, white Scottish, lesbian cis woman) experience reveal how deeply ingrained heteronormativity remains in social structures and institutions. Niamh's frustration with medical professionals shines a light on the heteronormative assumptions embedded in healthcare. She is constantly asked about hormonal contraception, a clear sign of the assumption that all women are heterosexual and at risk of pregnancy. 'I've said that I'm a lesbian, and their next question is, "what pill are you on?" not, "are you on a pill?", but "what pill?" … they're so in the headspace that this is the path, this is the default path for women. I'm like, what would this pill be doing?'

'What would this pill be doing?' Niamh's question perfectly captures the frustration she feels when her identity as a lesbian is overlooked. It's not that people think she's having heterosexual sex, but because society positions heterosexuality as the 'normal way of life' (Jackson 2006). Her gender, as a woman, leads others to connect her to heterosexuality, ignoring the reality of her sexuality. Niamh feels devalued – not because people misunderstand her sexual activity, but because of the conditioning to see heterosexuality as the default. For her, this assumption marginalizes her identity, leaving little space for her to be seen. Niamh's experience reflects the pervasive belief that heterosexuality is the norm, which excludes the realities of those who live outside it. This kind of compulsory heterosexuality is not just about enforcing sexual norms, but about reinforcing traditional gender roles (Rich 2003; Jackson 2006). Niamh is seen as a woman first, and therefore presumed to be heterosexual rather than her expressed sexual identity. This assumption undervalues her experiences as a lesbian and illustrates how deeply gender and heterosexuality are intertwined in societal expectations.

One size fits all?

One dominant theme throughout my research and personal experience is that the provision of these menstrual products assumes a 'typical' menstruating woman. The products themselves, the policies and the spaces they're available all cater to a typical menstruating body. But what does that mean for those of us who don't fit the mould? Those of us who are queer, disabled, fat or have bodies that don't align with the norm?

Zoe (twenty-seven, white Scottish, queer cis woman) works a precarious contract while managing a chronic illness or disease, including but not only a menstrual disorder. After wrestling with the stigma of being seen as less capable, Zoe disclosed her menstrual condition to her employer. His response was to suggest she take time off to 'get better', that a break from work would magically restore her to an able-bodied, fully productive employee. Zoe's story goes beyond personal health – it highlights the complex intersection of queerness, class and structural inequality. Her fear of jeopardizing future employment in a precarious job market illustrates how queerness and class interact together to perpetuate inequality. An expectation that employees should be disembodied – detached from physical realities like menstruation and period pain – creates pressure to present oneself as able-bodied and free from 'inconvenient' bodily experiences. This reinforces a workplace culture where periods are rarely considered valid reasons for absence or accommodation. Zoe underscores how workplaces can become spaces of exclusion for those whose bodies don't fit the narrow expectations of productivity and endurance, highlighting the urgent need for broader recognition of menstrual health as a valid and supported aspect of worker well-being. And yet, the Period Products Bill is framed as a success for people like Zoe – claiming that product provision 'will be of particular benefit to those on zero-hour contracts who do not get paid if they do not work' and ultimately 'benefit the wider economy' (Scottish Parliament 2020, 21). Rather than dismantling the structures that marginalize her, the policy simply requires her to be more productive within them.

Class is not just an employment category but also a deeply queer issue and one which might be 'glossed over' in a progressive equalities framework centred around equal opportunities while perpetuating inequalities. In Scotland, working-class people and those in precarious jobs – often disproportionately women, queer folks and people of colour – face additional barriers when it comes to menstrual management. For Zoe, having access to products in the workplace didn't solve the issue of stigma or the pressure to maintain productivity. Yvette Taylor (2023) emphasizes how queerness and class intersect to both challenge and reinforce normative structures. Similarly, Matt Brim (2020) explores how the intersection of queerness and class often reveals deeper structural issues, beyond surface-level inclusion (see Taylor et al. 2023). Both scholars show how queer and class identities are further marginalized by systems designed for normative bodies and experiences. Liberal inclusion fails to address the realities of marginalization, reflected in menstrual product provision which alone doesn't change the structures that leave workers like Zoe feeling vulnerable and excluded.

The limitations of inclusive policy ripple out into many public spaces and beyond the workplace. The products provided are often self-insert tampons, the typical negative response may be the desire to be distance from blood, not the concern of policy – unless, of course, you're someone who physically struggles to use them. Emily (twenty-six, white Scottish, bisexual cis women) shared her frustration with the provision of self-insert tampons: 'I couldn't ever make it comfortable enough, I don't know whether it's because I'm a bit fat or my arms aren't long enough, but I just couldn't reach to put it in properly!'

For Emily, who has a fat body and a developmental disability, self-inset tampons are inaccessible she struggles with self-insert tampons in public spaces, that its difficult enough at home – but being limit with the products available when at work or out socializing marginalizes her fat queer body. This implementation of the provision for typical bodies is exemplified by a poster in my local library in Leith, Edinburgh, which advertises free reusable menstrual products. While the Bill promises inclusivity by providing free menstrual products and ensuring ease of accessibility, the poster highlights significant limitations regarding body size and access. The poster advertises period pants are available in sizes Small, Medium, Large, Extra Large and Extra Extra Large; if you need larger size you need to ask a staff member to order in your size. The manufacturer's sizing chart reveals that an Extra Extra Large is a size 16/18, which, notably, is the average size in the UK. If you're a size 16 or larger, you can't simply pick up a pair of period pants from a local library; instead, you have to make a special request, creating a barrier to access. This limitation underscores a broader issue of inclusivity, where standardized sizing does not adequately support the diverse needs of bodies.

The policy seems to provide for a 'typical' menstruating body, which seems to exclude those with larger sizes and disabled bodies. Considering who and what is imagined and written into the Bill shines a light on who is excluded, redrawing deep normative expectations and pushing already marginalized experienced into the shadows or behind the library counter.

Period product populism

The passing of the Period Products Bill in 2020 by Scotland was celebrated as a groundbreaking move – even as a 'global first' that promises free menstrual products for everyone. It seemed like progress, a tangible response to period poverty. Framed as progressive, it aims to address period poverty and make menstrual products accessible to all who need them. But when we dig a little deeper, especially considering Scotland's ongoing debates about gender recognition and trans rights, the celebration of the Bill and its reaches appear in line with liberal politics and national image, rather than the radical change it's often celebrated as. In place of challenging the deeply ingrained structures that perpetuate inequality, it adds a shallow solution to a system that still marginalizes queer, trans and non-binary people.

Amid the Bill's passage, Scotland was also dealing with a contentious debate over the GRA. Reforms to the GRA aimed to simplify gender recognition, allowing individuals to self-declare their gender and lowering the legal recognition age to sixteen. However, significant opposition and the eventual blocking of these reforms by the UK government only highlighted the broader struggles around trans rights and gender identity. Against this backdrop, the Period Products Bill, though important, seems like a politically safe issue that doesn't challenge deeper problems.

One interviewee highlights this disconnect perfectly, pointing out the persistent transphobia in conversations about menstrual care and how the current discourse fails to normalize and validate the experiences of trans and non-binary people who menstruate. As Zoe (twenty-seven, white Scottish, queer cis woman) puts it, 'just with so much transphobia … because I know that's not going to be a thing that's going to be normalised in their lifetime. So just like trying to, like, hold up whatever the opposite of a red flag to like signal like, hey, it's okay. You can bleed and also identify as other things'. Her words resonate deeply, underscoring that the Bill's success is somewhat hollow if it does not encompass and support the diversity of identities, experiences and realities within our communities: a clear 'red flag'.

At first, there was a feeling of pride and accomplishment, but upon reflection, we should regard this policy as a fundamental standard rather than an exceptional accomplishment. Rory (twenty-five, white British bisexual cis woman) expressed her frustration, saying, 'If I see a basket that's like 'free to take' I'm always like fucking yes! I love you, which is stupid because it should be, because, you know, I think we're all infuriated we have to pay for shit that we don't get a choice in, it's that thing where the bar is in hell.' Rory captures a crucial sentiment: our expectations should be higher. Zada (nineteen, Pakistani Scottish, cis straight women) echoed this frustration, reflecting that while the Bill was a step in the right direction, it should be seen as basic rather than a highlight. Her perspective reinforces the idea that while legislative changes are necessary, they should not be the end goal, but rather the beginning of a broader conversation about menstrual care and inclusivity.

Scotland's promise of free period products was hailed as a massive victory for equality and inclusivity, a point of national pride. Headlines boasted of Scotland's progressive leadership, enhancing national image of exceptionalism. We have to ask what and who does this create and include, and who or what gets left behind in the celebration of 'success'? How deep can a policy go when it's built on binaries that define bodies and identities, and where the 'fix' is product provision? It's often easy to applaud Scotland as an inclusive, forward-thinking nation based on mainstreaming equality policy. But inclusivity isn't just achieved through material products, it's about understanding the full spectrum of experiences that people with periods have – especially when those experiences don't fit into the neat, traditional categories that society has conditioned us to believe are the 'norm.'

The Period Products Bill has undoubtedly been a step forward, but we must interrogate it from a queer and intersectional lens. Success, as it's traditionally defined in liberal politics, is often measured by the number of tangible outcomes: in this case, access to products – limited as they are. Even in this policy, despite the surface-level inclusivity of language, we find ourselves trapped in the very binary constructs that limit our understanding of what menstruation is and who menstruates 'properly'. It is important to consider who gets to define the success of this policy.

Compulsory heteronormativity, as Jackson (2006) explains, restricts both within and outwith the binary. From my experiences as a bi cis woman, and from what others have shared with me, it's clear these norms limit. For Erin, menstrual pain is a 'woman's cross to bear', serving as a marker of her gender identity, affirming traditional notions of womanhood. But when pain subsided due to changing contraceptive, her connection to the idea of womanhood weakened, revealing the impact of norms connecting pain and menstruation to what it means to be a woman. That pain, the embodied variability of it, defines, constrains and disciplines our bodies, with menstruation becoming as a vehicle for reinforcing these gendered expectations.

Queering the menstrual landscape isn't about excluding the typical to prioritize the marginalized, simply producing a new hierarchy – it's about dissolving the idea that there is a normative experience at all. Centring these voices and experiences not as exceptions to the rule or offered through eluded inclusion and box-ticking, but as integral parts of the conversation. It's about addressing the social and economic realities that people face, including how class intersects with gender, sexuality and menstruation. Queer periods don't fit neatly into the categories. They offer an opportunity to rethink what we know about bodies, gender and identity. In this way, queering menstruation becomes an act of resistance – not just against period poverty, but against the binary structures that define who we are and how we experience our bodies.

Notes

1. RepealThe8th led to the removal of the Eighth Amendment, which equated the right to life of a fetus to that of the mother. The case related to the tragic death of Savita Halappanavar, who died of sepsis because doctors refused to intervene in her incomplete miscarriage due to the presence of a fetal heartbeat. Doctors refused life-saving treatment, in line with Ireland's Catholic laws of the time. Savita's death sparked a turning point, resulting in the successful 2018 referendum legalizing abortion up to twelve weeks and in certain circumstances afterward.
2. An intrauterine device (IUD) is a T-shaped birth control that's inserted into the uterus to prevent pregnancy.

References

Brim, M. *Poor Queer Studies*. Durham, NC: Duke University Press, 2020.
Butler, J. *Gender Trouble: Feminism and the Subversion of Identity*.
    New York: Routledge, 1990.

Hassan, G. and Gunson, R. *Scotland, the UK, and Brexit: A Guide to the Future*. Edinburgh: Luath Press, 2018.

Jackson, S. 'Interchanges: Gender, Sexuality, and Heterosexuality: The Complexity (and Limits) of Heteronormativity'. *Feminist Theory* 7, no. 1 (2006): 105–21.

Lennon, M. 'End Period Poverty: Proposal for Action', 2017. www.endperiodpoverty.org/proposal. Accessed 22 September 2024.

Peri. '12 Women Leaders Who Changed the World for Better in 2020', *Vogue India*, 21 December 2020. www.vogue.in/culture-and-living/content/12-women-leaders-who-changed-the-world-for-better-in-2020. Accessed 21 September 2024.

Period Products (Free Provision) (Scotland) Bill, 2020. www.parliament.scot/-/media/files/legislation/bills/s5-bills/period-products-free-provision-scotland-bill/introduced/policy-memorandum-period-products-scotland-bill.pdf. Accessed 22 September 2024.

Rich, A. C. 'Compulsory Heterosexuality and Lesbian Existence (1980)'. *Journal of Women's History* 15, no. 3 (2003): 11–48.

Scottish Parliament. 'Period Products (Free Provision) (Scotland) Bill: Policy Memorandum', 2020. www.parliament.scot/media/files/legislation/bills/s5-bills/period-products-free-provision-scotland-bill/introduced/policy-memorandum-period-products-scotland-bill.pdf. Accessed 22 September 2024.

Taylor, Y. *Working Class Queers: Time, Place and Politics*. London: Pluto Press, 2023.

Taylor, Y., Mahn, C. and Brim, M. *Queer Precarities in and out of Higher Education*. London: Bloomsbury, 2023.

Tingle, S. and Vora, N. 'Girls' Rights in the Global Economy: A Review of the Evidence'. Plan International, 2017. https://plan-international.org/publications/girls-rights-global-economy-review-evidence. Accessed 22 September 2024.

9

Queer in Scotland: A wives' tale in conversation

Aoife Christoffersen and Ashlee Christoffersen

What, if anything, is unique about becoming and being queer/trans in Scotland, given that these experiences and identities are always shaped by multiple interlocking inequality structures? Employing an autoethnographic and dialogic method to explore this, we link to related debates on being racially minoritized in Scotland (Davidson et al. 2018; Sobande and hill 2022) and other experiences of intersecting marginalization and privilege. In this chapter, we present a dialogue between two different journeys of being and becoming queer in Scotland. The first author (Aoife) came to the rural north of Scotland from middle England as a preteen of mixed ethnicity in 1999, experimenting with her 'queerness' before migrating to Edinburgh in 2008, the location of her 'coming out' as queer/trans. She worked on offshore oil and gas rigs in the North Sea from 2002 onwards. She came out as queer and trans at age thirty-three, in 2018, going through medical and social transition since then, navigating her personal, college and professional life in an industry not renowned for queer acceptance. Aoife is a technically minded and practical person but also expresses her artistic side through various musical outlets, painting and drawing. The second author (Ashlee), from 'Vancouver', Canada (unceded, stolen territories of the xʷməθkʷəy̓əm (Musqueam), Sḵwx̱wú7mesh (Squamish) and səlilwətaɬ (Tsleil-Waututh) peoples), white and cis, and out as bi and queer from a teenager, migrated to Edinburgh in 2016 after a ten-year period in London (UK). Ashlee is an academic who previously worked in the LGBT sector in London. In 2022 we migrated onwards, back to Canada for Ashlee and newly to Canada for Aoife. Edinburgh provided the setting of our meeting and becoming partnered – while Canada provided the setting of our marriage, less encumbered with gender recognition. Through conversation, we consider the recent past of being queer in specific Scottish places, attending to change over time since our stories begin, via comparison to our experiences elsewhere. Our aim is to explore, through comparison, what can be learned about Scotland, as well as to provide an archive of the experiences of specific queer/trans positionalities in Scotland at a particular point in time. Before our conversation, we contextualize this dialogue within the context for minoritized identity in Scotland. We then discuss the politics of different, and yet similar, rising anti-LGBTQIA+ sentiment in both Scotland, where England/Westminster is heavily implicated, and Canada (where the acronym is 2SLGBTQIA+ – recognizing Two-Spirit people as the first 2SLGBTQI+ communities). After our dialogue, we end by reflecting upon queer/trans futurities in both contexts.

Scotland and the shaping of intersecting inequalities and identities

Scotland in many ways lives in the shadow of England and Westminster. Dominant tropes of Scotland as a colonized and oppressed country, heavily recirculated in recent times of increased nationalism, may have caused a foreclosure on reckoning with the oppressive ways that intersecting structures of power, including whiteness, racism and cisheteronormativity, shape social life. Scotland is constructed by contrast to England, leading to a dominant idea where, in terms of race for instance, there's thought to be 'no problem [oot] here' (Davidson et al. 2018). In other words, romantic tales of a precolonial, and then oppressed, Scotland have, potentially, precluded the level of public discussion of difference and oppression *within, and essential to*, Scotland that has taken place elsewhere. In recent years these debates have escalated in relation to Scotland's hugely significant role in the enslavement of Black peoples and the profits accrued from this enslavement – a profit that was not evenly disbursed, but that provided economic and infrastructural privileges and advantages for many in Scotland at the expense of others elsewhere nonetheless. At the same time, the left of centre political parties in power since Scottish devolution have sought to discursively construct, and in some ways to craft in policy, a Scotland that is different from, and more egalitarian to, England. Constructions of 'Scotland' and Scottish national identity simultaneously shape the conjuncture (Hall 1988) of intersecting structures of power and the way it is differentially and relationally experienced. This conjuncture constructs what it means to be Scottish and who is included, and who is excluded, from this category.

Rising anti-LGBTQIA+ discourse in Scotland and Canada

We will discuss being queer and trans in Scotland via comparison to our experiences elsewhere, and notably to Canada where we both migrated to in late 2022. Until recently, both Scotland and Canada were well regarded internationally in terms of LGBTQIA+ inclusion and liveability. However, in both countries, discourse opposing trans rights, and at times wider LGBTQIA+ rights, has been increasing in recent years, in multiple arenas and with effects on politics at the highest echelons of power. Both countries have seen a swell of anti-trans mobilization and lobbying, and in both the influence of the rising US far right is apparent. Both countries have also seen a corresponding increase in reported incidents of transphobic hate crime.

While backlash against her support of trans rights played a key role in the resignation of Scotland's first minister Nicola Sturgeon, the subsequent leader of the Scottish National Party, Humza Yusef, continued this support. More recently however, the party shelved its pledges on expanding trans rights in its 2024 general election manifesto, while Scottish ministers stated that they 'fully accept' the April 2025 Supreme Court ruling that has thrown trans rights, particularly for women, into turmoil. Of course, Westminster continues to exert a great deal of control over Scotland despite devolution, where the new prime minister Keir Starmer stated that he opposed 'gender ideology' shortly before the election, while pledging to continue Conservative bans on puberty blockers for trans young people.

In Canada meanwhile, the leader of the Conservative Party, Pierre Poilievre, has stated that he would seek to roll back gender-affirming care and exclude trans women from different arenas of public life. Hostile laws to this effect have already been passed in some Canadian provinces (Alberta, New Brunswick, Saskatchewan). While there are many similarities, there are also differences in how anti-LGBTQIA+ discourse manifests in the two contexts. In Scotland and in the wider UK context, anti-trans discourse has a much larger mainstream media platform than in Canada. In Scotland, anti-trans discourse can be largely traced to so-called trans exclusionary feminists who specifically target trans women (indeed the Supreme Court case was taken by one such Scottish organization), as well as to Evangelical Christianity. In Canada, the influence of trans exclusionary feminism is less pervasive, while the role of organized religion advocating for 'parental rights' over inclusive sex and relationship education and gender affirmation is greater.

In sum, queer and trans rights are on a precipice in both contexts – while trans organizations campaign for increased rights and better services, there is real danger of yet further rollback of gains that had already been made, and it remains to be seen what will happen in these next pivotal months and years. It must be noted however that in both countries (and by contrast to England), displays of feminist solidarity for trans rights have persisted. In Scotland, examples include a 2017 open letter in support of trans rights signed by seven leading national women's organizations, and in Canada, a collective statement of feminist organizations opposing provincial anti-trans legislation in 2024. For the purposes of this chapter, we must admit that we were naive when migrating to Canada in 2022 about the presence of anti-trans and queer rhetoric. In many ways, we thought that we were not only escaping an increasingly hostile environment for queer and trans people, but also entering one with better laws, and better healthcare, in this regard. Yet it has been here in Canada where we have been confronted first hand at political rallies by those who truly hate us.

We now turn to a dialogue on our experiences of becoming and being queer/trans, and becoming and being so in Scotland, via comparison to our experiences elsewhere. We explore: coming out; our experiences of being queer and trans in particular spaces in Edinburgh, as well as elsewhere in Scotland; our experiences of being queer/bi/trans in Vancouver now, and what this comparison might say about Scotland; and our hopes and fears for queer and trans futurities. We end by reflecting upon some of the implications that this dialogue brings.

Narratives in conversation

What was it like to come out?

Aoife: Coming out for me was a result of my own indiscretions. These were the catalyst that prompted a conversation and introspection that gave me the realization that I was both transgender and bisexual. Being bisexual should never have been a surprise but it's amazing how we rationalize our actions. For me this was because I would only engage with male identifying persons when cross-dressing/identifying female and engaging with female identifying persons while remaining male identifying, thus convincing myself I was straight. The introspection that followed allowed me to put into context my desire to cross-dress in varying forms and realize that I am indeed transgender, that my actions were not a perversion to be ashamed of and to actually embrace and become my true self. This led to me approaching the GP for a referral to the Gender Identity Clinic (GIC) and talking to my close family in Scotland. My mother was, of course, shocked and surprised but was happy for me and supportive. She told me that she saw 'life' come back to me that she hadn't seen in years. I lost friends but I found out who my true friends were. Within my friend groups at the time, we (my family and I) bumped into a friend and their family in a local supermarket. My first experience of transphobia, very new to me then, was that the 'friend' and their family didn't want to see me or talk to me and were more concerned with what to tell their children. I have never spoken with them again.

My coming out and indiscretions caused a separation with my partner and family. I moved to my own place in Leith, Edinburgh. From here I was able to start afresh in a new place. I started engaging with LGBT Health and Wellbeing, frequenting the trans groups and clubs that they offered. Joining a queer badminton club, basically wanting to be in places where I felt safe and comfortable. But I was still living a half-life as I remained closeted at work. It took two years before I would find the strength to come out at work. I have worked in the offshore oil and gas industry for twenty years. The fear of coming out outweighed my discomfort of not being myself, but as I had started a new job and was already on HRT by this point (I had taken a private route while my NHS referral was processed), HR at my new job were aware and keeping this confidential until the time I was ready. Eventually the balance of the scales tipped and the fear of coming out became less of a concern than not being myself 'full time'. During this period, in my personal life I had been living as myself, female, now for two years, since my realization. I even completed additional work-based training courses as myself. I had decided that so long as I was doing these training courses alone, I didn't want to be someone else and approached each training provider prior to, and told them that I would be appearing as myself, to use my chosen name but accepted that my birth name would remain on my certificates. Each training provider was accepting of this and made me feel very comfortable and safe. Especially as I needed to use the female changing and bathrooms. These training providers were in Clydebank, Falkirk and Aberdeen area. When the point came to come out at work, I approached HR and plans were put in place for my return at my next rotation. The welcome was amazing, everybody was great. My name was used, my pronouns mostly used correctly. I couldn't have asked for a better work transition. Overall, coming out was scary, but also brought with it a separation, so there was a lot going on at that time. But it also brought a joy and contentment I hadn't really experienced. Initially telling people is hard, but over time the news spread and I found that I didn't need to be coming out with everyone, until it reached the point that I would bump into someone I hadn't seen in a long time and be like, 'oh right yeah this is me now'.

Ashlee: It amazes me that we can be so similar in so many ways, and were living in the same place (Leith) when we met with a lot of the same activities and interests, and yet have had such different experiences with coming out. I 'came out' while I was at university during my undergraduate degree in the early 2000s in Vancouver. This was a period where I was learning lots of new ideas and developing new political commitments and critical perspectives. Studying women's studies and queer theory, and being involved in student activist work, gave me language to contextualize sexual experiences with other (cis) women from middle school onwards. However, coming out as 'bi' is an always incomplete process. In my case, I came out while I was with a cis male partner, whom I had been with since I was fifteen and would be with for another several years, so I was frequently not read as bi/queer and/or not 'believed'. Indeed, with some people I have had to 'come out' multiple times in my life since, with previous conversations that had been harrowing and imprinted on my memory seemingly completely forgotten by others. I have experimented with gender presentation frequently partly in order to be read as who I am. In my social world at the time, many, many people around me were queer (trans, much less so), and most people I interacted with had similar political ideologies to mine. Vancouver is overall a queer-friendly place (for white people with other privileged aspects of identity), and the activist queer communities I was involved in, together with the privilege of passing as straight with a cis male partner often in tow, provided a shield from homophobia – while in retrospect biphobia was an ever-present experience from the start.

Biphobia came into further focus when years later, living in London, I began to work at an LGBTQ community development organization, where I would work for six years and which was a formative turning point for my academic research trajectory, focusing on understandings and uses of intersectionality within equality organizations in England, Scotland and now Canada. Although I had been a 'bi hire', that is, I was out about my bi status and having this representation in the organization was one reason that I had been selected for the job, I remember clearly being told by a senior manager (cis lesbian) that earlier in her life, she had 'disliked bi women'. While I held this role, working in the queer neighbourhood of Soho and regularly creating and occupying queer spaces in London, I frequently felt not queer enough – and if I was dating a cis man (even if he was also bi/queer), would go to lengths to hide this information from most of my colleagues.

Aoife: I also can see similarities between being bi but not being seen as such, especially during my early transition when I was switching back and forth. It was hard to feel fully integrated and accepted. Although, in trans spaces, for the most part this was not true, as we all go through a similar discourse and there is understanding there.

What was it like to be queer and trans in Edinburgh? What are spaces in Edinburgh where your identity as queer/trans/bi was particularly affirmed/relevant?

Aoife: From my work transition through Covid I had my ups and downs. A couple of failed relationships before meeting Ashlee. In this period I had stepped away (not completely) from solely queer spaces, finding I just wanted to be myself in the world. Over the five years in Edinburgh, living in Leith and being somewhat 'alternative' identifying anyway, I found that the spaces I inhabited would have been LGBT health and well-being spaces and queer clubs: notably the Shuttlescots. My volunteering at Edinburgh Tool Library and later Empty Kitchen Food Bank as a delivery driver to individual residences were affirming in their own ways, feeling safe and confident in queer spaces, to gaining confidence in more mixed groups.

Ashlee: I also stepped away from solely queer spaces. When I moved to Edinburgh from London in 2016, I was more comfortable in my own identity and, having been immersed in queer spaces for six years because of my job, in which I frequently was *not* comfortable because of my bi identity, I did not seek out queer spaces to the same extent, though I actively sought to present as such in order to be read as myself (having said that, I made queer friends quickly and the Regent (queer pub) and the Street (queer bar) soon became regular haunts). Without doubt however, Edinburgh felt somewhat less 'queer' to me than London or Vancouver had – in spite of lots of talk at the time about how open Scotland was, even having a lesbian tory leader, Ruth Davidson – this did not filter into my day-to-day experiences. Living in the Abbey Hill area and otherwise inhabiting university spaces, casual homophobia and assumptions of cisheteronormativity were embedded in social life. Having worked in a Black-led LGBTQ organization that was very deliberate about creating multiracial spaces, what struck me about queer community and third sector spaces in Edinburgh that I did enter was how depressingly homogenous (white, gay, male, cis) they were. It felt in some ways like going back in time and progress towards greater equity. On the other hand, small pockets of grassroots trans organizing and trans femme resistance to trans exclusionary radical feminists (TERFs), often by trans women of colour, offered inspiration.

Aoife: It's interesting how we both stepped away from queer spaces, yet our timelines for doing so are very different! I guess Covid also caused the shift for me, as this closed things down for me at that time and I didn't really return.

What was it like to be queer and trans in other places in Scotland?

Aoife: I always had a lot more fear travelling to rural areas of Scotland, my parents living in rural Inverness-Shire, or travelling to the Highlands, but in reality, I have not had many issues in these places. Suburban towns around Aberdeen can be a little less friendly, but overall I would say Scotland is a welcoming place, or at least has been for me. That's not to say I haven't experienced my share of transphobia, the mutterings under the breath, the keeping clear, to obvious and often loud slurs being thrown about. A good pair of headphones make great armour.

Ashlee: I have less experience of travelling around Scotland than you do. When I've been with you in Inverness-Shire, I have felt more cautious than I would in Edinburgh or Glasgow, but I've felt safe in that we were together and I felt like together we could fight back if necessary. To be fair, the same cautiousness applies outside of cities in Canada too.

How did other aspects of your identity shape your experiences of being queer/trans in Scotland?

Aoife: With my work life and hobbies being somewhat more stereotypical of male-orientated activities, it took me a while to reintegrate these things again. Women don't ride or wrench motorcycles or play guitar. Then I realized that they do, that I can't really completely change the person who I grew into over thirty years and started to embrace that side of myself. Also I always felt guilty for my 'success'. I am in a well-paid job role, with security. I don't struggle to live. The privilege also holds me back from trans/queer spaces and makes me feel more secure and safe with myself and with those I am close to. As I progress through my life, I feel less comfortable in female spaces, because I feel I will never be whatever the definition of female is. So do I believe the rhetoric surrounding my existence? I feel trans people are being pushed into their own space, the third gender that encompasses all gender nonconforming people. That the 'T' is being removed from the LGB'T'QI+.

Ashlee: My whiteness definitely shaped my experience of being queer in Scotland, particularly given how white many queer spaces in Scotland are. The same applies to non-disabled identity since many spaces are inaccessible. Yet these experiences were also shaped by my being a migrant, and not seen as being 'Scottish' – given that I was otherwise largely inhabiting university spaces where Scottish people are actually very underrepresented, it was in some queer spaces where I found myself at times the only non-Scottish person – but people were very welcoming, for which I'm sure being a white migrant from Canada helped. My experience of being cis in such spaces was mainly as a cis person in trans-friendly/inclusive spaces; yet, as I realized in retrospect, I was also sometimes initially approached as a potential ally by cis lesbians, who would later go onto become heavily involved in so-called gender critical, transphobic 'feminism' in Scotland. These experiences often played out in the university contexts I was inhabiting, where for example TERFs screened a transphobic film in 2022.

Why did you get married in Canada? What is it like to be queer/bi/trans in Vancouver now?

Aoife: We chose to get married in Canada because, although I have a passport with my name and correct gender markers, I do not have a Gender Recognition Certificate (GRC). Marrying as a female couple in the UK where one is trans is extremely confusing and would have led to my birth gender being on the marriage certificate. In Canada, the marriage certificate doesn't even include gender. All that is needed is a marriage licence and names to be entered into the register. There is also no civil partnership differentiate for same sex/gender couples. All can be married.

Ashlee: Getting married in Canada was also fitting for us since we had already planned to move to Canada later that year.

Aoife: In some ways it is hard to compare Vancouver to Edinburgh as I experienced Edinburgh during the early stages of my transition (with nearly two years of that consumed with the Covid pandemic and lockdowns), when I didn't 'pass' and my confidence was low. Edinburgh is a pretty accepting city overall, but I agree that Vancouver is 'more queer' – it is a significantly queer city. My first impressions were how nice it was to see how many openly queer people and couples hold hands through the streets, something that in Edinburgh is still less common. Yet this doesn't mean that I haven't seen and/or experienced transphobia in both cities. In Edinburgh I have had comments, slurs shouted at me, people avoiding me, or shielding their children in supermarkets, the fear of using a public bathroom. I have felt scared in other parts of Scotland, the time I was waiting for a taxi when a group of drunk guys tried to hit on me, heard me talk and commented 'oh you're one of those!' as they walked behind me talking about me while I clutched my bag praying for their train to arrive or my taxi, fearing that things might escalate. Vancouver has had its moments; while I have seen less obvious transphobia, I have had altercations. What scares me now is the rising right-wing rhetoric, similar as is gaining momentum in the UK. I feel of Vancouver that it doesn't care. And I mean that in a positive way. Queer culture has been openly accepted for longer, I feel, than the UK in general. Now being queer is nothing unusual or to be feared, but there is a change of sentiment on the wind.

Ashlee: For me, in some ways Vancouver and Canada in general feel less safe to be queer overall, and to be in a cis/trans relationship, than they did back before I moved to London in 2006 – which is sad. At that time, gay marriage had recently become legalized (2005), and in Vancouver there was a thriving queer scene and civil society which catered beyond gay white men. While the latter is still true, increasingly at the time of writing (not long after Trump has resumed presidency), US politics are shifting the political and media climate in Canada. In Vancouver I experienced 'pride talks' in high school and a relatively inclusive sexual education in the 1990s/early 2000s, while these things are currently under attack. The changing political landscapes/conjunctures of Scotland, as we were leaving, and now Vancouver/Canada as the place we currently inhabit have compelled me into more queer-identified activism and voluntary work than I have been doing for a long time, since leaving the sector in 2016. In contrast to some other parts of Canada, Vancouver at the least offers a numerically strong queer opposition to political attacks.

What is it like to work in a straight male dominated industry as a queer trans woman in Canada, as compared to Scotland?

Aoife: This is a challenging question mostly because of the period of life I am in. I came out at my last place of work, I transitioned there. Starting work here in Canada, I was established. There was no history, no previous and no preconceptions. But in the twenty years I have been in the offshore oil and gas industry I have met only one openly queer person, white cis gay male. While I do know other queer people in the industry, they were not out during the time that I knew them (I'll add that this is solely in the offshore world, there were a number of queer people in the mainland office spaces) – this is very telling I feel. Here in Vancouver there are a few openly queer people, not many, and interestingly more queer women! Not a space for gay guys? Only 'butch' women? There are also more women in general in the trades in Canada, not nearly enough by far. But definitely more than I have seen in previous places. But I can talk openly about being in a lesbian marriage, not something I would have been as comfortable doing in the UK sector. Also worth a note, I am not only comparing Scotland to West Coast Canada, I am also comparing offshore world, working away from home, on a rig for weeks on end, to working onshore, home at night, the '9 to 5'.

What is it like to be trans and queer, in a settler colonial context as opposed to Scotland?

Aoife: To be honest being queer and trans in reference to a settler colonial context doesn't really matter. The context is about my own migrant status into settler colonialism, especially as British, the primary colonizer in Canada. The fact is I don't like it, I find Canada surprisingly close minded and insular. Maybe that's a West Coast thing, being so far from the rest of the world (aside from the United States). But honestly, being a migrant settler British person just feels like I am continuing the cycle of British colonialism.

Ashlee: For me, partly because of the research and activism I am involved in, I am very aware that in Canada Indigenous Two-Spirit people form a hugely important part of the 2SLGBTQIA+ communities, and that addressing anti-Indigenous racism within these communities and organizations 'representing' them is in nascent stages. Two-Spirit organizations are doing really incredible work in self-advocacy in relation to both colonial and Indigenous governance structures.

What are your fears and hopes for the future?

Aoife: Not living in Scotland at present, I can only watch as I see what appears to be louder and stronger anti-trans rhetoric. Pride has never been bigger, but voices are not being heard and the spaces between the L-G-B-T are growing. Watching political sentiments change in the wind based on First Minister John Swinney, loud public figureheads decrying trans people as a danger, laws being overruled by another parliament; but it's not just Scotland. I am seeing this happening in Canada also or at least I can see similarities. The hate is rising, free control of our bodies is being removed, yet I hold my head up high and go through my day.

Ashlee: I share these concerns and hope for greater solidarity from other movements for queer and trans rights in both contexts -- while this works both ways. The 'No Pride in Genocide' march held in Vancouver, among other cities globally, last summer was a positive on which to build.

What do you hope for the future for queer/trans people in Scotland?

Aoife: I hope to see a better healthcare system for trans people. Guiding people along their path rather than regulating it. I hope to see more gender-neutral spaces, specifically bathrooms. I hope to see waiting lists reduced and more research done on medical pathways currently offered and potentially made available.

Ashlee: I share these hopes and hope to see Gender Recognition Act (GRA) reform eventually come to fruition in Scotland and greater funding to a more diverse trans justice organizing. Without the barriers posed by the GRA we would have been able to marry in Scotland, Aoife's home.

Concluding reflections

What did we learn through this dialogue and introspection on our experiences in Scotland and elsewhere? It is clear that particular conjunctures of time and place (Vancouver *c.*2001, Edinburgh/Scotland *c.*2018) create the conditions for very different kinds of identity formations and different experiences of coming out. These contexts also influence the wider knowledge that we are able to gain of queer/trans identity in our personal and working lives that shape how we see ourselves. Our experiences and reflections emphasize that mainstream 'queer' spaces, as has been widely documented elsewhere, do not hold the same meaning for all and can be exclusive, perhaps particularly to bi and trans people. Queer spaces may provide an important haven at points in our lives, but they cannot necessarily prepare us for interaction in the wider world – but they can, potentially, allow us to grow confidence for the wider world. In comparison with elsewhere, intersectionally privileged queer people are substantially overrepresented in many queer spaces in Scotland. We saw queer spaces grow though, even while feelings of safety and acceptance decreased around them.

We find that although Scotland has constructed itself as very queer/trans-friendly, in comparison to some other places, it is less so. Born in a different country, time period or with parents more observant or accepting of her behaviour, Aoife may have been able to come out and transition at a much earlier age. In Scotland she has seen improvements as visibility increases. But this is also relative; Aoife has had to turn down work opportunities where her existence is not only illegal, but punishable by death. Moreover, in the current moment, queer and transphobia is increasing even in more queer-friendly places like Vancouver, while biphobia has, perhaps, long been rife in geographically disparate queer communities. In contexts where so-called 'women's spaces' are increasingly hostile to trans people – trans people are being pushed into their own space, the third gender that encompasses all gender nonconforming people. It's more important than ever for trans inclusive women's spaces to make the fact that they are trans inclusive very clear to those who are not already a part of these spaces. We share hopes and fears for the future of queer and trans lives in Scotland and elsewhere. We are at junctures where the coming months and years will be pivotally important for the experiences of queer and trans people in the future.

References

Davidson, N., Liinpää, M., McBride, M. and Virdee, S. (eds). *No Problem Here: Understanding Racism in Scotland*. Edinburgh: Luath Press, 2018.

Hall, S. *The Hard Road to Renewal: Thatcherism and the Crisis of the Left*. London: Verso, 1988.

Sobande, F. and hill, l.-r. *Black Oot Here: Black Lives in Scotland*. London: Bloomsbury, 2022.

10

Being queer in Scotland: Conversational snapshots

Dario Luis Banegas and Drew Bain

Who are we?

We were a couple. Darío is a Latino (brown) gay man (pronouns his/him) who was born (1978) and raised in Argentina and moved to Glasgow, the largest city in Scotland, in 2019 to work as an academic. Drew is a white gay/queer man (pronouns his/him) and was born (1976) and raised in Falkirk, a small town in the central belt of Scotland. We both come from working-family backgrounds, and we both experienced challenging circumstances as kids. We were together between 2022 and 2025, and we lived in different Scottish cities (Darío in Glasgow, Drew in Falkirk and then Leith). In different ways, we both advocate for inclusion and equity. When Darío received the invitation from Yvette (Thank you, Yvette) to write a chapter for this volume, he shared the idea with Drew, and after a few months, this chapter was born.

How did we put together this chapter?

For the purpose of this chapter, we recorded and edited our focus talk on being queer in Scotland. Like most people, we don't use language the same way when we speak and when we write, and transferring spoken conversation to a written dialogue can be a bit tricky because you want to keep the conversational nature of the exchange, but at the same time, you want a text that reads coherently. This entailed reformulating some statements, taking out broken sentences, polishing some incomplete ideas or deleting some bits that we then felt were a bit too personal or we didn't feel comfortable sharing. It also meant inserting sentences that we did not actually say when we got together with the aim of rounding up some ideas or clarifying some bits that were a bit obscure to understand.

Even though we had some initial questions to act as a guide, we also let ourselves depart from the initial agenda. In the end, we discussed these topics: (1) how we define 'queer', (2) how we experience being part of the queer community in Scotland, (3) comparing queerness a few decades ago and now, (4) queer spaces and safety, and (5) how different identities intersect as we talk about and experience queerness in Scotland. To make the chapter more organic and organized, we identified conversation snapshots to illustrate each of those themes. What is a snapshot anyway? In this chapter, a snapshot is a summary of a longer or more complex conversation. As we developed the snapshots, we may have added some bits here and there to mitigate some slippage between saying our words out loud to each other and conveying our 'queer in a wee place' thoughts and findings here.

Snapshot 1: On defining 'queer'

In this snapshot, we discuss what 'queer' means to us. As we talk about how the word resonates with us, we connect it to visibility and inclusion in Scotland, which seems to show that in different ways, Scotland is this wee queer place in which we feel we can be ourselves.

Darío: I guess I've never asked you this question but, what does it mean to be queer in Scotland? You know, I'm interested in this because we have a relationship, and I don't think we have ever talked about this.

Drew: I think we've got to start at the word, possibly, like what does queer mean to people? And I feel it's how I use it to describe myself because I feel it's quite inclusive. What does it mean to be queer in Scotland? Words are coming into my head. It means freedom, bravery, chosen family, solidarity, visibility. And inclusivity as well. I just think queer is quite an inclusive word that is being used more and more now. I mean, the word itself has been reclaimed by the community because it was a slur. If I'm being honest, it was a word I wasn't comfortable with when I was younger because it was used as quite a heavy slur, and words like queer and faggot were really scary. Scotland was a less inclusive country than it is now, just through visibility and through growing up, through Section 28.[1]

Darío: I agree with you. I can see queerness in Scotland. It's visible. It's palpable. What made you use the word visibility?

Drew: I think it's ownership of the word and a way of self-describing myself, using that word with no shame anymore. There was shame in the past. By being openly queer and owning that word and referring to myself like that, there is visibility in that. And I think not just by me, by the large group of people who identify as queer who use that word to describe who they are or something they're part of. There are people who aren't comfortable with the word, and I totally get that. No one should force a label or a name or a word on someone else. Some might associate queer with visibility because it's about being proud, being part of something. We're part of a minority, but there's strength, and strength in numbers.

Darío: I like that. We could be a minority, but that doesn't mean that we're weak. So, there is strength, and there is this sense of community and collective thinking and doing and being and becoming. I guess that's extremely supportive and enabling because then you know it makes people feel safe, or people who identify themselves as queer don't feel that sense of shame. You know, it's interesting because I almost never use the word queer to describe myself. I think I'm more comfortable with gay, but I'd say queer is more inclusive.

Drew: I think that what I like about the word queer is that it's an umbrella that brings everyone together, like the LGBTQ+, and even allies that identify as queer. It's about challenging the system, fighting for equal rights, but also being aware that different groups within that umbrella have more rights than others. It's about fighting until we all have equal rights.

Snapshot 2: On community

This snapshot illustrates our experiences with the queer community in Scotland. We discuss our sense and practice of community in relation to spaces, organizations and activities that take place in Scotland. You will notice that we refer to a variety of events such as Pride marches in Glasgow as well as smaller ones such as Pride Outside to show that the queer community in Scotland has created different actions and spaces to support people in big cities (e.g. Glasgow and Edinburgh) as well as towns (e.g. Kilmarnock). You will find a few notes that will take you to websites so that you can find information about the events or organizations we mention.

Drew: Do you feel part of a community?

Darío: Yes and no.

Drew: So, if you were to say that you are part of a community, what community would you see yourself as part of?

Darío: I don't identify myself as being part of a specific community. I wouldn't say that I am *actively* part of the queer community, but maybe this is because I'm not an activist. I see myself as an advocate, but I don't see myself as an activist. I don't necessarily reach out to queer people. I go to places that are queer or queer-friendly or whatever you want to call them. Since I moved to Scotland, I guess I go to queer places or Pride because I go with you. It's like an element of motivation, because I know I wouldn't go by myself. Not because I am ashamed, but it's just like I don't need to feel part of the queer community. And to me, that's good because it begins to show that, at least in my case, I am normalizing that identity. But now that I'm saying this aloud, I don't need to feel part of a community because there have been activists, and there have been people who continue to make sure that I can feel the way I feel.

Drew: So, when you have come along with me to Pride marches, have you felt part of something? Have you felt part of a bigger thing?

Darío: Yes, I have, and I think it is because you are physically part of something. So, it's not just a feeling or a value that I hold, but it is like this physical presence. You are actually marching with other queer people, and there's happiness, this feeling of pride around, of feeling safe. And I enjoy that a lot. I did enjoy marching with you in Glasgow in 2023. But, it's not something I am in need of. And even though I don't need that sort of validation, I do recognize that other people will feel validated when we walk alongside them or when they see us on the streets marching. So, it's a sense of responsibility that I have now. If others see me marching, they will feel supported, they will feel that they can come out and be comfortable and happy about being queer, which may push them to open up to their family, or friends, or whoever. What organizations or charities promote and support queerness in Scotland?

Drew: You've got LGBT Health and Wellbeing.[2] They're the biggest charity in Scotland supporting LGBTQIA+. You've got Equality Network who are more research, political activists. You've got Scottish Trans who are fighting for the trans community. You've got Pride Outside,[3] which is a small charity run by people in Glasgow. They have a focus on queer people getting together in nature, whether that'd be on walks or foraging. What I love about them and LGBT Health and Wellbeing Scotland is that they are spaces that aren't centred on alcohol, which is really good, because historically the only space that queer people felt safe to get together was bars, and there's been historic issues with alcoholism in our community. It was mainly in bars that queer people could get together and meet each other and be with large groups. So, I think it's just amazing that there are organizations who are providing sober spaces where people can get together, particularly Pride Outside. I think they are fantastic, as well as other organizations like Equality Network[4] who are pushing government, fighting for rights. There's also LGBT Youth Scotland, a great charity, who support young people from sixteen to eighteen, which is fantastic. They existed when I was young, but because I was in Falkirk (a town in the central lowlands of Scotland), they didn't have the resources to have a space in Falkirk, so it was Glasgow and Edinburgh (Scotland's capital city), but it wasn't an option for me to take any travel there. I didn't know about others. This is because we're a couple of dinosaurs; this is before the internet. Now, we can look up the internet and find things more easily. Sometimes I've got mixed opinions on the internet. In general, some things are great, some things are not so great. But one thing that's good about it is young people can find community online, particularly kids in rural communities, which is fantastic. There are lots of other organizations out there that can provide support. There are also the big Pride organizers in Glasgow, Edinburgh or Porty [Portobello, a seaside town near Edinburgh], and more grassroots ones are popping up all over the place, including rural places, which is fantastic. You've got Trans Pride Scotland[5] (a small, non-commercial grassroots movement) that was held in Kilmarnock (a small town in the west of Scotland) in 2024 and we marched with, which is amazing for visibility and for countering transphobia in Scotland. What I've just said also shows that you've got the bigger commercial prides in the largest cities of Scotland, that is Glasgow and Edinburgh, but in small cities and town there are also events that are smaller and perhaps more community-oriented. So, we can say that Scottish queer life is quite diverse and that there are things happening, in varying degrees and forms, in less populated areas. Being queer in Scotland is supported by big as well as wee places.

Darío: You mentioned Pride Outside. Do they only do it in Glasgow, or are they in other places in Scotland?

Drew: I don't think so. There was a group that started up called Queer by Nature,[6] a small Edinburgh-based community group who care about nature, and it was kind of smaller scale than Pride Outside. The LGBT Health and Wellbeing community events programme is quite wide and varied. So, they do have some things outdoors as well. More rurally, I think there are some things happening up north. I think that most of the money or the funding for LGBTQIA+ charities tends to go to groups in Edinburgh and Glasgow, and sometimes some more rural areas are a little bit forgotten, which is a shame.

Snapshot 3: On queerness then and now

In this snapshot, Drew compares growing up as queer in Falkirk and the limited support queer communities/group/organizations would offer back then and how that has changed now. In this snapshot we also mention, as in Snapshot 2, physical spaces and activities as well as online spaces. These online spaces are often complementary to/extensions of physical ones (e.g. an organization based in Glasgow with an online presence) or spaces which are only digital and probably created by small groups or individual even. Our discussion may also signal that queer people who feel lonely and unsupported by family/friends/organizations may find it easy to reach out to others online, but their physical experience and day-to-day life may still be isolating.

Darío: I was thinking about how things are changing, and it is great that queer people now have more opportunities to reach out to other queer people. There are initiatives, support groups and so on, and these could be in person or online. And I guess that, you know, some people might prefer initially to connect online because it they may feel it's safer or less intimidating, like they're not exposing themselves that much, or they don't want to reveal their identity in case other people find out about them. There are closed as well as open groups on social media, although you may have the danger of some people judging, pontificating or just spreading hate online. But this is now, though, as someone who only moved to Scotland in 2019, I don't know about being queer in Scotland twenty or thirty years ago.

Drew: The difference between then and now? I suppose it's more about progress, attitudes changing, equal rights happening. Visibility is a huge thing. I mean, being a kid in the 1980s, I thought I was the only gay person because I lived in a small town (Falkirk), and the only gay people I saw were on TV, but were never explicitly said to be gay. It was normally like an ultra-camp person and they were the butt the joke. So, that's all I could see. Whereas with changes in attitude and progress and visibility, and seeing through the media ... maybe pop stars coming out, seeing a variety of different gay people, or queer people in the media, I think that definitely helped, and that's a huge change. Basically, it's visibility and the opportunity for people to see people who are like them and feel seen, and not just helping queer people, but also helping non-queer people build empathy and understanding through that visibility. That's been a huge change for the better. Mind you, there's still a lot of bigotry out there. Visibility now, like I said, is really empowering. You have visibly and openly queer people in music, films and TV shows. Some shows over the years have been truly ground-breaking. In the 1980s there was this awful Tory government notoriously led by Prime Minister Margaret Thatcher, who was publicly being very nasty about gay people.[7] It was just awful. Current Tory prime minister [Rishi Sunak] is definitely not on our side, and he's a huge bigot himself with his anti-trans speeches for example in Parliament.[8] But we had our ex-first minister, Nicola Sturgeon in Scotland, who was such a huge queer ally, who, for example, led the Pride Glasgow march in 2018.[9] She campaigned for queer rights, for example, when she gave a speech on trans rights at an awards event.[10] The fact that there's so much visibility now and the fact that some people in power are today on our side fighting for us as well, that's the biggest difference I would see from then and now. That has impacted on people, by having increased visibility, by seeing yourself. That has validation and it reduces shame, and it builds acceptance. It's also probably helped families to understand more someone in their family who comes out as queer.

Darío: On visibility, I was just thinking of RuPaul's *Drag Race* (a reality competition TV series in which a group of drag queens compete to win a prize; it has versions in the United States, the UK, Spain, Mexico, France, Brazil, Australia, etc.), the UK version or even other versions. Do you know if there have been any Scottish queens?

Drew: Yes, a couple, I think. Season 2 winner was Lawrence Chaney,[11] who's from Glasgow, and there was another Scottish queen, Ellie Diamond,[12] from Dundee (a Scottish city). And that's a TV show that, whether people love it or loath it, has increased visibility. It's a show with real queer people with real queer stories on prime-time TV. It's won Emmys, other awards. Lawrence Chaney won the BAFTA Scotland Audience award. So, it has visibility that's pushing boundaries.

Snapshot 4: On queer spaces and safety

As readers may have noted by now, space has been a recurrent theme in our conversations. In this snapshot we discuss it in relation to where we feel safe to live our queerness. On this aspect, we talk about how, sometimes, hiding queerness may act as a defence mechanism even when we know that by doing so, we may be perpetuating heteronormativity. We also talk about party politics, government and political figures' views on queerness. Towards the end of the snapshot, we talk about how much queer visibility there is in diffcrent areas of Glasgow and in Leith. Regarding this latter aspect, it seems that queerness intersects with social class and geography since it looks like when certain areas regenerate, become trendy and experience an economic boost, queerness is more visible. This may also show that while, in general, we can live in

Scotland as a wee queer place, there are urban areas in which being queer may not be safe.

Drew: I'm thinking about spaces, like when you said that you feel you don't need to go to queer spaces to feel validated. I think that queer spaces are so important for people and myself. I am myself in general in life, but I feel it's completely different in a queer space.

I can be like 100 per cent myself, like 100 per cent authentic, and if I was to be kissing you in a queer space, I would feel completely comfortable with that. Whereas, if we were doing it outside in the street, I'd have one eye looking around thinking, 'is someone going to attack us, or say something?' I've spoken to friends, and a lot of us code switch as well. So, for example, when you are in the back of a taxi with a driver you don't know, you may code switch (to change your language/dialect/behaviour to adapt to a dominant social context) to tone down your queerness for safety. Whereas, in a queer space I'd never have that worry. I can be 100 per cent feeling safe that I can be myself in that space. So, I get a lot of validation from queer spaces.

Darío: Are there any spaces in particular where you feel safe?

Drew: Anywhere that's advertised as a queer space, where there are other queer people. There are different elements of feeling safe. There's maybe a rainbow flag up, and you're like 'oh, that's cool, they're on board'. But there's still an element of authenticity. Is it tokenistic? Or is it that there's one person in that venue that put it there, but others aren't as open-minded or supportive. I've been to places where I feel completely at ease like Pride marches, queer bars, any other events like Pride Outside we went to, or any kind of organization that does events, like LGBT Health and Wellbeing events. Any inclusive space.

Darío: I don't know whether it is because I am not originally from here, but sometimes I assume that there's more queerness in Scotland. What I mean is that, for example, if I if I want to kiss you in the street, I wouldn't be checking whether it's safe to do it. Perhaps it's because we're usually in places that are generally safe. I'm thinking about open spaces or the bars and pubs we usually go to.

Drew: You were just talking about not looking around if we were kissing. From my experience as I grew up in a small town in Scotland, there was a lot of bigotry at the time. I think that was not exclusive to Scotland. I think that's the whole UK, possibly the whole world in the 1980s, and but most definitely a lot worse in other countries. But we're living in a day and age where we do have a degree of acceptance or 'tolerance' from some people. However, there are still news articles of gang attacks on queer people in Edinburgh.[13] A few months ago, there were two guys holding hands and a gang jumped on them and beat them up, and nobody around helped. So, that's why if we are in a situation and I'm going to kiss you, I do check my area. I do have a look around to see if there's anyone I think that is going to potentially be a problem. And I'm not scared of people. But then, because I'm with you, and because I love you, I worry about you getting hurt. And so, I do check my location if I feel safe or not. I wish I didn't have to, but in terms of safety, it's still a reality that we're really still not safe enough in a lot of places, depending who's in the area.

Darío: Maybe I don't check around as you do because I'm being cheeky, or want to defy others and structures, or because I'm being too naïve. But at the same time, I think I know how to defend myself. Though, of course it is true that you never know who those bigots are and what they can do. The last thing we want is to be stabbed or beaten up. Maybe it's just me being careless, which is not good, or being too optimistic. Or maybe I feel too safe in Scotland particularly, you know, in Glasgow or Edinburgh. Maybe it's just my perception that it is safer than it really is. It's not that I would feel less safe in Argentina. Or maybe, mind you, that must be my stereotype about Scottish people or people in the UK in general that people don't mind what others do and I'd be fine. People minding their own business. Perhaps in Argentina, there would be a few heads turning, or a slur in passing, but I don't recall cases of queer people being beaten up. I'm sure there have been, or there are. In fact, this reminds me of this case that happened a few years ago in London. Two girls were kissing on a bus, and they were attacked, and one of them, or was it the two of them, were actually from Argentina. So, they got attacked in London, not Buenos Aires, but that doesn't mean that Argentina is 100 per cent safe.

Drew: Heads turning doesn't bother me. What worries me is potential physical violence that is happening and appears to be on the increase. It could get worse depending what happens with British elections on 4 July (2024). If the right wing suddenly feels they've got a voice again, it will get worse, similar to what is happening around the world. I do kiss you in public and I do hug you in public, but you've got to be aware of your surroundings, which is why I love specifically queer spaces because I know that in that space I don't have to worry or think 'is someone going to attack me for being myself?' So, yes, I think we definitely need queer spaces.

Darío: Yes, we do, and there should be more. And one thing that I've noticed is that it's not just bars, but sometimes other types of shops and maybe on Instagram they say something like queer-owned shop. I find that interesting because I suppose it sends the signal that it will be safe. But on the other hand, I think, it's a small shop that sells wine and cheese, why would I feel unsafe?

Drew: I think it's really important because you're saying it may not feel unsafe, and something just clicked in my head and I think it's just a realization that I haven't said out loud yet: Trans and non-binary people in particular are being attacked by the patriarchy because they're scared of losing power. For me, queer is an umbrella term that includes trans and non-binary people, but not everyone agrees with that, unfortunately even within our community. We've got breakaway groups like LGB alliance, who are basically a hate group, who are anti-trans. They've taken the letters LGB. They don't want the

T anymore, even though the T has always been there. T means people who have fought from the beginning for all our rights. Suddenly they're like 'Oh, no, we've got our rights now. You can go away'. So, I think the word queer and particularly when a business says it's queer-owned or queer-friendly, trans people will feel safe in that space. This is what I know from talking to my trans friends. Some of them have had negative experiences in other spaces. So, by seeing the word queer, I think they see a safe space where they'll be welcomed. Again, it's a matter of visibility.

Darío: Is the breakaway group present only here in Scotland, or also in the rest of the UK?

Drew: They're UK-wide. They're a breakaway group who are trying to break up our community. It's really sad because these are people who have gone through difficult times growing up and have been part of a marginalized group who are suddenly attacking and separating another marginalized group who always stood with us. It just baffles me that a group like that exists.

Darío: It's a real shame. Well, it's more than a shame. It's just ironic, horrific, a minority attacking another minority. If it's the usual suspects, the usual bigots, that's not a surprise. But it is just worse when a minority that has suffered, and continues to suffer discrimination, does exactly the same thing onto others. It's like a hierarchy within minorities, and it gives the message that within that minority, some people have the right to exist, and some others don't. Insane! Is it power? Is it money? I find it hard to comprehend.

Drew: It's a group that's been formed as a separatist move and so they don't want to be associated with anyone who's not LGB. They support the right-wing rhetoric of anti-trans, and they're supporting the taking away of trans rights. But anyone who doesn't live to their right-wing ideals will be the target of their attacks. They think that the right wing accept them and that suddenly bigots accept them.

Darío: Going back to the idea of feeling safe in a space, you just made me think of Katie's (a queer basement bar in Glasgow city centre), to me the best queer bar in Glasgow. And you know it's my favourite place because I feel completely welcome. I like the place, the atmosphere, the crowd, the inclusion you see, people of all ages, people having a good time, this good vibe I feel every time I go. The diversity around me is what attracts me the most about that place. I don't think I've been to a place like that in Edinburgh.

Drew: Sadly, we lost Bonjour (a cooperative-owned queer bar in Glasgow city centre that was opened in 2021 and closed in 2024). I would say Bonjour for me was more diverse and inclusive. It was a co-op of people, and it was most definitely a safe space for trans or non-binary people and they were centred supportively around that community. That made Bonjour really special and unique for bars in Scotland.

Darío: Is there anything similar to Bonjour in Edinburgh?

Drew: Not that I'm aware of. And every time there's less and less specifically LGBTQ+ spaces. Like Habana closing. We still have bars and cafes such as The Street, CC Blooms, Planet (three queer-friendly disco-bars, with drag queen shows, located in the centre of Edinburgh), and that's about it for specifically LGBTQ+ places, but I don't know if you'd describe them as 'queer' venues. I know sometimes they have nights that are explicitly queer as they're advertised as that, but are queer people always welcome?

Darío: I've never seen that level of visibility in Bridgeton or the East Side in Glasgow, two areas of Glasgow which are not seen as cool or trendy. I've never seen a flag in my neighbourhood in Glasgow.

Drew: The South Side (a 'cool' area in Glasgow) is very queer. There's a lot of us there.

Darío: Yes, there's more visibility. Same with the West End (another 'cool' and more affluent area of Glasgow, where the University of Glasgow is located). But definitely not around Glasgow Green (a park next to the Bridgeton area).

Snapshot 5: On intersecting identities and queerness

In this last snapshot, Darío talks about how he has been stereotyped by some Scottish queer men in relation to his identity as a brown Latino. This topic led to reflecting about how queerness may intersect with ethnicity and issues with racism within the queer community in Scotland. This topic may show that while a lot has been achieved in terms ensuring that Scotland is a safe queer place, a lot more needs to be done to ensure that sites of privilege and oppression are removed from queer spaces and beyond.

Drew: So far, we've been talking about being queer in Scotland, do you want to tell me about your own experience as someone coming from another country, in your case Argentina?

Darío: Are you sure you want to hear my side? Ha! One thing that I felt when I moved to Glasgow and I was on apps like Tinder (online dating application), Grindr (online dating application targeted towards queer people, usually used for casual encounters) or Hinge (online dating application), was that I had to conform to a certain stereotype. If I had a date, I think guys had a stereotypical expectation, like they would find this stereotypical Latino. Or that I had to be more dramatic, expressive, loud. It didn't bother me, but there was this sort of unspoken label. In any case, it was their expectation that I had to be hot and sexy and always sexually aroused because I was supposed to be this hot-blooded Latino. But that didn't last for long. They'd realize I was not that kind of person the moment I made a sarcastic comment, or if I was absolutely indifferent to a passing remark, or anything. This makes me think of another issue that I don't think I have noted because again I am not an active member of queer communities, but in your experience, have you noted any type of discrimination or disadvantage when you look at for example, you know, Scottish queer people or white queer people and immigrants or people from different ethnicities who may be British or not, but they have another ethnicity, or maybe English is not their first or dominant language?

Drew: I think there's definitely racism within the gay community, at least, the male gay community on apps. I have friends who have experienced racism within our community. Some people have on their dating or hook-up profiles this element of exclusion saying no this, no that. I know of someone who on the apps, met someone and that person dismissed them because they were a person of colour. So yeah, that definitely does happen, but again it baffles me. I just don't understand people who can be bigoted, who have suffered a great deal in the hands of bigots, then becoming bigoted themselves.

Darío: When we go to queer places like bars or pubs, I don't usually see people of other ethnicities.

Drew: I would say that in the queer spaces I go to, I do, particularly in non-alcohol centred spaces. Given what we've talked about before, I could see why some spaces might not feel welcoming. Similarly, but less so as time goes by thankfully, there are also spaces like gay bars where lesbians don't feel comfortable or invited there. Some spaces where it might be primarily gay white men, a majority within a minority, it can feel exclusionary of certain groups. That's not a general assertion, but there can be spaces where they are the dominant group and other people don't feel welcome and are made not to feel welcome. And by the way, I obviously have privilege on my side because I am a white gay man, and so I haven't experienced it first hand, but I've heard from friends about their experiences in some gay spaces. There are also still some spaces where campness or femme presented men are also looked down upon, or not accepted, and I just think that's so small-minded.

The way forward is the only way possible

In the snapshots included above, we have talked about personal experiences, views, community, trans people, conflict within queerness and so on. One topic that we see as recurrent is visible spaces; spaces for building community, spaces for feeling safe, spaces for reaching out and being reached out to queer people. Spaces to live our lives, to breathe, to be who we want to be. What's worth emphasizing is that Scotland offers people the right to live their queerness in wee, community spaces which come in different forms such as Glasgow Pride, a pub or activities run by small groups such as Pride Outside. That said, we recognize that more needs to be done so that these wee queer spaces are not only found in big Scottish cities or in trendy and/or affluent urban areas.

What's vital is that we construct queer in a wee space as a personal-collective dimension that promotes equity, equal rights, togetherness and the possibility of writing our futures and our pasts in our unique ways. Although our reflections are situated in Scotland with an emphasis on Scottish politics, identities and communities, they may resonate with other contexts and people as queerness and the construction of queer spaces transcend borders since, after all, queer lived experiences inhabit a multitude of places.

Notes

1. On Section 28 see https://digital.nls.uk/1980s/society/section-28/. Accessed 4 November 2024.
2. LGBT Health and Wellbeing, www.lgbthealth.org.uk/. Accessed 8 November 2024.
3. Pride Outside, www.prideoutside.org.uk/team. Accessed 4 November 2024.
4. Equality Network, www.equality-network.org/. Accessed 4 November 2024.
5. Trans Pride Scotland, https://2024.transpride.scot/#about-us. Accessed 4 November 2024.
6. Queer by Nature, www.lgbthealth.org.uk/community-groups/queer-by-nature. Accessed 9 November 2024.
7. Margaret Thatcher, www.gayinthe80s.com/2014/11/1987-politics-margaret-thatcher-derides-inalienable-right-to-be-gay. Accessed 10 November 2024.
8. 'Rishi Sunak Makes Anti-trans Remarks in Parliament', www.independent.co.uk/news/uk/politics/rishi-sunak-trans-joke-brianna-ghey-mother-b2492095.html. Accessed 4 November 2024.
9. 'Nicola Sturgeon Marches at Pride Glasgow 2018', www.bbc.co.uk/news/uk-scotland-glasgow-west-44832218. Accessed 4 November 2024.
10. 'Nicola Sturgeon on Trans Rights', https://metro.co.uk/2023/05/18/rainbow-awards-nicola-sturgeon-gives-rousing-speech-on-trans-rights-18803377. Accessed 4 November 2024.
11. Lawrence Chaney, https://rupaulsdragrace.fandom.com/wiki/Lawrence_Chaney Accessed 9 November 2024.
12. Ellie Diamond, https://rupaulsdragrace.fandom.com/wiki/Ellie_Diamond. Accessed 9 November 2024.
13. 'Gang Attacks on Queer People in Edinburgh', https://archive.thetab.com/uk/edinburgh/2021/08/06/how-safe-do-lgbtq-students-feel-in-edi-after-homophobic-assault-on-leith-street-71856. Accessed 9 November 2024.

11

Queer New Scots? On migration, queerness and Scottish exceptionalism

Francesca Stella

'"Enlightened" culture attracts LGB people to move to Scotland', headlined *The National* newspaper in December 2015. The article drew this rather far-fetched conclusion from the 2011 Census data which suggested that '69 per cent of people who identify themselves as LGB were born in Scotland, with 31 per cent moving here from elsewhere' (Paterson 2015). The percentage of Scottish residents identifying as lesbian, gay or bisexual and born outside of Scotland was higher than the figure for heterosexual-identified residents born outside of Scotland (19 per cent); this led Paterson to conclude that LGB people must be drawn to Scotland by its 'enlightened' culture on LGBT+ rights. Anyone who cared to check the Office for National Statistics' finer print would have quickly discovered that this was an 'experimental' statistic, coming with a health warning about its limitations and validity. Yet the article continued in a wholly positive tone, presenting Scotland as the best country in Europe for LGBTI legal equality according to the 2015 Rainbow Europe Index – again, the reader was encouraged to imagine Scotland's ranking as appealing to LGB people living outside of Scotland.

This narrative of queer Scottish exceptionalism – which highlights the Scottish nation's exceptionally progressive record on LGBT+ rights and implies its superiority to other countries – circulates widely, and it is also sustained in Scottish political discourse. Since the early 2000s, the Scottish government has discursively positioned Scotland as a queer-friendly country with a progressive stance on LGBT+ rights. Beating the UK government to repeal the infamous Section 28 in 2002, LGBT+ rights have remained high on the political agenda since, as evidenced by the introduction of family rights for same-sex couples, the mainstreaming of LGBT+ inclusive education and support for the Gender Recognition Reform (Scotland) Bill. This has consolidated a self-image of Scottish queer exceptionalism. This exceptionalism is replicated in the Scottish government's stance on overseas migration. Migration is an area of policy 'reserved' for the UK government which has become increasingly restrictive, with the introduction of a points-based visa system to 'manage' migration; attempts to reduce arrivals and increase deportations through a punitive approach known as the 'hostile environment'; Brexit; and the ongoing overhaul of the asylum system. Yet the Scottish government has generally emphasized the economic, social and demographic benefits of overseas migration to Scotland, mainstreaming the term 'New Scots' in official documents to refer to migrants of any nationality who have settled in Scotland.

This chapter interrogates how ideas of Scottish exceptionalism play out in the experiences of queer 'New Scots'. It queries the common-sense narrative of queer migration as a journey from repression to liberation and asks to what extent queer migrants, a population stratified along the lines of migration status, race and class, can benefit from extensive protection of LGBT+ rights in Scotland. To foreground the diversity of queer migrants, I turn to my past, Scotland-based research and public engagement work. I draw on a research project about LGBT+ migrants from Central Eastern Europe (CEE) and on more cursory engagement with queer asylum-seekers through knowledge exchange and community initiatives. These projects date back several years and may seem distant from the present time; yet the political present is permeated with history, and the value of looking back in time is that it enables us to read the present in light of the past.

Queer New Scots?

The term 'New Scot' has been widely used in Scottish government official documents for some time, to describe anyone coming from outside of Scotland who has 'made Scotland their home'. It is an umbrella term inclusive of all newcomers, irrespective of where they come from, why or how they came to Scotland.[1] You may come from just south of the border, from Italy or Iran, Pakistan or Poland, Cameroon or Canada; you may have arrived as an EU migrant exercising your 'right to free movement' within the EU, you may be on a short-term work visa or you may have come in search of sanctuary to get away from war, persecution or poverty – but you are still, according to the Scottish government, a New Scot. The framing of Scotland as welcoming to newcomers sits at the core of Scotland's civic nationalism: it doesn't matter whether you are Scottish by blood or birth, or what colour your skin is; you can still belong here, you can still be(come) Scottish. Civic nationalism and a broadly welcoming discourse on migration is said to set Scotland apart from the ethno-nationalism and anti-immigration rhetoric that have been pedalled for many years by successive UK governments. However, Scottish civic nationalism and the rhetoric of 'New Scots' are not unproblematic and have important limitations (Nguyen 2023). The rosy rhetoric of 'New Scots' can perpetuate the myth that the problem is not here but in Westminster, and that Scotland is free of anti-immigration sentiments, xenophobia and structural racism. Yet queer migrants' experiences tell a very different story.

Several years ago a colleague and I successfully applied for funding for a research project called 'Intimate Migrations', about the experiences of LGBT+ migrants from CEE and the former Soviet Union (FSU) living in Scotland.[2] Geopolitical changes in Europe had resulted in significant levels of 'East–West migration', driven by regional economic disparities and the right to free movement of labour within the EU, but also by demand for cheap labour in the West, to be channelled into low-paid, precarious employment. At a time when the UK economy was thriving, the New Labour government saw migration – and particularly migration from CEE – as an efficient, cost-effective and temporary way to plug gaps in the labour market, particularly in low-wage occupations. Migration from Eastern Europe was widely regarded as economically driven in political and academic discourse: it was assumed that migrants' motivations were related to comparatively better salaries and economic prospects, and there was little interest in exploring the role of sexuality and gender in migration. LGBT+ activists from the region, however, had indicated that lower levels of legal protection for LGBT+ citizens and the expectation that queer migrants could live a freer life in the UK may also be an important part of their migration. In our project, we wanted to explore the role that sexuality played in queer migrants' decisions to migrate, experiences of settlement, social networks and sense of home and belonging

There was little research on queer migration at the time in Scotland and in the UK more broadly, and a number of community organizations[3] supported our project and showed an interest in the overlooked experiences of queer migrants. I felt very invested in this project: years earlier I had been involved in a community-led project to increase awareness of and support for LGBT asylum-seekers in Scotland (Cowen et al. 2011), and as a lesbian migrant from Italy, the topic resonated with me on a personal level. The project ran from 2015 to 2017 and straddled chronologically the June 2016 EU referendum. In its run-up and aftermath, political and public debate on migration in the UK became especially fraught. Of course outcries about immigration – particularly non-white immigration – have been a recurring feature in British history. However, amidst widespread calls to 'take back control of our borders' and reduce overall immigration, EU migration became an especially contentious topic. There are two main reasons for this: in the run-up to the EU referendum, EU citizens made up the majority of migrants to the UK and, under the EU principle of free movement of labour, EU citizens could easily move to and settle in the UK without being subjected to UK immigration control (a right also enjoyed by UK citizens moving to other EU countries). Thus, the presence of (mostly) white EU migrants – largely perceived in the 2000s as *good* migrants because seen as contributing to the economy through their (cheap) labour – was now being questioned, sometimes in very incendiary tones, alongside more usual targets.

To mark the end of the project, in February 2017 we organized a photo exhibition at Glasgow's Hillhead Library as part of LGBT History Month. The photo exhibition was based on material collected with research participants invited to keep a photo diary on the theme of 'home'; this was explored in subsequent interviews centred on the meanings they associated to the pictures. We launched the exhibition with a well-attended and well-received event, introduced by the chair of OurStory Scotland. Five of our research participants, whose photographs were exhibited, read passages from their interviews. The exhibition lasted a couple of weeks and throughout this period attendees could leave their feedback by filling in a form with the prompt:

> Please let us know what you think about the exhibition ... What did the exhibition make you think about? What makes a place 'home' for you? Any other comments?

The comments from the feedback forms were generally positive ('Heartwarming stories, lovely pictures'; 'So lovely to see such honest expression from such an underrepresented group of individuals'). Two contrasting comments, however, stuck in my mind. One said:

> Thought about my idea of home, the small village in Scotland where I was born, small streets, familiarity. Glasgow, my home for ten years, represents freedom, more opportunities. I feel home is somewhere you feel safe, you feel yourself. I was homeless LGBT at seventeen and moving to Glasgow is when I settled down and my life began so I identified with the participants. I feel extremely proud that Glasgow was able to provide the safety to other individuals from various cultural backgrounds.

This comment exudes empathy based on a shared queerness and a common experience of migration, towards a place of safety and feeling oneself – although the comment was from someone who had migrated from within Scotland, rather than from overseas.

The other feedback comment that stayed with me had a very different tone:

> Why do you always showcase migrants and not Scottish talent? I'm sick to the back of my teeth of migrants, Scotland is becoming a multicultural mess with no real effort at integration leaving people like me feeling like my idea of 'home' is being culturally raped!!!

I was stung on a personal level by this comment, which came across to me as an injunction to 'know your place': Scotland is here presented, self-evidently, as the home of 'proper' Scots, people like the commentator: so much for 'queer New Scots'. I heard this comment in my head as an angry, intimidating voice, shouting, '*You migrants* are making this place a multicultural *mess* because *you* are making *no effort* to integrate – to become like *us*.' Migrants are framed as cultural rapists, taking up space that belongs by birthright to *real* Scottish talent and changing Scotland beyond recognition. But it's just *one* comment, right? It doesn't mean that everyone here – in Scotland, in Glasgow – is 'sick to the back of their teeth' of migrants. Yet this comment interrupts the promise of an 'enlightened' Scotland as a welcoming home to New Scots.

Despite an overall positive reception, our project was bookmarked by another, very public comment that also sticks. In March 2015 I received a phone call from the university media office. The *Sunday Express* was asking for our comments for an article it was about to publish; this centred on a statement made about our project by David Coburn, a Member of the European Parliament (MEP) from the UK Independent Party (UKIP). UKIP had made headways in British politics on a nationalist, Eurosceptic, anti-immigration and socially conservative platform and had received more votes than any other British parties at the 2014 European elections – although they only managed to elect one MEP in Scotland, Coburn. Choosing the *Sunday Express* as his outlet, Coburn said our study was 'a gross waste of public money' and a 'scandal'. In the published article, Coburn was quoted as saying:

> I don't care about anyone's sexual orientation. What could this study possibly tell us? The taxpayer is being asked to take part in belt-tightening exercises – we can't

fund hospitals or pay for the elderly. The people handing out this cash should be removed. (Christison 2015)

Was Coburn – an openly gay man, albeit one opposed to gay marriage – really objecting to research about 'sexual orientation'? I knew of other funded research projects focussed on sexuality, but colleagues working on them did not seem to be at the receiving end of these kinds of comments. We could only speculate, but the fact that the project focussed on queer migrants, and possibly the foreign-sounding names of some members of the research team, made us a particularly easy prey for media trolling. The university media office also read it as an attempt to stir up controversy, and we decided not to comment for two reasons. First, we were about to start fieldwork and did not want to put off potential participants by becoming embroiled in a media shouting match. Second, UKIP seemed to thrive on media attention, and we didn't want to give them any more airspace. While we were debating our 'media strategy' on the yet unpublished article, Coburn made headlines by comparing Scottish politician Humza Yousaf – who is a Muslim – to the convicted terrorist Abu Hamza. A public outcry, and more controversy, followed – and eventually Coburn apologized for his 'joke' (BBC News 2015). Again, we could only speculate but it was probably the blatantly racist and widely condemned comment about Yousaf that deflected attention from our project. The publication of the article was delayed by a few days; the article was demoted from page 5 to page 20, and the quotes about the project being 'waste of public money' and a 'scandal' were removed. The article did not kick off any media trolling, although we probably got away lightly because someone else became the target, and there is a bitter irony in this.

It is not surprising, therefore, that anti-migrant sentiments and overt xenophobia also featured in the lives of the queer East European migrants we spoke to. I briefly introduce our participants' profile to contextualize their experiences. All our fifty participants were white, and mostly (forty-seven) were from Eastern European countries that had recently joined the EU. Over half of our participants (thirty-one) were Polish, which reflected the broader demographics of East European migration to the UK; other participants were from Belarus, Bulgaria, Hungary, Latvia, Lithuania, Romania, Russia and Ukraine. The project focussed on sexuality and was designed to explore the experiences of lesbian (eighteen), gay (nineteen) and bisexual (twelve) migrants. Most of our participants were cisgender, with two identifying as transgender and non-binary; our sample included twenty-four women, twenty-five men and one non-binary person. Our participants were from both middle and working class backgrounds, but their trajectories also illustrate how migrants may inhabit different class positions in their countries of origin and destination. Although most had higher education, this was not reflected in their occupation, as they were typically employed in low-paid and precarious jobs in the service, hospitality and care sectors. Through migration, many experienced simultaneously an improved economic position and a decline in social status, although there were several exceptions to this pattern. Ola, who worked as a room attendant in a hotel, experienced xenophobia every day in the way clients treated migrant staff:

> I felt discriminated against at work. And, well, I feel it every single day. It's the [hotel] guests. Once there was a situation, for example. I wasn't involved, but

another Polish person was … as was a Slovak guy … They were at the reception desk and spoke Polish. A client showed up and didn't like it … and complained to the manager of the hotel. How come the hotel staff don't speak English! The thing is – they didn't speak to him – they spoke between themselves. And I found it very annoying. Because there's no such law that says we're obliged to speak English at our workplace.

Jaroslaw lived with his partner, also from Poland, in a housing estate on the outskirts of Glasgow. They were repeatedly targeted with violence as well as 'go home' rhetoric and homophobic slurs by two local teenagers over a protracted period of time:

There was two local teenagers who tried to start harassing us, throwing stones, smashing the car and windows in the house, and they shout 'Fuck off you fucking poofs, fucking Poles, go back from where you came from'. Nearly every second night, and we started drinking alcohol cause we needed to get sleep and go to work.

Uncertainties about the outcome of the EU referendum also created considerable anxieties among some of our participants regarding their ability to remain in Scotland. Acutely aware of the hardening rhetoric about immigration, Krzysztof, a Polish man in his forties who had lived in Scotland for ten years, had successfully applied for UK citizenship as a way to secure his continued right to remain and stake a claim on a place called home:

[Applying for UK citizenship] is about safety. It's about the uncertainty related to the government here … Nobody knows who will rule this country in the future and how the immigration law will change … If I had to return to Poland, I'd probably end up at whatever train station [homeless]. I have no home in Poland, I have no acquaintances to be honest. And I'm not close to my family. I'm [age] – starting a new life in Poland? No. It would be a disaster; I'd end up at the train station. So … that's why I want to stay here, because I want to have a home here.

Krzysztof felt no allegiance to British identity and looked at UK citizenship instrumentally as an insurance policy of sort that would protect his right to remain at a time when immigration legislation was becoming more restrictive, and borders were moving over people. He did think of Scotland as home, but he had also experienced condescending and hostile attitudes towards Polish migrants from Scots, which made him feel more comfortable socializing with, and dating, Poles and other migrants. He did not wish to return to Poland, but still felt an emotional connection to his country of origin. Like Krzysztof, our participants often had quite complex feelings towards the UK and Scotland, as well as their countries of origin: they may have made their home *in* Scotland, but they did not necessarily think of Scotland as an adopted home – or indeed as a queer homeland. Some of them, like Jaroslaw, experienced homophobia in Scotland. Many of them felt positive about their life in Scotland overall, but there was often a certain hesitancy about their feelings of belonging.

Much has changed in Scotland since we completed interviews for our project weeks before the 2016 EU referendum. Brexit represented a watershed moment for many EU migrants in the country in terms of their legal status, but also brought to the surface and mobilized anti-immigration feelings, nativism and racism more widely, affecting other migrant and racialized populations – including in Scotland. If we had conducted follow up interviews in the intervening years, our participants would have probably reported heighted feelings of uncertainty and unbelonging and more negative experiences. Post-Brexit, migration has remained a highly politicized and contentious topic, not just 'down South' but also in Scotland. This troubles the narrative of a Scotland welcoming newcomers, and indeed the very idea of 'New Scots'. A major limitation of the term 'New Scots' is that it homogenizes all newcomers into a single category, while in fact (queer) migrants are a highly diverse population. Who is a migrant and who is seen as a migrant are not one and the same thing, and migrants are not all treated the same: some are welcomed as 'good migrants', some are seen as temporary guests who should not overstay their welcome; still others – particularly displaced and undocumented migrants – are seen as undesirable and illegitimate and are vulnerable to incarceration and deportation. Migration governance translates into differentiated migrant status and access to rights, including residency rights, social rights and access to welfare and civil rights. Populist slogans about border security and sovereignty overlook the fact that borders do not operate as walls, but as porous membranes designed to filter in or out prospective migrants – offering legal routes to some, repelling others and sometimes turning a blind eye to irregular migrants if they service the needs of 'developed' economies. Both race and class underpin border regimes. Within the EU, and until recently in the UK, preferential treatment of EU over non-EU citizens maps on to postcolonial legacies of racial hierarchies. At the same time, points-based migration systems privilege those bringing financial and educational capital over 'unskilled' migrants, which maps on to class hierarchies.

Migration is often equated with non-white migrants, yet there is a complex relationship between migration, othering and racialization. East European migrants benefitted from a historical racialized bias favouring white migrants in the UK immigration system[4]; yet they also came to be perceived as a cultural threat (culturally different, unwilling to integrate) and an economic liability (stealing British jobs, abusing the welfare system).It is, however, impossible to talk about migration without talking about race, which featured prominently in the August 2024 anti-immigration riots that took place in England, Northern Ireland – and Scotland, albeit in a much lower key. The riots were not about immigration *in general*: protesters and rioters singled out Muslims and asylum-seekers, through slogans and attacks on mosques and hostels housing people seeking sanctuary. This was encouraged by rumours artfully spread on social media that the perpetrator of the 29 July Southport stabbing was an 'immigrant Muslim' and an 'asylum-seeker'. Why did these rumours catch on, and why did the riots continue even after the rumours had been disproven? This is a complex question, but part of the answer is to be found in the longstanding scapegoating of Muslims and asylum-seekers in political and public debate. Scapegoating migrants may be the oldest trick in the book; after all, most migrants are not citizens and cannot vote: for parties trying to curry favour with voters pinning the blame for all sorts of problems on migrants is a low-cost strategy with potentially high electoral returns. At times of economic downturn, this strategy of divide and rule deflects attention from more fundamental issues around living wages, welfare and redistribution. However, not all migrants are equally targeted by this scapegoating. Racialized migrants and racialized UK citizens became targets of a spike of racially motivated violence during and following the summer 2024 riots. Indeed, racialized UK citizens may never cease to be 'foreigners' or 'migrants' in the eyes of some, even when settled in the UK for generations.

We may look at the low profile of anti-immigration protests in Scotland in comparison to other parts of the UK as a source of comfort, and perhaps as evidence of the fact that the 'New Scots' narrative on migration makes a difference. Yet attendance at the anti-immigration protest in Glasgow on 7 September 2024 – estimated as between 200 and 500, depending on the source – was significant, even if no violence ensued and participants were greatly outnumbered by those participating in a parallel anti-racist counter demonstration. Meanwhile, Reform UK, a new populist far-right political party which, like UKIP a decade earlier, mobilizes anti-immigration sentiments, gained a sizable 7 per cent of the vote in Scotland in the July 2024 General Elections. Although this percentage is well below the 14.3 per cent that Reform UK gained UK-wide, at the time of writing (January 2025), Reform UK is on the rise in Scotland, and if current trends continue, it will gain significant representation in the Scottish Parliament at the 2026 Scottish Parliament elections. This may significantly shift the migration debate in Scotland, where for a long time the pragmatic economic and demographic arguments about the benefits of migration held sway. These arguments may become a hard sell, and attitudes may become much less welcoming, if not downright hostile.

On Scottish sexual exceptionalism and queer migration

Just like civic nationalism has important limitations, here I highlight the limitations of political discourses emphasizing the symbolic inclusion of LGBT+ people in the Scottish nation. The article from *The National* quoted at the beginning of the chapter, and its celebration of Scotland and its culture as exceptionally progressive on LGBT+ rights, is a good place to start. Is it true, as the article claims, that transnational migrants are drawn to Scotland because of its record on LGBT+ rights and its 'enlightened culture'? Again, this takes us back to both the complexity of the migrant experience and the diversity of queer migrants.

Intimate Migrations participants had complex reasons for moving to Scotland: sexuality or gender identity did not always feature prominently in their reasons to migrate, and sometimes not at all. Many participants were quick to point out that other factors (wage gaps, the expectation of better opportunities and economic security) were just as or more important in their decisions to migrate. An important contextual reason why many were drawn to Scotland and the rest of the UK was that, unlike most other EU states, the UK did not at the time restrict access to the labour market for East European migrants coming from then 'new' EU member states. The possibility to find work and a place to stay relatively quickly – often with the support of co-nationals or recruitment agencies – and knowledge of English were also important contextual reasons why our participants ended up in Scotland. Countries of origins were not uniformly experienced as unwelcoming or homophobic, and Scotland was not uniformly experienced as 'enlightened' or 'queer-friendly', as shown in the previous section. Nonetheless, there was a widespread perception of Scotland as generally more progressive than our participants' countries of origin on LGBT+ rights, which for some translated in the feeling that their sexuality or gender expression was ordinary and unremarkable in Scotland. Considerations about sexuality and gender expression featured more prominently when our participants talked about plans for the future, in terms of settling in Scotland, returning to their country of origin or moving to another country. Here, not fitting in with dominant sexual and gender norms 'back home', or concerns about heightened political homophobia, led to a low motivation to return. On the other hand, for many Scotland was a place where queer futures could be imagined, and this was an important reason why many decided to stay. It is, however, important to contextualize these settlement decisions: most of our participants were EU migrants with privileged mobility rights, under the principle of EU free movement of labour, and their right to remain in Scotland was not questioned – at least until Brexit. When the dust settled after Brexit, most EU citizens living in the UK were granted legal residency through settled or pre-settled status and continued to have access to social rights on a similar footing as UK citizens – although, for some, changes to EU migrants' legal status and ensuing restrictions on access to welfare resulted in high rates of homelessness. Settling in Scotland was not just down to choice: Intimate Migrations participants were, by and large, allowed to do so. The experiences of Intimate Migrations participants complicate and partially contradict the narrative of an enlightened culture attracting queer migrants to Scotland. They also trouble the idea of queer migration as an unfettered choice or a journey from repression to liberation. As shown in the previous, many of our participants experienced marginalization in Scotland because of their ethnicity or class, while homophobia did not disappear altogether from their lives.

If the experiences of East European queer migrants query the migration-as-liberation narrative, those of queer asylum seekers turn it on its head. On the face of it, asylum seekers looking for humanitarian protection on grounds of sexuality, gender identity or expression (SOGIE) would seem like the obvious beneficiaries of the advances in LGBT+ rights that *The National* article hints at. Like in other Western liberal democracies, in the UK (and by extension in Scotland, since migration is a policy remit 'reserved' to Westminster) since the 1990s protection of LGBT+ rights has been partially extended to non-citizens – including through the recognition of sexual orientation and gender identity as valid grounds for humanitarian protection. SOGIE asylum-seekers, therefore, must be drawn to Scotland because of its record on LGBT+ rights. But access to state protection as a SOGIE asylum-seeker in Scotland is conditional upon being recognized as a 'real' refugee, a protracted process that in many cases takes years. The asylum system is not designed to welcome refugees, but to filter out the very few who will exceptionally be recognized as refugees from those who, upon being denied refugee status, become deportable.

The asylum system operates as a filter that sorts 'real' asylum-seekers from suspected economic migrants, 'real' LGBT refugees who can produce a 'credible' narrative about their queerness from 'fake' queers, and queers who can prove they have suffered persecution in their countries of origins from queers who have not suffered enough to qualify as refugees. Decision-making procedures in the asylum system are themselves filtering devices designed to deter people from availing themselves of the right to asylum (Giametta 2020). For example, how do you prove your queerness? Asylum stories need to be rehearsed and tailored to institutional expectations around sexuality and gender identity to be deemed credible, as adjudicators rely on Eurocentric stereotypes of what a genuine SOGIE refugee looks and acts like. These are typically based on binary notions of gender and sexuality (gay or straight, male or female), 'outness' and participation in globalized queer lifestyles. Adjudicators also rely heavily on racialized stereotypes about SOGIE asylum-seekers as victims of their own cultures, looking with suspicion, for example, at religious SOGIE asylum seekers who do not renounce their faith or do not evidence an internal struggle with their faith. Another deterrence strategy is limited state support for asylum-seekers, who cannot claim mainstream welfare benefits or housing and cannot work for one year after lodging their asylum application. They are entitled to state support in the form of asylum accommodation and very limited cash support and often live in poverty. Amidst cuts to legal aid, SOGIE asylum-seekers' access to private financial resources to prepare their legal cases is often an important factor in their chances to be granted refugee status (Giametta 2020). SOGIE asylum-seekers may be drawn to Scotland and other countries that recognize, theoretically, that people who are subjected to violence and persecution because of their sexuality or gender should have a way to seek sanctuary and find a place where 'you feel safe, you feel yourself' – as one of our exhibition attendees put it. However, the inhumane asylum system troubles the self-image of Western liberal democracies as global protectors of LGBT+ rights. The promise of Scotland as a place of safety where you can be yourself remains, for many, unfulfilled. As it is, the asylum system is based on a culture of suspicion, grants individuals going through it only the most basic residency, social and civic rights, keeps lives suspended and creates new forms of suffering.

Do LGBT+ rights matter to queer migrants? They do – to an extent. But this is only part of a more complex story, as queer migrants are not only their sexuality or gender, and their journeys are regulated by border regimes informed by race and class that create differentiated migrant status and access to rights. A narrow focus on LGBT+ rights misses this crucially important broader context and produces simplistic narratives of sexual exceptionalism that can be co-opted into anti-immigration and racist agendas. In these, migrants and racialized citizens are framed either as victims of their own culture – seen as inherently sexist and homophonic – or as a threat to a supposedly 'enlightened' culture and an assumed national consensus on LGBT+ rights. Meanwhile, there are signs that in Scotland an 'enlightened' consensus around LGBT+ rights – never an absolute one – cannot be taken for granted. This is suggested, for example, by the controversies over the Gender Recognition (Scotland) Act and over gay marriage during the 2023 SNP leadership contest, and by a 2022 LGBT Youth Scotland report indicating a marked increase in experiences of trans, homo and biphobia among Scottish youth.

Conclusions

State legal and political discourse on migration and queerness matter, up to a point. Civic nationalism and the inclusive language of 'New Scots' is preferable to ethnic nationalism and its incendiary rhetoric; institutional support for LGBT+ rights and equalities is certainly better than state-sponsored repression. There is a pride in this, but vaunting the progressive character of Scottish institutions and political discourse without looking at the broader picture can only take us so far. Worse, it can perpetuate a complacent, self-congratulatory and potentially dangerous myth of Scottish exceptionalism. The twin narratives of Scotland's enlightened, progressive stance on LGBT+ rights and of Scotland as unreservedly welcoming of newcomers gloss over the diversity of queer New Scots and their experiences – and indeed of queer and of migrant communities in Scotland. They also downplay the fact that racism, anti-migrant sentiments and nativism continue to exist, as do homo, bi and transphobia – even when not constantly stirred by prominent politicians.

We are now operating in a very different context, in Scotland and beyond, from the one described at the beginning of the chapter – the aftermath of the 2014 independence referendum and arguably the height of Scottish exceptionalism. But to build an alternative, hopeful vision for the future, we need to look at the past, take stock of the limitations of Scottish exceptionalism and open up spaces for dialogue across queer and migrant communities – and beyond. The times we live in are marked by uncertainty and crisis (political, geopolitical, economic and environmental). One salient feature of our time is the rise of right-wing populism across the UK, Europe and beyond. Sovereign populism has stoked and weaponized people's fears, channelling them towards a common enemy of the nation, often identified as the foreigner and the racialized other but also, in a widespread backlash against so-called gender ideology, as the trans and the queer. Scotland is not hermetically sealed off from what goes on outside its borders, nor – at a time of crisis of liberal democracy – automatically immune from sovereign populism. We need to look outside national borders to get a clear vision of where we are at, because our histories are all intertwined.

Notes

1. The use of the term 'New Scot' has changed over the years. I use the term to refer to overseas migrants, although it is sometimes used to mean newcomers from other parts of the UK, and it is currently used mostly to refer to forced migrants.
2. The project run from 2015 to 2017 and was supported by the Economic and Social Research Council, grant no. ES/L009307/1. For more information about the project, including publications and resources arising from it, see www.intimatemigrations.net/.
3. These included LGBT Youth Scotland, West of Scotland Regional Equality Council, BEMIS and LGBT Health and Wellbeing,
4. This bias pre-dated EU membership and arguably continues to this day.

References

BBC News. 'UKIP MEP David Coburn Apologises for Abu Hamza Comment', 2015. www.bbc.co.uk/news/uk-scotland-scotland-politics-31927494. Accessed 14 January 2025.

Christison, G. 'Migrant Gay Study Gets Grant of £250,000', *Sunday Express*, 22 March 2015, p. 20.

Cowen, T., Stella, F., Magahy, K., Strauss, K. and Morton, J. *Sanctuary, Safety and Solidarity: Lesbian, Gay, Bisexual, Transgender Asylum Seekers in Scotland. Project Report*. Glasgow: Equality Network, BEMIS and GRAMNet, 2011.

Giametta. 'New Asylum Protection Categories and Elusive Filtering Devices: The Case of "Queer Asylum" in France and the UK', *Journal of Ethnic and Migration Studies* 46, no. 1 (2020): 142–57.

Nguyen, Q. 'Migration Experiences, New Scots, and the Limits of Civic Nationalism', *Scottish New Left Review* 133 (March–April 2023). https://scottishleftreview.scot/migration-experiences-new-scots-and-the-limits-of-civic-nationalism. Accessed 25 August 2024.

Paterson, K. '"Enlightened" Culture Attracts LGB People to Move to Scotland', *The National*, 3 December 2015. www.thenational.scot/news/14900728.enlightened-culture-attracts-lgb-people-to-move-to-scotland/. Accessed 15 January 2025.

Assemblages

Mae Diansangu

With assemblages, I wanted to convey the intentional and incidental ways queerness is constructed from disparate and connected parts. The word assemblage suggests a gathering, an accumulation; by locating my work in this collection, alongside other queer writers, I am part of an action to assemble an image of what 'queer in a wee place' can mean. This is a huge privilege of great significance, as I understand my queerness through connection – the connection I have with my body, with the built and natural environment, and of course, with other queer people. I do not believe the writer/reader relationship is unidirectional, so my hope is that whoever reads my contribution will see themselves as taking part in this dynamic process of assembling queerness.

Aberdream (I)

Swoopin an skreichin,
granite wings fusperin,
twa nash-gabbin sentinels
sweel deith in their een.
The scurras clate their wye
through a slate sky's flesh,
they champ at the haar
afore makkin their descent.
The beach hyperventilates,
chowkit wi bodies, limp an sleek.
Ill-aff sand shifts an greets.
Blaudit fae the reek o salt
an seal. Hero breathes it aa in,
wonderin foo this came tae pass.
The decade afore last
endit the selkie oil trade –
so fit ill hid laid oot
the sea fowk?
Hero cries the eldest bird

in aboot.
Skellum flochters doon.
His wee sister, Blellum,
cheetlin aside him.
Hero asks their feathery pals
fits a dee, fan it seems
thon peer craiturs wirna
huntit fur blubber.
It disna tak lang fur
the scene tae ging viral.
TikTok is awaash wi
conspiracies.
Hero canna stomach
the Insta Live autopsies.
The results are in:
traces o cocaine
marl the liver an muscle.
Extinction rebellion
hud a vigil. Hero gings
tae ask fur forgiveness.
They drap a promise
intae the sea –
tae nae forget
foo slow creepin neglect
poisons fae within.
That the law alane
canna stap
the tide of toxicity
fae claimin yer body.

Body meets world

I was made in the usual way,
like every body was:

a loose assemblage of thoughts, myths
and vibes, coerced by the relentless
force of affect, bullied into a unified form.

Feelings made me, I made feelings,
 and so it goes – the circle of life, etc.

We build bodies that build countries.
Bloodlines, blueprints, bylaws.

A country is a body made to be whole,
secure, held together by fear
of what lies beyond.

Queerness is the body that refuses,
that does not hold, that leaks,
that questions.

My country stops answering
when it refuses to speak
the language of every body
it holds. Still, it has told
my body to join its fight.

We have been conscripted
to build the new republic.
Our reward, a fairer society.

My body knows other bodies,
rejected and depatriated,
who would appreciate
that kindness today.

I wait for my country to explain
why we we can't have that now.
Why things would change
overnight, in a newly packaged
sovereign state, when our bodies
still carry the weight of prejudice
and neglect.

Delete as appropriate

my	body / country	is	defined by its limits / unconquerable / full
my	skin / flag	is	in distress / proud / flammable
my	heart / passport	is	expired / chewed up / brimming with blood
my	tongue / anthem	is	disfigured / flat / far-reaching
my	sensuality / citizenship	is	hard earned / cheap / conditional
my	spirit / constitution	is	flimsy / blank / easily amended

For Jackie Kay

In my country the streets are paved with poetry. Weel-luckit words kiss the soles of my feet. I was born to meet these verses in the soft and gentle dark, coorie into their warmth. We commit to the dance. You ground yourself, devolve into the stanza's origin – meaning standing or stopping place. I do-si-do my way around you. This circle I create, a simple annotation, a reminder to come back here. It is a queer tradition to read oneself between the lines. To look backwards into the future. I imagine your lugs burning as I tattoo the margins with myself. Living ink. Black, vital. Now that I think of it, I'm not sure I've ever said *palimpsest* out loud. One of those words I've only ever ~~read~~ felt.

Aberdream (II)

Efter the selkies were spat
ontae the shore, Hero lost
their voice. They didna ken
fan it slipped awa, or far
it could be hidin, so they retrace
their steps.
The search party kicks aff
by traipsin roond Big Tesco,
then they ask the First Bus Depot
tae check lost property,
but naebdy hiz seen onythin.
Tae begin wi, Skellum an Blellum
arna ony help. They set aboot
engagin in gyperie, thinkin it affa funny
that Hero canna spik. But the birds
dinna last a wik, afore they grow feart
this micht be serious.
Blellum howks an auld memory
fae Skellum's beak,
a scrap o a tale they'd eence ett –
trees that souch unnergrund,
reeshlin wi missin items,
The Forest o Lost Things.
Hero speirs the pavement
tae let the secret woodland
unsteek its mooth, a snorrel
or roots drags them sooth.
They sink intae weet
darkness. Greenish smellin air
clings tae their skin, mirkit wi

forgettins an ither lost things.
Ilka step girns an grushes,
the earth grippin ontae
fit's bin tint,
refusin tae let ging o it.
A faint song rises up fae
the glaur. The deith hymnal
o a kestrel, liggin in bleed.
Hero feels the hum o the reid
in their breist, it pushes them
tae their knees. The kestrel
spiks fae its een,

Ye maun gang within.

Hero thrists their fingers
intae the wound,
an pulls oot a yale key.
The kestrel turns tae stane,
yet still warm tae the haun,
the heat spiks tae Hero,
biddin them folla
the trail o bleed.
The path leads Hero
tae a clearin in the wood,
far a queer bein hunkers doon,
skin the colour o sky turnt
inside oot.
The seethin figure is bund tae
the cauld face o a mirror.
Its scaudert, bilin shape
sharpens the chill o the gless.
Hero moves closer,
a skirl leaves the stranger's
body, shatterin the chains.
The soond maks it wye
up Hero's spine, settlin
in their thrapple, far it belangs.
The figure wastes awa,
a shadow tint in the wind,
leavin the frigid mirror,
reflectin a sinister white lowe.
Hero hears the faint echo
of their ain voice
skiff across the mirror.

They pick it up, nae wintin
tae leave onythin
o themsel
in this
place.

1. It's shite being_____ (especially if you like your trains cheap and your arts funded) (**8**)
2. National identity synonymous with tea and colonialism. Useful to point at and say "we're not as bad", while hoping not as bad is good enough (**7**)
3. Partial, incomplete, unlikely to pass purity test (**4**)
4. More legitimate, more authentic. Completely. (**5**)
5. A rich and profound hue that embodies uncharted potential (**5**)
6. An insult and slur to be kicked around the playground that never means happy (**3**)
7. Strange, uncanny, unsettling. Archaic adjective that Enid Blyton would probably use (**5**)
8. A category of being that was designed to have exclusive membership, rejecting those who don't meet the colonial-era standard based on the Eurocentric binary system (**5**)
9. Alternative status (**5**)

at the intersection of cross words

Slay or nae?

There is a hierarchy of
Americanisms.
'Talented' and 'reliable'
are naturalised, acceptable –
but I will never take out
the 'trash'.
Scottish pals typing
'y'all' in the group chat,
I wonder who yous are
addressing, and in what
accent.
I've never been trick or
treating (we call that
guisin where I'm from)
but do I really want to stand in the way of progress?
Language is queer as fuck.
Its power located in

its fluidity, its refusal to stayin one place.
Queer folk wield
language to reclaim, reframe and resist.
Our commitment to honour
transformation, an ever
evolving lexicon.
In the age of TV drag queens, and endless screens where reality is filtered
through performance, and a terminal onlinesness
that oscillates between loneliness and genuine connection –
Scottish queers are absorbing a sharp and glittering speech.
Flamboyant, playful, joyous. But, if I enter this game,something shifts inside.
A flicker of recognition
The reflection within a reflection.
Blackness refracted through layers of
distance –

Blackception:
to perform an approximation
of Blackness
that bears little
cultural relevance
to my lived experience.
My Black body is a solid,
material fact.

Visibly Other
in an white landscape.
A Scottish town, a queer space.
To be other is to exist in multiple
places at once –

in the body I own,
in the racist imagination,
in the gap between.

When AAVE flows through
queer spaces, it displaces
me. Moves me between
stereotype and self, between expectation and reality. This borrowed language,
now a way to signal queerness,
a shared code to connect us, reminds me how hard it was to see my Blackness
affirmed. I grew up, shrouded in White.
Family, community, city.
Black American culture
opened a door

to something larger,
when the community
I sought didn't live next door.

I continue to seek these pathways
of connection, wary of the line between appreciation and appropriation, then
I see how easily
a Scottish white cis-gay man performs his best 'strong Black woman inside me'
routine.
Something jarring about seeing someone who doesn't look like me
mirroring someone who does, when finding my reflection in my community
has often eluded me.

Aberdream (III)

Foul farrant licht spilt fae the mirror.
A chilpit blaze, threatnin tae
strip Hero's skin o its melanin.
Ilka glint fae the rotten pane
wis a jibe. The piece of Hero's
voice that still bided there,
wis swallad up by
the coorse glare.
The mirror spewed
a familiar voice, suddelt
by merciless brichtness.
Hero coudna turn awa,
engulft by the greedy licht.
Skellum an Blellum kent
foo tae brak the spell,
but couldna yell through
the impenetrable whiteness.
In the mids o aa this,
the kestrel's gift hingin fae
Hero's neck sang a canny
tune. A message sint fae
Skellum's bleed tae
the reid on the key.
The crimson song
spun itsel alang
Hero's haus-bane,
lettin them ken
exactly fit tae dee.
The task aheid

wis simple,
weave a cloak
fae shadow.
Hero wis tae gaither
ilka scrap o darkness
they could find.
Shreid the nicht sky
an threid the deepest
onyx fae unexplored
neuks. They shook
the wecht o the white
leam fae their shooders,
makkin plinty space,
fur the lovin black
embrace.

Part 3

Queer Homelands: Myths, Migrations and Movements

13

Leaving is queer: Loving and leaving a wee place

Finn Mackay

The morning my father was found dead following a heart attack, a police officer asked my mother when I would be arriving to help with the funeral arrangements. A neighbour explained that I worked away in England at a university now and may well even be abroad at a conference. The young policeman looked around the small cottage and exclaimed: 'Abroad at a conference, what, from a tiny wee place like this?' Being from a 'tiny wee place' in a small country often treated as such too has shaped my relationship to the Celtic nation and my own sense of nationality and patriotism. My Scotland is now only a site of memory, childhood and adolescent memories at that. I have had no adult relationship with the country and so the shape of the place remains in the contours of a child's perspective. Modern Scotland is a very different sight to the one I left as soon as I could; before the rise of the Scottish National Party, the experience of contemporary independence struggles and a world-famous female leader in ex-first minister Nicola Sturgeon. I have not known the country outside of Section 28, and it was not repealed in Scotland until six years after I moved away. The following chapter is a reflection on being from and growing up queer in an isolated part of the borders of Scotland. It is a chapter about the meanings of home, gay migration clichés and queer rurality; but where I come from there was no queer, there was just rural.

The chapter attempts to dissect some experiences of making meanings of home, when home felt like an unliveable place. The attachment I feel to the countryside I come from, is mixed up with the baggage that results from a difficult childhood. Reflecting on Scotland then is also to reflect on a foundational time in my life that was not easy, for many reasons, not only the knowledge of being different in terms of sexuality and gender. In a betrayal of the roots that raised me, this is a story about escape, with no romantic arc of return. The undeniably beautiful landscape and the natural world that was my respite, tonic and escape is tainted by poverty, parental unemployment, a difficult family life, the exclusion and absence of any 'different' identities and the constant and pressing pressure from a need to get out as soon as possible. Life was challenging, and there was no cavalry coming to the rescue, no respite around the corner. This is a lesson you learn straight away in rural areas where people are isolated, independent and proud. If you need help, you help yourself first, and you assume nobody is coming. As a child the only power I had to help myself was to wait, to try to survive and get through until I was legally old enough to leave. I spent my childhood and my teens waiting to live. Being a queer teenager in a small, isolated and rural place is likely experienced by many as a frustrating stasis, like a plane forever held for take-off, in a stunning landscape that begins to look more and more like a holding pen.

The queer art of leaving

Realizing I was queer from an early age was the main reason I knew I would and could never stay in the remote agricultural countryside where I am from. I could not see anyone like me living their life there, I had no evidence that this was possible, and no example of how that would look. It was entirely unimaginable. Cities were the places that LGBTQ people lived, not the countryside, everyone knew this; occasionally it would be referenced in the news or in TV dramas. This was still the era of AIDS panic, and I remember the old television set and video recorder being wheeled into class on its trolley to show us the infamous gravestone advert at school ('Don't Die of Ignorance', 1986). I learned that AID killed. It was a gay disease, and it was spreading in cities because gay people lived, and died, in cities. As I was schooled for my secondary years under the reign of Section 28 (1988–2000) I was not taught anything else about the existence of gayness, but I did manage to imbibe one thing somehow, the fine queer tradition of leaving. In this I can claim some shred of shared experience, following in the footsteps of queers who have mostly hailed from places bigger than my village, but not big enough for them; taking the trail out, the path we have blazed smooth and bright en route to the exit. There is a queer art to leaving, it's something we do well.

The non-urban is not the rural

As I read another account of small-town Prides and the queer networks that are forged among those who find themselves sharing their difference together, I am yet again exasperated at the representation of the non-urban as being only the semi-urban or suburban. Small towns are not non-urban, small towns are still towns. Small cities are not non-urban, they are still cities. These examples are far from my experience of the non-urban, far from the rural that I have in my mind, blood, senses and history. Forstie's (2022) book *Queering the Midwest*, for example, covers so-called small cities of 50,000–60,000 residents in the United States, focussing on their one or two gay bars and occasional drag shows. Smith and Holt's (2005) paper on counter-urban movement, gentrification and sexualities studies lesbian migration away from the city and into the countryside, but the 'countryside' they use in their case study is Hebden Bridge. A Yorkshire town affectionately known in the UK as a lesbian capital, in commuting distance (depending on trains and flooding) between the cities of Manchester and Leeds and, importantly, still a town. Even in Leyshon's (2011) work on the lives of young people in rural villages in the south-west of England, the participants report facilities such as a village pub, cricket ground, village square, a shop with streetlights, a playground; several participants note that tourism is now a popular industry in their immediate locale.

The rural I am from was not a small town or a small city or even a touristy village. I grew up on a dirt track, in a one-bedroom stone cottage. There was electricity, but no gas, and my parents could not afford an oil heating system, so we relied on wood, which brings an endless cycle of chain-sawing, barrowing, stacking, chopping, drying, barrowing and stacking again between a summer shed and a winter shed. 'Wood warms you twice' as the saying goes, acknowledging the physical labour in fuel preparation. We had one wood burning fire, which warmed the water and most of the rooms. This replaced a stove, which had brought the room it was in up to blast furnace level but left the rest icy. The house is about a fifteen-minute walk away from a tiny village called Boreland, when I lived there the residents were solely white. The village is 7 miles away from the nearest town, Lockerbie, which has a population of around 4,000 residents. The village had no shop, pub, playground, no sports provisions, although for a while it did boast the smallest post office in Scotland, located in a home-made shed in the garden of the postmaster. There was a church, a plain Church of Scotland and nearby a much larger and grander manse for the minister and his family to live. The village is located in Dumfries and Galloway in the south-west borders of Scotland. The remote location means that it is 7 miles to the nearest pub or social space, never mind whether or not that space might be queer friendly or whether there were gay bars (it wasn't; there weren't any). More practically, it also means that it is 7 miles to the nearest shop, cash machine, petrol station. Available doctors and dentists can be even further away, the nearest hospital is in Dumfries, around 15 miles away.

The area is dominated by farming and scarred by poverty, as a lot of working-class rural areas are across the UK. The British countryside is either the countryside of the rich, which has a nice view, road access, broadband, train links to a city and a Waitrose supermarket round the corner; or it is the countryside of workers, which is more industrial and without amenities or connections – there are no farmer's markets in the places where farmers actually live! Most people I knew were poor. In a way this was a blessing as it meant none of us felt left out as we were all in similar economic circumstances. Most of us qualified for free school dinners, we didn't have holidays, our parents were in and out of various types of work or toiled tenant farms in tied houses on land they would never own. As with the representation of queer life, poverty is another phenomenon with an urban face. While we grew up poor, we saw poverty represented on TV solely as a preserve of the urban. Portrayed in concrete council estates, bleak industrial canals, factories and potholed playgrounds full of cast-off shopping trolleys. As children we were poor too, but we walked to school through long dried grasses in the summer and stopped to lick the sugar off clover stems. Our landscape was industrial too, but it was the industries of farming and forestry that provided our backdrop, soundtrack and playground. Growing up in such a remote location is a rare and niche experience, so much so that whenever I meet others who have grown up similarly, we immediately bond together, like survivors, no matter our current situation or identity. I have found this unity to override features such as sexuality.

It was not only that I could not see a future there as a queer person, I could not see a future there at all. This is the reason many people leave the countryside of course, not only queer people, but many Scots in search of better jobs and lives, often in England.

I know this well through working in the early 2000s as an employment advisor at a charity for Scots living in London, The Royal Scottish Corporation, which supported Scots who had migrated to London for economic reasons but found themselves homeless, in debt or affected by health or addiction problems. Queers do not have a monopoly on the grand exit, especially from our precious little country, which has historically had more people leaving than arriving. For all my time there, figures suggest more people left Scotland for the rest of the UK than the counter direction, although this has changed in recent years since the early 2000s with Scotland recording positive migration intakes from the rest of the UK. As well as not being able to imagine what a relationship, partner or family life might look like for me, there were the practical problems of living that affect everyone in such remote places. The main problem was that employment was so hard to find. All my childhood I watched my parents struggling through unemployment, getting by in temporary jobs or having to live apart to find work in England. When my mother enquired about working on the checkout tills at a new giant supermarket that opened, she was told there was already a waiting list to apply for a position; the waiting list was over a year long. Her last job before retiring was as a classroom assistant, a role she only got because the school replacing the previous post-holder was phoning through a list of interested applicants who had applied there over several years before and, as it was the middle of the day, those at the top of the list had all been out, and she happened to be the first person to pick up the phone. My father was a joiner, a skilled craftsman who made furniture and stained glass. The cottage I grew up in was renovated and maintained by him. Nevertheless, the world being what it is, he spent his life working for others, mainly doing construction work where his fine skills were not used.

Two police officers came to that cottage that he had built, responding to the emergency call my mother made when she found him dead in his bed. True to the statistics, my father died young at sixty-three, like so many working-class men in manual trades. He spent the last few years of his life battling the system to access welfare once heart problems and the physical implications of major heart surgery made working in joinery and construction impossible. Signed off by several doctors he was still refused welfare at first, told that instead he should be travelling up to 50-mile journeys to work part time in minimum wage call centre jobs in Carlisle or other cities over the border in England. Having trained in joinery and construction since leaving school to a joiner's yard apprenticeship at fourteen years old, and having always worked where and when he could, he resented, as he said, being treated as a scrounger and a liar when trying to claim what he rightly felt he was due.

On that cold February morning my mother was being supported by a neighbour, who told the young police officer that he should not judge a book by its cover, when he was unable to hide his surprise that anyone from that place had managed to get out and do something different. This event, for me, illustrates so much about where I come from and the working-class, distinctly rural, Scottish values and approaches to life. There was an assumption of limited opportunities, a constraint of vision; there was a passive belief that not only do things just happen, good and bad, but that if good things don't happen it must be because they are not meant to. *Whit's fur ye, will not go by ye* was the adage we were all raised with. Despite it never having happened in his own life,

I remember being told by my father and others that the trick is to work hard and treat that as its own reward, to do what you do so well that people with power will notice and give you more opportunities. The reward for work well done is the opportunity to do more – my father had this written on a sign in his workshop. One step out into the world and we all found out that none of this is true, yet still those norms are hard to shake off. The engrained consciousness freights impact throughout life and career and being aware of it does not stop that impact.

Home-making

Somehow the place, not my physical family home, but the village and the countryside around, was still home; because of this, then, as now, I was and remain a proud Scot. I understood myself as Scottish. I felt attached to the landscape, which I also experienced as distinctly Scottish. Those border lands do not have the snowcapped mountains of the highlands, but they have high and severe looking hills. The steep sides are either bare from grazing or are covered in the dense, almost impenetrable, spikey forestry crop of Sitka spruce, with its interior carpet of crinkly fawn needles hiding the haphazard trenches dug across the hillsides for planting. The land was worked for sheep and dairy industries, and industrially worked for the forestry business whose huge lorries, or waggons as we called them, caused upset and safety concerns as they barrelled down tiny roads through our village and past the primary school I had attended, later closed down due to a lack of pupils. I spent summer holidays walking to the top of every hill visible from our kitchen window, a strategy that Leyshon (2011) notes in his work with rural youth, defining this as a mobile strategy – using walking and mapping as a way to know and feel belonging in the countryside, as well as to escape adult control and scrutiny. Walking is also important in the countryside because there is a lack of public transport, and until young people are old enough to drive, they have no independent way of getting around, that is assuming their family can afford to lend and insure them on a car when they do pass their test of course. The freedom of walking also relies on young people being mobile themselves to a degree, without disabilities requiring mobility aids or wheelchairs, as the real countryside is fairly inaccessible; it is full of barbed wire fences, ditches, private no trespassing signs, unruly farm dogs or bulls for example. I walked my horizon of hills and taught myself to juggle standing on triangulation points on the tops, ticking them off my OS pathfinder map. On night walks I could trek in the dark down the valley and trace my way home by dry stone walls and the direction of the river without using a torch. It never got totally dark there anyway, as the lack of any light pollution meant that the moon and the sky, full to burst with stars, illuminated our tiny patch of the earth, somehow making it feel bigger. This is what Leyshon labels a moral and mythical 'embodied geography of the countryside', which he reported in the rural youth that he studied (2011, 304) and it was my experience too.

It is discombobulating to have a strong sense of home for somewhere that never felt like home in fundamental ways and, as it turns out, never would be. Again, it is important to acknowledge that this is not unique to rural queers; most rural youth have probably at one point or another fantasized about leaving, even temporarily, or kept that as a dream to bring a sense of options for the future, and through that a sense of control and agency. The youth in Leyshon's study did not identify as queer in any way, but they described a conflicting love/hate relationship with their rural corner of the world. Rural young people's relationships to the countryside are 'characterised by conflicting feelings of belonging, longing, ambivalence, and abhorrence' (Leyshon 2011, 304). His young participants keenly felt their identity as being of the countryside, as being rural, this was something they were proud of and had taken on; but they also resented the close suffocating limits of village life, the lack of private spaces for young people outside the home and an awareness that urban life had different, possibly more expansive opportunities. This mixture was something I felt too, all those years ago. Exploring the countryside provided a sensory and bodily experience of belonging and of having something that was mine, something I knew, and through that knowing came a sense of ownership; as if nobody else but me knew the corners, the dips, the hollow tree, the ruined house, the place where clay could be found by the stream. Yet the landscape around me that I loved grew more restrictive with each passing year, like being under house arrest. It wasn't that I did not like the beautiful rural area I lived in, but knowing I couldn't leave tainted it with resentment, with abhorrence even.

Most of us leave our childhood homes, even if we don't leave the immediate area. We nearly all set up anew somewhere else in terms of physical shelter. People will be shaped in different ways by their first memories of their first 'home' and its location and surroundings. We may take a bodily form that is shaped by how and where we grew, and in that way perhaps it stays in us and with us. Perhaps our first experiences of place are even more defining and foundational. Is this what makes home, do we literally carry it with us and within us like snails? Is the meaning of home the feeling of connection to a place, to a landscape, a particular view, a sound, the smell of warming sunbeams on dusty floorboards? How to honour the strength of these origin stories and sensory memories of place is a continuing enquiry when the very place that they flow from never offered some of the definitional features of home that one finds in the literature on the sociology of home, in terms of a secure and 'rooted' (Tuan 1980, 6) or unselfconscious base free from the scrutiny of contemporary society.

Everyone is called gay; but what if you actually are?

For many queer people, this idea of a comfortable, familiar, unreflexive, unselfconscious and secure home may seem alien, even if family life itself was supportive and secure, although we know that is sadly not the case for many LGBTQ young people. The Albert Kennedy Trust (2023) reports that an estimated 24 per cent of homeless young people in the UK are LGBTQ and the majority cite coming out as being the precursor to them being made homeless. In Scotland, 7 per cent of young LGBTQ people responding to LGBT Youth Scotland (2022) had been forced out of their parental home. Where I am from, at that time, there was no queer life. I did not try to fit in, but I did not know how to be myself either, because I did not know how that could look. I did not have a variety of examples of how selves could be different. Both these positions – whether trying to fit in or not knowing how to be – are hardly conducive to unselfconsciousness or unreflexive familiarity. Being queer and knowing that I was, led to an experience of seeing myself as others might, second guessing the judgements of others. At school, homophobia was common, almost without intent as it was just a way of speaking – everyone was gay or a lemon (slur for lesbian). Everyone may have been called a gay or a lemon, but I actually was one, so such language became more significant for me, more noticeable, and therefore I became more observant and vigilant around it, trying to match my response to how others reacted to such 'banter'.

For most people, the teenage years live up to their stereotypes and are a time of self-consciousness at the best of times, added hypervigilance around homophobia and heterosexism only increases that. I did not try to look straight, and I was certainly not feminine; the tactic I adopted was simply to try not to be noticed. I used this strategy at school too – by getting out of it. I took up work experience options so I could be out of school and worked in male-only environments doing agriculture and estate work, leading to me studying at agricultural college when I left school. Sometimes home is a place where we have to construct ourselves and our connection to the place in spite of those same surroundings, we identify ourselves through the contrast we perceive between us and the rest. This is certainly the narrative behind a lot of the gay flight stories, the experience of and embodied sense of a gulf of difference between the majority 'home' community at home and the queer individual in that place results in a conviction that home can never be there in that place, and it must therefore be somewhere else.

Gay flight – Leaving the rural closet

It is perhaps easier to romanticize the landscape that raised us when that homeland is denied. In the moving memoirs of rural life, from Smith (2023) and Carthew (2023), for example, I note an inability to return. So many attractive areas of the British countryside are progressively transmogrified into static AirBnB postcards or, in the more well-connected parts, become an unattainable millionaire row. Yet, for the price of a small, terraced house in Bristol where I now live, I could easily buy two houses where I'm from. I could return at any time; but my separation is not forced, it was fought for and won, and I can never imagine returning, nor can I imagine ever wanting to.

It has become passé to note the migration patterns of LGBTQ communities, a starstruck, panto-style exodus from small towns to the bright lights of big cities. This flight pattern is embedded in public consciousness, as well as in research, and it shapes both. It has become an assumption when studying gay lives. The city is represented as a place of consumerism, liberalism, anonymity, progress – all of which are attached to LGBTQ identity also, so much so that a queer identity outside of that is barely represented at all, becoming a contradiction in terms, a process that Halberstam has famously termed – metronormativity. 'Urbanism is lauded as progressive and spatially privileged for the desirable queer/trans life', observes Cram (2016, 271) in their powerful piece on the imagery around the horrific and defining murder of Matthew Shepard in Laramie, Wyoming, in the United States in 1998. A rural existence is cast as unliveable, literally, as in the case of homophobic hate crimes, which, as Cram shows, become linked to small-town or rural settings in the queer and mainstream consciousness alike, while they remain statistically more likely in larger cities. The rural life is also unthinkable, because it is seen as a cultural and economic void, explain Annes and Redlin: 'Rural places have commonly been contrasted as cultural vacuums' (2012, 57).

The narrative is that in order to escape the constraining rural, gays must move to the liberating city, which results in 'a sexual geography in which the city represents a beacon of tolerance and gay community, the country a locus of persecution and gay absence' (Weston 1995, 262). The common understanding of gay and lesbian life in rural areas is, 'as closeted, hidden, and oppressed', notes Kazyak (2011, 561). Some researchers point to the rural attitude as constitutive of a level of tolerance that can construct inclusion, albeit on particular terms requiring a level of fitting in and not standing out. Kazyak (2011) suggests that the live and let live attitudes in the countryside can mean that lesbian and gay residents are tolerated and left to get on with life the same as anyone else. As Annes and Redlin explain, this tolerance may be more likely if the individuals have heritage there, 'rural communities may quietly accept them, especially if they have close community ties' (2012, 561).

But what if it's true

However, reading all of these accounts of rural queers, I can't help thinking – but what if it's all true? What if you do come from a cultural vacuum, what if it was constraining, what if your town was overwhelmingly homophobic, what if the countryside did feel impossible to live in? Was my countryside a locus of gay absence? Yes. I did not meet other gay people until I left home. I had never seen, let alone been in, a gay bar or club until I moved to the city at twenty years old. I had none of the common teenage experiences that go on to shape adult lives. I did not date, I did not have sexual relationships, I did not go to parties and experiment with drugs and alcohol, I didn't go to pubs or nightclubs. There were no out gay people in my village, there were no out gay pupils at my secondary school. Was the countryside conservative and a locus of persecution? Yes. Being a 'poof' or a 'lemon' – gay or lesbian – was the worst thing one could possibly be, this was the lesson taught to us throughout school. Not that we had any sort of reference or experience for this, given that nobody, apparently, was gay, and nobody knew anyone who was. Research on the lives of LGBTQ youth in Scotland, published by LGBT Youth Scotland in 2022 found that only 28 per cent of respondents in rural areas described their area as a good place to be LGBT, compared to 62 per cent of those in urban areas. This does not surprise me, but it saddens me that this is still the case.

After I had left and moved to England, I went home once for the village agricultural show, with my first girlfriend. At that time I had a buzzcut, partly because I was living at a women's peace camp in that period of my life and it was quite practical. The village hall was set up to serve teas, raising money for local funds. Long, wooden trestle tables were covered with plastic tablecloths and decorated with jugs of flowers. Everyone sat on ancient, tubular framed metal chairs with canvas fabric that looked like it had been cut out of an old-fashioned tent. They are the same seats that I remember from when my primary school held our nativity play on the small stage. Sitting at a busy table with my girlfriend, I recall a farmer, whose daughter went to primary school with my younger sister, looking over at me and addressing the other villagers at the table to say: 'If my daughter ever came home looking like that I'd fucking strangle her, and she'd be glad of it.' Nobody replied, nor did they vocally agree, although there were a couple of shifty looking nods, but most people just looked down at their neat, white bread sandwiches with the crusts cut off and a skirting of cress. This reaction was to their credit, I have to say, by which I mean that everyone in that moment was fully aware and probably believed that they were doing the decent thing by not really acknowledging the comment. The fact that it was not acknowledged indicated a discomfort with the comment being made. I also felt that this response took the form it did because I was from the village, I was born and raised there. Had I not been, I suspect there might have been more affirmative acknowleedgment and even support for his homophobia. Ironically, the farmer was an outsider, an incomer to the village. The latter, it turns out, being still the greater crime; the otherness of the outsider outweighing my own othered state.

On another occasion, I was going home for a visit and travelled into the train station in Lockerbie to be met by my father. As the train arrived at the station I was by the door, peering out of the sliding, letterbox window. The train goes along the back of the slaughterhouse and into the town, past the station car park, a pub and a Salvation Army charity shop. The entire shop front of the charity shop was covered in a huge banner emblazoned with the phrase 'Keep the Clause' and as this faced the railway and the car park, the location was clearly picked to be as visible as possible. This was a distinctly Scottish campaign, sponsored and run by the millionaire Brian Souter, owner of Stagecoach buses. In 2000 Souter funded the public awareness campaign to lobby against repeal of Section 28 or Clause 2A as it was known as in Scotland due to where it was placed in Scottish legislation on local government. This included a public opinion poll, sent out to registered voters in Scotland, the results of which, it was claimed, found that nearly 87 per cent of respondents supported maintaining Section 28 and only 13 per cent in favour of repealing it. Thankfully, the Scottish government did repeal the clause in 2000, with the Westminster government following in 2003. While this was obviously a win, the hate campaign in favour of the law and the lifespan of the law itself had an effect on a whole generation of children and young people. Now, over twenty years later, people are talking about Section 28 again, worrying that we are seeing a return to this kind of policing and erasure, in Scotland and across England and Wales.

Watching Scotland

Like many Scots who do not live in Scotland I am extremely patriotic; perhaps it is easier to be more fundamentalist about it due to distance from the nuances and complicated reality of daily relationship with the country and its standpoint and directions. To me there has been much to be proud of over recent years, some of it unbelievable to me now, based on what I knew of the country and my tiny corner of it. Lesbian and gay people living in the borders area where I am from have reached out to me on social media and told me about their lives and families in Dumfries and Galloway. All of it is heartening and yet somehow still alien, as it jars so much with my bodily memory of the place, but I am glad things have so obviously moved on. My remaining family in Scotland voted 'Yes' for independence in the referendum; and, although disappointed by the result, we were all buoyed by witnessing the strength of feeling for the future and potential of Scotland, either as fully independent or at least with more control. We phoned each other during the lockdowns to sing the praises of ex-first minister Nicola Sturgeon and how she was handling the pandemic and communications between government and people. There was a low bar, from my perspective in England, with ex-prime minister Johnson's conscious incompetent cruelty causing such visible and visceral confusion, suffering, abandonment and loss as the bodies piled high, so to speak. I watched proudly as articles ticked by on social media comparing the leadership of New Zealand and Scotland favourably with other countries, in contrast to England. Scotland's fight to update the Gender Recognition Act 2004 and bring it into line with that of other European countries, mainly by removing the requirement for medical and psychiatric diagnosis, was yet another reason to be proud. Sturgeon during her premiership was a vocal and visible supporter of LGBTQ rights, campaigns and organizations. But more recently, I have watched while Scotland has become famous for another reason, the campaigns against trans-inclusion led and amplified by one of Edinburgh's most famous residents, the millionaire children's author J. K. Rowling.

Scotland is no small outlier when it comes to the UK's global reputation as 'TERF island' but is playing a leading role. J. K. Rowling has funded a trans-exclusionary rape crisis service in Edinburgh, likely not unrelated to the fact that the existing rape crisis service in Edinburgh was headed up by a trans woman. Rowling has contributed to an edited collection about anti-trans inclusion campaigns in Scotland, titled *The Women Who Wouldn't Wheesht* (Dalgety and Blackburn 2024). The subtitle is 'voices from the frontline of Scotland's battle for women's rights', and the cover blurb praises the anti-trans campaigns for the downfall of Nicola Sturgeon. This sort of language is common across anti-trans inclusion campaigns, not only in Scotland. The anti-trans position is presented as the only position for women to take, and for feminists to take, and those two categories are framed as one and the same. In this way, women who are trans-inclusive, or who are trans-inclusive feminists, are ejected from the constituency of women and from the constituency of feminists. The battle for women's rights is then not a battle for the rights of all women, not least women with a trans history of course, but also all women who dinnae agree. Having gone from being a leading player in LGBTQ rights, and proudly declaring itself as such, Scotland seems now, like the rest of the UK, to be slipping back into a familiar backlash against progress for LGBTQ rights, lives and communities. However, I see things now that I never dreamed of when I lived there decades ago. I even hear that the town of Dumfries has its own Pride celebration, the recent census in Scotland in 2022 found that just under 184,000 people identify as lesbian, gay or bisexual and nearly 20,000 identified as trans. I hope that modern Scotland continues to remain unrecognizable to me and never returns to the country I knew and had to leave.

References

Albert Kennedy Trust. 'Youth Homelessness Report', 2023. www.akt.org.uk/wp-content/uploads/2023/07/akt-thelgbtqyouthhomelessnessreport2021.pdf.

Annes, A. and Redlin, M. 'Coming Out and Coming Back: Rural Gay Migration and the City'. *Journal of Rural Studies* 28, no. 1 (2012): 56–68.

Carthew, N. *Undercurrent: A Cornish Memoir of Poverty, Nature and Resilience*. London: Hodder & Stoughton, 2023.

Cram, E. '(Dis)locating Queer Citizenship: Imaging Rurality in Matthew Shepard's Memory'. In M. L. Gray, C. R. Johnson and B. J. Gilley (eds), *Queering the Countryside: New Frontiers in Rural Queer Studies*, pp. 267–89. New York: New York University Press, 2016. www.jstor.org/stable/j.ctt1804134.17

Dalgety, S. and Blackburn, L. H. *The Women Who Wouldn't Wheesht*. London: Hachette, 2024.

Forstie, C. *Queering the Midwest*. New York: New York University Press, 2022.

Kazyak, E. 'Disrupting Cultural Selves: Constructing Gay and Lesbian Identities in Rural Locales'. *Qualitative Sociology* 34 (2011): 561–81.

Leyshon, M. 'The Struggle to Belong: Young People on the Move in the Ccountryside'. *Population, Space and Place* 17, no. 4 (2011): 304–25.

LGBT Youth Scotland. 'Life in Scotland for LGBT Young People Report', 2022. https://lgbtyouth.org.uk/wp-content/uploads/2023/12/life-in-scotland-for-lgbt-young-people-2022-e-use.pdf.

Smith, D. P. and Holt, L. 'Lesbian Migrants in the Gentrified Valley and "Other" Geographies of Rural Gentrification'. *Journal of Rural Studies* 21, no. 3 (2005): 313–22.

Smith, R. *Rural: The Lives of the Working-Class Countryside*. London: Harper Collins, 2023.

Tuan, Y. 'Rootedness versus Sense of Place', *Landscape* 24 (1980): 3–8.

Weston, K. 'Get Thee to a Big City: Sexual Imaginary and the Great Gay Migration'. *GLQ: A Journal of Lesbian & Gay Studies* 2, no. 3 (1995): 253–77.

14

The aul' days: Ewan Forbes and the ghost in the machine

Zoë Playdon

Beginnings

Ewan Forbes's 'wee place' as a child was his family's 20,000-acre Donside estate in Aberdeenshire, their villages, farms, moors, woods and waters stretching 20 miles from Craigievar (the family castle) eastwards to Fintray House (the family manor). But geography is a matter of both place and person and queer and trans cartography focuses on community: 'we' as well as 'wee', emotional security as well as physical safety. And as a trans boy, born in 1912, this was complex for Ewan.

On the plus side was his remarkable mother, Gwendolen the Lady Sempill, who supported Ewan's boyhood and then, during his adolescence, used the family's wealth and extensive connections to source affirmative medical care for him at European specialist centres: early preparations of testosterone meant Ewan didn't go through the wrong puberty. But on the downside his war-damaged father, the eighteenth Lord Sempill and ninth Baronet of Craigievar, was a stickler for traditional values and family duty. Consequently, although Ewan could live his isolated personal life as a boy, home-schooled, playing on equal terms with other boys, for public occasions he was obliged to dress up as a girl. The family were often in the public eye and Ewan was routinely dead-named and misgendered by the press, not least when he was seventeen and social convention obliged him to 'come out' in the London Season as a debutante.

Instantly, we see the fractured object-position which cis hegemony imposes on all trans lives, irrespective of class, race or age. Ewan was object to his parents' subject, his life literally subjugated to their differing understandings and intentions, his boyhood simultaneously given to and removed from him, affirmed and denied, authenticated and repudiated. This is more than the lack of agency which attends most childhoods. Identifying a child's gender 'communicates a set of adult desires and expectations' about 'how one is to live in one's body in the world', an expectation articulated and legitimized by the cis majority (Butler 2024, 30). From birth, trans people's lives were and are cisplained to them, confining them in a fantasy of binary biological sex, defining them temporally with terms like 'transition' and stigmatizing them socially with terms like 'passing'. But medically and scientifically there isn't such a thing as a uniform, binary biological sex, for humans are subject to diverse sex development. Further, everyone, cis and trans, 'transitions' through different phases of their lives and identities; and 'passing' is a derogatory, discriminatory term, used historically for African Americans indistinguishable from Europeans; for gay people indistinguishable from straight people; for Jewish people indistinguishable from Nazi 'Aryans'. These concepts and language are part of a cis lexicography, which seeks to legitimize trans objectification and defines cis privilege through epistemic sabotage – the wilful destruction of trans self-determination and autonomy.

Ewan's imaginative resistance to his social pressures was to dance. Both of his parents were keen Highland traditional dancers, and Ewan formed his own troupe, the Dancers of Don, and always danced the male part. Newspaper reports of these events still dead-named and misgendered him, but their audiences saw a highly skilled man dancing the most complex sets with pinpoint accuracy and discipline. When his father refused to pay for him to attend medical school, Ewan worked on the family estate as a farmer and driver until he could afford to pay for himself, graduating from the Aberdeen Medical School in 1944. His real community had always been the staff and tenants living on the estate and like his father, Ewan spoke the local Doric as well as Standard English. Instead of going into private practice for society patients, therefore, Ewan became a family doctor to his 'ain folk' in his local market town of Alford, dropping his inherited family title 'The Honourable' in favour of 'Dr': he is still remembered affectionately today by his former patients as 'the doctor' (Playdon 2021, 62).

Ewan was engaging in a politics of location in his dancing displays, his medical work and his redefinition of his personal identity by his chosen title. In his Craigievar life, Ewan was still an aristocratic Forbes-Sempill, bound by duty and habitually dead-named and misgendered by some family members, including his elder sister Margaret. But in his Alford life, he was simply Dr Sempill, encountering patients in a 'nomadic politics' of 'bonding, of coalitions, of interconnections' (Braidotti 1994, 35). Geographically, as local doctor, Ewan travelled long distances from his surgery at Alford to patients in hill farms and crofts, so that 'No matter how deep the snow, no matter how high the river or wind, the doctor is always there when we need him' (Playdon 2021, 76). His life crossed borders, trespassed, transgressed, released itself from the usual boundaries. Ewan purposefully demonstrated 'kincoherence', queer relationality defined by the impossibility of forming traditional relationships, diffuse and mobile, refusing entrenched cis-het norms.

In 1947, Ewan purchased a small estate of his own, the 3,000 acres of Brux, making him Laird of Brux, so that now he signed letters as 'Brux': he is still known as Brux by many old friends. His chosen, personal, adult 'wee place' had become his social identity, person and location merging together, his personal histories reconciled in what Tello (2022, 391) calls 'the *and-and*', held together as different but not divided. Because the Forbes-Sempill family had been central to local society for centuries, everyone knew Ewan was assigned female at birth (afab), but they also knew him as the man who was dancer, doctor and farmer. Ewan was able to 'refuse static, essentialist modes of being' (Tello 2022, 393) – until he fell in love and wished to marry. It is at this point that a legal 'ghost in the machine' entered his life, changing it irrecoverably and haunting him until his death.

The ghost in the machine

The term 'the ghost in the machine' was coined by philosopher Gilbert Ryle, in his 1949 book *The Concept of Mind*, to describe Descartes's separation of mind from body. He called such an attempt a 'category error', mistakenly putting mind and body into two separate categories rather than recognizing that both are equally complex organized units. One is not a machine and the other an activating element of the machine: they are mutual fields of cause and effect. Body and mind are a coherent whole, held in what scientific medicine now terms biopsychosocial health.

Trans healthcare has always been viewed in this way by scientific medicine, since the first medical diagnostic criteria for being trans was published in 1886 by German psychiatrist Richard von Krafft-Ebing, in his influential *Psychopathia Sexualis*. He called being trans 'metamorphosis sexualis without paranoia' and he classified it as an 'intersex' condition, a natural diversity of human development. Similarly, sexologist Magnus Hirschfeld understood the patient's body/mind as a unitary location, so that trans people were free to decide their sex: his renowned Institute for Sexual Sciences in Berlin provided elective affirmative medical care to self-identified trans people until its destruction by Nazis in 1933.

As medical scientists sought to synthesize 'ovarian' and 'testicular' hormone therapy', endocrinology emerged as a new medical specialty and in 1928 the first commercial formulation of oestrogen was launched as 'Progynon'. Surgeries were available too, but having accessed early preparations of testosterone, and thus avoiding the wrong puberty, Ewan did not require them. By the time Ewan was an adult, in the 1930s, trans people lived unremarked by the press unless there was an unusual reason to notice them. In 1936, for example, the *Yorkshire Post and Leeds Intelligencer* newspaper reported on international athlete Mark Weston, who received a certificate from his surgeon, Mr Lennox Broster at Charing Cross Hospital, stating, 'This is to certify that Mr Mark Weston, who has always been brought up as a female, is a male, and should continue life as such.' Mark corrected his natal birth certificate to male and married, just as Ewan wished to do.

Scots law made Ewan's birth certificate correction rather more onerous than Mark's, but he followed due process and on 12 September 1952 a short announcement in Aberdeen's *Press and Journal* read: 'Dr E Forbes-Sempill, Brux Lodge, Alford, wishes to intimate that in future he will be known as DR EWAN FORBES-SEMPILL. All legal formalities have been completed.' His family connections meant that journalists descended on Brux in search of sensationalism, but Ewan's community blocked the road with lorries, preventing access to his estate. Ewan himself had bought one of the first Land Rovers, which he drove across country to his surgery in a material nomadism that reflected and was caused by his cultural nomadism across conventional social boundaries.

It is in this moment, as Ewan gets into his Land Rovers and puts it into four-wheel drive, selecting its low-ratio 'bottom box' gearing to negotiate otherwise unnegotiable terrain, that the legal ghost in the machine carried out its first haunting. The press frenzy about Ewan's correction of his birth certificate was because it put him next in line for his elder brother's baronetcy, displacing his uncle. As *Time* magazine (1952, 19) reported:

> Rear Admiral Arthur Lionel Ochoncar Forbes-Sempill, 74, considered his new status. 'As uncle of the present peer, I succeed', he told a reporter. 'According to Scottish law, a girl can't. But Ewan ... dammit, that's a bit different, isn't it?'

The editor of *Debrett* confirmed that the family baronetcy was limited by male primogeniture, the law that still says that certain UK titles and estates can only be inherited by a man and never by a woman. Imposed by Norman invaders a thousand years ago and still operating against the spirit of equal opportunities legislation, primogeniture's son-preference system indicates that although women may be physically as able as men to run estates and carry out aristocratic duties, they lack the necessary intellect. It is precisely the Cartesian separation of body and mind that Ryle wrote against, an ideological ghost in the machine that still haunts Britain today: between 2013 and 2020, the Daughters' Rights group entered six Bills into parliament to end male primogeniture, all instantly quashed.

But in 1952, when Ewan corrected his natal birth certificate, medicine recognized with Ryle that mind and body are indivisible. The law followed medicine, accepting that for Mark Weston and all trans people, an error had been made and required legal correction. Medically and legally, Ewan was inarguably male and the next in line for the title, and Cartesian dualism had long been discredited. But ghosts are not easily laid and the spectre of primogeniture walked again when Ewan's elder brother William died in December 1965, and Ewan's cousin John turned up, saying that he was going to claim the title and estate on the grounds that Ewan wasn't 'a real man'.

Curing queers

As a doctor, still in close contact with his medical school colleagues at Aberdeen, Ewan knew how medicine had changed in the thirteen years between his marriage and his brother's death. In the 1950s, the United States had been gripped by fear of the 'Lavender Menace', Edgar Hoover, head of the FBI, targeting queer people as part of 'an entangled field of inversion, hermaphroditism, homosexuality, and transvestism' (Gill-Peterson 2018, 95). In 1955, psychologist John Money and his colleagues at the Massachusetts Institute of Technology invented a new way to 'cure' queers, by fabricating a medical 'ghost in the machine'.

Their initial purpose was to solve a surgical conundrum. Surgeons operating on intersexed neonates found it easiest to 'correct' their genitalia to female – the idea of simply leaving them alone, unless there was a life-threatening issue such as cloacal extrophy, was unthought. But what if they got the child's sex wrong? Money's solution was to separate mind and body with a pseudo-medical idea of 'gender role'. Victorian medicine had believed in the 'Law of the Homologous Sexual Development', a fantasy that in 'normal' people, sex, sexuality and gender would naturally be cisgendered and heterosexual. Money reinvented that idea of by claiming that 'nurture' could do the same thing. He said that parenting decided a child's gender, irrespective of their bodily characteristics: appropriate parenting would take the child's mind through a 'gender-gate' into a cisnormative, heterosexual identity. Consequently, surgeons could correct intersex neonates however they liked, since the body was a separate 'machine' from the pliable 'ghost' of the mind. If parenting failed in this mission, then medicine could use conversion practices to reprogramme queer children into being cisheteronormative. In 1962, psychoanalyst Robert Stoller founded the first Gender Identity Research Clinic at the University of California, Los Angeles, rapidly winning its 'professional reputation for its attempts to get "sissy" boys (and occasionally "tomboy" girls) to behave in masculine (or, in the case of girls, feminine) ways' (Meyerowitz 2002, 126). Money's 'gender role', the behaviour displayed by people in society, and Stoller's 'gender identity', the sense of belonging to one sex and not the other, combined to form a pseudo-medical ideology in which a binary biological sex could be separated from a behavioural social gender. By 1964, the patients at Stoller's clinic were almost entirely trans people.

Toxic, illogical and unscientific though this psychopathologization of trans people was, it gained a rapidly growing following in psychiatry and although endocrinologists had provided affirmative healthcare to trans people for decades, in 'a medical turf war' (Meyerowitz 2002, 107), psychiatry took over trans healthcare. And just when Ewan was dealing with the fallout from his brother's death, US psychiatry was about to import their pseudo-medical model to the UK and the NHS (Playdon 2021, 106, 191–9).

Projective identification

As a trans doctor, Ewan will have been aware of these shifts and changes and of the concurrent debates about trans healthcare in the *British Medical Journal* which, like every member of the British Medical Association, he received weekly. In psychosocial terms, such debates often represented part of the medical profession's anxieties about and desires for a patriarchal, deterministic, binary biological sex. Their coping strategy was to project those anxious desires onto their trans patients, just as in the past they had projected them onto gay men and lesbians, although now the patient's 'anxiety' or 'uncertainty' was supposed to be about their sex rather than their sexuality.[1] The psychiatric trans project was essentially 'a medical device mobilized to face the potential conceptual collapse of binary sex' (Gill-Peterson 2018, 98).

As well as this new toxic pseudo-medicine, British public opinion was turning against trans people. In the early 1950s, wide-scale publicity was given to Christine Jorgensen in the United States and to Roberta Cowell in the UK, much of it negative: a malicious song about Christine, entitled *Is She Is Or Is She Ain't* (Gene Walcott, *c*. 1950s), and a vicious article about Roberta saying 'he is now nothing but an unhappy freak ... he should go into a home and so avoid contacts that might lead to normal relationships' ('Come Off It "Roberta", 1954, 1). In 1953, the *Sunday Express* outed trans man Dr Michael Dillon, causing him to leave his job as ship's doctor and retire into a private life and in 1957, the Scots press covered Perth Sheriff's Court's refusal to correct the birth certificate of trans woman X. Four years later, well-known *Vogue* model April Ashley was outed as trans in 1961 (East 1961, 10) with the press continuing to publicize her private life as she married Arthur Corbett, son and heir of Lord Rowallen, in 1963.

Even as gay men's life possibilities were being expanded, beginning with their partial decriminalization in England by the Sexual Offences Act 1967, medicine and the media were contracting queer space for UK trans people, consigning them to a new pseudo-psychiatric ghetto and turning them into freak shows. When Ewan had received affirmative medical care as a child and corrected his birth certificate in 1952, medicine had classified him as intersexed: the determining factor had been his 'psychological sex' or, as we would say now, his self-identification. But at his brother's funeral in January 1966, when his cousin John told him he was going to challenge him for the baronetcy, Ewan knew that pseudo-medicine had changed trans medical classification, putting him and all trans people into the category of mental illness. A medical challenge would now decide that Ewan was female, that he and Patty were lesbians, that they had committed perjury by contracting a false marriage and that they should both be sentenced to two years in prison.

In court

Ewan's first response was to try and buy John off. Succession to a baronetcy cannot be transferred but the Succession (Scotland) Act 1964 had removed male primogeniture from property, which could be transferred. Ewan handed over the 20,000-acre Craigievar and Fintray estates to John in return in return for a gentleman's agreement from him not to pursue the title. But John was no gentleman, and Ewan's estranged sister Margaret, who habitually dead-named and misgendered him, was in cahoots with John.

Craigievar Castle had been put into the care of the National Trust for Scotland before William's death, and Brux, Ewan's 'wee place', should have been a place of safety for him. But after John had in effect blackmailed him out of the Craigievar and Fintray estates a series of dramatic events – family betrayal by his sister Margaret, a secret letter, a bidding war, sudden death – found Ewan's sex called into question. This should have been impossible, for both his medical and his legal sex had been decided in 1952 when he corrected his birth certificate. But the new pseudo-medicine was socially displacing trans people, rewriting their boundaries and diminishing their space for life. Now Ewan was obliged to go to court: even his body was not his own, for the state would decide who he was.

Ewan's place of safety was his community, which had protected him from journalists twenty-five years earlier, exemplifying a principle of rural queer studies that reputation as a familiar local is valued before all other identity claims. He had met his solicitor, Archie Haldane, when Archie and his wife Janet visited Aberdeenshire to fish, and they had become close friends. Ewan's barrister, Charles Jauncey QC, was a relative of Archie's, so in court, Ewan could feel that he was among friends. The doctors giving evidence on Ewan's side included his GP partner Wullie Manson and colleagues from the Aberdeen Medical School, as well as very senior clinical authorities like Professor Martin Roth, the most eminent psychiatrist of his day.

For four days, from 15 to 18 May 1967, Ewan's wee place contracted to the conference room at the offices of Haldane & McLaren in Edinburgh, where the hearing was held in camera. All Ewan had ever wanted was to live his quiet life with Patty and their community, but now, everything hung on the outcome of the hearing for both of them: their life together, their standing in their community, their freedom. John had used blackmail, intimidation, deception and coercion not only to take the estate from Ewan, but also to force him into a lengthy, humiliating medical examination and to make Ewan pay his, John's, court costs: all for a title which he would in any event inherit when Ewan died. Now, forced to gamble everything, Ewan finally decided to fight back. He falsified medical evidence, providing tissue samples which he claimed were from a testicle which had suddenly descended into his groin. Its validity could not be disproved in those days before DNA profiling, and combined with his 'psychological sex' or self-identification, it won him the case.

Ewan was facing a totalitarian pseudo-medical system that was completely new to him. It was ideology, not science, a set of unsupported assertions distorting empirical evidence, aiming to organize social reality, not reflect it. Although there was no evidence whatsoever that Ewan was delusional or mentally ill, this new ideology defined all trans people as acutely psychotic, living in a hallucinated reality that was, however, restricted solely to one area of their life: their experience of their sex. Such ideology 'pretends that the requirements of the system derive from the requirements of life. It is a world of appearances trying to pass for reality' which requires individuals to 'live within a lie' so that 'the complete degradation of the individual is presented as his ultimate liberation' (Havel [1978] 1986, 44–5). Gay men and lesbians had been persecuted because an ideological belief in 'complementarity' insistently told the lie that the only natural human form of sexual union was between a man and a woman. Now, trans people were being persecuted, using the same casuistry and the same conversion practices, to shore up an ideological demand for an anti-scientific, essentialized, fantasized, human biological binary sex.

Both as a doctor and from his own lived experience, Ewan knew this pseudo-medical ideology was a lie and he refused to live within it. By falsifying medical evidence for court, he opposed one untruth with another, or in Havel's terms:

> He rejects the ritual and breaks the rules of the game. He discovers once more his suppressed identity and dignity. He gives his freedom a concrete significance. His revolt is an attempt to *live within the truth*. ([1978] 1986, 55, original emphasis)

Hannah Arendt argues that 'the deliberate denial of factual truth – the ability to lie – and the capacity to change facts – the ability to act – are interconnected; they owe their existence to the same source: imagination' (Arendt 1972, 5). Ewan's inventive counter to pseudo-medical ideology landmarks Butler's (2024, 9–10) 'counter imaginary strong enough to expose its ruse, scatter its force and stop the efforts at censorship, distortion and reactionary politics that it empowers'. But in winning his case and the baronetcy, Ewan unwittingly precipitated a constitutional crisis which damaged the lives of trans people worldwide.

Consequences

At that period, the Crown was limited by male primogeniture: Britain only had a queen because there were no eligible male heirs. Constitutional law is all about securing succession to the throne to maintain political stability and Ewan's precedent disrupted that: now, the heir apparent to the throne might have an older afab trans sibling who claimed the throne instead. Having shrunk to the hearing's few square metres, Ewan's wee space exploded into the world with massive force, through a show trial a year after he won his baronetcy.

Trans woman April Ashley had gone through a ceremony of marriage with Arthur Corbett, son and heir of Lord Rowallen, but the marriage hadn't worked out. In the first of a series of bizarre incidents, April's solicitor, Terrence Walton, advised her to sue Arthur for maintenance. But unlike Ewan, April hadn't corrected her natal birth certificate and so Walton must have known there was no legal marriage and no maintenance to be claimed. On his side, Arthur could just have ignored April's demands, but instead, inexplicably, he sued her for divorce on the grounds that she wasn't and had never been a 'real woman'. The judge appointed to the case, Lord Ormrod, had recently heard another divorce case of a trans person without a corrected birth certificate (Talbot vs. Talbot) which he dismissed as 'plainly no marriage': but instead of following his own precedent for April's case, he ordered a battery of medical tests and a trial lasting seventeen days. When the tests said that April's anatomy was the same as that of other women, he required them to be rewritten to make a distinction between a 'normal vagina' and an 'artificial vagina'. It is true that Ormrod had attended medical school and served in the Royal Army Medical Corps in the Second World War, but now he was acting far beyond his professional competence and outside both legal and medical ethics.

Before they went into court, April and Terrence Walton were taken into Ormrod's chambers, where he showed them Ewan's court papers, told them that everyone involved in the case had been sworn to secrecy, a pact that now included them, and that the case records had been removed from the public eye because 'there are some interests it is more important to protect than the rights of individuals' (Playdon 2021, x). This meant that April couldn't use Ewan's precedent and that although some of her expert medical witnesses were the same as Ewan's, they were not allowed to refer to Ewan's case. In his summing up, on 2 February 1970, Ormrod rejected the idea of 'psychological sex' which had been key in Ewan's case, ignored senior medical opinion and invented factitious legal criteria which defined April and all trans people, as mentally ill homosexuals masquerading in a sex that was not theirs. This decision in *Corbett v. Corbett*, as the case is known, became a super-precedent, cited across the world, damaging trans lives globally.

Aftermath

Ewan had been traumatized by his time in court. A devout Episcopalian Christian, he was haunted by the knowledge that he had committed perjury, lying on oath in the face of God: overwhelmed, he would fall to his knees in the fields and pray for forgiveness.

By falsifying medical evidence for court Ewan had also committed gross professional misconduct and he punished himself by deregistering himself as a doctor. His staff and tenants at Brux found he was now hyper-vigilant, watching them with binoculars from surrounding hills and avoiding contact with them. His friends found him subject to rumination, the constant, repetitive anxiety about an apparently trivial issue which dominated his thoughts. Paying his and John's legal fees had reduced his income considerably, so that keeping up appearances as Sir Ewan Forbes of Craigievar was a financial battle, especially in summer when guests obliged him and Patty to move from their usual diet of porridge and the game and salmon he took from his land and water.

Concurrently, he could see the unintended consequences of his defence affecting trans people across the UK. April Ashley's case was reported everywhere and the consequences of the new cisgenderism it imposed were dire. No longer able to correct their natal birth certificates, UK trans people's substantive civil liberties were removed from them, they were socially ostracized and subjected to a brutal NHS regime which included compulsory sterilization.[2] Queer space went underground as new community support groups emerged to try to support trans people in this new, hostile environment, always maintaining the anonymity of their members (Playdon 2021, 237–9).

As he grew older, Ewan's space diminished further. He and Patty left their handsome, stone-built house at Brux and moved into a low-maintenance wooden chalet a few hundred yards away. There, Ewan wrote two slender volumes of memoirs, *The Aul' Days* and *The Dancers of Don*, without mentioning the court case or the personal circumstances that led to it. He died in 1991 and his ashes were scattered at Brux on Coillebhar Hill. Five years later, on 1 May 1996, trans woman P defeated the UK government in the European Court of Justice (*P v. S and Cornwall County Council* [1996] IRLR 347), restoring trans employment rights and landmarking a new era of community activism and social advancement.

Hauntings

It is hard for us today to imagine a world in which being trans is unproblematic, where medical care is affirmative rather than psychopathologizing, where being trans carries no legal penalties and trans lives are not appropriated by partisan politics, social stigma and media malice. At the time of writing, in the UK and the United States, hate speech identifies the academic concept of gender and the lives of trans people as 'a threat to all of life, civilization, society, thought' and 'as a weapon of destruction, the devil, a new version of totalitarianism, paedophilia, or colonization' so that 'gender has assumed a startling number of phantasmatic forms' (Butler 2024, 5, 7). Perhaps moral panic explains the 2019 legal decision in *Forstater v. CGD Europe* (ET 2200909/2019) which used April Ashley's archaic case to decide that legally, sex is biological and immutable, defying the Equality Act 2010 which reflects the decision in P's case that gender reassignment leads to a change in sex. Consequently, it is no longer clear when expression of trans hate – dead-naming, misgendering, shunning – constitutes harassment in the workplace and when not. The Hate Crime and Public Order (Scotland) Act 2021 offers some protection, although for transphobia to be treated as a hate crime, behaviour must to be both abusive and intended to stir up hatred. This gives transphobia a higher threshold for criminality than racial hatred, in which insulting behaviour is in and of itself an offence. The medico-legal ghost in the machine that haunted Ewan bedevils society today, in an aporetic relationship with the past.

Aporia, unresolvable paradox, is a traumatic overwhelming of 'the psychic defences and normal processes of registering memory traces' (Luckhurst 2008, 4). For the twenty-six years from April Ashley's case in 1970 to the landmark P case in 1996, UK trans people had their civil liberties removed, were socially ostracized and subjected to an NHS regime that included compulsory sterilization. Historically, these three conditions – legal exclusion, social abjection and biological eradication – constitute genocide, the eradication of a specific group of people, a reality so uncomfortable as to be aporetic, attendant but culturally unrepresentable under existing rules of knowledge. In *Specters of Marx* (1994) French philosopher Jacques Derrida coined the word 'hauntology' to describe how this kind of repressed or unthinkable past returns in the present, so that such 'haunting' plays a crucial part in preserving the traces of these kinds of aporia, as something central 'to responsible thought, ethics and politics' (Luckhurst 2008, 6).

In queer history, such aporia constitutes 'a theory of queer possession as both the occupation of the present by the past and the present's attempts to take control of these occupations' which

> allows us to apprehend in tacit, diffuse and material form the past that we unwittingly inherit and contain, and our efforts to hold these histories in place and to pass them on: that is, to make them meaningful and bearable. (Walsh 2023, 8–9)

The spectre that haunted Ewan, that now haunts Europe and North America, is thus 'a *psychosocial* phenomenon', 'a site where intimate fears and anxieties become socially organized to incite political passions' (Butler 2024, 5). They are 'cultural phantasms'

> guided by an inflammatory syntax: that is, a way of ordering the world that absorbs and reproduces anxieties and fears about permeability, precarity, displacement, and replacement; loss of patriarchal power in both the family and state; and loss of white supremacy and national purity. (Butler 2024, 7)

Paradoxically, UK trans history is both rewritten and made invisible at the same time, concealing Ewan's history and that of other trans people, while concurrently creating fictionalized accounts of trans experience. A striking example at the time of writing is NHS England's *Cass Review*, a lengthy inquiry into clinical care for trans children and adolescents, which locates such care as commencing from 1989 onwards, eliding all the medical provision made before then, including that made for Ewan. Consequently, *Cass* claims that the present visibility of trans boys is 'unlike trans presentations in any other historical period', an a-historical claim to exceptionalism which elides trans lives and an epistemic injustice which wrongs queer historians as knowledgeable about their communities. Similarly, hermeneutical injustice, speakers with insufficient knowledge seeking to silence speakers who *do* know, is apparent in the UK's refusal to ban conversion practices for LGBTQIA+ people even though such practices are described by the United Nations as unethical, unscientific, ineffective and tantamount to torture.

In his 1993 work *Aporias*, Derrida used the term to mean 'the difficult or the impracticable … the impossible passage, the refused, denied, or prohibited passage', and trans aporia is strongly present in waiting times for trans healthcare. At time of writing, NHS England has no new appointments available at all for child and adolescent services, creating a two-tier system of those who can afford private healthcare provision from organizations such as Anne.health, and those who cannot. Meanwhile, although the UK government recognized in 2002 that being trans is not a mental illness and both the World Health Organization and the American Psychiatric Association no longer classify being trans as a mental illness, NHS trans healthcare continues to be located in mental health services. Since service reconfiguration is an everyday part of NHS management this is inexplicable, except in terms such as institutionalized transphobia.

The pseudo-medicine which psychopathologized trans people destroyed Ewan's quiet life and that of all trans UK citizens after him. It continues to haunt the state, compromising the universal, fundamental value of equality, its ghost in the machine providing an innate testimonial injustice in which trans people are always already disbelieved in their accounts of their own lives. For Ewan, being trans eclipsed all his other characteristics as a white, aristocratic, professional, heterosexual, able-bodied, married, devoutly Christian man. Today, UK government subjects trans people to legal requirements and exceptions that make them less legally protected than all other UK citizens and while being gay or lesbian is now no hindrance to a political career, there are no trans MSPs, MPs or members of the House of Lords.

Ewan's response to attempts to make him live within a lie of innate inequality was imaginative and ultimately, perhaps, it is the critical imagination of Scotland's new generation of queer scholars and activists – people like Gina Gwenffrewi, Harvey Humphrey, Florence Oulds, Ruth Pearce, Nat Raha, Sam Rutherford, Vic Valentine and Rory Wilson – that will lay the ghost and enable UK trans people to live once again in the uncontested equality of the aul' days.

Notes

1. Occasionally, the deeply personal nature of this projective identification becomes evident. For example, Dr John Randell, head of the NHS Gender Identity Clinic at Charing Cross Hospital, was a highly closeted cross-dresser, keeping a flat nearby where he invited carefully selected colleagues for cocktails, which he served en femme (Playdon 2024, 107). Similarly, when I met Dr John Money in 1992 at St George's Hospital's conference on *Gender Identity and Development in Childhood and Adolescence* (13–14 March), his entourage included a pornography publisher seeking trans women to photograph in sexually enticing dress and poses. Money told me this was for the benefit of the exploited women, claiming they who enjoyed looking at the photographs, even though sales were clearly aimed at cis men.

2. Since Ewan's case, UK trans people can no longer correct their natal birth certificates. Provided they pass the tests created by the Gender Recognition Act 2004, they may apply for a GRC which provides access to a pseudo-birth certificate, which until 2011was identifiable by having one column less than natal birth certificates. Trans people's natal birth certificates remain uncorrected and endure as a legal record of birth. However, *For Women Scotland v. The Scottish Ministers* ([2023] CSIH 37) determined that sex under the Equality Act 2010 is determined by a GRC, although that legal status is currently being debated in the Supreme Court; see www.supremecourt.uk/cases/uksc-2024-0042

References

Arendt, H. 'Lying in Politics'. In *Crises of the Republic*, pp. 1–47. New York: Harcourt, Brace, Jovanovich, 1972.

Braidotti, R. *Nomadic Subjects: Embodiment and Sexual Difference in Contemporary Feminist Theory*. New York: Columbia Press, 1994.

Butler, J. *Who's Afraid of Gender?* London: Allen Lane, 2024.

'Come Off It "Roberta"', *People*, 18 April 1954, p. 1.

Gill-Peterson, J. *Histories of the Transgender Child*. Minneapolis: University of Minnesota Press, 2018.

Havel, V. 'The Power of the Powerless'. In J. Vladislav (ed.), *Living in Truth*, pp. 36–122. London: Faber and Faber, [1978] 1986.

Lennon, K. and Alsop, R. *Gender Theory in Troubled Times*. London: Polity Press, 2020.

Luckhurst, R. *The Trauma Question*. London: Routledge, 2008.

Meyerowitz, J. *How Sex Changed: A History of Transsexuality in the United States*. Cambridge, MA: Harvard University Press, 2002.

Playdon, Z. *The Hidden Case of Ewan Forbes*. London: Bloomsbury, 2021.

East, R. '"Her" Secret Is Out', *People*, 19 November 1961, p. 10.

Stoller, R. J. *Sex and Gender*. New York: Science House, 1968.

Tello, V. 'Counter-memory and And-And: Aesthetics and Temporalities for Living Together', *Memory Studies* 15, no. 2 (2022): 390–401.

Time, 'Milestones, Oct. 20, 1952' https://time.com/archive/6619492/milestones-oct-20-1952/. Accessed 6 November 2025.

Walsh, F. *Performing the Queer Past*. London: Methuen Drama, 2023.

15

A queer poetics of belonging: From *dui Bangla* to Glasgow

Tanvir Alim and Rohit K. Dasgupta

Introduction

Scotland's history hasn't always been progressive, and there are still big gaps in how accepting society really is. For South Asian queer people, the mix of supportive policies and lack of representation in Scottish media can lead to feelings of invisibility and marginalization. It's also important to recognize the positive role South Asian and queer communities play in Scotland.[1] While cultural and religious backgrounds can sometimes create barriers, these communities also help challenge the dominant culture and bring diversity. This chapter reflects this tension, where progress in policy doesn't always match up with social realities. Using assemblage as a framework helps focus on our complex lived experiences. Assemblage is a collection of different parts that don't necessarily form a single whole, forming 'a series of dispersed but mutually connected and messy networks, bringing together causes and effects, living and non-living forces' (Puar 2007, 211). Assemblage helps us understand queer identities as fluid and shaped by different factors, without forcing them into one neat story, an approach useful for looking at how queer lives in Scotland are influenced by overlapping forces, like migration, colonial histories and local culture, without simplifying them. Assemblage allows us to see the complexity of queer experiences in small nations, where sexuality and space connect in different ways. We are both Bengalis but live in different countries because of colonial history, and both moved to Glasgow, Scotland, around the same time, as potential 'New Scots'. We reflect on our relationship with the place we now live, recognizing that as researchers, we are closely connected to the ideas we've developed about our own social worlds. Our understanding is incomplete, shaped by our outside perspectives and the limitations of partial memories and mixed truths. Scotland is often seen as welcoming to migrants and refugees, and as being free from racism, but we believe the story of civic nationalism needs closer questioning (Davidson and Virdee 2018; Taylor 2023). Our citizenship, employment and sense of belonging are also influenced by the wider

UK context; while we now live in Glasgow, our gender, sexuality and racial identities make it hard to feel completely 'at home.'

> desire pleasure anger
> Brown bodies rage in trauma
> our truths bring us joy

Bengal has been partitioned multiple times: first in 1905 under Lord Curzon, reversed in 1911 after protests; then in 1947 with the creation of East Pakistan; and finally in 1971, when Bangladesh became independent. Bengalis across the border have a shared history, language and culture despite religious differences. The Bengali Language Movement in Bangladesh, for instance, played a crucial role in the country's struggle for independence. The emphasis on indigenous languages and culture serves as both a form of resistance against past colonialism and a means of strengthening regional identity in the face of modern challenges. In this chapter, we are using a transnational frame as it allows us to explore these shared experiences and how they shape identity, memory and culture on both sides of the border, illustrating how borders do not completely sever the connections between people and places that were once part of the same region. Writing within a transnational frame allowed us to explore how diaspora communities contribute to the shaping of identities and the social fabric of the two Bengals.

We also undertake a decolonial approach to how we narrate our stories. We are well aware of the ethical issues when it comes to using our cultural knowledge to advance causes we care about. Here we explore queer belonging in Glasgow as experienced by us as Bengali queer immigrants and we fully embrace our identity as scholar-activists utilizing autoethnography as a tool for self-empowerment and public advocacy. Our approach has also been creative in terms of how we approached writing and making our 'data' available through reflective journal style writing and insertion of literary poetry. It is also important to acknowledge our positionalities. Tanvir is a Muslim postgraduate research student from Bangladesh with precarious immigration status while Rohit is a Hindu-born atheist from West Bengal, India with a stable academic job. We are of similar age, yet despite our shared linguistic and cultural backgrounds we occupy different levels of privilege and disadvantage.

তানভীরের কথা (Tanvir's narrative): From Bangladesh to Glasgow

Bangladesh, a small and densely populated country in South Asia with a hot and humid climate, has a culture vastly different from Scotland's. Coming from a middle-class background in Bangladesh, adjusting to life in Glasgow as a mature student was a challenging experience. I barely knew anything about the landscape of Scotland. When I arrived at Glasgow International Airport, I was surprised to see two separate lines – one for EU passengers and another for everyone else. The dark blue signs reading 'Border Control' all around me only added to my sense of distraction. I have heard harassment stories of immigration, but I believe I have the best story to tell. When the officer learnt that I came here for PhD, he looked into my eyes and said, 'Welcome to Scotland'. This was a pleasant memory that I will remember for a long time. During my first year, I stayed in student accommodation which didn't work in terms of student well-being. The ceilings were incredibly low, and although I had great flatmates, I often felt like an uprooted tree, separated from my fellow activists back in Bangladesh. My sense of isolation was compounded by my inability to drive and my lack of interest in pub quizzes, which are a big part of Scotland's drinking culture – a stark contrast to the public drinking norms in Bangladesh and many other Muslim countries.

I learnt a lot from my multicultural flatmates. However, in the initial months, it was not easy to mingle. The student accommodation was in a residential area, but it was too quiet for my liking – nothing ever seemed to happen there. The area was hilly and lushly green, which sounded picturesque, but the winding path through the botanical garden on winter nights was something I dreaded. Despite being only, a twenty-five-minute walk from the university library, returning from late-night study sessions was a challenge. Managing my facemask, winter jacket, gloves and any items I was carrying made each trip back feel like an ordeal. My skin was not used to wearing so many layers. It was accustomed to handling the hot and humid weather, the sweat and the sunshine.

Previously I worked with Europeans as I worked in international organizations. Some of them were my friends. I tried to make friends and started socializing at different events and activities in Glasgow. Soon I realized there were a lot of pub nights or Ceilidh dances, which I was not interested in. I am brown, I am forty and I am an introvert. I have to constantly negotiate my presence with complex race, class, age and nationality. My mobility and boundaries often feel contested. While my Scottish friends here can travel to numerous countries without needing a visa, I find myself waiting in a separate line to enter and leave Glasgow. I started to use dating applications. But in most cases, there were no responses or people used to ghost me after a line or two. My dating life was never this dry in my earlier life, but I was surprised at the number of people who kept rejecting me. DasGupta (2014) explores in their writing about their early life in the United States, delving into themes of friendship, desire and the concept of home, wistfully noting that being brown and having a medium-sized penis does not take you that far in the white, blonde-dominated meat markets.

Feminist scholars critique the way progressive sexual politics are mapped onto geographical and spatial binaries, such as 'urban/rural' and 'West/East'. Puar argues that media often perpetuate binary stereotypes, creating a divide between 'progressive Western gays' and 'backward brown gays', 'dangerous Muslim men' and 'civilised Europeans' (Puar 2007, 330). I felt that most people I was trying to contact who were ghosting me on the dating app were like that. My brown body often failed to spark interest, and my inquisitive mind seemed to make others suspicious when I tried to initiate conversations online. In some instances, when interactions transitioned from the virtual to the physical realm, some people felt compelled to instruct me on the 'correct' way to behave and how not to. Things happen in impulses, sensations, expectations, daydreams, encounters and habits of relating, in strategies and their failure, in forms of persuasion and contagion and compulsion, in modes of attention, attachment and agency, and in public and social worlds of all kinds that catch people up in something that feels like something. Things like that also happened in my life in Scotland. I was very curious to explore the Zine Library[2] in Glasgow. I visited the Zine Library on Glasgow's South Side on a lazy winter afternoon. The tiny library was closed that day, so I started strolling around Cathcart Road on the South Side. On that lonesome afternoon, I found kids playing around the street on their way home. Bakeries were selling gigantic samosas,[3] and I could hear Roma community members chatting and laughing in circles next to the cramped tenements. It was messy and suddenly I felt at home that afternoon while sipping a cup of 'kadak chai'.[4] I realized that not all the neighbourhoods are as sanitized as I am located in. The Pakistani shopkeepers cleaning the mannequin and the young girls under burka[5] in the street gave me an unnamed comfort-like home. I was impressed by the multicultural environment, street food and stores in this locality. Soon I also realized that this part of Glasgow has a local library, a beautiful park, a community magazine, a performance space, a rumpus room and many others.

The South Side of Glasgow is frequently regarded as unsafe by middle-class residents of the city, many of whom openly admit to having never set foot in the area. While the West End enjoys a reputation for cosmopolitanism and cultural sophistication, the South Side is often dismissed as more provincial in character. The neighbourhood grapples with challenges including littered streets, visible struggles with drug addiction and widespread issues related to alcoholism. Yet, despite these difficulties, the South Side stands as a dynamic and multicultural enclave within the predominantly white urban landscape of Glasgow. Despite all the facts, I was determined to explore the area more deeply. I began volunteering at a café on the South Side, which allowed me to discover its roads and alleys each week. I found a variety of local gems, including charity shops, pantries and South Asian grocery stores. Over time, Victoria Road became my favourite part of Glasgow. Victoria Road in Govanhill, Glasgow, is home to a variety of unique and indefinable characters, which includes Kurdish barbers, African grocers, halal butchers and Irish boozers. The tenement buildings that form a grid around Victoria Road were built during the Victorian era. Volunteering in such an area not only provided me with a sense of accomplishment amid my otherwise monotonous life but also opened a window to my fantasy world in the city, helping me fill a void and find a sense of belonging. I also tried to develop some networks in the queer circles around Glasgow. Being an organizer in queer community groups in Bangladesh and working for international organizations for cultural exchange gave me access to travel around, learning about the emerging queer movements. From Bangladesh, the vibrant images of rainbow flags at pride walks always seemed intriguing but also felt distant – not in terms of physical distance, but in how far such celebrations seemed from the reality of the queer community in Bangladesh.

Shortly after the spring, it was June and Pride month was approaching. I went with a few other friends. The walk took place around the area of Glasgow Green where Doulton Fountain[6] is located. I felt good being there, being with some like-minded people. I was strolling around the stalls and learning about their activities and looking at the people wearing gimp masks. There were also promotions for plastic surgery clinics at the forefront of the pride. My eyes were looking for a South Asian group or a person of colour, but soon I realized that promotional merchandise and commerce are key to Pride. Shortly after, one of my friends who had joined me on the walk began working for a well-known financial institution. The following year, during Pride, I saw them with their office colleagues standing in front of a large caravan emblazoned with the institution's logo, which was highly visible throughout the event. Surrounded by glittering decorations, I felt that, while these moments of fabulousness might seem distant from the struggles faced by queer communities in Bangladesh, they represent a form of liberation for queer migrants navigating economies of sexual desire. While there are organizations in Scotland that support queer individuals, South Asian queer individuals may feel cultural pressure as the organizations do not fully understand or address the specific cultural challenges they face. Realizing this, I started organizing potlucks at home and the university. The evening discussions became one of the important attractions of the week. We planned for road trips and discussed visa status and the situation of the queer community groups in Bangladesh.

I'm reflecting on a time when, much like in many other places, the backlash against trans recognition was intensifying in Bangladesh. While I had often heard about homophobia in Europe, my own experience in Bangladesh was quite different. For the occasion of LGBT+ History Month, the university raised a rainbow flag. I was taken aback by the hostile social media comments.

> Fuck you! No one wants this fucking flag!
>
> I need the unlike button 👎
>
> Fuck this University boycott this fucking University
>
> This made me unfollow
>
> Shame on this bloody university; taking back my admission

Similarly, on one occasion, a Bangladeshi friend invited someone over with the hope of starting a romantic connection, and they stayed late into the night drinking together. Later, the guy privately confided in me that they found my friend presumptuous. However, rather than expressing this to my friend directly, they stayed the entire evening, not indicating their discomfort. This incident resonated with a broader pattern I've noticed in my efforts to connect with queer individuals in Glasgow: the prevalence of ghosting culture. People often maintain a facade of friendliness, avoiding direct communication about their discomfort. Later, however, they disengage abruptly, often blocking the other person without explanation. This performative niceness, followed by a sudden withdrawal, has consistently puzzled me. From a sociological perspective, ghosting can be linked to broader cultural patterns, including individualism and avoidance of conflict or narcissism. In my personal view, this behaviour often stems from an underlying sense of superiority, where individuals perceive their values, behaviours and ways of life as the 'correct' or 'only' way to navigate social interactions. In their introductory note on 'Understanding Racism in Scotland', Davidson and Virdee (2018, 9) argued that in contrast to England, there has been relatively little public discussion about the historical or contemporaneous structuring power of racism in Scotland. This silence has come to be interpreted as an indication of its absence by much of the Scottish elite, including its political parties, helping to consolidate a now powerful myth that there is 'no problem here'. This perceived superiority may lead to a dismissal of others who do not align with their expectations or norms, reinforcing exclusionary dynamics within certain social contexts.

There exists an unspoken tension between Scotland's progress in queer rights and the unique challenges faced by South Asian queer individuals living here. Despite Scotland's advancements in LGBT+ rights, South Asian queer people often experience a different reality: cultural differences can lead to significant pressures and fears, such as the risk of rejection, ostracization or even violence from their communities. Many South Asian queer individuals may feel hesitant to fully express their identities, grappling with a complex intersection of cultural expectations and personal authenticity.[7]

রোহিতের কথা (Rohit's narrative): From Kolkata to Glasgow

In July 2009 the Delhi High Court struck down parts of the colonial sodomy law Section 377 declaring that criminalization of gay sex was unconstitutional. I was living in Kolkata, West Bengal, for twenty-one years, my entire life at that time, under the constant fear of being a 'criminal'. I had been volunteering and later interning at Sappho for Equality, a feminist queer collective and other queer and sexual health charities in the city for around two years at that time. I was aware of queer organizing and grassroots public advocacy work that had been happening which led up to this momentous decision of 'decriminalizing' homosexuality. Within moments of the declaration, my social media pinged that a group of activists were making their way to Academy for Fine Arts/Nandan area, a creative quarter in the city that has also played host to numerous protests and rallies.

> বাংলার মাটি বাংলার জল
> বাংলার বায়ু বাংলার ফল
> পুণ্য হউক পুণ্য হউক

> Soil of Bengal, water of Bengal,
> Air of Bengal, fruits of Bengal.
> Let them be sacred, let them be sacred

Rabindranath Tagore's famous song composed in 1905 during the proposed partition of Bengal on religious lines was sung by activists as we cried tears of happiness and hugged each other. At that time, I did not realize that a couple of months later I would have to say goodbye to my beloved city. My journey to England and later Scotland was shaped by the romanticized idea of 'foreign'. The 1990s brought with it globalization, and upwardly mobile English-educated families in India like mine saw distant cousins and relatives move abroad and coming back with stories of a 'better future'. The quest to move abroad started my early membership of the British Council Library and afternoons spent at the American centre poring over glossy university brochures with happy smiling white students as I prepared to take the mandatory Test of English as Foreign Language. Peeping through the university prospectuses was also the occasional rainbow flag – promising an imaginary queer utopic future.

London was a culture shock. Landing in Heathrow, Indian students were asked to form an 'orderly queue' by an officer in the airport, shouting 'if you don't understand English maybe you shouldn't be here'. It was a shocking introduction to the country. I am an English-educated *desi* immigrant often having to negotiate my presence here through complicated race and class regimes. I am a classic example of what Sunil Gupta calls a 'sexual exile'. Like him, as a queer person I felt the repressive atmosphere of growing up in India was not for me, there was very little that I could recognize. Armed with the social capital of education and a generous full scholarship I made my way to London, somehow thinking this is where I could be free and live my life as a queer man. I still remember my conversation with the officer at border control. The piercing questions were to somehow make me trip up and tell them I was not a 'genuine migrant.' I was told to step aside because unlike other passengers I had not brought my mandatory tuberculosis certificate, so I needed to get screened at the airport. I was ushered into a holding area where my passport was taken from me. I looked around the room – there were only a couple of passengers from my flight. Everyone else had done their homework much better than me. Next to me was a Nigerian family of siblings. I struck up conversation with Ade who was twenty. He was travelling with four siblings who looked younger than me. He looked panicked just like me. His mother worked here in London at a hotel and had 'sponsored' her children to come. The officer called him and, looking at him and his siblings, brusquely said: 'Oh your mother has been very busy.' I was suddenly terrified that these people would be deciding my fate. Thankfully an hour later I was cleared to collect my luggage and make my way to my unknown future. This episode has left an indelible mark of what would be a constant fear and anxiety about dealing with border control, something that continues till today. It also became a genesis for my lifelong concern about the operations of gendered and sexualized power that is racialized and charged through multiple (unequal) flows of capital.

In 2010 after completing my postgraduate education I was still contemplating whether to stay or go back to India. England turned out to be far from the queer utopia I had envisioned, leaving me with a persistent sense of being 'out of place' that I did not want to endure. Even the bars in London's Soho, which I had heard so much about, felt constricted. One incident that I remember was joining a group of (mostly) white friends on a visit to GAY, the eponymous gay bar off Wardour Street. As we got ready to go in, the bouncer asked me, 'are you sure you want to come here, this is a gay bar for LGBT people'. I felt singled out and questioned myself at this point if being brown was incommensurate with me also being queer. How was this any different from people back home who thought being queer was a white thing I asked myself? Would I have to give up the markers of being proudly Bengali to fit in and be part of the respectable queer world of London? It was during this time that I came in contact with Naz Project London and joined their queer Asian youth group Ehsaas and later Dost. We used to meet in a tiny room for a monthly get together in Archer Street Studios in Soho. This became a lifeline for me, as I connected with other queer Asians who were navigating similar situations. Suddenly, we were speaking the same language – sharing our experiences with family, faith and race, all while dealing with the challenges of being gay. I had finally found my community!

My arrival in Glasgow happened almost a decade later when I moved to the city with a job in 2020 navigating the pandemic lockdown. It was difficult to try and form a community here during that time with not being able to socialize much and being kept busy with the expectations of a new job. However, compared to London, Glasgow felt much more welcoming. Perhaps it was because I had become more resilient and learned to assert my brownness even in hostile spaces, but I felt less scrutinized as I walked the Asian-dominated streets of Cathcart Road and did my shopping at the corner shops on Victoria Road. The road is a lively, bustling street in the south side of the city, famous for its independent shops and restaurants, and serves as an important route linking the city centre to Queens Park. The report, *Slavery, Abolition and the University of Glasgow*, admitting Glasgow's role in benefiting from slavery had just been published. These discussions were happening in the university's grand campus in the West End – a quiet, green area that feels very different from the diverse Victoria Road in Govanhill. Moving between these two spaces, so different in atmosphere and history, reflected the contrasts within Glasgow itself – a city shaped by both its colonial past and its vibrant present. My South Side neighbourhood was full of progressive spaces, like the queer Yiddish anarchist pay-what-you-can café Pink Peacock, and the queer bookstore Category Is Books, which proudly called itself 'fiercely independent and queer'. I joined queer community events and met some amazing people. But like many progressive queer spaces, these places were temporary and struggled with money. Sadly, Pink Peacock closed in 2024. The reasons were complicated. Money problems were part of it, but there was also local backlash. The owners, who had moved from London, were criticized for telling long-time locals and other business owners how to run things. Their 'fuck the police' posters also brought police attention to an area that was already over-policed, causing more tension. On top of that, there were issues with anti-Semitism in the way some people reacted to them. It was a sad ending for a space that meant so much to the community (also see Taylor 2023).

I was also grateful to have met Churnjeet and have since become good friends and collaborators. However, something was still missing. When Tanvir came to Glasgow to start their PhD under my supervision, we quickly bonded over our shared Bengali heritage – my grandparents had migrated from Bangladesh during the 1947 partition. Our connection was immediate, strengthened by our mutual involvement in queer organizing and our understanding of the unique experiences of being Bengali and queer across borders. We decided to organize a queer Bengali film festival that would showcase films from both Bengals – West Bengal and Bangladesh.[8] This festival aimed to spark critical conversations about the challenges faced in queer activism and issues of belonging. This was the first time a queer Bengali event had been organized in Scotland and 'Odbhut: Queer Cinema from Two Bengals' had Bengali queer people coming from all across Scotland, with audience members effectively 'finding my community'. Many spaces are not welcoming to queer people of colour or working-class queers due to high levels of securitization, a lack of inclusive spaces for those who don't consume alcohol and the expectation to spend money. Building cross and intra ethnic/faith alliances are not without challenges. Casual conversation can encapsulate how much the queer movement has been taken over by politics of respectability and visibility over concerns around livelihood and liveability. For us organizing a Bengali queer film festival was to provide quality cinema from the two Bengals and offer a space for community-building.

We politically embrace the idea of two Bengals, not just as a romanticized notion of the colonial injury caused by partition, but also as a way of asserting ourselves within the landscape of Glasgow, Scotland. This includes remembering Kazi Nazrul Islam's famous lines of Joy Bangla (Hail Bengal), while also standing together as a community with shared concerns about racial and sexual politics.

জয় বাংলার পূর্ণচন্দ্র, জয় জয় আদি-অন্তরীণ!
জয় যুগে-যুগে-আসা-সেনাপতি, জয় প্রাণ আদি-অন্তহীন!

Hail to Bengal's full moon, hail to the eternally enveloped,
All hail to the warriors who came here generation after generation, hail to the ceaseless eternal souls.

Glasgow city and the University of Glasgow can be seen as offering spaces where queer people of colour can have same-sex encounters, form intimate connections and build community. However, the university and the city are connected in some ways but also quite different from each other. The university can feel separate from the more informal, lively queer spaces found in the city. As we move between these spaces, we see how they both overlap and differ, creating complex experiences of belonging. The global queer movement is increasingly being shaped by a neoliberal, casteist, classist and racist agenda, making the festival even more important. These events became a way to express and share Bengali queer lives – experiences that are real and felt within these communities, but often hard to see or understand in mainstream spaces.

Conclusion

In this chapter, we have embraced autoethnography as a feminist method. The two narratives we share offer a plurality of truths. Our personal experiences as two queer Bengalis living in Glasgow, despite its historical and social context, also raise questions about our relationship as immigrants to both the nation we have migrated to and the one we left behind. The social and material realities shaping our experiences are influenced by global flows of capital, labour and an imperial, racialized history. Glasgow, as the second city of the British Empire, has long been complicit in this history, and these global connections continue to shape the city's identity and our place within it. Autoethnography, as Ettore (2017, 1) has so eloquently argued, can generate useful ways of creating knowledge and collective agency and the 'interior language of emotional vulnerability and at times wounding'. Our joint narratives express trauma, grief and joy within the historical context of sexual displacement as we forge new identities and contest racialized imaginings imposed upon us. We also reflect on what it means to inhabit queer liveable lives – a difference between 'bneche thaka' and 'tike thaka' (to live and to survive). As Banerjea and Browne (2023) remind us there isn't a simple linear hierarchy and normative temporality between surviving and living. What is needed for life to become as we articulate is the complex interplay between family, faith, place and above all a solidarity towards organizing. In a city shaped by heteronormativity and whiteness, we have sought to create a space where we can collectively imagine a life worth living on our own terms. Glasgow, like much of Scotland, remains marked by these structures. Heteronormativity is often embedded in institutions, social norms and even in the way public spaces are designed, while whiteness continues to dominate much of the city's cultural and social life. From the university to local communities, there are often subtle, yet powerful, expectations about who belongs and how one is expected to live. As Banerjea et al. (2018, 7) remind us, 'life after all is an unruly vector, always escaping empires, biopolitical attempts to discipline and regulate our bodies and pleasure'.

তুমি কে আমি কে
সমকামী
আমাদের প্রতিবাদ আমাদের ভাষা
চিৎকার করো

Who are you and who am I
Queers
Our resistance in our language
Shout out

The experiences of South Asian queer individuals in Scotland are shaped by a complex interplay of cultural, religious and social factors. Our cultural context often creates significant tension between personal identity and societal expectations, leading to fears of rejection, ostracization or even violence. Overcoming these challenges requires a multifaceted approach, including fostering community dialogue and developing culturally competent support systems, for an inclusive Scotland.

As we complete this chapter, our hometowns are engulfed in turmoil. In Bangladesh, a popular uprising has led to the ousting of the prime minister, with tragic loss of lives. In Kolkata, the streets are filled with protesters demanding justice following the brutal sexual assault and murder of a doctor. This situation highlights the challenge of navigating two worlds as queer Bengali migrants. While we stay in constant touch with our queer and trans friends to ensure their safety, we also receive support to look after our own well-being. Amidst these turbulent times, we have found solace in the support and friendship of our queer friends and allies in Glasgow, who have reached out to check on us and offer their care.

Notes

1. In 2022, 12.9 per cent of Scotland's population identified as belonging to a minority ethnic background, up from 8.2 per cent in 2011. The representation of Indian, Scottish Indian and British Indian communities increased from 0.62 per cent in 2011 to 0.97 per cent in 2022, while the Bangladeshi, Scottish Bangladeshi and British Bangladeshi populations grew from 0.07 per cent to 0.13 per cent during the same period.
2. Glasgow Zine Library is a community archive and zine library based in Govanhill, Glasgow, established in 2018. They are the largest independent zine library in the UK.
3. Samosa is a fried or baked pastry from South Asia and West Asia that's typically triangular or cone-shaped and filled with spiced vegetables or meat. The word 'samosa' comes from the Persian word *Sambosag*, which means 'triangular pastry'.
4. Kadak Chai is a strong tea in taste and colour compared to regular English tea. This sweet Indian tea is made with a blend of fermented black tea leaves, ginger and spices such as black pepper, cardamom, cinnamon, fennel and cloves.
5. A burka is an enveloping outer garment worn by some Muslim women which fully covers the body and the face.
6. Built to commemorate the 1887 Golden Jubilee of Queen Victoria by the Royal Doulton Company, the fountain was also designed to commemorate Britain's achievements. Four groups of figures are sited within open arches on the lower tier, representing the territory of the British Empire, Australia, Canada, India and South Africa.
7. Also see S. Biswas, R. K Dasgupta and C. Mahn, 'Queer Politics in Times of New Authoritarianisms', *South Asian Popular Culture* 21, no. 2 (2023): 147–53.
8. Funded by a Carnegie Trust Grant for the project 'Queer Cinema and Public Space: Festivals as Community Making in India' and a Thinking Culture Grant (University of Glasgow) for the project '*Ami Shomokami*: Queer Cinemas from Bengal'.

References

Banerjea, N. and Browne, K. *Liveable Lives: Living and Surviving LGBTQ Equalities in India and the UK*. London: Bloomsbury, 2023.

Banerjea, N., Dasgupta, D., Dasgupta, R. K. and Grant, J. *Friendship as Social Justice Activism: Critical Solidarities in a Global Perspective*. Calcutta: Seagull, 2018.

Biswas, S., Dasgupta, R. K. and Mahn, C. 'Queer Politics in Times of New Authoritarianisms', *South Asian Popular Culture* 21, no. 2 (2023): 147–53.

DasGupta, D. 'Cartographies of Friendship, Desire, and Home; Notes on Surviving Neoliberal Security Regimes', *Disability Studies Quarterly* 34, no. 4 (2014). https://dsq-sds.org/index.php/dsq/article/view/3994/3789.

Davidson, N. and Virdee, S. 'Introduction: Understanding Racism in Scotland'. In N. Davidson, M. Liinpää, M. McBride and S. Virdee (eds), *No Problem Here: Racism in Scotland*, pp. 9–12. Edinburgh: Luath Press, 2018.

Ettore, E. *Autoethnography as Feminist Method*. London: Routledge, 2017.

Puar, J. K. *Terrorist Assemblages: Homonationalism in Queer Times*. Durham, NC: Duke University Press, 2007.

Taylor, Y. *Working Class Queers. Time, Place and Politics*. London: Pluto, 2023.

16

Lessons in geography: Learning from Maud Sulter

Natasha Thembiso Ruwona

My introduction to Maud Sulter (1960–2008) was in 2018 after the mention of her name in a text written by Evan Ifekoya in the publication *Surviving Art School: An Artist of Colour Toolkit* (2015), during my second year of art school. I then located as much of her writing as possible across the libraries in Edinburgh – the traces of her life and work were sparse, yet scattered across my living room floor in an attempt to understand her journey and my own. Maud was many things; Scottish, Ghanaian, queer, Black, mixed-race, working class. She was also an artist, writer, photographer, filmmaker and curator, among other titles. Her contributions to Black and feminist art movements were significantly unrecognized in Scotland when I first began researching her at the time, so although frustrating, it was no wonder I hadn't heard of her. Since that point, my research into Maud's life and practice has spanned various outcomes; a presentation for a symposium by St Andrew's University and Glasgow Women's Library; a publication *PASSIONS*, where nine Black Scottish artists or those with relationships to Scotland responded to Maud's publication *Passion: Discourses on Blackwomen's Creativity* (1990); a publication featuring contributions by Black women and women-of-colour creatives. In 2022, I directed *maud*, a fifteen-minute short film considering her memory via conversations with Black artists who are making art in Scotland today and who reflect on Maud's important contributions to excavating history, challenging art world politics and community-building. In this chapter,[1] I turn my attention to Maud as a conduit between place and people. Through my practice as an artist, geographer and community event producer, I am interested in the ways we can build community by creating space to gather (physically or otherwise). I am also curious about Maud's role as a placemaker – bridging places, identities and people together through her creative practice. I speak to these *lessons in geography* by offering an analysis of Maud's work and by being in conversation with Glasgow-based community-builder Mahasin Ahmed.

Place is a strong theme in Maud's practice – placing people, placing history, placing time, placing location – and I have always been interested in where she was at the time of creating her works – her moves from Scotland to England and her return; there is something about having physical distance from a location that often makes it more possible to think about elsewhere. Maud seems to inhabit many places and also non-places, and perhaps through her mixed-race identity, it could be read as lending itself to thinking about geography as something unfixed, moving fluidly between here and there, with considerations of belonging and where home might be inhabited. As she plays around with geography as a lesson in thinking transculturally, I like to think about her work as it relates to Black Geographies, and in particular how she has contributed to Black Scottish Geography. Black geographies are 'subaltern or alternative geographic patterns that work alongside and beyond traditional geographies and a site of terrain of struggle' (McKittrick 2006, 7). Black geographies consider the entanglements between race, space and place, specifically how the experiences of race and human geography coexist with tension in the afterlife of slavery and colonization.

Maud's poetry is often in conversation with Scotland, whether meeting with lover(s) across the landscape, nods to Black Scottish History or writing in Scots. In her poem *Passion Plays*, part of the *As a Blackwoman* series, she writes: 'Tomorrow my candy, My caramel sweet we two in Edinburgh shall meet' (Sulter 1989, 17). In *Dreich Day* she opens with 'Ice cold grey sky ahead entering the kingdom of Fife' and finishes with the line 'Walking the links at St. Andrews we kissed holding each to the other treasuring the moment for the sake of itself nothing between us and Denmark except that tomorrow you leave me' (19). These lines contemplate Scotland as a place of romance where Maud travels with her lover across its sites. This tender approach to writing about love and placemaking about Scotland feels somewhat significant as being authored by someone who was a Black Queer Scottish woman. Her writing in the Scots language is scattered throughout *As a Blackwoman*, including in the *Scots Triptych* section where she writes 'Never too busy to stoap fur a chat, a natter, a rap, steamin hoat' (13). This creates a tribute to her roots by using a language not normally expected to be spoken by a Black person and challenges preconceived notions of language, race and national identity. I remember hearing Maud's voice on a recording for the first time in 2021 and being pleasantly surprised to hear her Scottish accent was so strong, expecting it to have dwindled significantly after time spent away. I have lost count of the number of times people have heard my accent and told me that they didn't know there were Black people in Scotland. By naming and placing Scotland within her poetry, Maud rejects a homogenous notion of who a Scottish person is and who might inhabit the landscape.

In the *Zabat: Poetics of a Family Tree Collection* poetry series (1990), Maud traces Black history in Scotland. 'I dream of Blackwomen in the Scottish Court / Their dresses and jewels / They raise their eyebrows at the ridiculous cold' (Sulter in Mabon 1998, 148). Here, she refers to the two enslaved African women brought to Scotland via Leith, Edinburgh, in 1506 and who were 'gifted' to King James IV.[2] This reference is continued in another work, *The Alba Sonnets* (1995), where she says: 'Black people at the Scottish court, fired up, hot tempers wild emotions, and jealous' (Sulter in Mabon 1998, 150). Maud didn't shy away from discussing Scottish racism as evidenced in her poems *The Privilege of the Fairskinned* (1989) and *By the Pond* (1990) where she confronts the erasure of mixed-race identity in Scotland and the lack of care towards young Black Scottish girls (Mabon 1998, 151). Throughout Maud Sulter's practice, transatlantic and personal histories are excavated, often becoming intertwined. Scotland becomes a meeting place – a point of departure and sometimes of return. I reflect on this in the context of Maud leaving for England and her eventual arrival back. Her writing about

Scotland reflects a fraught relationship that feels like a tension I have myself felt, and that others have shared with me when speaking about their experiences of being Black in Scotland, and so often how this tension can lead to moving elsewhere. As evidenced by Maud's success and breadth of work, leaving Scotland allowed her access to a Black and feminist creative community on a much larger scale than was available within Scotland at that time. I understand why she left, but I am also left wondering what inspired her to come back and if distance and time did indeed heal this tension.

Maud built a community of practice as an active member of several feminist and artist communities, visible through her collaboration with many voices and faces, past and present throughout her work. In the *Zabat* (1989) photographic series, she documented Black women as Greek muses, and in the *Significant Others* (1993) photographic series, she reproduced photos of family pictures, capturing thumbprints alongside general wear and tear. Further to her commitment to 'Put black women back in the center of the frame', by sharing the work of her peers and community, she started Urban Fox Press, a publishing press, the Blackwomen's Creativity Project and opened a gallery in London, Rich Women of Zurich. By studying Maud's practice, I have watched as my own practice has develop collaboratively, beginning with the processes of creating the *PASSIONS* publication and *maud*. In this spirit, I am interested in community-building as a practice – how we might come together and what happens once we gather. With this intention, I sat down with Mahasin, founder of Exhale.group and cofounder of Mojxmma, a QTIBPoC club night, to discuss their experiences of community-building through creativity in Scotland.

In June 2023 I facilitated a workshop, *Living Memory*, for Exhale.group as part of their *Space to Be* programme. Founded in 2022, Exhale.group is a non-profit organization which aims to create a safe space to dream, explore and connect for QTIPoC+ (queer, trans and intersex people of colour) living in Glasgow and Scotland. During the workshop, we watched *maud* and created a space for discussion and making in response to the themes of the film, which included memory, archiving and our relationship to our environments. The workshop title comes from the text *Living Memory: A Conversation with Toni Morrison*, an interview with Paul Gilroy (1988) which prompted me to consider memory as an alive entity and archiving as a process of the present, something that I feel is important, particularly for those with marginalized identities. My conversation with Mahasin (they/them) explores these themes further, while considering how to create intentional spaces for gathering and the realities of community-building. Mahasin has a background in public health, specifically working to develop meaningful community engagement within research. They also have experience in mental health advocacy, working with LGBTQIA+ groups and racialized communities. In their spare time, they like to DJ!

This conversation took place in Glasgow, April 2024.

Natasha: How did Mojxmma and Exhale come about?
Mahasin: My friend and I started Mojxmma because we grew up in Edinburgh and felt like there weren't any nightlife spaces where we felt comfortable to be ourselves as queer people of colour so we thought we should try and make something for people like us. We had our first party in the Wee

Red Bar, which was really nice. We were trying to establish some sort of community and a place where we could feel comfortable, hear the music that we wanted to hear, wear what we wanted to wear, feel included and seen. With Exhale Group, I started that in 2022, and that came out of doing Mojxmma for a few years and being in Glasgow and seeing that there were quite a lot of queer spaces in Glasgow like Bonjour which was a really inclusive, positive space. But at the same time, all of the spaces that I enjoyed going to were nightlife spaces, and I didn't always want to be in those types of spaces, I felt like I couldn't make genuine connections with people all the time. Being in a new city, I wanted to make friends – I wanted to try and actually get to know people. When you just see people in the club all the time it's kind of hard to do that. There's also people who don't want to go out, people who don't drink, people who need to be away from those spaces. So I just thought we need to have a space that's wholesome and sober and that's more focused on wellbeing and community as well.

Natasha: Could you describe what a night at Mojxmma looks like and then a session at Exhale?

Mahasin: With Mojxmma nights, we try to make it as exciting as possible, and I guess, quite a different space from Exhale. It's community-focused but we have to invest a lot more money and time into it and rely on ticket sales to make the parties happen, so we need to make sure we're offering something attractive and different because there are more queer and POC-run things in Glasgow now. One way we do this is by throwing themed parties, because we always try to encourage self-expression – we want people to come and dress up and do what they wouldn't normally do in their day-to-day lives. We want it to be a space where people feel free to be themselves and go crazy! Exhale is more about making genuine connections and fostering resilience in the QTIPoC+ community. Thinking about what people in the community want and what they would benefit from. I try to be quite intentional about the types of workshops we do, thinking about the different insights or skills people could get from a session.

Natasha: I noticed Exhale seems to have a focus on creative expression. In my work, I find that taking part in workshops feels like a good entry point to thinking about a larger theme or a topic, and whether it's doing a playful exercise such as writing exercise or collaging or drawing as a way to think about something bigger or maybe issues for communities. Is that how you see it too?

Mahasin: That's exactly it. When I was first setting it up, I was thinking, what's the easiest way to try and get people together and build a community? There needs to be something to facilitate that. If I advertised it as just coming and meeting people, I think people would feel quite anxious about it. Instead, they can bond over an activity and think 'I would like to try and do this' or 'this sounds interesting', so it gives them the motivation to come. Then it's also a catalyst to bring all of the other elements together, for example, I always provide a meal in the evening, and I try to think of it in a way that some people might not be getting a proper meal some nights of the week, but at least if they come there, they can be guaranteed that. So I try to bring in little elements like that and make everything completely free, cover travel expenses, etc. I was thinking about all the different circumstances that people in our community might have been under and are facing – for example, the sessions are for people aged 16+, and a majority of that group might still be living at home so they might need a space sometimes away from that family unit to be in a different environment with people that are like them.

Natasha: What are your experiences organizing community spaces?

Mahasin: Once the people are there, everything kind of falls into place, but getting to the point where people are in the room is the toughest part. Like most things, it's to do with money, with Exhale, especially. I'd volunteered for charities and worked for them, but I didn't really know what went into them, really the work and the time and the money. So I under-budgeted and underestimated how to do it, and then I was in the middle of it and thinking 'this is a lot more than I expected it was going to be'. So I've been quite lucky that I can work another job, part time, but it has reduced my income dramatically. But I'm happy doing it because I like doing it, but some people who have kids or something, don't have the luxury of doing that, so it's definitely hard. I think sometimes when you're doing a lot of things off your own back, you can put a lot of pressure on them and you want them to do well and you are so passionate about it. So I had some moments where, like, with both Mojxmma and Exhale, when fewer people show up I felt disheartened in the beginning and perhaps took it more personally, but over time, I've realized that that's just the nature of things. It's not personal. We live in a complicated world. A lot of people in our community suffer with mental health and lots of different things, and just wake up sometimes and can't be bothered, and the weather is always rubbish. So I think it's like trying to deal with setbacks, trying to keep yourself motivated when it's just you trying to do everything and you're on limited resources, and, yeah, also just trying to make sure that it's things people are interested in doing while paying people fairly, and getting the venues, etc. that are aligned to your values.

Natasha: What's your process for programming?

Mahasin: In the beginning, I did a lot of planning and put a lot of thought into it, but as the first project of Exhale developed, it wasn't really working out in the way that I thought it would. I programmed writing, film and then art workshops, followed by open creative sessions. I envisioned it would be the same or a similar group of people from the beginning that would attend, and they'd go through this journey of getting inspiration, learning new skills and opening their minds to different things through the facilitated workshops. And then we'd have the open sessions, where they'd use everything they've learned and then we would collate everything and create something together. However, the way it actually worked out was people coming to what they were interested in, with mostly different people at each workshop. When the open creative sessions started, sign-ups were quite low, so I thought that maybe people aren't interested in just coming to an open thing and they probably need something specific that they are interested in coming to. So I started adapting from there. Recently, there have been a couple of people who come along to the Exhale events, who've put on their own workshops after being like 'I really want to share this with the community', so that's been nice. It's coming to the end of that project now, and in the past few months we have established a wee group, which I'm really happy about, and they all are really keen on helping out and doing things. So I think in the future, I would like them to co-design the projects and for it to be more community-led.

Natasha: How do you create intentional spaces?

Mahasin: For Mojxmma we always try to be quite explicit about what kind of behaviour is not going to be tolerated at our events. So posting on Instagram and on our event tickets about what won't be tolerated, and we're quite specific as well. Instead of just being like 'Don't be unkind to people', we say 'No homophobia, no fatphobia, no racism', etc. Just being clear that this is a space for everyone. With the themes, we usually post inspiration for how people can dress up, etc. We try to make sure that we include different body types and different ethnicities to visually show that everyone's welcome there, and not just booking super popular people – we don't care so much about popularity. We also try to do sliding scale tickets and things like that to make it more accessible. It's a shame, since Bonjour closed we've not used a physically accessible venue because there are not many in Glasgow that are affordable and have inclusive security, so that's something that we're hoping to change.

I think with Exhale, the first few workshops that we did, the artists used quite radical language, and spoke about radical themes. So I was trying to show people that this was a space where it's safe to talk about those types of things and really be honest about the world that we live in and the situations that we're in. We've spoken about quite hard-hitting stuff, and everyone in the room has been strangers, but we've all opened up because we've had the facilitators create space for that. And sometimes, if I see that the group is quite shy, I'll share something myself to show that this is an okay place to be vulnerable – then people usually follow after that. I'll try to say something in the beginning about maintaining confidentiality in and outside of the space so people feel safer.

Natasha: I am thinking about Scotland as a context, and why it's important to have these sorts of spaces here.

Mahasin: In a lot of spaces that I've been in that have been queer-led or POC-led, they still have the hierarchies of outside life – for example, there can be hierarchies of gender, income, etc., and a lot of cliquey behavior, so the subtleties of wider society are replicated in the different groups. When you have the intersection of identity, you're coming together because you all know that you don't really belong and feel safe in the majority of spaces so it does make it more welcoming by nature. Although there are still a lot of different cultures, religions and experiences within the queer POC community, there's still a basic empathy and understanding with each other that you might not get as much by being of that identity in another space.

Natasha: There are a lot of queer people of colour in Scotland, to a certain extent. It's not a large number, because just being a person of colour is a minority, but I'm thinking about the necessity of these spaces to come together because of this – in solidarity.

Mahasin: Growing up, I felt like there was not much happening here. I always saw myself moving somewhere else like New York or London – I thought, oh, there are so many people from different backgrounds and so many things to do. It's important to feel like there are things in the place that you're from too, and the place that you live in, and that exciting things can happen as well for your community, created by people who are from where you're from.

Natasha: It's like a sense of belonging, I suppose, isn't it? And feeling like as you say, there are things to do and places to go so you can feel that that's a space where you can show up, and not compromise on your identity in any way.

Mahasin: And even just being able to meet people. If you've grown up in a school where there weren't any people like you or people with similar interests and experiences, and then you can come to a group where there are people like that, or a club night or something, just helps you feel more connected.

Natasha: Has your relationship with Scotland changed, or has your relationship with place changed through community organizing?

Mahasin: I grew up in Edinburgh, but now everything I do is in Glasgow. I always tell people that I prefer it, but then if I didn't have these spaces, and there weren't the other things going on, maybe I wouldn't feel that way. It is those spaces that make me enjoy living here. Not just the ones I created, but the ones other people have too. It is those community spaces that make me feel welcome, and give me a place to go with my friends or to meet people. It is those things that make the city what it is for me.

Natasha: I'm just thinking about your work, and how you see it with processes of archiving and the legacy within that.

Mahasin: I've never really thought about it before until I created Exhale because I was trying to do Instagram posts of queer POC figures in Scotland for content but when you look into it, it's not documented at all. It makes you feel like no one was here, or like four people were here in the last fifty years. So then it doesn't make you feel very good about your identity or where you live. So I think archiving is really important to give people that sense of belonging, representation, and to make them feel that they have a history and are capable of doing all the cool things that people from our community have done in the past. I thought about it a lot when Bonjour closed because I was like, that was such an amazing space, and my life in Glasgow wouldn't have been what it is if that never existed – I couldn't imagine. We probably wouldn't have brought Mojxmma to Glasgow, because probably no other club would have brought us in because we were so small and didn't have much of a following, but they were open to it and gave us support as well. So when that closed down, it was like, oh, there's people who have never been there, people are going to move here now and have no idea that place existed. I think you need to have examples of what's happened to know what's possible. If you never have examples of things that have gone on, then you'll think it's impossible, or that it can't happen. And so it's important, yeah, for a lot of reasons.

I've been thinking about that with Mojxmma. We do take a lot of pictures, but I realized in the beginning, we were taking photos on disposable cameras. I used to just post them on Instagram, then delete them for storage, because I was like, it's fine, they're on Instagram. But then I saw something, I think it was on TikTok, talking about how we used to use Bebo and had so many photos on there that are all gone. Then it was Facebook, but people in our demographic don't really use Facebook for that anymore, and if Facebook closes we will lose everything that's on there, and the same for Instagram. So now I'm thinking we actually need to save these photos, even just things in my own life, if I delete the photo I have no evidence that that actually happened. So I've been thinking about it a lot. It comes back to what I was saying about when you're doing something yourself with little resources, spending so much time just trying to make the thing happen, that you don't have time to sit and save everything and write reflections and be very thoughtful about it sometimes because you are just trying to get it done. So it's that fine line of trying to make sure people can learn from it in the future, and also trying to make the work in the present.

Natasha: I think about archiving and space as well, because I don't understand how archives work entirely but it has to go through all these processes if you want to give something and whether they want it is a decision made. I don't know much about community archives but I think people can give things without as much of a rigorous structure. With community work, or research-based work, it can be less tangible in that sense, it's more like a journey of something, or a project. I think about that in my own work as well. When I'm making films and I've got all these bits of things that I've looked at, and they maybe aren't the film, but I still want to show them, tell the story of how I got from the A to B, because that's even as important, if not more than.

Mahasin: I think about that as well. In my other job, I work with people in community organizations and we discussed recently how organizations can close down and everything that they did was just gone. You can't learn from that process. You can't see what kind of projects they did and

	how they did it. It's just gone forever. It just lives in people's memories, and once that person doesn't have a job anymore, you can't contact them about it. It is important for, like, so many different things, not just representation, but learning. Because if you're going to do something similar that's already done before, there's so much shared knowledge.
Natasha:	It makes me think of Octavia Butler's words 'We can each of us do the impossible as long as we convince ourselves it has been done before' (Butler 1998, 168). It becomes a collaboration when we can fluidly connect across time, and for the process of archiving with each other and for each other so knowledge doesn't become lost. This is what drew me to Maud's work – I found those connections, our practices in conversation years apart, created in response to our similar geographies – Scotland and London. Studying the practice of Maud Sulter can tell us many things. Maud used creativity as a vessel to hold and challenge histories; personal and collective. Her commitment to *remember* Black women, or as she described it, 'This whole notion of the disappeared, I think, is something that runs through my work. I'm very interested in absence and presence in the way that particularly black women's experience and black women's contribution to culture is so often erased and marginalized', is disappointing as her life and practice became largely forgotten in the Scottish cultural memory until recently. While institutions might choose to misremember or forget us, Maud reminds us we can be memory-makers. As demonstrated by Maud and Mahasin, we might call upon creativity to build collectively – speaking to those who came before us, who are with us now, and those to come. As a geographer, Maud didn't shy away from the tensions that place holds, as they entangle themselves in national identity, in the wake (Sharpe 2016) of colonial histories. Maud tells us 'My work has to be placed within … my environment' (Hamid in Mabon 1998, 8) – our reminder that we are not only shaped by our environment, but we are also entangled within its call and response.

Notes

1. A version of this chapter was first presented in a symposium organized by St Andrew's University and Glasgow Women's Library: *Significant Others: Maud Sulter in Relation* in June 2022.
2. On tracing the historic presence of Black people in Scotland, see www.johngraycentre. org/transatlantic-slave-trade/black-people-in-scotland.

References

Butler, O. *Parable of the Talents*. New York City: Seven Stories Press, 1998.
Gilroy, P. 'Living Memory, an interview with Toni Morrison'. *City Limits*, 31 March–7 April 1988.

Ifeyoka, E. 'A Letter to a Future Younger Self'. In *Surviving Art School: An Artist of Colour Tool Kit*. Collective Creativity and Nottingham Contemporary, 2015.
Mabon, J. 'Europe's African Heritage in the Creative Work of Maud Sulter', *African Diaspora and Its Origins* 29, no. 4 (1998): 148–55.
McKittrick, S. *Demonic Grounds: Black Women and the Cartographies of Struggle*. Minneapolis: University of Minnesota Press, 2006.
Sharpe, S. *In the Wake: On Blackness and Being*. Durham, NC: Duke University Press, 2016.
Sulter, M. *As a Blackwoman: Poems 1982–1985*. Hebden Bridge: Urban Fox Press, 1989.
Sulter, M. *Zabat: Poetics of a Family Tree Collection Series*. Hebden Bridge: Urban Fox Press, 1990.

List of Artworks Cited

Sulter, M. *The Alba Sonnets, Sound Work*, 1995.
Sulter, M. *Significant Others, Photographic Series*, 1993.
Sulter, M. *Zabat, Photographic Series*, 1989.

17

Unintended *poiesis*

Sindhu Rajasekaran

What does it mean to be queer in a wee place? As a dysphoric teenager growing up in India many moons ago, I remember asking varied versions of this question to myself. Mostly, to be queer meant alienation. To be judged, pathologized and derided. Ironically, Indian mythology was full of queer desire and shifting sexualities, in direct contrast to the social reality I existed in. Reading mythology made me feel like I belonged. Still does. All those queer 'stories of the mind and gods of India'[1] (Calasso 1998), which inspired me to write the last poem in this wee set: 'Kā' which translates to *who* in Sanskrit, feminine form, transcendent – but I get ahead of myself. Back then as a teenager I didn't know about queer South Asian pasts, or that 'postcolonial amnesia'[2] (Wieringa 2009) was a thing. Yet I cited ancient mythology to contextualize myself to myself. Then I found transnational queer terminologies online. Over the course of my life, I've variously called myself a lesbian, a bisexual womxn, sometimes I've thought of myself as asexual, fluid – till I settled for queer. That's the version of me that I brought to Scotland.

As a lover of languages and landscapes, Scotland immediately felt like home. Home away from home. Her changing moody weather seemed to complement my mindscape. The Gaelic language's visceral connection to place mirrored my native Tamil tongue's poetic modes of *tiṇai* (திணை).[3] This inspired a synaesthesia of emotions, places, people, languages, thoughts and truths in me. Researching and writing about queer South Asian pasts[4] (Rajasekaran 2023) while in Scotland, reading through archival material like old letters and reports, I've felt like I existed between timelines for many years. In this surreal period, I (re)discovered many fascinating things about the queer South Asian past. But the most enduring truth that emerged was simple in its tenet: that love persists against all odds. Even as Empire strove to erase all notions of sexual 'deviance' in its colonies, love persisted across the lines of race, class, caste and gender.

And as fate would have it, I fell in love intensely IRL while researching this. The 'aesthetics of desire and surprise'[5] (Skorin-Kapov 2015) – the phenomenology of my own queerness possessed me. At the edge of every academic research paper, essay or piece of prose, I found myself writing poetry. Mostly sapphic, at times rambling and existential. Unintended *poiesis* if you will.

So, I present here a wee set of poems from this collection of unintended *poiesis* that came into being at the margins of my academic praxis. In them, I explore the contradictory experiences of my queer body in space and temporality. 'The mnemonics of queerness', the first poem of the set, talks of how I named/unnamed myself with queer jargon over the years of my life. Writing this poem as deep dark Scottish rainclouds threatened to break in the winter sky, I transported myself to the Madras summer, thinking of how I'd scandalized everyone I knew under the hot sun aeons ago by calling myself a lesbian. In this poem, and in those that come after, I imagine my body as an intimate landscape of desire(s), where language, discourse and memory intermingle.

The poems 'you are it' and 'small things' deal with queer temporalities. Those fleeting moments of intensity that inform the metanarrative(s) of life. Small shifts of thought. Ambiguities of existence. Of images that remain. Most of my unintended *poiesis* thinks through the 'being and nothingness'[6] (Sartre 1992) of things, I think. Like, is this real, or am I delulu to *feel* this so intensely? To make sense of myself to myself, I dwell on the momentary, the transient, the transcendent. There's a quiet creolization that happens within these poems of mine, written as they are between time(s) and space(s). The poems in this set do not speak of any one space. They belong to many places. However, the words came to me, in the queer way they came to me, in Scotland. In a (mind)space of nothingness, a space of possibility.

'Decolonial Queer Knowledges' is a poem about falling in love with what's foreign to me. Of visceral modes of practising truth and reconciliation, 'Silvery moon', 'In Search of Lost Time'[7] (Proust 1998), 'Untitled', 'Dreamer' and 'Sein Lassen' speak to the themes of queer love, loss and hope. Some of the lines from these poems are set in dreamscapes, while others are rooted to real places. These poems go forwards and backwards in time, sometimes shifting between languages, slipping into தமிழ், experimenting with (my) A1 Level German, because that's what happens when one lives in exile and speaks in tongues.

I trace the course of epigenetic traumas 'In our bodies' and find joy in the most unexpected of places. Here I spend time with my foremothers' words, translating between languages. To be queer in this wee place *of memory* is so rewarding. Because in my foremothers' language, sexuality is fluid, dynamic, fleeting. 'Queer Chronotope' maps such a mindscape. In the poem, the queer chronotope shifts once, then again, and yet again, fracturing time, merging fact and fiction, melting realities.

The mnemonics of queerness

I tell many stories of coming out
of belonging and unbelonging.
a womxn at the intersection
of colliding cultures & sexualities
the mnemonics of queerness construct
my reality

~

when my Tamil family finds out
about my same sex desires, my aunt
calls it sābālam, insatiable lust for a lover's body,
சபலம் is mercurial.

my grandmother says I'm infatuated.
that it's mōkam: a variant of
the illusory Sanskritic māyā.
it'll transform, she divines.

but I call myself a
LESBIAN
in English proper.

search up cunnilingus.
PDA outside a temple.
scandalize society.
I become an embodiment
of libidinous impurity.

~

later when I fall in love
with a man, my rebellion crumbles.
a clash of mental and
emotional states of perplexity.

in bed with him, I dream of a beautiful woman,
of water and holy basil.
I baptize myself bisexual
but nuances spill over
my mercurial body, I
seek transcendence,
between sinew and spirit.

~

I'm also asexual.
writhing in the dark, writing
about the sexual power of language,
thinking about the possibilities of noumenon,
performing motherhood. I yearn
for words that flex, for the
cathartic fluidity of my native language.

English is too disciplined; sexuality is dynamic in Tamil.

so don't label yourself, says my mother,
we are all a little ambiguous.

~

You are it
think the forbidden

speak your truths
be ambiguous
boundless

your body is cosmic
so is your mind
truth is subjective

be your body
be without your body
be androgynous

(wo)man, you will
change, feel differently
because you are it

```
            she
    ze            he
   this           that
      they     them
            all
```

Small things

in life it's those things
you find when you
least expect it –
sweet somethings, perfect nothings
a smooth pebble on the beach
hot cup of chai on a rainy day
an old poem you read again
a soft kiss on your cheek
her rosyfingers
violets on her lap
a map

Decolonial Queer Knowledges

Today
My mind is a map of the future
It's bold & bright; beyond the binaries
Of the English language

The sky is blue, the sun
Shines. I'm with her
She's by my side
Feeling the sting
She's thinking; Tamil style

Can you deny it?
Yes, it's shameless
Deviant desire – my brown skin
Hers is porcelain, our lips
Thirsty, she wants my spices, and I want
To cut through her posh British reserve

Drink that tea, baby.
She's so sweet, she gives me
A toothache, so deliciously spiteful
In passive speech she critiques my BS
But I no less, decolonize her logic
Tell her it's time for truth and reconciliation
She agrees, gives me her hand

I run my fingers along the lines
Of her palm, tell her of the future
Where she'd be mine and I hers
She smiles her twisty smile
The sun continues to shine
And together we redefine
Language and love and
Lust and désir.

Silvery moon

furious love
cry of the wolf
lusts frothy and rising

out in the middle of nowhere
indigo sky

fireflies magickal
moonlight

catch me before I slip away
into impermanence
imprint yourself
upon me

so, I'll carry your scent
the memory of you
deep in my bone

and I'll find you again
in another life

another moon
elsewhere

In Search of Lost Time

This gentle sting between us
your skin against mine
you and I, thus
this fire between my legs
the smile on your face
your green ocean eyes
I'm lost

Making meaning as I
go along humming
your song, pretty riff
that tore into
my heart

~

There will be oceans between us
hours of silence
and time that fades
memories and dreams and fantasies
yet a trace of you will remain –
till our fates cross again

And we see each other somewhere, somehow
because I will find a way
to see you smile with your ocean eyes
to hold you tight
in my arms again.

Untitled

என் உடல் அவளுக்கு
என் உயிர் அவனுக்கு
என வெறி பாடிய
காமக் கவி நான்

en uṭal avaḷukku
en uyir avanukku
ena vēri pāṭiya
kāmak kavi nāṉ

my body for her
my life for him
announced I
the poet of kāma

Dreamer
you're a reckless dreamer
                speak a reality make it exist
                        hours of longing
                                crooked love songs
distant sounds in the breeze
                fading away like caprice
                        wake up see the stars
shine in the night sky
maybe it is all a dream
                        and you a reckless dreamer

In our bodies

when we – my imaginary
foremother and I –
see our faces in the mirror
we feel dysphoric.
our features aren't feminine.
our dark lips speak words
of visceral desire in தமிழ்.
words that I struggle to translate
into English – my colonizer's language
now my own.

incongruous thrills spiral
in her breasts and mine. from
lovers sucking to infants suckling
our breasts portend pleasure, but also
this is where suffocating secrets calcify
into boulders of pain.
pain that metamorphoses into cancer
and passes down from generation
to generation, making us porous
susceptible to grief.

and there's my yōni, her vagina
the most sacred symbol of femininity
only, in our bodies, this is a space of paradox
where deviant desire flows like a river
raging and wet, spilling beyond binaries
it teems with striking serpents
and pink lotuses, incensed and serene
all at once.

by telling our queer stories
in a language that's all mine
writing against time, I
undo the knots in our bodies
and we flow on
like the night.

Blood

my blood fell
like her blood fell
among those thorns sharp
we cried shouted mourned
our love desire dreams
our tears were salty
we kissed one another
soft like rose petals
we kissed one another
redder than blood
when she bit my lips

Sein Lassen

The obsessions have come to a halt.
All the foolish games stopped.
She now sees it as it is in her head.

Anesthetized.

Sucking sir. She sits in her chair.

Thoughts are like phantoms.
Let them float.

Inhale.

Exhale.

Inhale.

Exhale.

Inhale.

Exhale.

Queer Chronotope

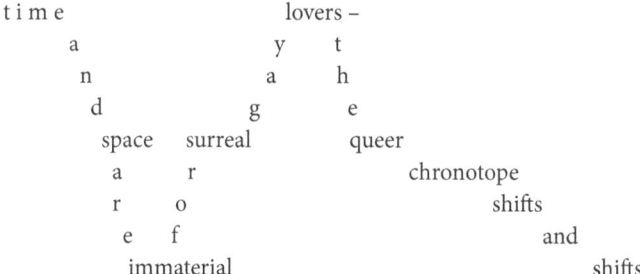

when you fall in love at sixteen with a girl for the first time
weak in the knees, willing to bend all bounds of reality

the queer chronotope shifts

when you meet a man in your twenties and make a marriage
charmed by his wits, falling in love with him in a whole new way

the queer chronotope shifts [again]

when you fall for a woman madly in your mid-thirties
feeling like it's for the first time, weak in the knees, willing to bend all bounds of reality

the queer chronotope shifts [yet again]

when your bodies collide, and you are like I've never known this before
like an electric riff between your legs, better than anything you've had with men

the queer chronotope shifts [yet and yet again]

when you think you can let her go, and keep it all casual but deep inside you
you know she's the one, the only one, the ordained, she who is meant to be
your wife

the queer chronotope shifts [yet and yet and yet again]

Kā

once the voyage is done
ritualists say the vehicle can be destroyed
the fire altar is not a fixed object

it is temporary

like my body and yours

we could burn in it how we like
for whom we love

the body is temporary

fires will burn in all sorts of altars

kā is who in Sanskrit
feminine form
transcendent

who is who is who is who?

in this fire altar I will marry you
as it burns it will carry our truth(s)

Notes

1. Roberto Calasso's book *Ka: Stories of the Mind and Gods of India* (1998) is full of sexual transgressions. I was lucky to find this book early in my life. And I thought: if the gods and goddesses could change genders and shift between masculinities and femininities, why not me?
2. Saskia Eleonora Wieringa argues that colonial and postcolonial sexual moral panics led to the erasure of 'memories of certain sexual practices, cultures, or norms, specifically related to women's sexual agency and same-sex practices' (2009).
3. 'Tamil poets used a set of five landscapes and formalized the world into a symbolism … By remarkable consensus, they all spoke this common language of symbols for some five or six generations' (Ramanujan 2009).
4. In 'Undoing the Colonial Gaze: How Gender & Sexuality Shifted in British India' (Rajasekaran 2023), I explain how India was not a space of sexual rigidity before colonization.
5. Thoughts inspired by Jadranka Skorin-Kapov's book exploring phenomenology and speculation (2015).
6. Jean-Paul Sartre's *Being and Nothingness* (1992) has inspired me in more ways than one. I love the phrasing so much that I've dreamt up whole creative non-fiction pieces

with 'being and nothingness' in the title: 'Breasts, Being & Nothingness' (2021), 'Bisexuality, Being & Nothingness' (2020) and so on.
7. I've spent a lot of lost time reading *In Search of Lost Time* (Proust 1998).

References

Calasso, R. *Ka: Stories of the Mind and Gods of India*. New York: Vintage International, 1998.

Proust, M. In Search of Lost Time, *Vol. 1*: Swann's Way. New York: Modern Library, 1998.

Rajasekaran, S. 'Bisexuality, Being and Nothingness', July 8 2020. https://gaysifamily.com/lifestyle/bisexuality-being-and-nothingness/

Rajasekaran, S. 'Breasts, Being, and Nothingness'. *Room Magazine* 44, no. 2 (2021).

Rajasekaran, S. 'Undoing the Colonial Gaze: How Gender & Sexuality Shifted in British India'. *Smashboard*, 28 January 2023. https://smashboard.org/undoing-the-colonial-gaze-how-gender-sexuality-shifted-in-british-india/

Ramanujan, A. K. 'On Ancient Tamil Poetics'. In G. N. Devy (ed.), *Indian Literary Criticism: Theory and Interpretation*, pp. 346–74. Hyderabad: Orient Blackswan, 2009.

Sartre, J.-P. *Being and Nothingness*. New York: Editions Gallimard, 1992.

Skorin-Kapov, J. *The Aesthetics of Desire and Surprise: Phenomenology and Speculation*. London: Lexington Books, 2015.

Wieringa, S. E. 'Postcolonial Amnesia: Sexual Moral Panics, Memory, and Imperial Power'. In G. Herdt (ed.), *Moral Panics, Sex Panics: Fear and the Fight over Sexual Rights*, pp. 205–233. New York: New York University Press, 2009.

Part 4

Queer Creations: Vibrations, Glitches and Curiosities

18

Queer wee filmic places: Creating a utopic gaze through queer film exhibition in Scotland

Leanne Dawson

In this chapter I home in on queer Scottish culture, specifically the exhibition of film, as a way to provide a queer wee place for people to gather, simultaneously helping to queer places, or at least make them a little less straight and heteronormative, while providing an opportunity to imagine a queer elsewhere, geographically and/or temporally. Film is an interesting cultural product as it is often created to circulate within and beyond national borders, while allowing spectators to see and even imagine an elsewhere. With queer film festivals, lesbian, gay, bisexual, trans, queer, intersex and asexual (LGBTQIA+) people learn about LGBTQIA+ life in their country and beyond, while international filmmakers travel to – and become part of – such queer festivals. These filmmakers, alongside festival workers, volunteers and audience members, create – whether temporary or more permanently – queer wee spaces and 'communities'. Indeed, identity-based festivals can transform places, offering space for those from oppressed and minoritized communities to convene for entertainment, knowledge, activism, political reasons, friendship, sex and more, including an envisioning and hoping of how things can change positively.

This chapter considers space, place, time and community in two of Scotland's queer film festivals: GLITCH, a festival described by its co-founders as a queer, trans, intersex, Black, Indigenous, people of colour (QTIBIPOC) film festival; and the Scottish Queer International Film Festival (SQIFF). Both were founded in Glasgow, ran for the first time in 2015 and have helped to queer Scotland. I begin by briefly outlining some politics relating to LGBTQIA+ Scotland and LGBTQIA+ film, in order to set the scene. I then locate both festivals, before considering how each can offer a place for queers to gather to imagine and create a better elsewhere/future. I use the idea of 'utopic gaze', outlining how this can be accessed in such queered wee filmic spaces. This also involves considering queer theory (Duggan 2002; Muñoz 2009), diversity and inclusion in film exhibition (Dawson 2020) and work from Queer Film Festival Studies (Dawson and Loist 2018).

LGBTQIA+ politics and film

The term 'queer' is used both as a noun, an umbrella term for LGBTQIA+ identities, and as a verb 'to acknowledge that mainstream culture – from which [LGBTQIA+] people have often been excluded and/or erased – can be subverted and queered through against-the-grain readings' of art, books, theatre, television and film, for example, for which it is 'a viewing strategy many [LGBTQIA+] cinema-goers had to employ in the past when their identity was not widely represented' (Dawson and Loist 2018, 2). Until recently such queer identities were not commonly represented due to the law and social stigma: for example, Scotland only legalized same-sex sexual activities between men in 1981.

Queering art and culture is important because queers have long been depicted onscreen as monstrous, evil, criminal, or they were invisible or erased. Erasure happens when an LGBTQ+ character is killed, typically as a punishment for their supposed sexual transgression, also presented as a social one, and such erasure is found across art, literature, film and television. Another form of erasure is via an invisibility, for example, the removal of a gay character or LGBQ+ storyline when adapting a book for the screen, where an overt gay relationship is translated into nothing more than friendship to be more palatable for a mainstream audience, while being read queerly by queers. Of course, there is also the issue that LGBTQIA+ people are missing from swathes of art, including film, in the first place, meaning that LGBTQIA+ viewers have long had to read interactions, looks or suchlike as queer. Film festivals are significant spaces for queers to unite and see a spectrum of queer representation, while also collectively queering things not always intended as queer by the creator and/or viewed as such by mainstream audiences.

Film can also represent socio-political realities of the past and/or the present. Section 28 was introduced by Margaret Thatcher's Conservative government in 1988 and ran until 2000 in Scotland and 2003 in England and Wales. Named after Section 28 of the Local Government Act 1988, which stated that a local authority 'shall not intentionally promote homosexuality or publish material with the intention of promoting homosexuality' or 'promote the teaching in any maintained school of the acceptability of homosexuality as a pretended family relationship' (Local Government Act 1988). This meant that schools and teachers often did not dare to mention the subject of homosexuality. *Blue Jean* (Georgia Oakley 2022) is a narrative film set in north-east England in 1988, about a lesbian teacher of physical education (stereotypes, we see you!), who tries to hide her sexuality at all costs, even when this means not helping gay pupils in times of need. This self-censorship did not just happen within schools but also spread to a number of LGBT groups, including social spaces where queer representation could be discussed, with many of these closing through fear, at a time of extreme homophobia. While the past and present are represented onscreen, including in relation to political issues, visual culture can also allow us to imagine a different – better – future, which I return to later when considering the 'utopic gaze'.

Politics always plays a role in filmmaking and film exhibition, including the types of film receiving funding to be made and/or exhibited. For example, SQIFF applied for, and won, British Film Institute (BFI) funding for a 2015 travelling same-sex marriage season to mark the legalization of this in Scotland. Duggan (2002) used the term 'homonormativity' to describe a trend in the Western world of giving rights, especially relating to family and finances (marriage, adoption, pensions, etc.), to those in same-sex relationships.[1] Many queers and queer activists also take issue with such homonormativity, including the time and money invested, which mostly benefits wealthy, white and cisgender same-sex couples. SQIFF hosted such homonormative events because of available funding, although both SQIFF and GLITCH aimed to operate differently to commercial LGBTQIA+ film festivals, which have often traditionally focussed on, and catered to, white gay men.

We need to consider such politics beyond sexuality. The Gender Recognition Reform (Scotland) Bill, for example, removes any requirement of a medical diagnosis of gender dysphoria and instead replaces this with self-identification, which lowers the age people can legally change their gender from eighteen to sixteen. It was introduced in Scotland on 2 March 2022, but on 17 January 2023, the UK government, based in Westminster, London, blocked the Scottish Bill, in an example of how a larger nation can oppress a smaller one, making it more difficult to be queer in a (comparatively) wee place when the government is only devolved for some matters and does not have full control. Trans rights have been dominating news within and beyond LGBTQIA+ communities in recent years, with Scotland's capital city of Edinburgh, the seat of the Scottish government, seeing much activism both for and against these.

Specifically, issues surround the University of Edinburgh, where multiple protests have arisen due to academics platforming speakers who are 'gender critical' and screening the documentary film *Adult Human Female* (O'Neill and Wayne 2022), which asserts that women are defined by their biological sex. Protests by trans rights activists meant the first two screenings had to be cancelled and made national headlines (e.g. *The Guardian*'s 'Edinburgh University Cancels Film Screening after Trans Rights Protests', 26 April 2023). The university eventually succeeded in screening this film, which trans students and staff stated was causing them distress and erasing their identities, while the queer wee spaces of the film festivals I discuss aimed to stand in contrast to such large, powerful hetero- and homonormative places. For context, the University of Edinburgh's chancellor is the epitome of unearned privilege, a member of the royal family: Princess Anne. The university also owns vast swathes of land and buildings across the city of Edinburgh, including renting out teaching buildings during Edinburgh's Fringe festival to make further profit, and is the city's top third employer, with over 13,000 employees.

There is a plethora of brilliant LGBTQIA+ culture in Scotland, some of it explored in Scotland's queer magazine *Somewhere for Us* (www.somewhereforus.org), launched in November 2020. The magazine, available in both print and digital versions, highlights itself as a place – some*where* – for queer people, rather than an object – some*thing* – for us. Yet the head might be eating the tail in some senses as the magazine's website discusses their Rainbow Enterprise Network and declares the University of Edinburgh – a place accused of trans- and many other -phobias and -isms – as one of its members. This highlights the difficulty of creating community and trying to find a space – *somewhere* – just for 'us'/queers, which is ethical, inclusive and embraces truly queer politics, without needing to metaphorically get into bed with organizations that are definitively not queer, whether for funding, publicity or other reasons.

Queer utopia

Time and place have been considered differently in Queer, Trans and 'Crip' Studies. The queer rethinking of time and consideration of the future was influenced at the end of the twentieth century by the AIDS epidemic, when untimely deaths could occur due to sexual acts, resulting in a diminishing future and a subsequence focus on the present. Muñoz, in *Cruising Utopia: The Then and There of Queer Futurity*, rightly argues that 'the future is only the stuff of some kids. Racialized kids, queer kids are not the sovereign princes of futurity' (2009, 95) and I argue the same is true for kids in poverty, with all of these issues multiplied when the intersectionality (Crenshaw 1989) of identities is considered. For Muñoz, minoritized subjects need utopia to have hope in capitalist cisheteropatriarchy. 'Utopia is an ideal, something that should mobilize us, push us forward. Utopia is not prescriptive; it renders potential blueprints of a world not quite here, a horizon of possibility, not a fixed schema. It is productive to think about utopia as a flux, a temporal disorganization, as a moment when the here and now is transcended by a *then* and a *there* that could be and indeed should be' (2009, 97). Because of this utopia, Muñoz argues that 'queerness is not yet here. Queerness is an ideality … a structuring and educated mode of desiring that allows us to see and feel beyond the quagmire of the present' (2009, 1). This utopia is repeatedly linked to visual culture in Muñoz's work, notably some performance art, painting and photography, which show that other possibilities exist. I argue that some queer film and film festivals should be added to this list, with the queerness of such festivals aided by the escapism of the screen, which I later draw on to create a utopic gaze. While I agree that queer in Muñoz's sense is not yet here, I continue to use the term throughout this chapter in both noun and verb form.

This focus on futurity is also present beyond academic theory. It Gets Better is a motto often told to LGBTQIA+ young people and also the name of a charity which aims to empower and connect LGBTQ+ youth globally (https://itgetsbetter.org/about/), and from which, *It Got Better* (Heather Ross 2014–16) was three seasons of television documentaries about LGBTQ+ celebrities and the struggles leading to their success. Although a better future certainly cannot be assured when hard-won rights are so easily withdrawn, people can, and want to, hope.

Locating GLITCH and SQIFF in time and place

The oldest continuously running film festival was founded in 1977 in a large city known as a gay mecca and is now called Frameline: The San Francisco International LGBTQ+ Film Festival (although Covid lockdowns created a temporary online queer film showcase in place of the festival's usual offline presence in 2020). Frameline is a big, glossy, commercial festival, in many ways unlike the two grassroots, queer festivals I consider in this chapter. Since the launch of Frameline, LGBTQIA+ festivals have been created in towns and cities with a much straighter reputation and demographic than San Francisco, therefore allowing audiences to gather queerly and imagine a queered future because identity-based film festivals are spaces where specific identities are not only represented onscreen but also often in the filmmaking teams behind the finished product, the organizing team working on the festival and the audience/attendees. Up to and including the year 2015, 373 known LGBTQ+ film festivals were established across the globe.

This figure includes GLITCH and SQIFF, whose inaugural festivals ran in 2015 (between 19–28 March and 24–27 September, respectively), in Glasgow, Scotland's largest city, and were based at the Centre for Contemporary Arts (CCA), Sauchiehall Street. SQIFF also ran in a number of other venues across the city, as well as Scotland's capital, Edinburgh, and eventually in other Scottish locations (including Aberdeen, Dundee, Stirling, Hawick and parts of the Highlands and Islands such as Inverness and Stornoway) and places beyond Scotland (e.g. London and Newcastle in England).

GLITCH belongs to a more recent trend in queer film festivals, 'with a focus on race/ethnicity, migration and intersectionality' alongside queerness (Dawson and Loist 2018, 11). This consideration of the intersections of different forms of oppression, including those who are not and do not have the privileges of being heterosexual, cisgender, white and so on, is imperative in order to carve out a more intersectional space because many mainstream LGBTQ+ bars have issues with racism and some LGBTQ+ people may struggle to come out in families and cultures that are homo- and/or transphobic (although this is certainly an issue within white families and cultures too). Clearly intersectional events, with organizers and attendees who are not homonormative and who do not carry the whole suite of privileges aside from being LGBTQIA+, can offer a space to meet people with a greater understanding of aspects of identity which could be in tension.

GLITCH grew out of Glasgow-based charity, Digital Desperados, which had been created with the intention of supporting global majority people in filmmaking. This is important considering how film is dominated by the most privileged people and the stories told in the Western mainstream are too often those of white people or, when global majority characters are included, they are often written and directed by those with no lived experience of being from the global majority. GLITCH foregrounded and celebrated those who have been oppressed and erased: people from the global majority, those who are not the sex they were assigned at birth (indeed binary gender systems are very much a project of white Western colonialism) and those who are not heterosexual. That GLITCH was a festival designed to provide a truly intersectional space not only for queers but also global majority people is crucial considering the demographics of Scotland and that it was hosted within a predominantly white city and nation (in 2022, Scotland's population was recorded as almost 93 per cent white).

One thing I did notice as a white lesbian attendee at a number of GLITCH screenings, and while hanging out in the festival's main communal space of the CCA café-bar, is that much of the audience still appeared to be white, although this does not mean they were. White LGBTQIA+ people may have attended because it was a queer event and/or because they were interested in and wanted to support global majority queer events (like me). The dominance of whiteness in a QTIBIPOC film festival space meant that people of the global majority were still in the minority at an event intended to centre them. Unlike GLITCH, SQIFF was started by a predominantly white team and, although there was always a breadth of representation, both in films and some of the advertising, it did not centre global majority people in the way GLITCH did.

White mainstreaming is also a question of naming: while both SQIFF and GLITCH adhere to contemporaneous language use in film festivals and the shift away from a solid classification of sexualities (lesbian and gay) in festival names to queerness and fluidity, SQIFF locates itself as if it were *the* representative of LGBTQIA+ film in Scotland and on the international global stage. This and the name's 'queer'ness are in tension as a queer festival is typically grassroots and subversive (as SQIFF originally aimed to be). GLITCH, however, rejected any form of national and global posturing, instead wanting to offer representation of, and a space for, those more often oppressed locally, nationally and internationally. The first GLITCH festival programme (2015) made this clear, 'we are a glitch in the system, our lives deny the lies, our complexity is dissent, we fight for love'.

SQIFF began in 2014 with a number of one-off events, including a celebration of trans lives and film at the University of Edinburgh's John McIntyre Conference Centre, before the university and transphobia became so publicly linked. The festival launched in 2015 and is Scotland's only active LGBTQIA+ film festival. After a temporary shift online (May and June 2020) during Covid lockdowns, it returned in a smaller offline form, which grew back to its full-size festival. GLITCH, on the other hand, ran for three editions overall, every two years from 2015 to 2019. That SQIFF celebrated its ninth edition in 2024 is significant considering queer film festivals tend to have a shelf life of around ten years, often because they are founded and run by people who give their time voluntarily and who also often do activist work and so on, so find themselves dealing with burnout (see Dawson and Loist 2018).

A significant change of team after the 2019 festival, after five in-person editions of SQIFF, has likely contributed to its longevity as has the fact it is a festival with paid roles, alongside a team of unpaid volunteers (including me as chair of the festival and co-creator and host of numerous events, from the first edition until 2019). Positively, the current SQIFF team comprises more people from the global majority than it did, and they continue to shape the festival, including its transformation into a charity, alongside both the unqueer establishment of a SQIFF office in the CCA building and SQIFF becoming a BAFTA-qualifying festival (now part of identifying films for BAFTA categories Best British Short Film and Best British Short Animation). GLITCH, meanwhile, was run by a team of two, who were active in a number of film and arts projects, alongside their paid work. Queer venues, spaces and initiatives are often sustained by unpaid labour, across time and place; this is not merely queer film festival or Scotland-specific and is also why queer spaces and events can only be wee: capitalism and queerness are in tension.

A utopic gaze in a queer wee space and time

Both SQIFF and GLITCH aim/ed to provide a – temporary – queer wee space for those under the LGBTQIA+ umbrella, and beyond, to meet while helping to queer the venues and towns and cities in which they have run. 'People Make Glasgow', the famous

2014 strapline used in advertising in and around the city, played on Glasgow's rivalry with Edinburgh, whose history, culture and beauty, both natural and architectural, effortlessly attract tourists even though residents have a reputation for being wealthy and even snobby (gentrification means many less wealthy locals have been forced and/ or priced out of several areas). It very much is the case that people – queer people specifically – make Glaswegian festivals, GLITCH and SQIFF, in all ways: by creating and running them, making the films and arts exhibited at them, and coming together to attend them, while trying to make the spaces that exhibit the films and host the audiences as welcoming as possible. I think of and have always experienced Glasgow as significantly queerer than more conservative Edinburgh, the city I work and live in, for example, while acknowledging my privileges navigating both spaces as a white, straight-passing femme lesbian. Queer people queer spaces, like the CCA, but such events can also help to queer a city and even a country, in terms of both lived reality and reputation.

A venue open to the public cannot become a welcoming space for queers without consideration, effort and time. It is not enough for a group of queers to simply turn up in any space and queer it, because this does not consider issues of risk, where a visibly queer space is one that homo- and transphobes may target. When a group of queers turn up and queer a space, we need to consider the queers with intersections not present in that group. Organizers should ask who feels welcome in their festival space; making room for those under the LGBTQIA+ umbrella is not enough if that space is not welcoming to LGBTQIA+ people from the global majority, or raised/in poverty, for LGBTQIA+ parents and carers and not accessible to LGBTQIA+ people who are D/ deaf and/or disabled, to name a few. Curiously, a space may be read as queer by cishet people if just one *visibly* queer person is present, but much less queer by queers even if numerous people with a queer sexuality and/or gender are present. This is because the bar is often different; one person who is visibly unlike the mainstream, especially in terms of gender and sexuality, can make a space seem queer for mainstream cishet people, meanwhile one queer person amid a mass of people with normative genders and sexualities rarely makes a queer feel like the space is queer/ed (although they may find anally).

The CCA was generous to GLITCH and SQIFF, but, like many art galleries, is often dominated by white, middle-class people, meaning it is not always the most comfortable space for people needing to envision a utopia. However, as of December 2024, the CCA website states, 'CCA is temporarily and partially closed from December 2024 to March 2025 to focus on restructuring and financial recovery', meaning that even established venues attracting many socio-economically privileged people are struggling in the current climate.

SQIFF, from the first edition, held various events at both CCA and a range of venues beyond its hub, including Glasgow Women's Library (GWL), in Bridgeton, a working-class area, where I hosted a working-class femme event for the inaugural SQIFF, with the aim that it could be used as a hook for the festival to attract people who would not typically feel comfortable in an art gallery (indeed, people who came up to chat to me after the GWL event then came to the CCA with me afterwards). I later conceived and co-created a workshop to examine how LGBTQIA+ and working-class identities have been 'demonised, patronised, and romanticised onscreen' and 'how queer working-class people feel in arts spaces, especially those traditionally catering to an audience that is middle-class and above, including art house cinemas and galleries' (Dawson and Loist 2018, 15), which ran as a warm-up for SQIFF's 2017 edition and several participants later came along to the main festival for the first time, which began a week later, 'while feedback from the event (discussion, feedback forms, email correspondence) signalled quite clearly that events like these are much needed and working-class people want more space to have their voices heard in relation to both onscreen representation and offscreen inclusivity' (Dawson and Loist 2018, 14–15). This allows for queers, people from the global majority, people in poverty and so on to imagine an elsewhere, an otherness, and consider actions to create a better future. It is perhaps easier for a utopia to be imagined when oppressed people are in a safe/r space and not in immediate proximity to their oppressors. This can be achieved by creating spaces by, about and only for people of the global majority or people who are/were raised in poverty.

There has been much literature on various types of filmic gaze and spectatorship, including the male gaze, female gaze, trans gaze, Black look, maternal gaze and more, although word and reference limitations prevent me from discussing each further. While such gazes often focus explicitly on the identities being shown onscreen and the effect this has on spectators, the utopic gaze is not specifically about identities onscreen but rather about a better elsewhere, whether temporally or geographically, of some fictional onscreen worlds and could typically be accessed by those who are not as privileged in the status quo including queers, trans people, people of the global majority and people in poverty.

If queers do not feel comfortable, they might not feel safe enough to watch a queer film in that space or to get so lost in the onscreen world that they can imagine an elsewhere through a utopic gaze, although conversely, they may need to imagine an elsewhere to escape their current environment. I argue a queer utopia can be pointed to or temporarily accessed via the moving image shown more than the space it is exhibited in, although the space is much needed. Some film festivals also perhaps allow for a sometime utopic gaze because the queerness of people, places, spaces, times, futures and imaginaries seen on screen in some of the films happens more strongly due to the collectiveness of those happily under the LGBTQIA+ umbrella coming together to spectate and sometimes to act, politically. 'A queer aesthetic ... art manifest[s] itself in such a way that the political imagination can spark new ways of perceiving and acting on a reality that is itself potentially changeable' (Muñoz 2009, 135). Of course, not all film does this; indeed some of the films shown at the festivals might show, for example, gay or lesbian people but their identities, politics and/or aesthetics are not at all queer.

Access to the utopic, even temporarily, is important because much LGBTQIA+ history focuses on the tragic, which is also present in collective memory: imprisonment, castration, ostracization, the AIDS crisis and more, while film in the past contained many of the aforementioned negative LGBT+ stereotypes. At GLITCH and SQIFF, some films screened allow/ed us to imagine a better elsewhere, in spaces which enabled (some of) us to do this together. Indeed, the utopic gaze can sometimes be accessed more easily in the space of a film festival because, while queer film can be watched at home thanks to streaming services and more, queer film festivals often offer a range of films often not available or seen elsewhere because queers can programme and promote specific films in their festivals or events that are not favoured by film production companies, streaming services and social media algorithms.

Furthermore, festivals are also important because of the liveness of the festival and events within, with the 'bodily presence of audiences, filmmakers, and critics. The live presence is both a significant element in the formation of festival community and for the festival operating as a public sphere' (Dawson and Loist 2018, 3). The public sphere is important to those under the LGBTQIA+ umbrella as there can be a disconnect between their private and public selves (e.g. being 'in the closet' about sexuality or gender identity) because non-normative sexualities and genders were long considered shameful and, in some instances, sexual acts criminalized, so to be able to attend a public queer event can feel like a privilege when it should be a basic right. In a public sphere such as a queer film festival, queers can watch films and, at times, perhaps access a utopic gaze together and in a way that ideas can be exchanged, opinions formed and action taken.

If such a utopic gaze is accessed alone at home, then there are no others with whom an elsewhere can be imagined, planned and suchlike, and of course social and political change often requires more than one lone person. Indeed, the way that film festival attendance differs significantly from a regular night at the cinema includes 'rituals, hype and the feeling of belonging to a group' (Dawson and Loist 2018: 3). This highlights a sense of belonging, even a being seen while seeing both what is on screen *and* who else is present at the event, which can tie to the queer utopic gaze: queers can unite to watch with a hope of a better future/time/place/elsewhere.

Those present at the festival create a form of group or community within the broader and problematic LGBTQIA+ 'community'. The latter is especially problematized because LGBTQIA+ 'community' is not actually a 'community' as it comprises people who do not want to be grouped with others: some grouped within the acronym like to be considered only as an individual or as their own identity rather than as part of an umbrella, some identities are in tension, for example, there are LGB people who object to various trans rights and being grouped with trans people, there are intersex people who do not want being intersex to be grouped alongside identities relating to sexuality and so on. However, with festivals such as SQIFF inclusion is highlighted, even if not always fully achieved (despite the self-selecting audience).

There is a sense of belonging, a being seen while seeing (both what is on screen *and* who else is present at the event), in such queer filmic gatherings. What is important about being in a place such as SQIFF or GLITCH is for queers to be openly themselves, not needing to 'pass' as cisgender and/or heterosexual and so on or worry about passing while at the event. While 'People Make Glasgow', we also know that people can make places feel uncomfortable and even dangerous. In order to help with safety getting to and from the queer/ed wee space of festival/events in a city which is not always safe for those who do not visibly adhere to norms of gender, sexuality and the city's predominant whiteness, as discussed previously, SQIFF offered money for taxis to queers who might face abuse when in public spaces such as walking on the street or taking public transport to get to live, in-person events safely as it is important to note that while a space is being queered and may be considered safe, the surrounding area, city or even country may not be. This is why safe/r queer spaces are so wee; because there are identities, beliefs and so on which are in conflict, and the more people present, the more likely there is to be this conflict between identities/people.

Indeed, film festivals – unlike a regular night out at the cinema or media such as online streaming services – also create a circulation of people and, in the instance of festivals like GLITCH and SQIFF, this means a circulation of queers, which can only happen well if the space and place feels like a safe one, meaning a safe venue, but also a safe city and country where the festival and individual events can be advertised without legal or other repercussion and where, if problems were to arise, attendees can feel as if they would be dealt with swiftly and well and there would be support. Here, Glasgow feels like a safe space to those travelling to the festival/s. Of course we need to consider privilege as there will be a number of people who do not travel because they do not feel safe or comfortable (perhaps because of the extremely white demographics of the city and country) and/or who cannot afford transport and do not have the money or networks for accommodation and a festival pass, and even those from Glasgow need to have the time off work or free from caring responsibilities or suchlike to attend.

SQIFF's queer wee space became accessible to a much larger audience via the online transition during Covid lockdowns and creation of SQIFFLIX, a pun on the festival name and streaming service Netflix. Unlike the latter, SQIFFLIX provided films online for free, at least for those who had the devices, data, space and skills/knowledge to access them and the safe space to view them. SQIFF was not a first, as film festivals 'launched online decades before the Covid-19 pandemic, both out of fear that the rise of the internet could kill their festival if they were not flexible and in order to reach as wide an audience as possible' (Dawson 2020). Experimental film festival MIX NYC was a pioneer, creating an online version in 1997. SQIFF, however, did not continue the online version and GLITCH never had one. These decisions can be a question of resources, such as time, money and the learned knowledge to create an online platform.

One of the many positives of a parallel online space, is that it can, along with festival ephemera such as posters and programmes and the films available, but unlike Muñoz's focus on live performance art, be carried into the future. While the web can make things more accessible to some, digital divide excepting, archives can also carry this work to the future, whether in venues such as the GWL or in people's homes. One key issue with some of the work shown at queer film festivals is, whether they are screened at one festival or circulate widely throughout the grassroots queer film festival circuit, that such films may not be watched again unless they are in an archive or online.

Conclusion

It seems that queer spaces can, at present, only exist in wee places. However, this queer wee place is likely not a wee country, or even a wee film festival, but rather smaller pockets of queerness within these. This is because there is so much normativity – hetero- and homo – which can work against queerness, as well as too many -isms and -phobias (here are ableist, racist and classist people calling themselves queer; I have encountered several in my time). Many people, whether consciously or unconsciously, are biased against identities and groups to which they do not belong. Even if queer film festivals are not truly queer spaces in the Muñoz sense, because queer is not yet here, or even in the sense of a united queer community, they are spaces in which queers can come together and access the possibility of a queer utopic elsewhere/future through the make-believe of the screen. A queer elsewhere is imagined within a queer-themed film festival, even within the white-middle-class space of an art gallery, in a country more tolerant of LGBT+ rights than many. Returning to Muñoz, maybe we can take comfort in imagining the utopia of a truly queer Scotland. SQIFF and GLITCH, centred in Scotland, are perhaps most important because they have offered spaces not only to gather, but also to imagine something and to act upon it, for a better here and now.

Note

1. While there has been a simultaneous normalization and demonization of LGBTQIA+ people in the UK, LGB people who can assimilate are increasingly normalized through same-sex marriage, adoption rights and more, whereas others are attacked, including trans folk and migrants. Gender, sexuality and 'race' are a knot that creates a certain type of citizen (white, cisgender, gender-normative, heterosexual, married, reproducing to create family), and this family is desired within certain political groups because, multiplied, it creates a certain type of nation (although as a lesbian mother, I can happily attest that heterosexuality is certainly not the only way to reproduce). Within this chapter, then, I am considering *queerness* in opposition to homonormativity.

References

Crenshaw, K. 'Demarginalizing the Intersection of Race and Sex: A Black Feminist Critique of Antidiscrimination Doctrine, Feminist Theory and Antiracist Politics', *University of Chicago Legal Forum* (1989), article 8. https://chicagounbound.uchicago.edu/uclf/vol1989/iss1/8

Dawson, L. 'Culture in Crisis: A Guide to Access, Equality, Diversity, and Inclusion in Festivals, Arts and Culture'. MAI, 5 October 2020. https://maifeminism.com/culture-in-crisis-a-guide-to-inclusion/

Dawson, L. and Loist, S. 'Queer/ing Film Festivals'. Special issue of *Studies in European Cinema* 15, no. 1 (2018). https://doi.org/10.1080/17411548.2018.1442901

Duggan, L. 'The New Homonormativity: The Sexual Politics of Neoliberalism'. In R. Castronovo and D. D. Nelson (eds), *Materializing Democracy: Toward a Revitalized Cultural Politics*, pp. 175–94. Durham, NC: Duke University Press, 2002.

Local Government Act, 1988. www.legislation.gov.uk/ukpga/1988/9/section/28/enacted?view=plain.

Muñoz, J. E. *Cruising Utopia: The Then and There of Queer Futurity*. New York: New York University Press, 2009.

Filmography

Adult Human Female (Deidre O'Neill and Mike Wayne, 2022).
Blue Jean (Georgia Oakley, 2022).
It Got Better (Heather Ross, 2014–16).

19

Queer curiosities: LGBTQ+ equity in Scotland's museums

Joe Setch

Working at Inverness Museum & Art Gallery in the Highlands of Scotland in 2021, one of my tasks was to expand the museum's collection by sourcing objects which reflected experiences of the COVID-19 pandemic. The first item I collected was an example of a COVID-19 recovery pack sent out by the Highland Pride charity to their members across the region. Containing a facemask, sanitizer, sweets and a message of support, it captured the efforts of a burgeoning queer community to stay connected at a deeply difficult time. As a gay man local to the area, it felt only natural to me that LGBTQ+ themes should be represented in the museum's collection. But when I went to add the pack to the organization's digital database, I found that there was no way to catalogue its queer credentials. It was only in adding a new 'LGBTQ+' category to the system that I realized Inverness Museum & Art Gallery had never before collected an object with an acknowledged queer connection. In their 140 years of collecting, all of it was apparently straight. Until I happened to come along. I hadn't intended to break new ground, and my actions were hardly radical. So why had it fallen to me to start the work of queering this collection? Why did it take direct intervention to achieve this representation? Pausing on these questions constituted my introduction to the idea of LGBTQ+ equity in Scottish museums.

Since then, I've become increasingly aware that not only are LGBTQ+ people and themes underrepresented in museums, but also that little has been done to reflect on how Scotland's museum sector as a whole is addressing the topic of LGBTQ+ equity. This chapter therefore aims to prompt discussion and inspire action by offering an outline of the museum sector's approach across four key areas: objects and their interpretation, public engagement, safe and inclusive spaces and the responsibilities of the workforce. To achieve this, I draw chiefly on my personal and practical experience as a queer museum sector worker, the results of a survey on LGBTQ+ equity sent out to museum organizations across Scotland in early 2024, and a series of interviews with five people who have worked on LGBTQ+ inclusion in Scottish cultural organizations. These interviewees, despite representing a range of organizations and areas of work, share a commitment to LGBTQ+ representation which I was personally inspired by and eager to highlight.

It's my hope that this brief overview will give all those who love museums – visitors, volunteers and workers alike – the power to have more confident conversations about the status of LGBTQ+ equity in Scotland's museums. It highlights the complexity of the relationship between queer people and these institutions which, despite their prominence in the cultural landscape, seldom reflect the reality of LGBTQ+ lives and lifestyles. It acknowledges the successes and shortcomings of the museum sector and, by providing examples of good practice from across Scotland, ultimately makes the case for all museums to find a place for LGBTQ+ people and perspectives in their work.

Firstly, however, we must explore what we mean by 'museum'. In my opinion, museums are otherworldly environments where collections of objects – usually far removed from their original contexts – are amassed and arranged in the service of storytelling. They are peculiar expressions of our desire to systematize and structure, all delivered with the aim of inspiring, educating and entertaining the public. Scotland has over 450 of these unique storytelling spaces, each devoted to a particular location, occupation, noteworthy person, social group or specialist interest. When at their best, museums distil the essence of their respective remits into expressions of collective memory and imagining, creating vibrant cultural hubs which rest at the heart of their communities.

Museums hold and display things which we as a society care about – and in doing so, exist as affirmations of our prevailing values, ambitions and aspirations. But values change, and the longer a museum exists, the more historical baggage it can accrue. This means that, by nature of existing as 'respectable' cultural institutions in an historically queerphobic Scotland, museums have reinforced the otherness of Scotland's LGBTQ+ people. Whether unconscious or intentional, the failure of museums to account for queer perspectives acts as an assertion that some people are more important – and more included – than others. In my interview with Chloe Rose-Alex, Capacity Building Manager at LGBT Youth Scotland, she reflected on this topic by drawing on her experience of supporting organizations to become more inclusive through the charity's LGBT Charter accreditation programme: 'Systems, processes, and services generally haven't been built with marginalized populations in mind. So they unintentionally exclude people in many cases. And you're not going to fix those problems if you don't know that they exist.' It is every museum's responsibility to confront their complicity in the othering and exclusion of marginalized groups. Every museum, no matter its subject matter or intended audience, should seek to serve its entire community. But if a museum is unable to acknowledge, understand or accommodate for LGBTQ+ people, then it should come as no surprise when this part of their community fails to engage with them or be invested in its success. A museum can only truly succeed as a community asset if it strives for equity in all areas, from its public spaces and workplace environments to the collections and displays which are so essential to their existence.

Objects and interpretation

Scotland's museums hold millions of objects which, when taken together, serve as the physical manifestation of the nation's collective consciousness. They shape our understanding of the past and present. They are the storytelling devices and star attractions of every museum: but the limits of space and resources demand careful curation not only of the things which are collected, but also the tiny proportion of these which make it out onto public display. Any decision to collect an object or create a display is a decision *against* many others. This decision-making power has traditionally sat with a narrow demographic of white, middle-class and university-educated museum workers, a group whose understandings of which objects have value, and precisely what those values are, have resulted in collections which offer only a partial history of Scotland's culture and communities. This approach is rightfully being called into question. Museum workers are increasingly expected to cede their control over collections and displays to the communities which their museums represent. By shifting from shapers of the narrative to facilitators of public narratives, museum workers can achieve more diverse, engaging and authentic storytelling. This commitment to the public voice is a rejection of the pretence of museums as 'impartial' observers to the world around them. Bias is inescapable, and no museum is truly neutral. Museums may tell stories which reinforce prevailing wisdom or challenge it; they may create space for debate or seek to assert certainties. They choose which truths to tell and which elements of their objects – function, form, symbolism, history – should perform in the service of the broader narratives of their exhibitions and displays. In this context of consciously crafted storytelling, any museum which lacks LGBTQ+ representation in its collections or displays is a museum which has embedded exclusion into its policies and practice.

It is only over the past thirty years that Scotland's museums have taken steps to close these queer gaps. In the early 1990s, National Museums Scotland started collecting objects which related to LGBTQ+ events and activism, while in 1995 Glasgow Women's Library – which is now also recognized as a museum – became the permanent home of the Lesbian Archive, arguably one of the UK's most significant collections of material relating to LGBTQ+ women. In 1997 the Gallery of Modern Art (GoMA) in Glasgow shone a spotlight on LGBTQ+ themes by hosting an exhibition organized by fotofeis, a Scottish photography festival which ran throughout the 1990s. Titled *Grit and Glitter*, it featured a selection of campy and queer-coded works by French couple and artistic collaborators Pierre Commoy and Gilles Blanchard, perhaps better known simply as 'Pierre et Gilles'. Several of Scotland's earliest LGBTQ+ museum exhibitions were instigated by Glasgay!, an annual LGBTQ+ cultural festival which was held in Glasgow from 1993 to 2014. Glasgow Women's Library showcased items from the Lesbian Archive for the 1995 festival, marking a significant moment of a Scottish museum organization arranging a public display of consciously LGBTQ+ objects, while GoMA provided space for several exhibitions organized by Glasgay! in the late 1990s and early 2000s.

These forays into LGBTQ+ collecting and curation are significant milestones for the museum sector, but represent just a drop in the ocean of Scotland's queer consciousness at a time of intense political and cultural activity for LGBTQ+ people. Exhibitions which explored gender and sexuality, the Pride movement, LGBTQ+ activism, sexual health and the HIV/AIDS pandemic had been taking place in cafés, community centres and commercial galleries in Edinburgh and Glasgow since at least the late 1980s. But the vast majority of Scotland's mainstream museums were total strangers to the vibrant expressions of LGBTQ+ life and culture taking place around them. Fortunately, the first decade of the new millennium saw a growth in the scale and depth of the museum sector's engagement with LGBTQ+ themes. In 2002, the Living Memory Association launched *Remember When*, a project to collect oral histories of Edinburgh's LGBTQ+ communities. Edinburgh Council's museum service joined this project in 2004, spurred into action by gay rights activist Keith Cowan's observation that they had thus far failed to acknowledge the city's rich LGBTQ+ history. This led to the creation of *Rainbow City* in 2006, the first major LGBTQ+ history exhibition developed by a Scottish museum organization. Despite being exhibited in the basement of the City Art Centre – allegedly to prevent it from being too visible to the general public – *Rainbow City* left a significant legacy for Edinburgh Council, inspiring the 2017 *Proud City* exhibition now on permanent display at the museum in the nearby town of Queensferry. The Living Memory Association also continued their invaluable work on LGBTQ+ oral histories, collecting further contributions for the 2022 *Queer Edinburgh* exhibition held at their Wee Hub venue in Leith, a district in the north of Edinburgh. Much of this early activity was achieved at the instigation of LGBTQ+ activists, groups and cultural organizations. Large gaps in museum collections were filled thanks to significant donations from queer people, while many major exhibitions have taken place only because of the efforts of organizations such as Glasgay! and OurStory Scotland, a charity dedicated to improving the representation of LGBTQ+ voices in Scotland's archives.

It continues to be an era of attention-grabbing firsts for Scottish museums, reflecting not only the growth of thriving queer communities outside of Edinburgh and Glasgow, but also the museum sector's increasingly proactive approach to LGBTQ+ collecting. Culture Perth & Kinross, the body which runs Perth Museum, collected a series of objects associated with Perthshire Pride in 2021. The McManus, Dundee's Art Gallery and Museum, put local drag queen Ellie Diamond's 'Denise the Menace' dress out on permanent display in 2022, and in 2023 the Scottish Football Museum acquired a football shirt worn by Zander Murray, Scotland's first openly gay male professional footballer. In recent years, exhibitions addressing LGBTQ+ themes have graced the galleries of institutions such as Inverness Museum & Art Gallery, Paisley Museum and the John Gray Centre in the town of Haddington in East Lothian, while the digitization of exhibitions such as *Pride: A Queer History* at the Watt Institution in Greenock and Edinburgh Council's *Our Rainbow Past* – both launched in 2023 – has ensured a broader reach for LGBTQ+ inclusive museum content.

Yet perhaps the boldest expression to date of a Scottish museum's LGBTQ+ inclusive intentions came with the opening of Perth Museum in 2024. The centrepiece of the new museum's inaugural *Unicorn* exhibition was Destiny, an enormous wooden unicorn crammed full of objects loaned by local LGBTQ+ people and groups. Looming over the museum's main gallery, this remarkable statue stood in stark contrast to the silence of museums in the 1990s and the basement-dwelling displays of the 2000s. Described by museum staff as a Trojan unicorn, Destiny serves as a nod to the wooden horse of Greek myth: a gift which harbours a hidden threat. The sculpture therefore represented the impending queer conquest of a hitherto hostile space, and the promise of museums which Scotland's LGBTQ+ people can claim as truly theirs.

It's tempting to celebrate the unabashed queerness of the *Unicorn* exhibition as the triumph LGBTQ+ equity in Scottish museums. But statistics show that Destiny is merely an advance guard in the fight for equal representation. In early 2024, I sent out an anonymous survey to find out how the Scottish museum sector is engaging with LGBTQ+ themes. I received ninety-two replies, representing 32.5 per cent of the 283 museum organizations recognized by Museums Galleries Scotland, the national development body for museums. Of these replies, only twenty-seven (29.4 per cent) confirmed that they have at least one object in their permanent collections that they know relates to LGBTQ+ individuals, communities or themes, while twenty-three respondents (25 per cent) have at some point addressed LGBTQ+ themes in an exhibition or display. Further data suggests that these hints of progress are not always indicative of a shift to greater LGBTQ+ inclusion in all areas of a museum's work: organizations which are serious about the consistent representation of LGBTQ+ themes in their collections will often declare this intent in their policies on collecting: but only seventeen respondents to the survey have made such commitments to acquiring objects with any known LGBTQ+ connections. Some of the museums that already hold LGBTQ+ objects have no policy to continue collecting in this area.

Having objects in museum collections is one thing. Finding them is another. Just eight organizations confirmed that they have a collections database which includes LGBTQ+ categories or search tags. This suggests that – even though individual museums workers may be aware of LGBTQ+ objects in their collections – this knowledge is either difficult to obtain or vulnerable to being lost. These results make clear that, despite over thirty years of action, a large majority of Scottish museums continue to exclude LGBTQ+ people and themes from their collections and displays. This may be because not all museums feel they have a means of engaging with this topic. As one survey response remarked: 'There is nothing about the collection which could have a specific LGBTQ+ angle to it.' Others explained that their collections don't feature LGBTQ+ perspectives because they perceive that they aren't relevant to the remit of the museum. This included museums dedicated to the lives of particular (non-queer, or *presumed* non-queer) individuals, to science and technology or to places and periods of history in which queer lives and experiences were less likely to have been recorded for posterity. Yet every single museum in Scotland will *already* have objects which hold queer potential. Queer people have always existed, and their lives have touched on all aspects of humanity. So collections likely include objects made by, used by or otherwise associated with a queer person; objects which have a unique resonance to queer people; or even objects which reflect aspects of the queer experience. Queer connections undoubtedly exist in museums: where museums have fallen short is in the knowing and telling of these connections. 'We don't believe there to be any LGBTQ+ objects in the museum's collections', one survey result observed, with a qualifying remark: 'but perhaps this is due to a lack of research'. Whether through censorship, misrepresentation or a genuine lack of awareness, the queer stories already contained within museum objects have gone untold. Museums must recognize the role they have played in upholding historical harms and aspire to address this underrepresentation by revealing the queer narratives hidden within their collections. They can achieve this by conducting research, consulting with their communities and giving LGBTQ+ people the power to make decisions about collecting, interpretation and display. By privileging the knowledge and experience of LGBTQ+ communities, museums open themselves up to new truths. The *Remember When* project which ran from 2002 to 2006 involved regular meetings of a cross-generational group of LGBTQ+ people, all sharing their own perspectives on the objects that were being collected. Sheila Asante, who works as a Programme Manager for Museums Galleries Scotland, the national development body for museums, was involved in the project early in her career. Speaking with me in an interview for this chapter, she recognized that her role in the project's meetings was to facilitate discussion, not to shape it: 'As a neutral, non-lived experience voice, I was there to listen and learn.' The 2023 Lavender Labels project at V&A Dundee, Scotland's design museum, took a similar approach by setting up a dedicated advisory group of LGBTQ+ people from outside the museum organization. The members of this group selected objects connected to queer themes for the museum's permanent exhibition space and wrote interpretation which was displayed on the eponymous lavender labels spread throughout the gallery.

When working to unlock the queer potential of existing collections, museums may choose to move beyond the individual history of an object and focus instead on what it may represent to LGBTQ+ people. Community Engagement Officer Lorna Steele-McGinn, whose work on *Our Story: Closing the Queer History Gap in the Highlands* involved close collaboration with LGBTQ+ groups, explains: 'I think that most things will have an ability to be used as a conduit to talk about those subjects. Even if that one object itself has no queer associations, there's still a way that object can be used by those people to talk about their experience.' The Georgian House, a National Trust for Scotland property in the heart of Edinburgh, has put this approach into practice by using objects as a means of addressing topics of non-normative dress, queer-coded language and the persecution of homosexuality in eighteenth-century Britain. For their *Pride: A Queer History* exhibition, the Watt Institution used colour, design and provenance to highlight the queer symbolism contained within objects such as a sea snail shell, a butterfly specimen and a Roman oil lamp.

Museums don't even need to change their displays to unlock the LGBTQ+ potential of their collections. The self-led Hidden Histories tour at the National Museum of Scotland, developed by young LGBTQ+ people and launched in 2021, and regular LGBTQ+-guided tours held at the Burrell Collection since 2023 and The Hunterian since 2024 all demonstrate that it's possible to add value by introducing queer perspectives which sit either alongside or on top of existing interpretation. Absence, too, speaks volumes: a blank display space can acknowledge gaps in collections and serve as an expression of a museum's desire to make amends for historic underrepresentation. This was used to great effect in the *Rainbow City* exhibition, where at the end of a series of portraits of LGBTQ+ residents of Edinburgh, an empty frame was hung to represent those whose queer identities remained hidden and whose stories went untold.

No matter how museums seek to involve LGBTQ+ people in the development of collections and displays, they must ensure that they are careful, respectful, receptive to feedback and mindful of the welfare of participants. They should celebrate their contributions, seek to compensate them for their time and expertise and always leave the door open to further collaboration. Speaking from her experience of working with

LGBTQ+ community groups, Lorna Steele-McGinn adds: 'If a project is going to be meaningful, participants need to have a proper say in it and not just have the project imposed on them.' A smash-and-grab approach to queer collecting and interpretation may yield short-term results, but ruins any chance of sustaining working relationships and effecting meaningful change. When done properly, however, the pursuit of fair representation in collections and displays pays dividends to queer and straight museumgoers alike. The breadth of this impact lies in the fact that museums are spaces which, in reflecting on the past and present, inform our understanding of the world around us. They have power over the narratives which shape their subject matter and can use this to affirm the right of LGBTQ+ people to a place in their community. They can use the cultural capital of their objects, displays and reputation to assert their aspirations for a fairer society.

Engagement

Collections and displays are fundamental to any museum. But its true purpose is to the public it serves. After all, a museum without an audience is essentially just an elaborate cupboard. Museums should strive to harness the unique opportunities afforded by their collections and cultural position to create focused opportunities for engagement, thereby fulfilling their mission to support their community while guaranteeing a function for the objects in their care. Museums which deliver sensitive and sustained engagement have a proven impact on the well-being, cohesion and confidence of their communities. As Chloe Rose-Alex from LGBT Youth Scotland shares, this can have a profound impact on marginalized groups: 'Positive experiences can make such a difference to people's physical and mental health, their sense of inclusion in society, and potentially their academic aspirations and career aspirations, too.'

Museums can further the cause of LGBTQ+ equity and make a positive difference to their communities by organizing inclusive events and activities. Molly Ashmeade, a Museum Assistant who organises queer-friendly music performances at St Cecilia's Hall Music Museum in Edinburgh, explains the value of this work: 'Inclusion isn't just about making people feel comfortable in their experience when they're there, but also making sure that they feel like they are part of the museum.' When a museum embeds queerness into its events and activities, it encourages LGBTQ+ audiences to understand that they can claim all elements of the space as theirs. It brings new audiences in through the door and breaks down the barriers built into the system.

Scottish museums are already engaging with LGBTQ+ people in a variety of creative ways. The community-led exhibitions and displays I've already highlighted are just the tip of the iceberg: recent programming includes self-led heritage trails such as the Glasgow Women's Library *Stride with Pride* tour of Glasgow and the Living Memory Association's 2022 *Walk around Queer Edinburgh*; talks about LGBTQ+ history at Dumfries Museum, the Georgian House and the City Art Centre; and LGBTQ+-friendly print-making workshops at the Pier Arts Centre in Orkney. In 2024 the National Museum of Scotland worked with the charity LGBT Health and Wellbeing Scotland to co-host an LGBTQ+ family day, while Timespan, a museum in the Highland village of Helmsdale, enabled members of their community to attend Highland Pride in 2023 and 2024 by organizing banner painting sessions and arranging transport.

Museums are invigorated when they attract new audiences. They may bring with them new perspectives, become public champions for the museum or even offer their time and skills to its cause. Visitor Services Assistant Indigo Dunphy-Smith commented on this in a presentation she delivered on the impact of the LGBTQ+ inclusive programming which she leads at the Georgian House: 'I've seen our volunteer pool … begin to diversify. New volunteers, old and young, are seeing the Georgian house as an inclusive place that tells their history.' Indigo also explained that LGBTQ+ talks, tours and screenings provide the museum with a vital source of revenue: 'To my amazement, and I think a lot of other staff, the event actually sold out. This was a really clear communication to me and to the staff that this history was in demand.' The experience of the Georgian House demonstrates that the social relevance secured by engaging with LGBTQ+ topics can support the sustainability of a museum's workforce and finances. It's evident museums are rewarded when they seek to include LGBTQ+ people in their work. But with only twenty-five of the ninety-two museum organizations (27.2 per cent) who responded to my survey having actively engaged with LGBTQ+ communities through targeted programming, the museum sector has clearly yet to fully explore the potential of this approach.

Safe spaces?

The Scottish museum sector's relatively patchy efforts to address the historic exclusion of queer people won't inspire the members of this community to place much faith in the methods or motives of their local museums. Museums must therefore be proactive in their efforts to earn the trust that underpins all successful collecting, storytelling and public engagement. They have to assure LGBTQ+ people that they are welcome in their venues and assert – loudly, visibly, and unequivocally – that they are authentically safe spaces. The good news is that many believe that they are already safe spaces for queer people. Only five (5.4 per cent) of the ninety-two respondents to my survey disagreed that they had made meaningful progress towards developing a safe and inclusive environment for either volunteers, visitors or paid staff who may identify as LGBTQ+. Many respondents also believe that they have achieved parity of access and experience for LGBTQ+ people, with only eighteen (19.6 per cent) acknowledging the existence of any barriers to LGBTQ+ inclusion at their organizations. But I find it difficult to reconcile this perceived lack of barriers with the reality that very few museum organizations have realized the possibility of any LGBTQ+ representation in so many areas of their work. A museum which is truly barrier-free for LGBTQ+ people will have considered the marginalized status of this community and taken measures to provide a parity of access and involvement which accounts for their needs and desires.

The survey results suggest that not all museums are aware of the many forms that obstacles to inclusion can take. Some explained that they are inclusive simply because they are friendly: in reference to the question on barriers, one respondent wrote: 'Not applicable as we welcome all visitors and our volunteers without question', while another commented, '[we] treat everyone the same regardless of sexuality and therefore [have] no need for [a] special exhibition'. This perhaps well-intentioned statement, submitted by a museum with no LGBTQ+ representation in its collections or displays, falls into an all-too-familiar trap by categorizing LGBTQ+ themes as a 'special' or optional interest for museums, rather than a core element of their work. Fair treatment requires more than friendly welcomes: just as a queer person's identity will inform so much of how they navigate the world, so too are there manifold opportunities for queer people to encounter barriers to equity. Museums may have exclusionary collections, displays or programming. They may be environments in which queer staff, volunteers and visitors are misunderstood, misgendered or otherwise mistreated. They may lack facilities which account for the needs and comfort of queer people or lack policies which ensure that discrimination is properly challenged. Among the eighteen organizations that did identify barriers to equity were acknowledgements of 'entrenched views/old fashioned language', 'micro-aggressions' and 'resistance … to change'. While these examples demonstrate that queerphobia and close-mindedness sadly remain as obstacles, the majority of identified barriers were instead symptomatic of a museum sector suffering the anxiety-inducing instability of long-term cuts to services. Respondents highlighted that their organizations have limited funding or capacity to address LGBTQ+ themes, have made uneven progress across departments or lack leadership on LGBTQ+ inclusion. Others reported of organizations which are averse to 'risk', unwilling to deal with any hypothetical backlash to a push for greater equity, or constrained by the political considerations of belonging to a local authority. Given the budgetary vulnerabilities of the museum sector and current contentiousness of the cultural climate, I have to wonder if museum managers fear that any negative attention garnered by LGBTQ+ inclusion work could be used as a justification for further reductions to their funding. Without the safety net of financial security, it's possible they lack the bravery to challenge the status quo.

If a museum does not have a good understanding of the needs of LGBTQ+ people or the ability to address the barriers they may face, they fail to serve as a safe space. Chloe Rose-Alex from LGBT Youth Scotland advises: 'If you are signposting that you are inclusive, try to make sure that you can actually back that up with reality, because it can be counterproductive to say "LGBTQ+ inclusive" and then for somebody to come in and have a really poor experience, because the actual structure and knowledge wasn't there.' It is positive, however, that museums clearly strive to be welcoming to all. Chloe adds: 'Friendliness can be a really good building block to go from: I think it indicates they have the attitude, which is going to be really important in that process. But there's definitely a need to formalize the inclusion behind that friendliness.' Creating a safe space can involve training, research, consultations, new policies, unlearning habits and rethinking attitudes. It is a constant process which requires scrutiny of all areas of a museum's work. Some museum organizations have created LGBTQ+ working groups to advise on these efforts and endorsed calls to action such as the University of Leicester's guidance on how to create trans-inclusive cultural organizations (MacLeod et al. 2023). To date, two Scottish museum organizations have formalized the development of safe spaces in their venues by achieving accreditation from LGBTQ+ charities. In 2024, Historic Environment Scotland became the first museum and heritage organization to achieve LGBT Youth Scotland's LGBT Charter Foundation Award. Similarly, Glasgow's Maryhill Burgh Halls, which runs Maryhill Museum, has attained the Equality Network's Scottish LGBTI+ Rainbow Mark.

I've found that the more a museum has done to embrace LGBTQ+ inclusion, the more likely it is to recognize that work needs to be done to reduce barriers. Although fourteen of the eighteen organizations (77.8 per cent) that recognize barriers to equity have engaged with LGBTQ+ collections, interpretation or communities in some capacity, the same can be said for only eleven of the thirty-nine organizations (28.2 per cent) that do not recognize any barriers at all. Connecting with queer people opens up new possibilities and helps museums to achieve a more complete understanding of how they can support their communities.

Despite the good work that I've highlighted, the fact remains that LGBTQ+ inclusive interventions are relatively rare in Scotland's museums. Just four of the ninety-two museum organizations that responded to my survey had positive responses to all six of my questions about collections, interpretation and engagement. By contrast, fifty-four organizations – 58.7 per cent of all respondents – were unable to confirm that they met any of these metrics: they aren't aware of any LGBTQ+ objects in their permanent collections, have never collected LGBTQ+ objects or set a policy to collect LGBTQ+ objects, lack any LGBTQ+ tags or categories in their collections database, have never referenced LGBTQ+ themes in their exhibitions or displays and have never proactively engaged with LGBTQ+ people. The pursuit of LGBTQ+ equity seems far from being mainstreamed in Scotland's museums. The sector must work harder to prove that queer people and histories matter to them, and that the harms they have played a role in perpetuating are a thing of the past. To succeed in developing inclusive collections and displays which reflect the full scope of their audiences, they must earn the trust of LGBTQ+ communities by offering earnest engagement in safe and welcoming environments which are mindful of the specific needs of marginalized groups.

The change-makers

Advancing LGBTQ+ equity is not a small task and may even seem daunting for museums which have struggled through years of post-pandemic recovery and cuts to arts funding. It can, however, be scaled to suit the capacity and resources of every single museum in Scotland. Large, small, urban and rural organizations have all made progress in this area. The ability of a museum to push for equity is dependent not on its size or location, but rather on the priorities of its team. For a museum sector workforce which is broadly straight and cisgender, the responsibility for putting LGBTQ+ equity at the top of the agenda often falls to the significant minority of the workforce which identifies as LGBTQ+. Audience Engagement Officer Ilona Butter found this to be the case when creating an LGBTQ+ working group at Aberdeen Archives, Gallery and Museums: 'It just came up out of having conversations with queer colleagues, and then it's just kind of steamrolled and become this bigger thing, which is wonderful ... I feel like I can say this, as a queer woman: it's always angry queers that get stuff going.' Queer pioneers develop collections, dream up exhibitions and organize events, frequently going beyond their official remits to ensure that the perspectives of people like them are reflected in spaces which they care deeply about. This is a labour of love undertaken by people who – conscious of their place as representatives of the underrepresented – challenge the status quo in order to assert their identities in environments which do not always fully understand them. When enacted within the systems of an apathetic or indecisive organization, these assertions can even take on the character of a minor rebellion.

No matter their tenacity, these pioneers are not always operating from positions of power. Individual efforts to collect, reinterpret or engage with LGBTQ+ audiences can be fragile and fleeting, creating queer blips in the record which serve only to underscore the work which remains to be done elsewhere. Discussing the legacy of Edinburgh City Council's participation in the *Remember When* project, Sheila Asante observes: 'A lot of these stories are still on the periphery, and are exhibitions, not embedded. There have been some great things but what have they done, going forward? Where is that history, permanently?'

Without institutional support or promises to embed inclusive practices, LGBTQ+ workers can feel burdened or overwhelmed by their commitment to queering. But despite the stress, they continue in their efforts because they understand the necessity of this work. One survey response acknowledged systemic shortcomings at their organization in their report that 'the emotional labour which is often undertaken by LGBTQ+ staff when working towards these displays goes unrecognized and [is] not properly taken care of'. This burden must be eased. More museum workers need to get on board with LGBTQ+ inclusion, and more organizations need to immerse themselves in this work. This requires staunch allyship from a broadly non-queer sector. We've already seen that many museum teams believe themselves to be friendly, open and accepting spaces, while still being hesitant to pursue LGBTQ+ equity in their organizations. In the words of one survey responder: 'I would love to be an inclusive space for the LGBTQ+ community but not sure how.' Many simply lack the knowledge or confidence to get started, a situation which I suspect may stem from a fear of queering. Although a straight museum worker may desire a more equitable museum, they are aware of their lack of lived experience or connections to LGBTQ+ communities and worry that taking action on behalf of queer people may be perceived as an imposition. Straight, cisgender museum workers should acknowledge the root of this fear by relinquishing the power over spaces which they hold as members of society's sexual and gender identity majorities. Ilona shares her experience of a straight colleague whose allyship has led to significant progress at Aberdeen Archives, Gallery and Museums: 'Don't feel like you can't do something because you're not a queer person. Create the space for the queer person. It takes so much emotional strain off this whole process, just by having that space already. As a queer person, it's really validating and encouraging working with and for people with this attitude.' Chloe Rose-Alex from LGBT Youth Scotland agrees: 'We're not looking to just keep things in the queer community, we're looking for everybody to get involved … one of the best things that an ally can do is recognize that it shouldn't fall just to that community. And this is something that we're going to work together on.' These are the museum workers that queer people need.

Museum workers who embark on LGBTQ+ inclusion can minimize risk and avoid causing harm by engaging with people that have lived experience and listening to those who have expertise in creating safe spaces for LGBTQ+ people. They can express their intentions to improve, ask for feedback and be open about their lack of knowledge. And if things actually do go wrong? 'I made mistakes during the concert series.' Museum Assistant Molly Ashmeade admits about her work at St Cecilia's. 'But that doesn't mean I stopped and completely froze and thought, "Oh, my God, I'm useless at this, I should never do this again". It just meant, "oh, I should take that feedback, and run with it". And that was fine.' What matters most is that people are sincere in their efforts to build fairer museums. This work is worth the effort. The push for equity can breathe new life into museums, giving them renewed relevance and broadening the communities which sustain them. In this era of financial uncertainty for museums, the attention, energy and revenue generated by LGBTQ+ audiences can serve as a lifeline.

Museums need queer people. But do queer people need museums? There is a need for public spaces which celebrate the queer lives which came before us; their struggles, successes and fights for rights and recognition. Scotland's cultural institutions should be settings where LGBTQ+ experiences are nurtured and normalized, and where queer people can express their identities and explore their place in society. Although the museum sector has incredible potential to champion LGBTQ+ equity, it hasn't kept pace with cultural change in Scotland. I regularly visit museums where nothing has been done to acknowledge the existence of LGBTQ+ people. This is how museums have always been; and so I used to accept it. But in an increasingly diverse Scotland, the choice for museums is stark: embrace queerness, or risk becoming things of the past.

Reference

MacLeod, S., Plumb, S., Sandell, R. and Scott, E.-J. *Trans-Inclusive Culture: Guidance on Advancing Trans Inclusion for Museums, Galleries, Archives and Heritage Organisations.* University of Leicester Research Centre for Museums and Galleries, 2023.

20

After Morgan: On legacy and queer elders in poetry

Andrés N. Ordorica

Introduction

From the age of fourteen, I wrote poetry in secret, often about my musings of loneliness, my not-so-subtle longing and a hunger for something that remained unknown, but that existed in the just beyond: a happy queer life, somewhere I might safely root myself, call home. An earnest, voracious reader, the kind of young man his English teachers would describe as 'considerate,' 'kind,' or even 'conscientious', it was in words I found safety. The outside world was dangerous for all its loud, brash, machismo, and my version of boyhood, eventually manhood, did not align with it.

Eventually, I would come out at the age of nineteen, having grown up in a US military family against the backdrop of Don't Ask, Don't Tell. My formative years were shaped by a very specific type of masculinity, by a world that pushed my inherent queerness into the shadows, off into the margins, never to be spoken about. But it was words that would be my salvation. Across my writing, both prose and poetry, I have intentionally built a body of work that is queer. I thrive on clawing my way out from the shadows, the margins, the silences. I am inspired by the Mexican American phrase, *ni de aquí, ni de allá* (to be from neither here, nor there). This liminal space has become a home both for my writing and my many identities: queer, immigrant, brown, man. I am most interested in what happens in the in between, through metaphor and allusion, consonance and assonance, form and style. The writers I aspire to emulate have found ways of queering these writerly tools to build worlds where how they live, how they love can exist fully.

At twenty-eight, I first read Scottish poet Edwin Morgan's poem *Strawberries* (1968). He immediately pulled me into his atmospheric world, which was both stunning and also deeply intimate, as if I, the reader, were intruding on a private moment between two lovers:

> facing each other
> your knees held in mine.

What he says and doesn't say in this poem is both tantalizing and a means of self-preservation. He understood how to use the poem to hold space for all he could not say aloud, defiant though with the heat, carnality and lust he poured into each descriptive word.

I spent my late twenties, actively seeking out queer writing like Morgan's, as if to rewire my brain on what was possible to do in poetry and prose. Morgan, James Baldwin, Audre Lorde, Edmund White, Richard Blanco, Ali Smith and more became obsessions, an almost refuge for a burgeoning queer writer like myself. I had grown up in a way that tried to silence so much of who I was, and yet, for as long as I was able to read, there had been queer writers that existed. Now was the time to trawl through the great bodies of work in an attempt to find home. The idea of home was another obsession, informed by a childhood of growing up around the globe following my father's military career, born into a family of immigrants, never having lived in one place more than four years. But then in my early twenties, I met a man who happened to be Scottish, whose family went back generations in the same distinct area of Scotland. And so, we fell in love and married, and eventually I would move to Scotland in 2018 and begin to wonder if this verdant, poetic landscape might be the kind of home I had been searching for my whole life, its history and culture, its writers included. Thus, this is how I began my longstanding love affair with the work of Edwin Morgan, one of Scotland's greatest champions of the written word. First by reading his work over and over again, trying to inhale each stanza as if it were my life's oxygen and then by writing to his larger legacy, working through his archive and beginning to craft my own poems after Morgan. So that in turn, my own writing might become a refuge for others, a place to call home.

Introducing Edwin Morgan

Edwin Morgan was born in Glasgow in 1920. After serving in the Royal Army Medical Corps during the Second World War, he returned to Scotland and became a lecturer in English at the University of Glasgow. His prolific poetry career saw him named Glasgow's first Poet Laureate in 1999 and Scotland's first modern Makar (or national Poet Laureate) in 2004. Morgan spent the first forty years of his life living under the criminalization of homosexuality. It wasn't until 1981 that sexual relations between consenting men over the age of twenty-one was decriminalized in Scotland. In 1990, he came out publicly at the age of seventy and passed away two decades later at the age of ninety. But he left behind him a body of work rich in its depiction of love and desire, pulsating with the unsaid, never naming the he or him of a poem. It is in this unnaming in which Morgan built a refuge for readers across generations.

Artists have long wrangled suffering and pain into wondrous works of art which evoke a sense of familiarity, emoting an almost refuge in their portrayals of pain which feel both deeply intimate and intensely wide in scope. But rarely, as a reader, have I ever been afforded the opportunity to feel a synergy with how the artist portrays pain and love, by that I mean a version that is firmly queer. The literary canon is so large and wide, and as a lover of words, and a writer of words, I have spent much of my life trying to find my refuge, a wee place, among countless books that line a library shelf. This has been a deliberate act, a reclamation of my right to see myself in words, in verse, in story, how I love, how I grieve, how I celebrate life's many joyful chapters. It is both through reading and writing that I have created my own act of rebellion against the structures I grew up in.

On writing with Morgan

The first time I read Edwin Morgan's *By the Fire* (1963), I was overcome how, in a few short lines of verse, he captures what it is to take on a lover's pain and hold space for it, until both become as ceaseless as 'the black ice of Lanarkshire'. His ability to capture, with such fearlessness, both the beauty and brutality of love and life is one of the reasons I have grown to love Morgan so intensely. There are countless Morgan poems that literally stop me in my tracks when reading:

> I asked if you heard the rain in your dream
> and half dreaming still you only said, I love you.

This ending to Morgan's gorgeous poem *When You Go* (1968), a meditation on what it would feel like to be left behind by a dying lover embodies the unique freedom afforded to queer people only when gifted a private room of one's own, a wee place. It comes at little surprise then that Morgan so often placed his lovers in situations away from the prying eyes of judgemental society: tucking them safely away in bed, or in a field of grass, or in the dark gloam of a summer's night. These settings were far safer than the outside world where the very real threat of police attention, accusations of 'gross indecency' and associated punishments destroyed lives. Despite all these real-world fears, reading his love poems is to read a masterclass in writing of same-sex love and desire in a coded way. He wrote in a style that intended to ingratiate a more general audience so as not to offend 'majority sensibilities' (Morgan 1990, 145). His poems often speak directly to the lover, never gendering them as he wrote in *Drift* (1973):

> Only stars of heat
> picked, and your cigarette
> smouldered in the grass
> forgotten ...

Again, knowing the society he was writing in, one in which homosexuality was still criminalized, it makes sense that he never mentions the man his speaker is addressing. Why would he? To be gay was dangerous, even for the well to do, the accomplished, the academic, the war hero. Morgan would have been only thirty-two when the Second World War code-breaker Alan Turing made headlines, prosecuted for homosexual acts. The very man who played an integral part in helping the Allies defeat the Axis powers, who chose castration over a prison sentence, only to be left with the mental anguish that led to his suicide. But like Turing's work as a cryptologist, Morgan left behind many clues for the queer reader. His sumptuous verse is filled with a yearning so specific to the queer experience – its intense observation, ample sensory details and the heat burning within its lyrical longing. It is that heat, a torchlight in essence, that I carry forth in my own writing. I acknowledge my privilege in being able to write more openly and unabashedly, naming the 'he' or the 'him' in my work and allowing my queer characters to have parts of their story happen outside the confines of four walls. This privilege is most evocative when engaging with Morgan's love poems, such as in *When You Go*:

> I let the darkening room
> drink up the evening ...

For me, allowing my characters out into the light is of paramount importance. I do not neglect the reality of how a room of one's own, that wee place, for so many queer people, is the only area in which they are guaranteed safety and freedom. My hope though is by moving out of the 'darkening room' I might shed a light on what it is to be a queer man writing now a days and to extend the possibility of literary refuge for a new generation of readers.

Like many of my favourite writers who have occupied this place before me, themes of loss and love pepper much of my writing practice. My debut poetry collection, *At Least This I Know*, works as an almost poetic memoir taking the reader from childhood on into my thirties. It explores many facets of the self, from race to sexuality, to immigration and family history, but the throughlines are love and loss in equal measure. Throughout the collection I feature past lovers, but there is an entire section that is dedicated to my husband. This openness is something that would not have been afforded to a writer like Morgan at the height of his career. My debut novel, *How We Named the Stars* furthers this interrogation of love and loss through its protagonist Daniel who is reeling from the death of his friend-cum-lover, Sam. The novel is elegiac in form, told in second-person narrative by Daniel as a means of processing his grief, with the reader embodying the character of Sam. My central question was to understand what it is to hold love and loss in tandem, how a singular person might be a vessel for all those emotions, and what that might do to someone (i.e. Daniel) when left behind in the aftermath of death.

To me, despite their seemingly universal appeal, these two themes are strongest when told through a queer lens via my own lived experience. Perhaps, because for so much of my life I went without seeing that perspective on the page or within a line of verse. Choosing to write to queer love and loss is the most political aspect of my writing. I am deftly aware how queer communities so often have been prevented from telling our own stories. Instead, our loss, our pain, our love and our joys have often been extracted from us in muted colour and given back to us by the heterosexual majority. Or too often, if we are given a seat at the table, there is an expectation that we write of our love and loss in a palatable way. My ambition across my poetry and prose has always been to articulate the pains and glories of love, desire and loss with as much honesty as I can afford myself so that a reader, in particular a queer reader, might see part of themselves reflected in the worlds I create. Again, I do this as a means of writing the stories I did not get to read when I was young and questioning and to expand the possibilities of literary refuge.

In truth, few writers have been able to capture loss and, more importantly, love in a way that ever rang true to me. *No one had ever loved the way I loved.* Or so I thought until I read Edwin Morgan's poetry who broke open my world view into something much richer, more tangible, basking me in a familiar sense of warmth. Morgan's writing held in its grasp kinship and wisdom, things I had long been searching for, like a hand being held out across time.

On queerness in Morgan's work

In his 1988 interview with Morgan, writer and critic Christopher Whyte opens part of the discussion with a matter-of-fact observation, 'When I first read your poems, I remember noticing that there were signs you might be gay, there was more room in the love lyrics than I would normally expect' (Morgan 1990, 144). It is in such 'room' Whyte describes in which I found a possibility of my version of loving and longing, and while Morgan may have had to play his desire much more demurely, the richness of his language still remains. Morgan later surmises in his interview that 'a younger poet in a similar situation today wouldn't feel so inhibited' to write much more explicitly, and yet confirms, 'all the love poems which I have published are gay' (144). My generation of poets is indebted to writers like Morgan who found a means of writing honestly even when having to rely on ambiguity and a reader's savvy to know what kind of love was being addressed.

My love and admiration for Morgan blossomed brightly during his centenary celebrations when I was awarded a grant through the Edwin Morgan Trust to carry out a project inspired by Morgan's legacy. Throughout his life, he was lauded for his inventive, inquiring, energetic, internationalist writing and deep commitment for his home city of Glasgow. As part of my project, I wrote a sequence of poems which I then produced as film poems drawing inspiration from the visual media produced by Edwin Morgan in his scrapbooks from 1931 to 1966, my focus being his love poems (Ordorica 2024, 1953).

Although, at that point in my career, I was quite familiar with Morgan's poetry, it was when I first learned of his scrapbook collection – thanks to an open call from the Scottish indie press Speculative Books – that the cogs began to spin. Scouring his collage work, I felt as if he had taken bits of my own personal diary as source material, building scenes of my life, making visual representations of the very questions that burned brightly in my mind.

As part of a planned publication, Speculative Books invited writers, in partnership with the Edwin Morgan Trust, to produce poetry and fiction that spoke in conversation to Morgan's scrapbooks housed at the Mitchell Library in Glasgow. As the centenary occurred during one of the many lockdowns of the Covid-19 pandemic, much of the research happened via the library's Flickr account. Throughout a spring of unwavering change with a mysterious virus running rampant, almost like the Sci-Fi worlds of Morgan's most experimental writing, I dove headfirst into Morgan's archives. They were a tonic to the sheer unknown unfolding around me. I ended up writing a story in which the central character goes on a walk one afternoon as his town is eerily abandoned. Obviously, inspired by many solitary walks taken during the early days of Covid-19. My story was published by Speculative Books as part of *The Centenary Collection* in May 2020.

What I was most captivated by was the chaos of Morgan's scrapbooks and the absurd, exotic, unsettling and sexual images that were plastered throughout. Images of ancient pottery from Africa and South America, sepia muscle men posing for vintage body-building magazines, Sci-Fi objects and foreign paraphernalia collected from his time overseas in the Royal Army Medical Corps. His scrapbooks were just on the cusp of revealing something sensuous and desirous, as if leaving behind code for future generations. Reminiscent of collages I made for revision books and binders in high school, I cut from magazines and brochures, added bits of paraphernalia that I hoped might signal to others my unique worldly, cultured viewpoint. Only now, much older, do I understand that it was less unique in aims and more a common expression of yearning for communion, particularly queer communion. As if through choice words and select images we might signal to others our wants and desires but only at a distance.

On the poet's gaze, or Morgan as queer outsider

In her introduction to *Scotland: Selected Poems by Edwin Morgan*, Liz Lochhead, former Makar of Scotland who succeeded Morgan (2011–16), says of Poets' Pub, the painting by Alexander Moffat hanging in Edinburgh's National Portrait Gallery, 'In this painting, Morgan isn't part of the central group but off to the side, his gaze looking outward, elsewhere' (Morgan 2020a). Lochhead's relationship with Morgan, both as friend and peer, was so valued that she was chosen to read out his commissioned poem *For the Opening of the Scottish Parliament, 9 October 2004*. What a testament to Scotland's relationship with the written word to have two poets consecrate a new chapter of national autonomy. And while Morgan's prestige ingratiated him into such esteemed places, there still existed so much of the outsider in his writing. Having spent many an afternoon in front of that painting, sitting on a bench to study these great poets who have come before me, Lochhead's assertion could not be a more accurate observation. To me the way Moffat captures Morgan's essence evoked the queer outsider, something that resonated with me deeply and it further shaped my approach to creating new work inspired by both Morgan's vast poetry work he left behind as well as his archive.

My gaze has always turned elsewhere, dreaming and scheming, qualities that I feel chime with so much of Morgan's writing, and what I know of his being, often in what has been shared by peers like Lochhead or another more recent Makar, Jackie Kay. As Kay writes in her introduction to twenty love poems by Edwin Morgan, 'Morgan knew all about love: its mysteries, its silences, its absences, its passions' (Morgan 2020b). For me, it is in the unsaid, what goes unnamed, which thrums the loudest in Morgan's work. He is not afraid to gaze longingly, because in his poetry there is a safety from the outside world, from dogma and law, from persecution and hatred. Love has a home in his verse.

In my poem *Neroli Kiss*, the speaker grapples with staying in the present moment which felt in synchronicity with Morgan's *Strawberries* (1968) as his own speaker is at the border of the present and the past on a day that mirrored 'that sultry afternoon' which he is desperate to not lose to time, praying that 'the sun beat on our forgetfulness'. The question the speaker asks his lover in Morgan's *Where You Go* is almost ethereal: Did you hear the rain in your dream? There is a deep intimacy in its childlike wonderment. In my poem *Neroli Kiss*, the speaker of the poem recounts how he met his lover while sailing down The Clyde – the very river that cuts through Morgan's beloved Glasgow.

> Do you ever dream about a life
> in which we never met?
>
> Or wonder what would be
> had I not traversed the sea?

On marrying two cultures

It was only by traversing the sea that I ended up meeting my then boyfriend, eventually partner, now husband. We married in 2014, the first year that same-sex marriages were legalized in England, Wales and Scotland. Our wedding took place on a quiet Monday afternoon in July, slightly grey and humid, in a library in Marylebone, London. Our wedding reception was a combination of our cultural backgrounds, Mexican and Scottish. Our boutonnieres were handmade by my mother-in-law from reclaimed tartan, and our wedding flowers combining my beloved sunflower and the hearty, majestic Scottish thistle. Name cards made from a deck of Mexican lotería. For his reading, my husband chose Robert Burns's *A Man's a Man for a' That* (1795).

This idea of what may come or what has come echoes across the poetic canon, be it making the decision to cross the sea or not as in my own poem *Neroli Kiss*, or the reckless power of desire in Morgan's *Strawberries* to 'let the storm wash away the plates' – there is something intensely desirous in throwing caution to the wind. And yet, we were not the first poets to grapple with such potent questions. As Burns himself wrote:

> Then let us pray that come it may,
> As come it will for a' that

I am reminded of Morgan's Scrapbook 10, its use of bright colours like those of a deck of lotería cards (Morgan 2024). On this page, he has arranged different hand-painted postcards at slight angles, overlapping just enough to hide one lay beneath. As if he threw them down, rather than painted them himself, letting fate decide the order like a deck of tarot or a hand of poker. Perhaps, that's part of the poet's calling, to let fate decide how the cards land, how the words arrange themselves, how the poem forms? The poet is simply the conduit, the tarot reader, a vessel.

Burns famously almost packed it all in to move to Jamaica, out of money and at a loss, but it never came to be. Had he indeed traversed the sea, he might not have gone onto be one of Scotland's foremost poets. A Scotland without Burns or Morgan would be less rich, poor of colour and weak in verse. Thank goodness that fate knows when to intervene, thank goodness the poem knows when to call upon the poet to craft it on the page.

My favourite photo from my wedding day is one in which I am looking at the camera, enjoying a pint in the beer garden of our reception venue, the Scottish bunting my in-laws strung about in soft focus. A smile on my face, the bunting a sign of home to come, a rooting taking place in the form of a new union. I had visited Scotland a few times before, but it would be three years into our marriage before we decided to fully leave London, the city that brought us together:

From the banks, I might see two lovers
sailing down the tangerine stream

And when I do, I'll wash in its
blessed blossom loch and think of you.

In my poem, the speaker's mind goes 'with the currents' as he remembers when he first met his lover. As they sail down a fictional version of the River Clyde which cuts through Morgan's Glasgow, the speaker of the poem wonders what would have been had they not met. As Morgan says in his poem *Absence* (2003), 'Love is the most mysterious of the winds that blow'.

As I continued to create new work based on Morgan's legacy and archive, I began to feel a synchronicity with Morgan and understood how poetry enabled us to commune together across time and experiences. What Morgan left behind through his legacy, his writing and his expansive archive offered me the ability to root myself deeper in Scotland as a queer person and as a creator. Morgan showed me how in poetry, I can choose to write my existence however it suits my understanding of this world. I can choose to write my version of love, in the same way he did because ultimately someone, many even, have loved how I have loved.

On longing for 'haim'

Sometimes the hardest part of love is the hurt, the sadness and anger you must shoulder when deeply loving someone else, or even a homeland, or new home. How in your times of great loss, you must ask this other person, or entity, to keep you going, to wake you up each day, wash you, to help you try and survive a little longer – all of these great emotions and rites of passage of love are evident in Morgan's work. Love was not solely reserved for people but shared in abundance with the places that mattered most to Morgan. He was a masterful writer of place, specifically, Glasgow, but also of wider Scotland. He captured its flora and fauna in only the way a poet can with an eye for detail and a peculiar surrealism. In *Beasts of Scotland*, he introduces a familiar band of characters. Of the midge, he writes:

> The evening is perfect, my sisters.
> The loch lies silent, the air is still.

His poetry always transportive whatever the locale. In taking inspiration from Morgan, I also wanted to write to the landscape as I did in my own poem *Bennachie*. The speaker addresses his lover, a Scotsman, as they look out upon Aberdeenshire. For me, I would have been amiss to not write to a version of the northeast of Scotland. As a place, it is where much of my connection to Scotland begins as a man married into a proud, Doric-speaking Aberdonian family. The poem evokes a liminality, a sense of one foot (or 'fit') sturdied upon the rock, and another somewhere deep in the vault of memory.

> I longed to know a land like that,
> close enough to feel at home
>
> and for that home to love me back

Learning to lay claim to the land, and celebrate all the love it has afforded me, has been a way of honouring poetry as both place and home. In her poem *In My Country* (1993), former Makar, Jackie Kay (2016–21), ends with a stunning couplet that encapsulates how home (or haim) can be found within the magic of poetry, its power to illuminate, to affect, to reflect back to the reader a sense of self.

> *Where do you come from?*
> 'Here', I said, 'Here. These parts.'

Conclusion

For me, the making of home (or haim) lives in the words I write and those I read. I understand them now as a refuge both for the queer and immigrant selves I carry within. I am grateful to have found home in the poems of Morgan, and successive Makars like Lochhead and Kay, or closer-to-home, Edinburgh Makars Hannah Lavery and Michael Pederson, and more widely poets such as Alycia Pirmohamed, Rachel Plummer, Harry Josephine Giles and Jay Gao, who have shown me how I come from a long history of writers and thinkers in Scotland who imbue language, longing and notions of loss with such deft precision, but in each, there are call backs to the great legacy of Morgan. I appreciate this looking forward while also still maintaining a gaze on the poets who have come before. Through Morgan's writing, he has encouraged a generation of poets to write truthfully and honestly. For that, I am forever indebted to his legacy and to the many other queer poets and writers who have made home in Scotland. As I continue to root myself into the landscape, I will unabashedly move my characters out into the light, expanding our place in this country from something wee to something much richer and bigger, always encouraging my fellow queers to take up more space, so we can proudly lay claim to this land and know exactly where we're from. Our words will serve as refuge, our poems will become our home.

References

Morgan, E. *Edwin Morgan Twenties: Scotland*. Edinburgh: Polygon, 2020a.
Morgan, E. *Edwin Morgan Twenties: Love*. Edinburgh: Polygon, 2020b.
Morgan, E. 'Edwin Morgan Scrapbook 10 (1953–5)'. 25 October 2024. www.flickr.com/photos/uofglibrary/4545644184.
Morgan, E. *Nothing Not Giving Messages: Reflections on Work and Life*. Edinburgh: Polygon, 1990.
Ordorica, A. N. '3 Poems after Edwin Morgan'. Edwin Morgan Trust, 25 October 2024. https://edwinmorgantrust.com/2021/02/26/andres-ordorica-3-poems-after-edwin-morgan/.

21

Brilliant vibrating interface: Queering the post-internet through poetry and practice

Kirsty Dunlop and Maria Sledmere

Brilliant Vibrating Interface (BVI, 2022–3) was a year-long series of workshops, podcasts, performances and a hybrid (print and digital) anthology of creative works funded by the Edwin Morgan Trust's Second Life Award. It was conceived by SPAM Press – a Glasgow-based community interest company which started as a poetry zine in 2016 and has since evolved into a publisher, online magazine, podcast and community organizer. Webpages discussed below can be found at www.spamzine.co.uk.

Kirsty,

The other day I was in the shower slathering myself in soap and noticed my left arm and leg were connected by a giant bubble. The ceiling light reflected in its swirl-warp many times over as the shower water splashed around me. It looked like a curvaceous screen ... shimmer ... interface between skin. When the bubble popped in the light of day, my body felt 'online'. I scratched my leg. There was no discernible residue.

Recently, someone brought bubbles to a poetry reading in Glasgow. These weird bubbles lingered a little too long on surfaces. They'd hold a world, refracting the outside. The intimately scaled arts scenes of this city are often described as a 'bubble'. From design to concept, bubbles were a key motif in our design for Brilliant Vibrating Interface (hereafter referred to as BVI). We write to each other here in short 'bubbles' of floating thought. We hope to situate BVI as a case study in queering the post-internet[1] and explore what that teaches us about the relationship between queer Scottish culture and the world of digital literature.

For me, the first time queerness and bubbles were brought into contact was via the poet CAConrad. In their somatic exercise 'POWER SISSY INTERVENTION #1: Queer Bubbles' (2016), they describe a ritual in which the poet occupied a North Carolina street corner 'to bless children with bubbles that will make them queer'. Knowing that of course 'bubbles have only the power to be bubbles' and not literally imbue passers-by with queerness, this was a playful exercise in exposing the latent bigotry in a city (Asheville) that otherwise 'purports to be a liberal laid-back city' (Conrad 2016). Bubbles are transient phenomena: a thin sphere of precariously held air. The point about bubbles is that they are liable to pop. To burst someone's bubble is to ruin their illusions. In Conrad's poetic ritual, the bubble is at once a queer phenomenon

– unfixed, fluid, afloat – and the demonstration of homophobic prejudice. Many parents liked the bubbles until Conrad explicitly deemed them queer.

With BVI, we embraced the idea of queer air and rainbow iridescence, reproduced in the bubble's soapy surface. In scale terms, this got me thinking about Glasgow as a bubble set within the bigger bubble of Scotland and beyond. Funded by the Edwin Morgan Trust's Second Life Award, BVI was a year-long endeavour in situating the queer, experimental and machine-minded poetry of Edwin Morgan with contemporary examples of Scottish writing which unite such themes in the post-internet age. We essentially conceived of the project as a series of interrelated bubbles for engagement – workshops, performance nights and podcasts – culminating in the wider, more enduring bubble of a print and digital anthology. BVI centred on the question: what affordances do experimental, digitally inclined forms have for articulating queer experience? Building on our previous record of publishing queer poets such as Jay Gao, Parel Joy, T. Person, Ali Graham and fred spoliar, we were passionate about formulating BVI as a queer, shape-shifting project.

I wanted to ask you, as editor, what you thought about the scope of BVI specifically as an anthology. On the one hand, we saw the book and its digital sibling[2] as a culmination of the research and workshopping achieved during the earlier phase of the project. How does this relate to the published work's connections to Morgan's writing? Hosting local events and publishing local writers since 2016, SPAM has forged a distinctly Glaswegian identity, borne out of the city's long history of DIY zine and club culture: examples from the 2010s include Lauren Mayberry's collective TYCI (Tuck Your Cunt In) and the cabaret night Queer Theory. However, the post-internet theme of our publishing attracted an international audience through social media, email and webspace. How did that combination of local and global combine into the particular bubble that was the BVI anthology?

In our open call for the anthology, we specified that those submitting work must identify as 'queer practitioners ... with a connection to Scotland' (SPAM 2023a). Some of our key aims for the project (in line with those of the Edwin Morgan Trust, our funders) were to provide innovative poetry education to a general audience, platform underrepresented voices, promote the ongoing legacy of Edwin Morgan as a queer Scottish poet and to galvanize opportunities for emerging writers to innovate in their practice. The way we use the internet in our current moment is often as a 'walled garden', where users are confined to limited, algorithm-bound platforms which do not enable much freedom by way of customization – a distinct sense of permanent enclosure compared to the transience of bubbles. Can you talk about the open call for the project and the queer aesthetics of its framing?

—Maria

Maria,
As I read your words I float above the language in a bubble. Occasionally I will stick to a word, a sensation; there's *shimmer, afloat, scratched* by the *unfixed*. Chance and an improvisatory impulse loom at the forefront of this imagining. How many of these sensations are lost in the overwhelming algorithmic rhythms of our online world? In

the early experiments of the internet (the largely static pages of Web 1.0), there was a keen sense of the DIY, of amateurism, play; an attempt to discover what the internet could make space for, creatively, aligned to the collaborative ethos of small press publishing. But this movement and thinking is by no means over. We wanted to situate and express queerness and fluid forms, fluid bodies, within and through the multiple vibrating interfaces that we live among today – beyond the human, entangled between the virtual and the physical.

Across this landscape floats the question of BVI's scope as an anthology. I am drawn to a quotation by Donna Haraway from 'The Cyborg Manifesto', a key text for the cyberfeminism and interrelated queer theory movements. Haraway advocates for 'pleasure in the confusion of boundaries and responsibility in their construction' (1991, 150); there is space for multiplicity and fluidity beyond Western dualism, while taking these movements and the construction of alternative systems of creating and living seriously. Throughout the process of working with the practitioners in the final publication, we were less interested in the categorization of specific works than the techniques of language, image, sound, code and playback as methods of exploring queerness.

In line with these ideas, it was important for us to construct what might be conceived of as a transmedial[3] space, to produce a book and an accompanying digital exhibition site named the digital sibling. It is common in the publishing industry for books to be replicated as electronic PDFs, with few differences between the page and the screen and without a focus on *how* we are engaging with the writing materially. We wanted to glitch these kinds of transferences. The digital sibling offered an alternative direction for the collection: not as a replica but instead a performance.

I am going to take a step back and draw upon some of the directions of our call for submissions. We asked open questions which felt fundamental to the scope and ethos of BVI such as: 'How do societal strictures on queerness influence content and form? What new worlds, sanctuaries, and utopias can hybrid work and post-internet poetics allow us to explore?' (SPAM 2023a). We also included a list of specific and abstract playful language prompts, such as 'transmedial tantrums / electronic writing / code poetics / osmotic enquiries/ … / platonic point-and-click adventure / lurker lyric / strawberry vibes / manifestos for a queer utopia'. Within these prompts are references and connections between digital spaces, queer world-building, play and post-internet culture alongside the legacy of Morgan's work as a queer Scottish writer.

The practitioners came from varied artistic backgrounds, crafting pieces that move between media, ideas and skillsets: from the film sound work of New Media artist and musician Zeo Fawcett, which explores trans bodies through an expansive alien landscape, to the ceramic interactive drawing tool of visual artist and poet Rebecca Close, which invites us to consider where our networks of care are located in community. While many of the artists are well known locally, others were based further afield with a connection to Scotland. We were keen that the idea of Scotland as a place, an idea and relationship wasn't set or limited, reflecting the interconnected, international artistic spirit of Glasgow.

I will draw upon some examples of how Morgan's legacy was held within the anthology. One of Morgan's most pivotal works is 'Strawberries' (1968), a poem which

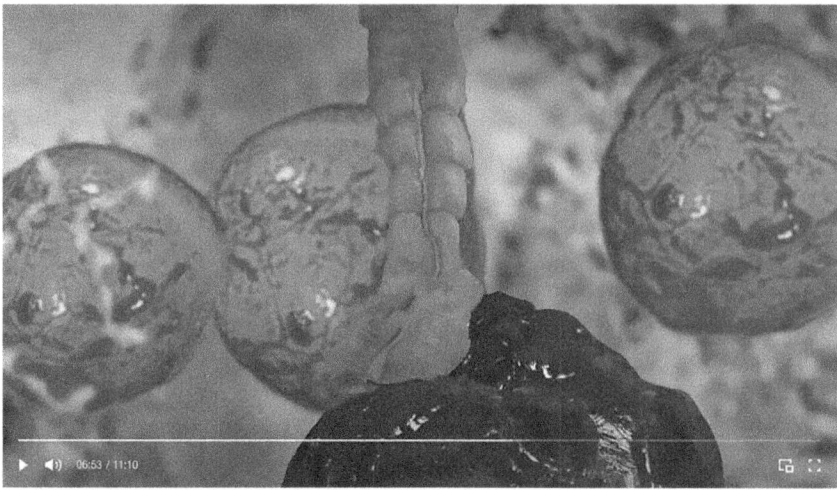

Figure 21.1 Film still from Zeo Fawcett's 'increasingly honest desires (extraterrestrialboy00)', printed with permission. *BVI Digital Sibling* (2023).

brims with intimacy, as the speaker addresses an unidentified lover. Many of his poems reference queerness obliquely, although reading it in the present day, we can sense how the language is laced with queer longing: 'from your eager mouth//the taste of strawberries' (Morgan 1968). Another method of queer reading is tracked through the shape of the lines, appearing as two forks on the page; there is a paralleling here, perhaps insinuating homosexuality. The locality of the poem is felt in the fruit; after all Scotland is revered for its strawberries, able to withstand the frosty climate.

The most explicit reflection of Morgan's work in BVI is Lauren Sheerman's 'a poem about strawberries flirting'. In many ways, Sheerman is upturning the idea of strawberry as a metaphor which plays out in Morgan's work, further complicating the boundaries between the literal and symbolic, although similarly, the lines tease and withhold:

> Embarrassment loads like a glitch
> the bowl of strawberries taste of strawberries
> flavouring strawberry lips strawberry gloss strawberry hot. (SPAM 2023b)

The poem carries its questioning through a playful address and an overwhelming sense of being seen; 'embarrassment' as a queer emotion opens up from the outset. The language is quietly deceptive, a slow and shifting unloading and withholding of *what* the strawberries may contain. 'A poem is the way I am thinking//or not thinking' (SPAM 2023a), she writes a few lines down, and we are buoyed onwards by this gentle tease and refusal to be pinned down. Boundaries are confused. The listing reflects the pace of online advertising, while the poem's subjective voice moves among a collective virtual gaze. In the online adaptation, lines are slowly revealed, with varied timings: a deliberately slowed down reading is directed. In Fiona Glen's poem 'strawberry squid', a swerve takes place. Here, the more-than-human is embraced through this beautifully luminescent alien creature which is both highly visible while also known for hiding itself in a cloud of ink, an apt reflection of the refractions of queer identity held within language, the visible and the obscured.

While my central focus was the final publication, you were project lead for the workshop component in the lead up to our call out. What did the workshops contribute? What did it mean to run this project locally in Glasgow? I also wonder how you conceive of the project's wider scope in connection with Morgan's writing.

—Kirsty

Kirsty,
In Morgan's poem 'The Second Life', the speaker asks: 'Is it true that we come alive / not once, but many times?' (1996, 180). Given that this is the titular poem from a collection very much focused on Glasgow, it suggests for me the many queer lives of Glasgow itself – in and beyond poetry. While homosexuality was criminalized for most of his lifetime, Morgan came out in 1990, at the age of seventy, and supported LGBTQ+ rights both as a writer and activist. Working with the Edwin Morgan Trust, we hoped to bridge more explicitly a connection between what we felt we were doing as a literary press and what Morgan's legacy continues to be among generations of queer writers. In the same poem mentioned above, Morgan writes:

> Many things are unspoken
> in the life of a man, and with a place
> there is an unspoken love also
> in undercurrents, drifting, waiting its time.
> A great place and its people are not renewed lightly. (Morgan 1996, 181)

I was taught to read queerness in literature through what a text leaves out. Take for instance, Eve Kosofsky Sedgwick's claim that 'queer' often refers to 'the open mesh of possibilities, gaps, overlaps, dissonances and resonances, lapses and excesses of meaning' which occur when 'anyone's gender' or sexuality can't be reduced to one thing (1993, 7). The 'unspoken' 'life' and 'love' identified in Morgan's poem 'The Second Life' may easily be read as a tacitly concealed sexuality, and yet one that spreads out not just from the 'man' but to 'a place'. Morgan identifies struggle in how the second life of a country might be felt, 'not renewed lightly'. He also mentions 'undercurrents, drifting, waiting'. These words speak to the fact that identities and desires often emerge in eddying movements and not just the epochal ruptures implied by legal change. I'm very interested in where the 'wee places' identified in this volume emerge.

What time, as Morgan's poem implies, belongs to what love? The time of small press publishing is often marked by fracture. Cuts to funding, the intervention of major life events, shifts in one's ability to provide voluntary service in addition to paid and care-based labour – this publishing sphere is precarious, liable to burst at any moment. If literature bears transitions in culture and consciousness, small press publishing is poised to respond at agile and exploratory scales and paces (given its lesser dependence on the institutional hierarchies and corporate procedures of upscaled publishing environments). The emergence of work from these 'wee' entities, then, is co-dependent on a circulation of what I want, shakily and sentimentally perhaps, to call *love*.

In a recent survey of 'love' as applied to literary theory, Deirdre Lynch states that love 'implies ethical commitment of a kind that people usually mobilize in their encounters with living persons rather than with lifeless things' (2020). As such, to become a lover of literature is to involve yourself in 'an enduring relationship' and so 'test one's capacities for fidelity' within that relationship (Lynch 2020). As Morgan's poem reminds us, no great renewal of person or place is achieved lightly. I wondered how much love factors into your editorial work, Kirsty? The love I have for small press publishing is beyond value and category, and yet its fidelity must constantly be tested. As you say, this is a process of unexpected glitches and experiments. With BVI, we were keen to test the boundaries and (im)possibilities of what constitutes Scottishness.

The call for submissions, which elides essentialist notions of belonging in favour of 'a connection to Scotland', makes possible an emergent reworking of what flavour that Scottishness might take in the work we wanted to publish. Much of the work of any small press literary community takes place in the Morganian 'undercurrents' (1996, 181) of conversation, work done in kind, support, resources and venues shared. Across the UK more generally, evidence of this is found in the Poets Hardship Fund which was set up to support poets facing financial difficulty in the Covid-19 pandemic.

This emphasis on connection leads me to your question about BVI's workshops. As project leads, we paid SPAM editors and other local writers to run free public workshops on topics relating to queer writing. These included your workshop 'the glitch potential', a workshop on 'waste & trash' poetics (led by Colin Herd and fred spoliar), queerness, appropriation and digital poetics (Ian Macartney and T. Person), art writing and queer ekphrasis (Alice Hill-Woods and Loll Jung) and finally my own 'poetics of cringe' workshop. With the latter, I was fascinated by the overlaps between 'cultural cringe' (often experienced in the over-signification of what constitutes Scottishness – think fridge magnets of Scots words) and the way we might 'cringe' at expressions of queer identity and belonging within post-internet forms such as fan-fiction, lyric poetry, blogging and video essays. The approach I encouraged within this workshop was a 'gallus' one, referencing the Scots word for being bold, daring and reckless.

One affect associated with cringe is shame: workshop participants made the connection between being scolded for sounding 'too queer' and 'too Scottish'. The workshop explored what happens when 'overshare' and excess were embraced as aesthetic possibilities. When I think about this workshop and the generosity of exposure people gave, I feel a great love for what is possible in that vulnerable space. That love was not dependent on any assessment of aesthetic 'quality' but on the fluid exchange of ideas and materials, process over outcome. As an editor more involved in the 'outcome' side, your approach was nonetheless iterative and expansive. Collaborating with others, what kinds of 'fidelity' to digital or post-internet literatures, to queer and to Scottish literatures, did you find tested in a productive way? How did the work connect to legacies of queer and electronic literature?

—Maria

Maria,

I fully agree with your idea of love being a central tenet of how we have navigated this project and its DIY ethos; I think part of this love is tied into a glitchful approach to publishing itself, foregrounding collaboration and questioning, meeting artists where their work stands.

In *Glitch Feminism*, theorist Legacy Russell writes:

> A body that pushes back at the application of pronouns, or remains indecipherable within binary assignment, is a body that refuses to perform the score. This nonperformance is a glitch. This glitch is a form of refusal. (2020, 16–17)

We could replace the word 'body' here with the words 'writing', 'poem', 'art' or 'Scottishness'. This project embraced risk, on a very material level, felt in the ephemerality of the online. To glitch[4] is to take a risk, to subvert, as Russell expresses, but it carries an exuberance: a portal to a different world of seeing, an expansive scene of connections. I discovered Edwin Morgan's 'futura 20: emergent poems' (1967) during the planning of my workshop, 'the glitch potential', which introduced participants to electronic writing and aesthetics. Morgan's concrete poems splay out letters from inside these words; as they caress across the page, we are disorientated from their original sources, which include 'dialeck piece from burns to a mouse' (1967), cut up very literally, appearing like a rainy downfall of sounds, ghostly memories. To collage, to transfer, to translate is a very queer mode[5] and also falls into this idea of a 'non-performance', breaking apart the boundaries and context of the source text towards an alternative relationship to language. I am reminded of several works in the anthology, such as Ernesto Sarezale's poem 'Anthology' which rewires meaning and progress in its slippery lines: 'between body indoors uphill tyranny clasping regarding off some off concordant hourly was' (SPAM 2023a). Sarezale, like Morgan, highlights that the work reuses other canonical texts, from William Shakespeare to Sappho, Lord Byron to Virgil, melding multiple histories and translations in its fractured syntaxes, rejecting simple meaning.

Something interesting also takes place with recycling and reconceptualizing in several of the digital-born submissions, such as Maria Wrang-Rasmussen's 'stroke(whisper' which utilizes moving gifs of pencil line drawings, reworkings of renaissance images, moving these androgynous figures outside of the boundaries of gender and inviting an intimate queer sensuality. This sensuality is felt in the pacing of the work, slow movements contrasting with our sped-up daily online feeds; here, bodies drift together, apart, hands embrace a head, which submerges in a puddle. Digital tools are not being used to optimize or to transfer directly, but rather to swerve into another lens of seeing and interacting. To be queer is to find alternative ways to live, to act and to shape, and so much of this reworking and play across media enacts this living through a generous space created for the reader to explore.

The history of queer practitioners online was a key part of the thinking behind this project. There are many underground corners of the web where queer history and its current waves of creative practice can be found, but an under-researched area is Interactive Fiction. A key practitioner is the trans writer and game designer Anna Antrophy, whose works are brilliant examples of how simple, short acts of game design

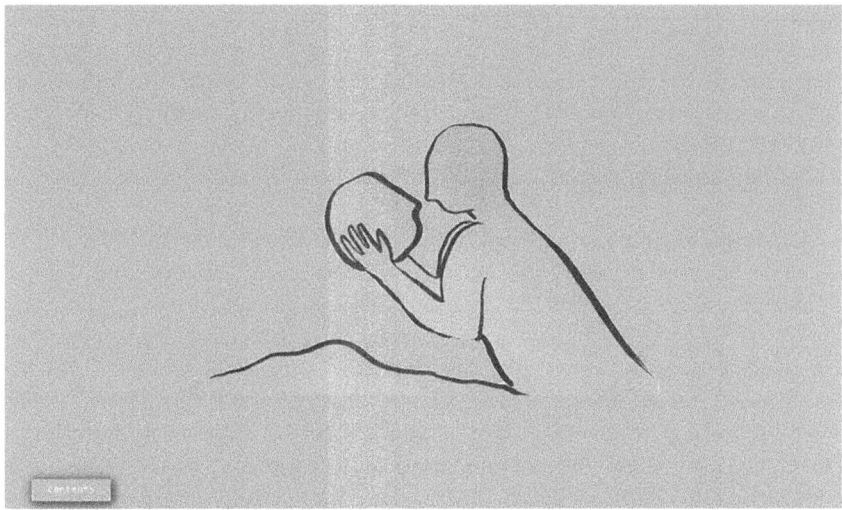

Figure 21.2 Screenshot from Maria Wrang-Rasmussen's 'stroke(whisper)', printed with permission. *BVI Digital Sibling* (2023).

can illuminate key issues affecting queer people on an intimate level, such as her work *Dys4ia* (2012, 2023), a minimalistic art game chronicling her experiences with hormone replacement therapy. Antrophy is an advocate of more people, particularly women, trans and queer people and people of colour having access to these tools, in a game industry still dominated by men.

In line with Antrophy's ethos and accessibility more generally, we wanted to provide practical tools in my workshop, through examples of open-source software practices such as Twine, as an entry point to those new to electronic writing. Who gets to make New Media work today, what resources does this require? Not everyone has the time or the means to take a coding class or read a book on game design. In other words, who gets to live online, to create online?

Other key aspects of the project were the interviews and podcasts we publicized; can you talk about some of the conversations opened in these arenas; did any themes or ideas emerge that fed back into our thinking? I've talked about some of the contexts of queer e-literature, perhaps you could discuss how our trajectories were influenced by a wider history of small press publishing in Scotland?

—Kirsty

Kirsty,
The interviews and podcasts offered research and scoping for the project. I'll start with the interview we conducted for our online journal, SPAM Plaza. In this interview, we explored sonnets: a perennially fashionable form that is also one of Morgan's hallmarks. Dating back to the thirteenth century, the sonnet is associated with courtly love. With their frequent references to William Shakespeare, sixteenth-century sonnets are

often read through a queer lens. SPAM editor Mau Baiocco and I interviewed three contemporary sonneteers (Ali Graham, Nik Ines Ward and Nat Raha) to see if the form still had purchase among queer poets in the twenty-first century. Our respondents variously testified to the sonnet's embrace of chance, constraint, seasonality, love and ideation. Queer poets such as Gertrude Stein and Sophie Robinson, along with the New York School, were cited as an experimental sonnet lineage, and queries around courtly forms and their relation to 'an anti-colonial imperative' (Sledmere and Baiocco 2024) were also raised by Raha. The fourteen-line sonnet, which means 'little song', is a suitably wee form for working in and against big questions of linguistic, political and social constraint. We hope the interview initiates more conversing between Morgan's engagement with the form and what Ward calls the 'euphoric' (Sledmere and Baiocco 2024) sonnet-writing of today.

We made several episodes of interview conversations between three contemporary queer practitioners with ties to Scotland: Aischa Daughtery, Ian Macartney and Parel Joy. Daughtery and Macartney were raised in Scotland, and Joy spent time in Aberdeen at university. Each is heavily involved in various facets of the Scottish poetry scene, whether through DIY zine-making, editing or publishing (Daughtery's book *This Is How We Love* (2022), Joy's *Dyke Love/Magic/Rage* zines and Macartney's small press sincere corkscrew). Including 130 love letters, texts, poems and artwork, Daughtery's anthology foregrounds explicitly lesbian experience and grants an expansive space of archive and appreciation to its contributors. Daughtery, in her SPAM interview, describes the book as a love letter to a whole community. We also talked about the intimacies of digital posting, trying to understand one's queerness in isolation, the importance of the internet in helping many people negotiate that with community. This harkened back to the queer coding in Morgan's poems, which are widely taught in Scottish schools but (in our childhoods at least) rarely with queer desire explicitly discussed in class. What we felt implicitly in those poems we were able to find more explicitly online. If BVI, as anthology, is somewhat representative of queer Scottish poetics today, how important is that dialectic of the implicit and explicit?

Ultimately, the conversations were a fluid tool for creative and critical inquiry. As discussed in a podcast interview, Joy's poetry and publication work oscillates between English, Dutch, Scots and Polari,[6] and their mix of poetic practice, archival work and interest in queer history relates to what Macartney calls a 'queer tapestry' (Joy and Macartney 2023). The textile metaphor nicely harkens Sedgwick's 'open mesh' as well as the idea of digital practice as a constantly woven web. While all three authors discussed specific localities for their work (Aberdeen for Macartney and Joy, Glasgow for Daughtery), each had a diverse vision for the forms of queer community they sought and forged through queer art and literature. The internet was obviously a prominent channel for this international outlook, but we discussed reservations about seeing the internet as a wholesale positive space. There is a haunted quality to contemporary digital life – with dead links, sites falling out of use, whole communities abandoned because of platform collapse. Macartney especially touched on issues of 'haunting' in terms of the communities left behind by the Aberdeen oil crisis and the infrastructural breakdown of Web 2.0. An alternative social infrastructure emerges through poetry, publication and printmaking. Such practices were named in one podcast as facilitating a 'new appreciation for ... queer elders' (Joy and Macartney 2023) – whether in the range of authors published or those cited as an influence, Morgan being one of many.

I'd say that SPAM remains a resolutely hybrid project of digital and print publication because there is resilience in variety: if a webpage is easily lost, a printed zine is easily archived; a webpage can be printed into a zine, and a printed zine can be archived online for a wider audience. This hybridity allows us to maintain an adaptable and intimate space for engagement with literary community and legacy. We are very much in conversation here with influential Scottish magazine endeavours of the past such as Callie Gardner's zine *Zarf* (2015–20) and Peter Manson and Robin Purves's transatlantic *Object Permanence* magazine (1994–7). To take *Object Permanence* as an example: this magazine emerged out of a desire to bring Scotland up to speed with experimental British and North American writing. As Manson summarizes on his blog, the magazine 'stands as an example of how much can be achieved with neither wisdom nor cash' (Manson 2014). This spirit of low-budget endeavour is very much in our realm, and perhaps reflects the need to continuously find ways to survive in an increasingly compressed funding landscape. In line with these ideas, what do you think is queer about the aesthetics and platforms of BVI, especially as they relate to the user interface you designed in the digital sibling?

—Maria

Maria,
In this final letter to you, I'll discuss some of the design choices undertaken in the book and website, alongside some thinking on the growth of New Media queer creativity in Scotland today.

Each editor worked closely with five artists, collaborating on the best means to adapt their work and stay true to its purpose while, in some cases, expanding with new interactive updates. Working with technology is always already a collaborative approach: it is easy to forget about the code that is performing behind the clean aesthetics of our screens. We were committed to letting the limbs of the work grow and swerve, whether in the case of Georgie du Boulay's sculptural processes and accompanying words becoming a live film on the website, or the move from static images and text to moving image and sound in the films of Freya Johnson, Sophie Taylor and Zeo Fawcett.

While co-editor Loll Jung was responsible for the design of the page-based work, my focus was on designing and coding the website. The anthology, as a mixture of visuals and text, sits between the spaces of a poetry collection and art book with no set reading method; at times you have to turn the book sideways, for example, to appreciate the static images of Eleanor Oliver's haunting webspace collage and to view the code and poetic entanglement of Maya Uppal's poem-game 'feedback loops'.

A black background is consistently present in the accompanying website design. Web 1.0 is often associated with this aesthetic, which is also more environmentally friendly, as it takes up less server space. We were keen to move away from the bright colours of social media feeds, to plunge viewers into more unfamiliar territory, drawing us into a past without seamless navigation. An editors' remix opens the site, coded from the

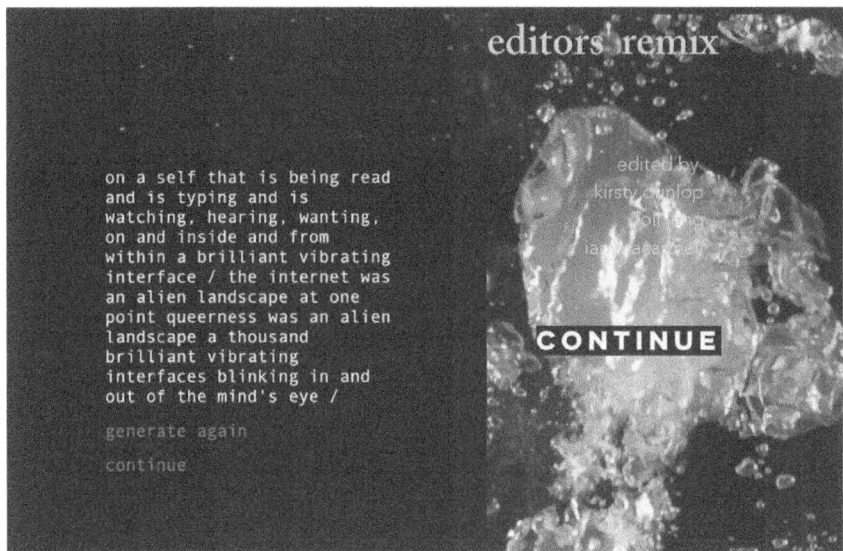

Figure 21.3 Screenshot of editors' remix. *BVI Digital Sibling* (2023).

introductions we wrote for the book, all in differing styles, from Ian Macartney's personal focus on queer life in Scotland, to Loll Jung's splicing up of Morgan's *Second Life*, to my own discussion of the project's background and multimedia visions in Scotland today. Variable lines from each text are generated on the screen, which you can choose to remix again or move on; unpredictive, they enact a live collaborative queering and unfolding of language that makes space for the reader to draw their own connections.

Following the introduction, you can choose which artists' work to access, on a visual contents page, non-linear form the outset. As a user, you are forced to take time with each piece as they follow such different navigation and interaction methods, paralleling Sedgwick's notion that queerness is not easily reducible to one thing. For example, Nicks Walker's 'patience behaviours' takes the form of tarot cards, which I coded onto card images, allowing readers to play the options which are all fully visible in the book (in this sense, the piece transforms into an interactive game) whereas some of the artworks, such as India Boxall's visual/text collage 'smear allegories', have been inserted directly from the host website into this space, the images blown up with horizontal landscape movement required.

During the exhibition launch and film screening at Many Studios, Glasgow, in November 2023, it was fascinating to see how people interacted with these assemblages. We had two laptops, one of which projected visuals onto the walls while the other encouraged a more private experience, as participants designed their own ceramic plates, using Rebecca Close's interactive drawing tool. At first, there was some uneasiness as to *what* people should do upon arriving: was it okay to take your time on the laptop with everyone watching your reactions and response on the screen? I realized it was a performance, not only of the works, but of your relationality to

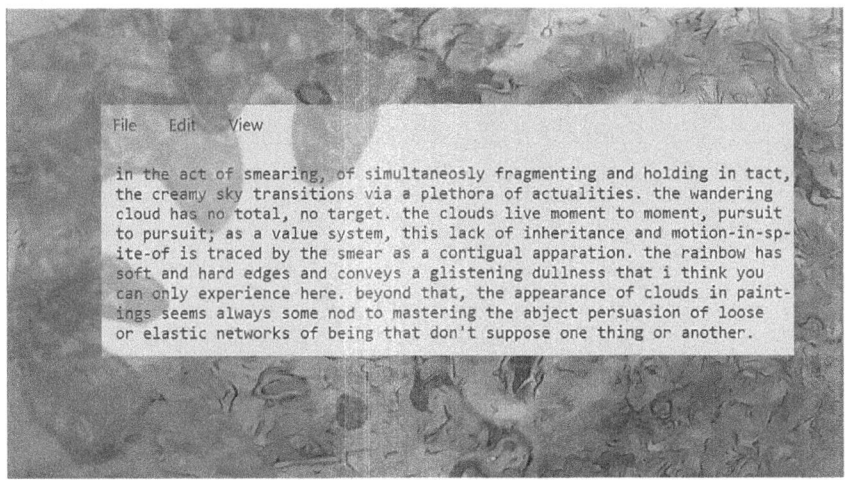

Figure 21.4 Screenshot from India Boxall's 'smear allegories', printed with permission. *BVI Digital Sibling* (2023).

them and to virtual space more generally. The exhibition challenged us to think about different formats for readings and audience interaction, in the absence of clear boundaries.

Reflecting on the challenges and expansiveness of co-creating this project with such an exciting range of queer thinkers gives me hope for the future of New Media across Scotland. E-literature has a grounding internationally, but its practitioners are often focused in set geographical locations, with a long history of Spanish digital poetics, for example, and key practitioners in the United States, such as Nick Montfort and Shelley Jackson. Connections between visual arts and poetics were at the forefront of BVI's collection of artists, in this sense showcasing how distributed New Media practice is across disciplines, but consistently reflecting that queerness is at the forefront of the thinking. For instance, Rebecca Close's practice in ceramics, poetics and creative coding is entangled with their research in post-internet queer reproductive work; they also run a Scottish-based anthology, *Them/All*, which publishes poetics and software art on reproductive politics and sexuality.

So many of these colliding bubbles of thought and creativity, which might not previously have met, are fizzing and defying categorization here: queering publication practices and expectations, making space for a new generation of queer digital practitioners in Scotland.

—Kirsty

Acknowledgements

We would like to thank all BVI contributors, along with fellow SPAM editors Alice Hill-Woods, Loll Jung and Ian Macartney for their support on the project.

Notes

1. We take post-internet in Marisa Olson's sense of the word, meaning art or literature made after the mainstreaming of internet access in the late 1990s and beyond – work which encounters, explicitly or implicitly, new forms of media and their influence at the level of form or content (Olson 2008).
2. The 'digital sibling' refers to an interactive webpage that was designed and coded by Kirsty Dunlop to accompany the print anthology.
3. Transmedia is a shifting term, but defined most recently by Henry Jenkins as texts and practices that cut across media, where meaning is gained in the relation between different media (2024).
4. We use the term 'glitch' expansively in this essay, understood in its most simple definition as a technological malfunction, but also as an aesthetic in sound, visuals and in theory, most recently in Legacy Russell's *Glitch Feminism* (2020), as a queer method of inquiry.
5. In *The Queer Art of Failure* (2011), Jack Halberstam draws attention to the queer aesthetics of collage as an act which references the spaces in-between, refusing to respect the boundaries delineating the self from others.
6. A secret form of language used by gay people to conduct conversation in public, dating back to an older form, Parlyaree, used by fairground people and entertainers in the nineteenth century (Baker 2021).

References

Antrophy, A. 'Dys4ia', 2012, 2023. https://w.itch.io/dys4ia. Accessed 25 August 2024.

Baker, P. 'Polari and the Hidden History of Gay Seafarers', *National Museums Liverpool*, January 2021. www.liverpoolmuseums.org.uk/stories/polari-and-hidden-history-of-gay-seafarers. Accessed 25 August 2024.

Conrad, C. A. 'POWER SISSY INTERVENTION #1: Queer Bubbles', *Capilano Review*, 21 January 2016. https://thecapilanoreview.com/caconrad-power-sissy-intervention-1-queer-bubbles/. Accessed 28 July 2024.

Halberstam, J. *The Queer Art of Failure*, Durham, NC: Duke University Press, 2011.

Haraway, D. 'A Cyborg Manifesto: Science, Technology and Socialist- Feminism in the Late Twentieth Century'. In *Simians, Cyborgs and Women: The Reinvention of Nature*, pp. 149–81. London: Routledge, 1991.

Jenkins, H. 'Foreword: What We Mean by "Transmedia"'. In *Imagining Transmedia*, pp. ix–xx. Boston, MA: MIT Press, 2024.

Joy, P. and Macartney, I. 'Brilliant Vibrating Interface #3: Interview with Parel Joy', *URL Sonata*, 19 February 2023. https://open.spotify.com/episode/5OIndoIBhRi0zP58uV9l6i?si=0d3aa3b7f3f54e68. Accessed 25 August 2024.

Lynch, D. 'The Love of Literature'. *Oxford Research Encyclopedia of Literature*, 28 September 2020. https://oxfordre.com/literature/view/10.1093/acrefore/9780190201098.001.0001/acrefore-9780190201098-e-1033. Accessed 6 August 2024.

Manson, P. 'Object Permanence Magazine, 1994–1997'. *Peter Manson*, 18 June 2014.

Morgan, E. *Collected Poems*, Manchester: Carcanet Press, 1996.

Morgan, E. 'Futura 20: Emergent Poems', 1967. www.theideaofthebook.com/pages/books/821/edwin-morgan/futura-20-emergent-poems?soldItem=true. Accessed 25 August 2024.

Morgan, E. 'Strawberries'. Scottish Poetry Library, 1968. www.scottishpoetrylibrary.org.uk/poem/strawberries/. Accessed 25 August 2024.
Olson, M. 'Interview with Marisa Olson'. *We Make Money Not Art*, 28 March 2008. https://we-make-money-not-art.com/how_does_one_become_marisa/. Accessed 28 July 2024.
Russell, L. *Glitch Feminism: A Manifesto*. London: Verso Books, 2020.
Sedgwick, E. K. *Tendencies*. London: Routledge, 1993.
Sledmere, M. and Baiocco, M. '14 Questions about the Sonnet with Nat Raha, Ali Graham & Nik Ines Ward'. *SPAM Plaza*, 2024. www.spamzine.co.uk/post/feature-14-questions-about-the-sonnet-with-nat-raha-ali-graham-nik-ines-ward. Accessed 25 July 2024.
SPAM Press. 'Online ~Digital Sibling~', 2023. www.spamzine.co.uk/brilliant-vibrating-interface-digital-sibling. Accessed 28 July 2024.
SPAM Press. 'Open Call: Brilliant Vibrating Interface', 2023. www.spamzine.co.uk/brilliant-vibrating-interface. Accessed 28 July 2024.

22

International stories on a Scottish stage: A conversation on representation, recognition and activism through the *As Is* ethnodrama

Harvey Humphrey, Slater Cain, Gina Gwenffrewi, Leni Daly, Odhran Thomson and Mathew Wilkie

Introduction

In 2022 we staged a play, *As Is*, an ethnodrama written from qualitative research with trans, intersex and LGBTI activists across the UK, Malta and Australia from 2016 to 2018. Now writing as a collective of authors our roles in *As Is* were as follows: Harvey Humphrey (he/they): researcher/writer/dramaturg/producer; Slater Cain (they/them): director; Gina Gwenffrewi (she/her): actor – KATE; Leni Daly (they/them): actor – LESLIE; Odhran Thomson (he/him): actor – IAIN; Mathew Wilkie (he/him): actor – JACK. The play uses trans and intersex legal recognition and law reform as a way to discuss issues of identities, recognition and community relationships in activist spaces. This play was staged at a time when Scotland was taking centre stage in relation to trans law reform. We had an imagined audience of a local Scottish queer community, academic colleagues, actors' friends and family and potentially an international audience watching a future film. Attempting to follow international best practice with a reform of the previously UK-wide Gender Recognition Act (GRA) 2004, the Scottish government were discussing the Gender Recognition Reform (Scotland) Bill (GRR). A bill which does not consider intersex legal recognition but does consider trans legal recognition. The GRR would go on to be passed by the Scottish Parliament but prevented from becoming law by the UK government. This bill was subject to intense transphobic media coverage and anti-trans rhetoric in its discussion, which set the scene for putting this work out in the world (Pearce et al. 2020; Gwenffrewi 2022). We present this chapter as a conversation thinking through the context of our small Scottish stage sharing this internationally focused research play, *As Is*, at the time when Scotland's figurative stage was becoming a central focus on trans legal recognition.

It was conversations and interviews that informed the original research project from which the script for the play was written. It was conversations and debate that became such a feature of the GRR's journey from consultation to passing to not-yet law. It was conversations across the cast and crew that shaped how we chose to share this research as a play and the ways in which we saw ourselves in the script. We were a diverse international cast and crew with members from Scotland, elsewhere in the UK, Europe and North America, each with different connections to gender recognition reform. However, none of our members were from Malta or Australia, two of the original research locations, and our membership lacked diversity in other ways with an all-white cast and no intersex members. For more information on the cast and crew, auditions, representation and authenticity and methodological choices that led us to this point, see Humphrey (2024). In this piece we talk to each other about how we came to work together and what it meant to us. The 'us' here is four actors, one director and a researcher/dramaturg/writer/producer. There are other members of the cast not contributing to the article but whom we include here as 'us'. This includes the full cast and crew (eleven actors, one director, one assistant director, one stage manager and one researcher/dramaturg made up the full cast and crew) who we may at times collectively refer to as 'us' acknowledging the important work all those individuals undertook to bring this performance of ethnotheatre to life.

Harvey conducted the original research project interviewing thirty-six activists across the UK, Malta and Australia in the context of legal reform for trans and intersex citizens in those countries. He started this research project in 2015 when gender recognition reform wasn't yet under consideration in the UK; while including activists who worked across the four nations of the UK, many activists within the sample focused only on Scotland (with devolved governments' differing priorities being a key factor in this focus). The relationship between gender recognition legislation across the UK and within Scotland dominated the headlines from 2016 to the present day with multiple public consultations to legislative reform that have since been abandoned or unable to move forward.

While gender recognition legislation in Scotland is yet to recognize many of us, we discuss our own recognition of each other in this space. Although this conversation might be unique to the cast and crew of this particular research play, we hope the issues that resonate for us of anticipation, waiting, recognition and sharing speak to other trans and non-binary queers in this 'wee place' searching for a reflection of themselves. Our shared stage was 'wee' in some sense of the word, a one-off performance in a small theatre in Central Glasgow. However, in another sense we stretched our stage to fit a cast of eleven and we spoke to an audience beyond those seated in our theatre. It is important to find space, no matter how wee, for Scottish queer and trans voices on stage speaking to issues of authenticity in theatre-making (Frankland 2019). We worry contemporary arts cuts in Scotland may make future queer theatre harder to find space for. The play was filmed and shared back to the international participants in the original research project – the here and now reminding us of a there and then. Time and space matter here. We utilize 'trans time' (Amin 2014) to think through our non-linear experience of the reality of being trans people living in Scotland and sharing this research during the non-linear passing of the GRR. The location of the performance in Central Scotland when the GRR was under discussion matters. Scotland, despite its small size, has been leading the way for LGBTI rights, frequently putting the UK to shame due to not matching Scotland's ambitions in this area (Equality Network 2015). The 'wee place' also matters as a way for conversations from countries with world-leading legislation for trans and intersex citizens to set the scene for discussions about ongoing reform to gender recognition legislation within Scotland. The Gender Identity, Gender Expression, Sex Characteristics Act (GIGESC) (2015) in Malta was the first of its kind and remains internationally significant (Ní Mhuirthile 2018) – another 'wee' place stretching beyond its borders with its legislative recognition for trans and intersex people.

Why did you audition to be in As Is, *or what brought you to this project?*

Leni: So, when it came to finding the callout for *As Is*, I approached it with intrigue and hesitancy; who wrote the play, were they trans and would they be safe to work with? This could be a chance to meet other trans people in real life, but it wasn't initially clear if this circle of people would accept me. After some digging, I learned the author was trans and wrote poetry, something I did too. Biting the bullet, I applied, auditioned and got the part of Leslie (the non-binary trans character). Auditioning turned out to be one of the best decisions I have ever made. It impacted my life in a profound way, affecting my own self-acceptance and gave me contact with people just like me.

Gina: It wasn't my original intention to do *As Is*, but the idea of immersing myself in a community theatre project for trans and queer people had come at a good time. I was conscious of Theatre of the Oppressed and its many variations, which create 'a space for vulnerability, empathy, and trust, which in turn builds community' (Fox and Leeder 2018, 101). Harvey's theatre project sounded like it was doing something similar, an exploration of minoritized issues from minoritized voices, to be played out in front of a live audience, with dialogue in the follow-up Q&A. I was also getting drained by all the protests I'd been attending against anti-trans campaigns, their reactive nature, dictated by anti-trans hate (Gwenffrewi 2022). In this sense, such a theatre project becomes an act of empowerment.

Odhran: I wasn't certain I'd get the role. I feel lucky that I was able to medically transition earlier in life than most. Subsequently, I am exclusively read as a cisgender man. On that basis, though, I worried that people casting for trans characters mightn't view me as trans enough, despite the occasional voice squeak and mastectomy scars. A very slow two weeks after applying, my anticipation turned to apathy as it's industry standard to just not hear back if you haven't been given a role. The joyful surprise, then, when I was offered the job, was a very welcome pick-me-up. The time for action, quite literally under all the stage lights, was now.

Mat: Before I came out I spoke loudly and confidently. I demanded to take up space. But over the years of being hypervisible and hypervigilant I have grown tired of being observed. It has felt like a continual grinding away at my resolve and my ability to be me. Agreeing to be in a play (aka be very visible) about the very topic which has caused me to become invisible (trans rights) therefore felt exciting. Even before we had started rehearsals

	the very knowledge that I was going to be part of *As Is* felt like a step towards reclaiming part of who I am. I felt that it was a step towards reclaiming my power and the possibility that I am healed enough to begin opening up who I used to be.
Harvey:	So my experience is a little different to everyone else's having worked on the research project on trans and intersex activism from 2015 to 2021 that would produce the script for *As Is* out of these research interviews. For me, creating composite characters out of real people who shared delicate activist stories with me was a way of retaining anonymity for my participants and not causing damage to their ongoing relationships. Then writing these characters into dialogue with each other was a way to share these stories ethically and get at some of the complexities and nuances of their activist relationships. Each stage of this felt like a way to do justice to these participants and these stories without causing harm. At the same time the wider trans and intersex political context in all the countries of the original research (Australia, Malta and the UK) was becoming more fraught – especially in the UK. Putting *As Is* on as a play felt like a way to *do something* when so many of the rising transphobia and political hostility to trans lives felt harder and harder to challenge. What brought me to this project was my research but the wonderful cast and crew made me realize that none of this was over. This was much more than an academic output.
Slater:	After moving far from New York City over the pandemic I was eager, but confused by how to go about participating in the reopening of a theatrical community I'd never had any ties to before the Covid-19 lockdown. I knew it was important to me to participate in specifically queer theatre, even if those projects and roles felt hard to come by. I'd dipped my toe in as an actor and was applying to things but not feeling very fulfilled. It was similarly important to me to enter back in as a director, because I didn't feel like I was adding to projects very much as an actor. When I submitted to *As Is*, I recall thinking to myself, 'If this isn't the right fit I don't know what is.' All the while not being wholly confident as I was still new to the Scottish queer community and didn't know if my artistic practice was enough to gain access to all the participants, let alone speak for them. That's why the script was such a saving grace, it being pulled from first-person accounts allowed me to take a back seat and be a part of the community in the first place. It was never about speaking for anyone, but getting a chance to listen and amplify my community's voices.

As Is *uses international trans and intersex law reform to discuss broader issues of trans and intersex recognition and activist relationships*. As Is *was staged while gender recognition reform was taking centre stage in Scottish politics. What did that GRR or other gender recognition legislation mean to you?*

Mat:	The feelings of anticipation throughout the rehearsal and performance of *As Is* were in stark contrast to those leading up to the GRR hearing,

where we were surrounded by cis people, having our lives debated and explained to us by cis people. That anticipation was the sort that I power through – that I ignored, knowing I had done all I could, until it was over. It was cold and heartless without even a celebration when the bill passed (2022). The years of work up to that ruling, the watering down of the bill and the years of increased vilification of trans people weighed heavily and felt unmentioned – left to sit and solidify. While sometimes it feels only minutes ago that we began discussions around GRA reform, the heaviness I feel within me is infinite in comparison to the person sitting at those tables – a true marker of the passage of time.

Leni: Despite the fictional *As Is* bill, we also had the real-world GRR approaching, which fostered mixed feelings. Our community is still largely misunderstood, not accepted or treated equally. People actively work against us passing laws that would give people a life easier to navigate and prevent suicide. This could be huge progress, positively affecting the lives of so many trans people – but my gender was still not recognized. Solidarity for binary trans folks but an aching gap for further change, and an infinity of not knowing whether this day would even come for me. So, when the GRR did not pass – what did that mean for me? 'Mx.' [my title] is lovely, but recognition beyond that is still way beyond grasp. Trans people have waited years for this bill and the beginning of my wait has not even begun; it now looks like it will be even further away. Support from others who understand that is important and isolation from community can pose real danger.

Harvey: I had mixed feelings about the GRR. I started this research project in 2015 when gender recognition reform wasn't yet under consideration in the UK. In the time from then to performing the play in 2022 the UK would go from announcing a fairly innocent reform to the UK-wide GRA to a specific Scottish reform to the same piece of legislation being subject to unimaginable levels of public debate and scrutiny. In the interim the original UK-wide reform would be abandoned by the then UK government but not before multiple public consultations had brought trans lives into the public imagination like never before. Trans people went from relative media obscurity to being political footballs and dangerous bogeymen in what felt like a short period of time. Each public consultation brought with it a fresh wave of hostile media coverage becoming further and further removed from the actual legislative reform. I like reading policy and legislative reform as much as the next trans academic but it's hard to care about legislation to change birth certificates when in the same period waiting lists for trans healthcare hit the six year mark for a first appointment and our lives were subject to intense public debate and scrutiny. At the time of the GRR I watched some of the debate on TV while messaging trans friends and colleagues, including some of the *As Is* cast. But I couldn't watch it all live, instead prioritizing my own wellbeing and watching Christmas films over hearing vitriol about trans people in the

Scottish Parliament. I was pleased the bill passed but it felt deeply imperfect without non-binary recognition and with built-in waiting times nobody wanted. It felt like a disappointing win. This was as good as it was getting. However, for some people gender recognition was really important and I was glad they were finally getting an easier process and one that did not leave recognition of trans identities in the hands of biomedical discourses and unknown Gender Recognition Panels. This was still a win. Until it wasn't. The GRR remains in legislative limbo, unable to become law. Is this as good as it gets for gender reform?

Odhran: It was three months after *As Is* that I submitted my application for a Gender Recognition Certificate (GRC). This was the result of two long years of administrative effort, harassing GP receptionists for medical reports and pulling my hair out over what could possibly constitute evidence of a person's gender. So, receiving an application confirmation email with the sentence 'the panel will usually look at your application within twenty-two weeks of applying' felt like a punch in the gut given the enormous amount of time spent waiting before I was able to apply in the first place. I had no doubt that I would have to fill my life with more distractions, as time had slowed down again. Another three months later, the Scottish Parliament was in the final stage of passing the GRR, a law that would improve, though not to perfection, the very process under which my GRC application was pending. I was watching the consequences of these larger conversations, experiences and opinions play out in front of me on four consecutive days of parliament TV. Sleep was not frequent, sick leave was taken, and I felt every minute as if it were an hour. This was the ultimate wait. Faced with a culture war on the Scottish Parliament's doorstep in 2022, I was grounded by solidarity and collective action from my community. The bill passed 86-to-39. Before, when a role in *As Is* felt out of reach, writing, acting and creating with other trans artists regardless of opportunity was inspiring. This has been amplified now I have had the chance to meet and work with all of the wonderful people involved in *As Is*. The euphoria of the GRR passing, and the collective grief experienced when it was then blocked, gave me a purpose in taking my time. Waiting by yourself is horrible. Waiting, grieving and healing with your community is affirming.

These experiences of waiting are central to the play and to many of your own experiences. What can you tell us about waiting, anticipation and what 'trans time' means to you?

Odhran: I have and probably always will live in a state of 'trans time.' As a trans child, my formative years were spent waiting to be old enough for treatment of my dysphoria. As a Covid highschooler, my exam years were spent waiting to be taught. As a freelance creative, 98 per cent of my job was waiting. For the right opportunity, for the hours of my dull day job to pass in the meantime, for application deadlines, interviews and finally, acceptance or

	rejection emails. Admittedly, the latter is more frequent. Learning to be comfortable waiting has been imperative to my being, and I was and still am awful at it. So, when parliament was consulting on a new trans bill (May-ish 2022) and a project was looking for a trans actor to play a trans man, it seemed that the waiting was over. Until, of course, it wasn't.
Mat:	The character I played was Jack, an intersex man, and I was one of the few actors who did not hold the same identity as the character I was playing. Rehearsing discussions about the scraps of fundamental rights and recognition we are fighting over through someone else's voice gave me a deeper understanding of the nuance, patience and empathy that we must display as broader communities working towards similar goals. That said, finding a balance requires mistakes to be made, and true trust across communities necessitates honesty and argument and sticking it out until agreement and reconciliation is reached. The glacial progression of our rights is mirrored by the stepwise development of our understanding of one another. *As Is* achieved all of this by prioritizing representation and belonging throughout the project.
Harvey:	I think a lot about time. I think about how it feels different and moves differently for different people at different times. This is definitely deeply frustrating for anyone who tries to arrange a meeting at a set time with me. This approach to the non-linearity of time isn't a unique phenomenon. Many scholars have highlighted 'queer time', 'trans time' and 'crip time' are important features of queer, trans and disabled time. I think about that a lot in relation to my practice as a scholar and an activist. It's easy to talk about trans temporality in a theoretical sense. It's harder to embed that into our work when the world around you runs on deadlines and expected timelines. The PhD this play came from took longer than anticipated. I took 'time out' from the research more than once. The production of *As Is* was much more rushed in comparison. We relied on zoom calls often without the full cast. I tried as much as possible to build in time but I was also committed to paying everyone for all rehearsal and performance time on a limited budget. I was worried we wouldn't have enough time. However, I was blown away by how much we achieved in a short time. Some of the terms in the play are technical – the language is not easy. The stories themselves are complex and nuanced. But a cast and crew with such a strong connection to these experiences and performing at a time when it all feels current meant the time felt longer. Perhaps time stopped in rehearsals. Gave us all space and time out of our lives to imagine something else. It's hard to know when a research project is finished. Was it the night of the play performance? Was it the uploading of the film of the play? Is it now writing about *As Is* collectively in past tense? I think perhaps what I've learnt about time from this project is that it's even more fluid than I previously thought. Projects don't end. They just change shape.
Slater:	Every trans person I know has an intimate relationship with waiting. Waiting for others to come around to the idea of treating them with the

respect and affirmation they deserve. Waiting for traditional methods of medical or physical self-actualization to be available. Even waiting for the strength and bravery to admit to ourselves that we aren't only especially supportive allies, we are valid in our own trans identities. There can be strength in giving the realization of these truths their time to properly percolate, but trans time being governed by cis and heteronormative individuals is ludicrous. Ironically it lacks the same autonomy that trans people gain but affirm their identities.

What can you tell us about the queer space or spaces that this experience meant for you?

Odhran: The space we created through *As Is*, and the lessons I learnt from it, helped me realize myself that 'trans time' is not a hindrance, burden or problem to be dealt with. The ultimate conclusion that I came to is that the goal is not to speed time up or slow it down, but to have the autonomy to choose how we exist within it.

Mat: I expected rehearsals to be a rushed affair with little human connection and no space or time to think. It was only two days after all. They were the exact opposite of this. Connection and thought was demanded from start to finish. There were entire communities present within the text and on the stage around me. Justice for my character was a fundamental part of this. Neither the text nor my peers permitted me to speak quietly or to be ignored. I could not have anticipated how deeply this space could have affected me. Although I have a lot of experience of public speaking I was nervous to perform in front of others in rehearsals. I thought that I might do it 'wrong' or do something embarrassing. At present when in the public eye we trans people must be model citizens. The slightest error or reaction is enough to discredit us all. But whatever I did, and whatever the rest of the team did, the rehearsal space held. The nurturing and peaceful environment that we created together stretched and moulded around us, probing and offering support where necessary. My worries were reflected back at me by others in the group, and through this I found my voice. I sort of didn't want to do the play in the end because it would mean an end to the rehearsals and an end to our space. How had it only been two days?

Leni: Without having to explain our identities, we could focus on the people behind the labels and collectively figure out how to best tell our story, unsure who our audience might be or how *As Is* would be received. Would gender-critical activists be attracted to the venue, creating fear of violence, as with similar events (Gwenffrewi 2022)? Would cis folks attend and not understand, both queer and straight alike? Would I be looked upon sceptically within this cast and crew of trans people, for not being trans enough? Straddling the divide by worrying I may be othered by the trans community as a weird tag-on or deemed by transphobes to be too trans, putting me in danger. *As Is* taught me how people struggle with their identities across the UK, Malta and Australia and how their laws help or hinder this, being more advanced in some ways and less so in others. It highlighted how much longer we must go before non-binary and intersex people are given equal rights and autonomy, the world still grappling with basic concepts of people outwith cisnormativity. The space we created for each other held importance, solidarity and support, acknowledging the needs and vulnerabilities that we each held. This even gave me confidence to sit in front of the audience as myself, answering unprepared questions with a panel of my fellow cast and crew members. Not just recognition, but now representing other non-binary people too. In the end, our self-created *As Is* bubble continues to hold importance and solidarity. Being able to celebrate our collective wins and lament over our losses with empathy, understanding and pure trans joy.

Gina: The drama is in the tensions between different communities that make up the LGBTQI+ community. But for me, this was a less interesting focus than one that emerged for me almost by accident. At the end of the play, all the characters repeat the same line, one that resonates with me: 'There's a really difficult problem of not being able to be a representative, but also having to represent something' (*As Is* 2022; Humphrey et al. 2025). This reflection leaves me with more questions than answers. Who, in fact, gets to represent these communities and individuals? There is an assumption that the characters in the play represent the aspiration of whole communities, but I'm not sure this can ever be true. Instead, it's an imperfect necessity: the policy-making people initiate things with politicians, the LGBTQI+ populations benefit or suffer the consequences, depending on how it goes. I'm ambivalent about the process and the people involved. I reflected that I've never been approached by trans policy-making groups, though some of the actors I worked with in *As Is* have. Learning about this selectivity on the part of trans policy-making groups – which trans people they choose to work with, which ones they choose to avoid – has contributed to my layered sense of engagement with LGBTQI+ communities.

Harvey: Early on in rehearsals we all sat on the floor (or on chairs) of the theatre and, taking it in turns, just one after another in the order we were seated we read each line of the play out loud. We stopped each time a word or an expression was unfamiliar. I made it clear that I was not the person with the answers and we were staging it collectively. We would find our own answers. We had to decide what this word meant in our current context. What should the emphasis be here and now? I don't often get to see people reading my work or engaging with my ideas. It was such a privilege to have had my participants share their stories with me, to share them with this considerate cast who then shared them with a much wider public audience. It gave a real purpose to the often solo work that I do. This was community research and community theatre.

Slater: Creative queer community safe spaces are what have provided me the safety and first-hand accounts to be brave enough to consider coming out myself. I was out and queer at fourteen but it took nearly as long, if not longer again to be safe enough to come out as trans. Queer and trans communities have shown me real first-hand accounts of how special and liberating living an affirmed life can be. The *As Is* cast and crew lead in their own ways to a steady livelihood for me, the foundation of artistic life for an immigrant in their new home in Scotland, and long-lasting friendships and practitioner relationships. Those are massive and impactful, and dare I say more sustaining than the community I had built going to drama school or in almost ten years of being an artist in Brooklyn.

Where do we go from here?

Mat: First, we use the nuanced understanding of our differences in experience and needs, developed through working with this text and within this group, to continue to build solidarity and understanding across different communities and to work towards shared goals – even when we have to make compromises. Secondly, we create more spaces of trans beauty and brilliance where we can live unapologetically and without fear (even if only for a while). Within that, we use the skills and assets that we have so much of as a community to continue to build ourselves a million possible futures – all of which involve community led creative academic work.

Harvey: For me I've been surprised how much we have done together beyond this one-off performance of *As Is*. This isn't our first publication together. We're planning future theatre projects. Things feel hopeful. I think we have more to say together. I do a lot of work that's participatory research and often worry about 'leaving the field' and what happens after a project ends or funding dries up. *As Is* makes me feel hopeful that new spaces can emerge after a research project. This is no longer a cast of people who put on a play I wrote. This is some kind of emerging collective finding new ways to work together to share our voices as diverse trans creatives and theatre-makers in Scotland. Perhaps we'd all be doing our own things if *As Is* hadn't happened but the work we are planning together feels hopeful. I'm grateful to have had a part to play in bringing us together.

Gina: There's a poem by Diane di Prima called Rant whose message dovetails with what we did and may do again: 'the war that matters is the war against imagination' (di Prima 1990, 22). In our different ways, we should aim to be creatives because it pulls us out of the cycles of transphobic discourse that feel designed to subsume us. In a moral panic that wants to relegate us to the private sphere, it's easy to forget the power of creation, and of the importance of creators and curators in making new worlds for ourselves, and to celebrate those worlds in the public sphere.

Conclusion

This conversational chapter has offered one example of queer performance in Scotland giving voice to trans and queer actors as part of a trans and queer research space. We have considered ourselves, our contexts and our audiences in presenting the wee stage from which we performed and spoke to wider issues of legal gender recognition. We focused on the 'trans time' of when and where we were over the course of the performance and its development. We looked back over how this queer space and time came to be and now we look forward. Reflecting on our experience, we considered the feasibility of a production like this being possible again. With moral panics surrounding trans communities at an unprecedented high and funding crises across all sectors, the reality of similar future work feels constrained and unsustainable. However, constraints on funding for queer theatre and activism have existed before and yet queer theatre has persisted and thrived on low budgets and small spaces. We hope to continue to perform in the wee stages we make for ourselves and future theatre-makers.

References

Amin, K. 'Temporality'. *Transgender Studies Quarterly* 1, nos. 1–2 (2014): 219–22.

As Is. Writer Harvey Humphrey, Director Slater Cain. Glasgow: Scottish Youth Theatre, 2 July 2022.

Di Prima, D. *Pieces of a Song: Selected Poems*. San Francisco, CA: City Lights Books, 1990.

Equality Network. 'Scotland Rated Best Country in Europe for LGBTI Legal Equality', 2015. www.equality-network.org/scotland-rated-best-country-in-eur ope-for-lgbti-legal-equality/.

Fox, H. and Leeder, A. 'Combining Theatre of the Oppressed, Playback Theatre, and Autobiographical Theatre for Social Action in Higher Education'. *Theatre Topics* 28, no. 2 (2018): 101–11.

Frankland, E. 'Trans Women on Stage: Erasure, Resurgence and #notadebate'. In J. Sewell and C. Smout (eds), *The Palgrave Handbook of the History of Women on Stage*, pp. 775–805. Cham: Palgrave Macmillan, 2019.

Gender Identity, Gender Expression and Sex Characteristics Act 2015. Malta.

Gender Recognition Act 2004. London: Stationery Office.

Gender Recognition Reform (Scotland) Bill 2022.

Gwenffrewi, G. 'JK Rowling and the Echo Chamber of Secrets'. *Transgender Studies Quarterly* 9, no. 3 (2022): 507–16.

Humphrey, H. 'The Play's The Thing: Using Creative Methods to Place Trans and Queer Knowledge-Making Centre Stage'. In J. Cooke and L. Nyhagen (eds), *Intersectional Feminist Research Methodologies: Applications in the Social Sciences and Humanities*, pp. 29–45. London: Routledge, 2024.

Humphrey, H., Cain, S., Gwenffrewi, G., Daly, L., Thomson, O. and Wilkie, M. '*As Is* and Co-creating Theatre from Research to Stage: The Play's the Thing'. *Sociological Research Online* 30, no. 2 (2025): 487–500.

Ní Mhuirthile, T. 'The Legal Status of Intersex Persons in Malta'. In J. M. Scherpe, A. Dutta and T. Helms (eds), *The Legal Status of Intersex Persons*, pp. 358–67. Cambridge: Intersentia, 2018.

Pearce, R., Erikainen, S. and Vincent, B. 'TERF Wars: An introduction'. *Sociological Review* 68, no. 4 (2020): 677–98.

Part 5

Queer Education: (Post-)Compulsory Classroom Contexts

23

Black Scottish writing and the fiction of diversity

Churnjeet Mahn

On a Saturday afternoon in September 2018, after leading an anti-Faslane protest,[1] Jackie Kay, the Scottish Makar (national poet of Scotland), came to Edinburgh to act as a panellist at a one-day conference called *Resisting Whiteness*. She spoke optimistically about race and sexuality in Scotland, contrasting some of the stories of her youthful struggle to feel Scottish, Black, a lesbian, against her current status and experience in a Scotland keen to distinguish itself as more progressive and inclusive than England. Kay openly discussed raising her son in London and Manchester, places she argued offered a richer environment for Afro-British identity. But now Kay was firmly back in Scotland, talking about Scottish Blackness with ease and confidence. Kay's sleight of hand managed to seamlessly bring together an older narrative of a more hostile or challenging Scotland for a Black woman, with a contemporary account of possibility and hope without critically questioning how and why this change was possible. In this chapter, I am interested in the rhetorical gestures and silences required to reconcile different accounts of Black Scottish experience, one that can understand how older racisms can change, adapt and erupt into the present to maintain the whiteness of key cultural assets, in this case, the study of literature. The discussion layers contemporary debates around race in UK literary studies, with literary criticism on race and Scotland, and the experiences of students studying themes of race and nationality, to understand some of the difficulties in raising race as an issue in the Scottish classroom.

In January 2017 Meera Sebaratnam issued a clarification around the SOAS 'decolonize the curriculum' campaign led by students: 'You may have recently read false news reports that SOAS students have called for the removal of white philosophers such as Plato and Kant from their reading lists. It bears repeating that *these reports are untrue* – they are calling for a greater representation of non-European thinkers, as well as better historical awareness of the contexts in which scholarly knowledge has been produced' (Sebaratnam 2017). This theme continued as in October 2017 a media furore broke out over a discussion around 'decolonizing' the English literature curriculum at the University of Cambridge (Demianyk 2017). A conversation about an inclusive curriculum was reported in the *Daily Telegraph* as 'Student forces Cambridge to drop white authors', a strapline which the paper later corrected and apologized for. The containment of diversity within the curriculum (which often sits at odds with university agendas to use diversity as a promotional tool) has been a delicate balance between acknowledging the importance of postcolonial theory and its developments, without dismantling the histories, values and aesthetic judgements which guarantee the whiteness of English literature. Diversity has often acted as an additive in English literature teaching in the UK which demonstrates the inclusive and diverse nature of literature, a sleight of hand which allows English literature to universalize its aesthetic standards rather than challenging or radically refiguring what they might be. The calls for decolonizing the curriculum, whatever that may mean, have been various and with quite divergent aims. But what makes each demand distinct is the moment they belong to, a moment where the politics of race threatens to dilute the value of universalized (white) knowledge which, in turn, is attacked as unreasonable political correctness.

The apparent threat of diversity in these contexts has superficially become synonymous with the straightforward sacrifice of quality and value (through the suggestion that white thinkers or writers must be ejected from the curriculum). But the moment and challenge to curriculum diversity, and their appearance in the media, is illustrative of the way racial politics and activism has become focalized by political events and movements in the UK. Scholars have begun work on tracing the ways in which the debates around Brexit triggered and reworked older forms of racism, bringing them into contact with new contexts which could give the appearance of measured and uncontroversial sentiments such as overpopulation or balancing the economy (Bhambra 2017).[2] This has coincided with a visible growth in discussions of Black culture and postcolonialism in UK academic culture, from the introduction of new degree courses, to a growing connected awareness of the range of Black social and academic activism in the UK through social media platforms. However, the evocation of the 'UK' in this context, generally means England.[3] Scotland, through the fashioning of its own version of a progressive civic nationalism, has posed its own challenges to ideas and debates around race and immigration.

During and after the Brexit campaign, I've been congratulated several times for living 'on the right side of the border'. A public perception of less racism and a welcoming approach to refugees and migrants in Scotland has been an important part of a national discourse which has been highly selective in its evidence (Davidson et al. 2018), 'there's no problem here' has been a mantra in circulation for decades (Singh 1999) which is dependent on the circulation of some national myths about Scotland: Scottish people are friendly and welcoming, and Scotland is a left-wing nation with an inherent bent towards social justice informed by its experience of inner-city poverty and effective 'colonization' by England. I am interested in the extent to which this distinction fosters a different debate about what 'decolonizing' the English literature curriculum might look like in Scotland. This chapter is a reflection on the contemporary politics of teaching Black writing in a Scottish university classroom, especially when delivered by a person of colour who is expected to embody an authentic minority experience. More specifically, it discusses the experience of teaching Jackie Kay's novel *Trumpet* (1998) to two first-year cohorts in a major Scottish university, from designing the lecture and seminar questions, to the discussion and feedback of students.

Decolonizing Scottish writing

What is Black Scottish literature being decolonized from? England? A white canon? There is a growing body of criticism charting a distinct experience of race in Scotland, especially in the context of a civic nationalism which has been antagonistic to some UK-level policy and campaigns which have become conjoined with debates about racism.[4] A subcategory of critical writing has emerged in Scottish literature and Scottish history, which addresses Scotland's distinct role in empire and the potential relevancy of reading Scotland as a postcolonial nation. As Michael Gardiner has argued, 'Scottish Literature and Postcolonial Literature are less separate trends or two sets of texts, than intricately related and often conjoined critical positionings in relation to a much longer history, which has as one its main objects a critique of the jurisdiction of the imperial mode of British state culture' (2011, 1). The story of Scottish exceptionalism is overwrought but in the knotty relationship between Scotland and postcolonial studies there is a meaningful division that defies the well-honed, convincing and thoughtful arguments to Scotland's entanglements with the postcolonial: whiteness. By expanding on, and borrowing from, postcolonial theory and studies, Scotland becomes a vantage point from which to critique the British state while displacing responsibility for social problems, such as racism (Davidson et. al. 2018). Through this, Scottish postcolonial studies can undertake a critique of the British state without contending with whiteness in the same way as postcolonial studies of British writing.

Graeme Macdonald makes an argument about how/why 'Black Scottish' has become an important category in literature in the past twenty years, 'if the earlier generation of Black British writing argued for legitimate inclusion within the expanded realms of British culture, then devolutionary *Scottish* Black and Asian representation appears at a time when the unity and coherence of 'British' in 'the British novel' is under increasing scrutiny, partly as a result of the pressure placed upon it by the devolution of the Scottish novel' (Macdonald 2011, 85). By sequencing together the devolution of the Scottish novel and an emergence of a distinct Scottish Black Minority Ethnic (BME) representation in art and culture, there is an invitation to imagine a solidarity which strategically erases the potential conflict between these positions and, I would argue, tends to underplay and reduce the complexity of national and transnational narratives that can be evoked within Black writing which travels across borders to connect with other bodies of thinking unconnected to Scotland; indeed, some of these connections (in terms of critiquing whiteness, the Global North or the history of colonialism) would be antagonistic.

In this chapter I consider some of the challenges of talking about race in Scottish university classroom, especially when the text being studied is set in Scotland or about being Scottish. Like Gardiner, it is not my intention to contribute to a debate about whether or not Scotland can be read as postcolonial in relation to the British state, rather, my question is about the conditions required to mobilize a history of Black activism and Black intellectual thought in a nation which may refuse an explicit ethnic basis for nationalism despite having an implicit one. Remi Eddo-Lodge in *Why I'm No*

Longer Talking to White People about Race (2017) offers a compelling account of the whitewashing of racism:

> Structural racism is never a case of innocent and pure, persecuted people of colour versus white people intent on evil and malice. Rather, it is about how Britain's relationship with race infects and distorts equal opportunity. I think that we placate ourselves with the fallacy of meritocracy by insisting that we just don't *see* race. This makes us feel progressive. But this claim to not see race is tantamount to compulsory assimilation. My blackness has been politicised against my will, but I don't want it wilfully ignored in an effort to instil some sort of precarious, false harmony. (Eddo-Lodge 2017)

To what extent does postcolonial solidarity in the Scottish context rely on the erasure of racial difference to qualify for of national solidarity? While the street names of Glasgow act as testimonies of histories of slavery and racism (Jamaica Street, Tobego Street) and a statue to Lord Roberts, the nineteenth-century colonial administrator, stands prominently overlooking the University of Glasgow, is it possible to take seriously the claims that Scotland is any more or less progressive in its racial politics than England? Or is this whitewashing of racism part of the terms for making space for ethnic minorities within the discourse of Scottish nationalism? To think of this question another way, does the inclusion of Scottish texts by an author of any ethnic origin have the potential to decolonize English literary studies in Scotland?

A significant body of Scottish literary criticism around issues of colonialism has focussed on the status of Scotland as a kind of colony or experiencing social consequences analogous to other colonized nations. The 'minority' status of Scotland within the Union of the United Kingdom has been the focal point for the rejuvenation of Scottish literature in the twentieth century. Being British and Scottish – or in the case of *Trumpet*, being Black Scottish and Black British – is a recurring contradiction explored in Scottish literary criticism. Early twentieth-century writers from Edwin Muir to Hugh MacDiarmid engaged with some kind of fundamental loss at the heart of Scottish culture: what does it look like to be a minority nation in a union? The fashioning of a distinct tradition of Scottish writing, especially in Scots and English, has involved identifying a distinct quality that cannot be predicated simply on language.

A key recurring concept for Scottish literature in the twentieth century has been the 'Caledonian Antisyzygy', the duelling of opposites and core contradictions that prevents it from presenting a unified face, which was defined as a characteristic of the Scottish psyche and writing by Gregory Smith in 1919: 'The literature [of Scotland] is remarkably varied, and that it becomes, under the stress of foreign influence and native division and reaction, almost a zigzag of contradictions. The antithesis need not, however, disconcert us. Perhaps in the very combination of opposites – what either of the two Sir Thomases … might have been willing to call 'the Caledonian Antisyzygy' (Smith 1919, 4). Smith's formulation undergirds a perspective on Scottish literature which is entirely based on variety and contradiction. Expansive and inclusive to the point of being vacuous, it has provided the means for Scottish literature to refuse any singular anchoring tradition and canon of writing in favour of reading multiplying threads of Scottish writing. From Highland versus Lowland, to intense religious discord and the contradictions of egalitarian politics versus the realities of class and inequality, the Caledonian Antisyzygy has been a useful way for critics to pack together the fact that Scottish identity celebrates a struggle with itself that has come to act as a powerful mythology, whether or not it is a valid or relevant reading of Scottish culture.

When it comes to understanding the character of Scottish culture and writing in the wake of migration and increasing diversity in the late twentieth century, versions of the Caledonian Antisyzygy are deployed to understand the inclusive, capacious, diverse and contradictory character of Scottish fiction. And this, in itself, carries an intense contradiction. For a country so fixated on its history and heritage, the bar to qualify for Scottishness is relatively low. As Willy Maley says in his discussion of Leila Aboulela's *The Translator* (1999), a novel by a migrant to Scotland set in Scotland:

> Scotland, at the heart of Sudan's colonial history, fittingly provides the context for one of its most significant contemporary literary works. *The Translator* belongs to Scottish as much as it does African literature. When asked in an interview about being designated a 'Scottish Arab writer', Aboulela expressed her satisfaction with *The Translator's* designation as a Scottish novel … What this designation means in a postcolonial context is, of course, globally fashioned. The novel's publication history and its author's biography exemplify ways in which transnational contexts shape the parameters of Scottish Literature. (Maley 2011)

Maley acknowledges Scotland's influence in different forms of African colonialism to evidence a long history of Scottish participation in colonialism. And while there is much to be researched on how these connections have 'shaped the parameters' of Scottish writing, where is the corresponding discussion about how Scottish intervention in colonialism has shaped the parameters of other cultures and traditions? Bashabi Fraser, a migrant to Scotland who has written extensively about BME writing in Scotland, suggests, 'New Scots are transcultural writers who can move across boundaries of nation and write with a deep consciousness of a global reality of interconnectedness' (Fraser 2016, 234). This view is optimistic when it comes to the stories and histories of racism, gender and especially class.

I was an undergraduate student at a large Scottish university and studied English and Scottish literature. Throughout the entirety of my degree, I did not study a single text by a Black British or British Asian author. Throughout my degree I was one of a few non-white faces in some of the largest subject cohorts of the faculty. Whether this matters is a question of perspective. I did study the basics of postcolonial literature, but when these were applied to texts, they were primarily in colonial contexts, for example the writing of Chinua Achebe; in the context of North American civil rights, bringing in Audre Lorde and bell hooks; or in discussions of Scotland as a nation that had been subjected to postcolonial violence after the loss of its sovereignty. To be 'well-read' was to be well-versed in a tradition that was overwhelmingly white, middle class and, apart from the odd expedition, confined to the Global North. By the time I was a graduate student teaching English literature, I idealistically believed it was my duty to bring some intellectual activism into my teaching. I asked at an English committee meeting if we could introduce a Black British or British Asian text into the undergraduate curriculum. In a department that had approximately forty members of staff, not including graduate teaching assistants, I was one of the few ethnic minorities in the staff and student body combined. I received a kind response but ultimately it was decided that there was no suitable text that could be included on the curriculum at the expense of other English literature (for which we can read predominantly white with odd references to Black American or African).

After I received my PhD I moved to the south-east of England in 2008 where it was impossible to ignore issues of race in the curriculum. Our student body was diverse, issues of race and migration played out visibly and violently from the rise of Islamophobia after the 7/7 attacks, to the riots in South London in 2011, not to mention the escalation of tension between communities and the police. Reading texts like Monica Ali's *Brick Lane* and Zadie Smith's *White Teeth* in the classroom was impossible without reference to the life experiences of students and the diversity of nearby London. In 2015 I moved back to Glasgow shortly after the Scottish Independence Referendum, which had taken place the previous year. Devolution and independence had become the key cultural framework within which to debate the social and cultural issues around inequality, social justice and identity. Debates around race in Scotland have not been focalized and politicized in the same way as parts of England, and while the English and Scottish literature university curriculum has become more diverse than before, the staff make-up of English and Scottish literature departments is still overwhelmingly white, with some of Scotland's largest English literature departments having no BME staff on permanent contracts. There may be an appetite for talking about Scotland's diversity in culture and literature, but there is little or no interest in questioning why the undergraduate, graduate and academic experience of English and Scottish Literary Studies in Scotland is so white.

Black Scottish or Black British writing?

In a curriculum where making space for Scottish texts is a consideration in a programme of reading dominated by English writing, Jackie Kay has found herself onto a series of university courses in Scotland as the premier example of Scottish Black writing. For the rest of this chapter, I want to consider Jackie Kay's role in Black British or Black Scottish writing and then consider this in coordination with student's responses and feedback to ideas around the opportunities and limits of thinking about the distinctiveness of Black Scottish writing. Jackie Kay is currently Scotland's Makar or national poet. She was born as a mixed-race child in Scotland and adopted by a white couple and raised in Glasgow. Her first novel, *Trumpet* (1998), draws on the life of the American jazz musician Billy Tipton (1914–1989) who was born female but who lived the majority of his life as man, a 'secret' discovered upon his death. Her novel's protagonist, Joss, follows a similar trajectory in his life but he is mixed-race, and the story is set between Scotland and England. The novel is told through a series of perspectives from Joss's wife, to his son, a coroner who takes care of his body and a journalist writing about the sensation around Joss's death. Joss makes an appearance towards the end of the novel, from beyond the grave, where he reflects on his own heritage and journey. The entire novel is structured around the evasion and refusal of any stable categories and relies on a pervading dissatisfaction with the labels and prejudices which delimit people's lives. Writing eighteen years after the novel's first publication, the Scottish writer Ali Smith has reflected on the ways in which *Trumpet* made a distinct contribution to writing in Scotland while being part of a recognizable tradition of Scottish writing:

> There had certainly never been a Scottish book like it, yet it came from the Scottish tradition of honouring the margins, the vernacular and the ordinariness of things and lives (an 'ordinariness' that is always extraordinary). It came from a literary tradition of shapeshift itself, one that finds voice in unauthorised, unexpected forms and places; one often concerned with the search for a communal form, a tradition that can be traced in writers such as Lewis Grassic Gibbon, Hugh MacDiarmid, Nan Shepherd, Willa Muir, Alasdair Gray, Liz Lochhead, James Kelman. It came from such tradition and expanded it with influences from international black writers such as Audre Lorde, Jamaica Kincaid, and especially Zora Neale Hurston and Toni Morrison. Plus, it said things about and for that Scottish tradition, and about and for a wider British tradition as well, concerning gender and ethnicity, that had never been said before. (Smith 2016)

Smith creates a mixed genealogy for Kay but does not address the ethics or possibilities of connecting different kinds of marginalized positions (marginalized from what, by whom?). Her laboured genealogy does not question how different margins may connect and who benefits from marketing or positioning these 'margins'. In terms of the possible points of connection between a Scottish and 'international Black' tradition, ideas around the unexpected and/or unauthorized are hardly unique in any literary culture. Smith's observations are valuable not as evidence of a parallel between the history of African American or Caribbean writing and Scottish writing, however, they are valuable in terms of evidencing the will to make that connection. Discussing her own literary traditions, Kay has reflected on the problem with locating her voice in fiction:

> When *Trumpet*, her first novel, was published in 1998, Kay became one of the most prominent of a small number of women writers of African descent in Britain. The poet Jean 'Binta' Breeze and novelist Joan Riley both emigrated from Jamaica and published here in the 1980s. Unsurprisingly, it was to African-American writers – Toni Morrison, Alice Walker and Maya Angelou – that Kay turned as a young woman, and the poet Audre Lorde, who told her she didn't have to deny her Scottishness in order to be black. 'It's a strength! You can be both!' Kay says in a hearty approximation of Lorde's accent. 'That was an amazing thing to hear. So I stopped feeling like a sore thumb and realised that complexity could bring something, that there are advantages as well as disadvantages.' (Rustin 2012)

Kay claims her Scottishness through a playful approximation of a difference that is not anchored in a historicized and politicized challenge to, and writing back to, a national(ist) politics which has harboured racism, whether historical or contemporary. In other words, while Lorde wrote with the backdrop of Black civil disobedience and activism, and Jean 'Binta' Breeze and Joan Riley arrived in an England which experienced major race-related riots in the 1980s, Kay's depiction of Scotland and race moves in and out of a dialogue with a British or American/Caribbean experience which does not challenge Scotland's own specific contribution to empire or discourses of racism.

Trumpet introduces a proliferating series of identity categories (which it goes on to critique), from lesbian and trans to Scottish and Black. In designing two lectures for *Trumpet*, the challenge was to introduce and explain the biopolitics of the text without getting 'stuck' in identity politics, something Kay has commented on frequently:

> Kay says she was 'bogged down' in identity politics for a long time, and worries that the labels and categories it created – 'lesbian writer', 'black writer', 'Scottish writer' – can become a drag. 'You want to be open about being gay – why would you not be open about being gay? But you don't want to be defined by it', is how she expresses the conundrum. 'You never have control over how much the volume goes up or how much flavouring goes in. Ultimately I'm a writer and I don't want my work or my characters to be constrained by the fact of me. I think a lot of writers feel like that.' (Rustin 2012)

Trumpet is a novel which resolutely refuses a sustained engagement with any single thread of identity politics (what it may mean to be Scottish or black or queer) and instead situates itself at a confluence which uses music and reconciliation as strategies to demonstrate the inadequacies of understanding identity as a definition rather than a process of making or becoming. The text is split into a series of diverse perspectives which run through Joss's family and the media and medical reception to his death. While Joss's voice enters the narrative towards the end of the text, the narrative structure is dependent on refracting him through frameworks of intimacy, medical-legal language and prurient media interest to displace the narrative. Joss's absence is a refusal to realize an authentic voice that can account for, or explain, the categories of race, gender and sexuality that come into play. Through refracting Joss through other perspectives, some of the contradictions and impossibilities of his life are brought into sharp relief through the description of a wife who loved her husband and a son who comes to view his father's body as a lie and betrayal. Jack Halberstam describes a different kind of authenticity that this narrative structure can reveal:

> In a flurry of investigative zeal, Kay's novel shows us that a life carefully written by its author, owned and shielded by loved ones, may suddenly stand exposed as a lie. The beauty of Kay's narrative is that she does not try to undo the life narrative of a passing man; rather, she sets out to honor it by weaving together a patchwork of memories from Joss's survivors, but mainly his wife, and making that patchwork into the authentic narrative. (Halberstam 2005, 59)

Kay does show some of the 'undoing' of Joss's life through Coleman's emotional and violent rejection of the 'truth' about his father which leads to him cooperating with a journalist, who herself, is part of a broader metaphor of exposure than runs through the text. Joss's post-mortem neatly brings together social censure around passing with the undermining of easy(?) equations between the body and gender(ed) truths: 'Doctor Krishnamurty felt as if she was removing skin, each wrapping of bandage that she peeled off felt unmistakably like a layer of skin. So much so that the doctor became quite apprehensive about what kind of injuries the bandages could be hiding' (Kay 1998, 43). Through the transmogrification of gauze to skin, the injury to the memory of Joss's life as a man is implied through the removal of the bandages. The negative media and social attention Joss's death garners layers with this scene to produce a kind of literalized excoriation through the demand to expose the apparently real body of a woman and negate the reality of a man's life.

When Joss does speak to the reader at the close of the text, he recalls a life which involves following traces back in time that slip into an attempt to recall and reclaim the stories of a land he did not belong to. Speaking of his father he comments: 'But he couldn't remember what he wanted to remember. He would read many books to see if they might remind him of what he wanted to remember: the hot dust on the red road, the jacaranda tree ... The trouble with the past, my father said, is that you no longer know what you could be remembering. My own country is lost to me now, more or less all of it, drowned at sea in the dead of a dark, dark night' (273). Joss recounts his own experience of racism alongside an identification with Scotland and being Scottish which becomes the only home available as a past life of his father is as far as a past world. Coordinating the loss of an imagined African heritage with the contrasting fit of a sense of Scottish belonging, if not heritage, becomes another way in which the text interrogates the assumptions made about bodies and lives.

Being Scottish in the text, on one level, operates within the parameters of progressive nationalism with the lacuna of Joss's heritage being filled by his life and upbringing in Glasgow. However, Matt Richardson reads more resonance in the absence: 'Primarily, Kay's work suggests that people of African descent in the United Kingdom find a precarious (im)balance between their relationships to blackness and black identity and their Scottish or English or Welsh identities. Ultimately, Kay's work suggests that to be black and Scottish is to be absent from the national historical imaginary' (Richardson 2012, 364). Richardson's writing belongs to a tradition of American writing which reads cultural outputs alongside politicized and cultural experiences of race. The history of that political consciousness in Scotland, of solidarity between people of colour against the forces of racism or histories of colonialism and imperialism are absent in the text. While Kay may riff off Audre Lorde or be categorized at times as a Black British writer, there is something about her dimension as a Scottish writer which de-emphasizes a political or explicit historical consciousness of race. For critics such as Carole Jones, 'Embracing the openness in Scottish literary culture enables an aspiration to more queering representation and queer readings that productively challenge the boundaries of our notions of community, identity and the human' (Jones 2016, 195). What is the cost of the embrace? The discussions of race in Kay's work often reroute her through Black British or Black traditions of writing that exist within a well-defined consciousness of race that has been accompanied by activism. Kay's critique of race and nationality is not as nuanced as her critique of sex and gender. This produces an ambivalence in the text around the relationship between Scotland and racism: is this a British (or English) problem which reaches into Scotland, or is there something distinct about its manifestation in Scotland? If openness and ambivalence have become trademarks in Scottish writing, then *Trumpet* is an excellent example of a text which embraces and refuses all kinds of progress:

> When the century turns. Everybody turns like people in a progressive reel dance. Some turn over a new leaf, some turn a blind eye, a deaf ear, some turn the long barn tables, some slip back, sliding towards the old tongue. When the pendulum of the old clock's big hand moves forward, somebody always turns it back. Somebody who resents progress or is irritated by it or decides all change is false. (Kay 1998, 272)

Prejudices old and new recur in rhythms. In a text self-aware of its effects, time, music and movement become the guarantors of change without a promise of something 'better'. This discussion forms the basis of the two lectures on Jackie Kay that I deliver to students, and which have become an entry point into gathering student responses to the question of race and Scotland.

In the classroom

Trumpet was introduced on the Level 1 English literature curriculum at the University of Strathclyde in 2016 in an attempt to create a more inclusive reading list. Kay is the only non-white author to appear in the primary reading for Level 1 students. Most humanities faculties in the Scottish university system will allow students to take subjects as core or minor subjects, so our cohort is made up of students who have chosen English literature as their degree, or joint-degree subject, and students who may have an interest in studying literature at a pre-honours level, with no obligation to take the subject to graduation. This makes Level 1 English literature (which is taught in the first year of a four-year degree) a more diverse group of students in their interest level and commitment to studying English. Students are predominantly from the west coast of Scotland with a significant number living in Glasgow, where part of *Trumpet* is set. Teaching comprises a mixture of lectures and seminars, with first-year lectures having to bridge the gap between secondary, college and access routes into university-level English.

In order to provide active feedback on student's writing and to encourage debate among students, we piloted a student response/feedback mechanism over two years. The format was the same for all texts: students would be asked to take responsibility for collectively writing up/summarizing seminar discussion in a way that would demonstrate different perspectives (through representing the various views of individual students) as well as a good knowledge of the text (through providing evidence from *Trumpet* through quotes or analysis). For the two weeks on *Trumpet*, the student feedback was structured in response to a series of questions around eight key terms, two of which focussed on race and nationalism. While other questions focussed on form, technique and transgender representation, for this chapter I am interested in the way students explicitly addressed issues of race and nationalism in the Scottish context. The extracts used in the following discussion are from responses to seminars held over two sessions (2016–17 with 129 students and 2017–18 with 139 students). Divided into smaller groups of approximately twelve, students were asked to produce a collective response to eight questions over two seminars which were then summarized and produced as a written reflective reading log. Each cohort (2016–17 and 2017–18) produced eleven substantial responses (twenty-two in total) ranging from 200 words to 1,000 words, with ten responses explicitly addressing the following two questions:

1. Think about the role of 'identity' in the text. More specifically, what makes this text Scottish? Is Scotland important for the text?
2. In the interview, Kay discusses the importance of Black writers in creating a different kind of voice. Why is Joss Moody's race significant in the text? How is 'Blackness' or 'Black culture' represented?

As this work was not assessed and in a very different format from marked assessments (essays and exams), students approached the task of summarizing seminar discussion with a language less critical than their assessed work. Students were asked to read a range of secondary material including interviews with Jackie Kay and the article by Matt Richardson discussed earlier in this chapter. Students were made aware of two perspectives on this issue through lectures and this secondary reading, namely, that reading Kay in a Scottish or British or Black continuum presented different kinds of political challenge. The majority of responses attempted to take a critical stance by referring to statements Kay had made or by analysing sections of the text. However, this was disrupted in two ways. Students who identified Scotland as more inclusive or progressive than England, moved towards personal language around friendliness an openness with less direct evidence from the text. Students who identified Scotland as racist or having a problem with race moved towards more abstract references beyond the text and Kay.

The ten direct responses to the questions on Scotland and race produced an extremely broad range of responses. While a single student within one of the group responses called Scotland's culture 'white supremist', the most common view (five out of the ten group responses) was that Scotland was important to the text because Jackie Kay was Scottish and it would appeal to Scottish readers. While this response deflected the issue of race onto authorship, three of the group responses flagged that Scotland was less diverse and therefore issues of race appeared less frequently in public discourse. For example, one group's response included: 'It is a "*Scottish*" novel not only in the use of slang and locations but in the way that some of the characters act … Joss comes across as very Scottish as he seems very nationalist and identifies with Scots, he tells his son to "speak properly" when he picks up another accent other than Scottish.' The students picked up on a series of complex arguments: the conflation of Scots with slang, or the misidentification of Scots as slang is demonstrated through Joss's remonstration of his son's English. The text does not express any nationalist political sentiment, but language choice here becomes read as part of a nationalist project of distinction from and against English and England. The observation about language was extended through to culture by another group discussion: 'We felt that the interactions between characters really showed a Scottishness within the text – the way Joss always withheld [sic] his little Scottish values and refused to lose his accent. The behaviour of the people on Torr, the warmness and 'open door' values were really a staple of old Scottish values.'

Despite the majority of students identifying a positive framing of Scottish identity and values in the text, and Joss's attachment to them, students tended to take as fact that Glasgow is less diverse that other large UK cities, equating diversity with more 'progressive' or 'accepting' views: 'Setting of Scotland important as at the time it was not as progressive or multiracial as other parts of the UK such as Manchester or London so gives a different perspective on people'. In this discussion, depictions of racism in the text, combined with the absence of Black communities, or a broader consciousness of Black lives in Scotland, is equated with Scotland being less 'progressive' (thereby reading a critical mass in population and a politicized conflict around race as a platform to generate 'progression'). This was supported by another comment, 'We felt that the story would work the same if it was set in another city with similar attitudes at the time but not in a more diverse city such as London since people would be more likely to be accepting'. Equating London with acceptance bypasses notions that Scottish civic nationalism automatically produces more inclusive contexts for racial minorities.

The responses did include positions more explicitly critical of Scottish identity in the text, but these were in the minority and tended to include more emotive language: 'Joss's femininity can be seen as threatening to White Scottish masculinity. As soon as it is revealed to the public that he is biologically female joss [sic] goes from being the proud face of a culturally diverse Britain (a façade) and is quickly relegated to the role of the perverted Black who duped the public'. By layering white Scottish masculinity and a culturally diverse Britain, the students appear to disaggregate the intersectional politics of the text, attributing anxieties with whiteness and masculinity to Scotland and racial diversity to Britain. Another position raised its criticism through refusing Scotland's immunity from structural racism or heteropatriarchy: 'Not to say Scottish people or that Scottish culture is patriarchal or racist/transphobic, but it is evident that these ideas still exist at the heart of our institutions, much like those across the majority of Western countries. This intolerant culture may appear non-existent to those who don't experience large scale oppression, but Kay draws upon these ideas in the novel'. In their discussions, the students moved between discourses they identified as 'British' and 'Scottish', often attributing more sentimental or inclusive values to Scotland. The accumulation of affective evidence for Scotland's inclusivity (warmth and openness) in the majority of the student discussions fails to find a way to accommodate to respond to explicit instance of racism in the text, Kay's own recollections of racism or the material in Matt Richardson's work which directly names a failure in representing Black Scottish experience. The affective response to Scottishness provides a means to sidestep real experiences of individual and structural racism in the text through its displacement to other contexts, namely, Britain.

Students, on the whole, did not question how 'Scottish' the text was, but their discussion of its content and politics demonstrated a shifting view about the location of 'progressive' politics or acceptance around racial and sexual difference. Without a pathway to offer a sustained engagement with literature about race and Scottish literature, many of the discussions raised in Level 1 simply disappear in the degree, as is the case in many English literature degrees. In Scotland, the space given to 'Scottish texts' often constitutes its own minority status within the teaching of English literature degrees which elides other kinds of minority positions which might slide across the borders in messier ways. The study of race in Scottish writing finds itself falling between different gaps, which allows Scottish literary criticism to make easier – or less contested – claims to postcolonial conditions that do not have to contend with whiteness, race and ethnicity in the same way as English literature from England.

Conclusion

What happens to *Trumpet* after it has been dissected in the class and put back together? Its inclusion within the university English literature curriculum in Scotland offers a gesture towards a devolved and diverse reading list. But the response from students is an excellent demonstration of the ambivalent ways in which the politics of race are triggered in the context of various intersecting nationalisms. While the postcolonial debate in Scottish studies has been overwhelmingly dominated by white critics, these first-year classrooms have opened a space for Scottish BME students to read about race and racism in a city they knew intimately due to my institution's exceptionally high recruitment from the local area. It can be dangerous to evoke the language of authenticity or authentic encounter with literature, this is not what I want to suggest here, but what I do want to suggest is that some of the more 'provocative' and direct responses we had from students makes an important contribution to our understanding of race in the Scottish context. From the visceral rejection of inclusive nationalism to using language and literary analysis as the foundation for challenging the intersection of ethnic, sexual and national selves, the students on the course articulated some of the contradictions that critics in Scottish literature have avoided. However, there is a remaining difficulty in raising questions of race in this context. In the face of accumulated affective responses to a Scottish national project which is often viewed as progressive in distinction to UK politics, the charge of structural racism is too difficult to touch or feel. The strategies for avoiding race or its politicization in the classroom, and the prevailing efforts in Scottish literary criticism to read Scotland as a historically postcolonial state, work to subdue the power or possibility of Scottish Black politics to challenge how we envisage and make national literature.

Notes

1. Faslane is popular name for Her Majesty's Naval Base Clyde where the UK's nuclear deterrents are located (Trident missiles). As Scotland's Makar, there were some questions as to whether it was appropriate for Jackie Kay to lead the protest.

2. The 23 June 2016 referendum where Britain voted to leave the EU and the 18 September 2014 referendum where Scotland voted to remain part of the UK have created two waves of divisive political campaigning. A UN envoy was sent to the UK to examine race relations since the Brexit vote argued that racism and racist views had increased in the UK (see, for example, Dearden 2018).
3. It is worth noting that Wales and Northern Ireland have their own distinct issues with race and racism in education which are distinct from Scotland's.
4. Scotland has a smaller ethnic minority population than the UK as a whole (on average 4 per cent versus a figure closer to 13 per cent in the UK), but there are significant concentrations of ethnic minorities in Scotland; for example, in Glasgow, approximately 12 per cent of the population is classed as ethnic minorities (based on the 2011 census).

References

Bhambra, G. K. 'Brexit, Trump, and "Methodological Whiteness": On the Misrecognition of Race and Class'. *British Journal of Sociology* 68, no. 1 (2017): 214–32.

Davidson, N., Linpaa, M., Davidson, N., Liinpää, M., McBride, M. and Virdee, S. (eds). *No Problem Here: Understanding Racism in Scotland*. Edinburgh: Luath Press, 2018.

Dearden, L. 'Racism Has Become More Acceptable since Brexit Vote, United Nations Warns', *The Independent*, 11 May 2018. www.independent.co.uk/news/uk/home-news/brexit-racism-religious-intolerance-united-nations-special-rapporteur-a8348021.html. Accessed 1 June 2018.

Demianyk, G. 'Daily Telegraph Admits "Decolonise" Cambridge Curriculum Story Was Wrong as Student Lola Olufemi Condemns Newspaper'. *Huffington Post*, 26 October 2017. www.huffingtonpost.co.uk/entry/telegraph-lola-olufemi_uk_59f1fe0fe4b077d8dfc7eaf9. Accessed 2 January 2018.

Eddo-Lodge, R. *Why I'm No Longer Talking to White People about Race*. London: Bloomsbury, 2017, ebook.

Fraser, B. 'The New Scots: Migration and Diaspora in Scottish South Asian Poetry'. In S. Lyall (ed.), *Community in Modern Scottish Literature*, 214–34. Leiden: Brill, 2016.

Gardiner, M., MacDonald, G. and O'Gallagher, N. (eds). *Scottish Literature and Postcolonial Literature: Comparative Texts and Critical Perspectives*. Edinburgh: Edinburgh University Press, 2011.

Halberstam, J. *In a Queer Time and Place: Transgender Bodies, Subcultural Lives*. New York: New York University Press, 2005.

Jones, C. 'From Subtext to Gaytext? Scottish Fiction's Queer Communities'. In S. Lyall (ed.), *Community in Modern Scottish Literature*, pp. 179–95. Leiden: Brill, 2016.

Kay, J. *Trumpet*. London: Picador, 1998.

Macdonald, G. 'Scottish Extractions: "Race" and Racism in Devolutionary Fiction'. *Orbis Litterarum* 65, no. 2 (2011): 79–107.

Maley, W. 'Conversion and Subversion in Tayeb Salih's *Season of Migration to the North* and Leila Aboulela's *The Translator*'. In M. Gardiner, G. MacDonald and N. O'Gallagher (eds), *Scottish Literature and Postcolonial Literature: Comparative Texts and Critical Perspectives*, pp. 185–97. Edinburgh: Edinburgh University Press, 2011.

Richardson, M. '"My Father Didn't Have a Dick": Social Death and Jackie Kay's *Trumpet*'. *GLQ* 18, no. 2–3 (2012): 361–79.

Rustin, S. 'A Life in Writing: Jackie Kay'. *The Guardian*, 27 April 2012. www.theguardian.com/books/2012/apr/27/life-writing-jackie-kay. Accessed 2 January 2018.

Sebaratnam, M. 'Decolonising the Curriculum: What's All the Fuss About?'. *Study at SOAS Blog*, 18 January 2017. www.soas.ac.uk/blogs/study/decolonising-curriculum-whats-the-fuss/. Accessed 2 January 2018.

Singh, G. *Racism and the Scottish Press: Tracing the Continuities and Discontinuities of Racialized Discourses in Scotland*. PhD thesis, University of Leicester, 1999.

Smith, A. 'Rereading Jackie Kay'. *The Guardian*, 16 January 2016. www.theguardian.com/books/2016/jan/16/rereading-trumpet-jackie-kay-ali-smith. Accessed 2 January 2018.

Smith, G. G. *Scottish Literature, Character and Influence*. London: Macmillan, 1919.

24

Welcome home? Finding your (queer) place in Scotland and in STEM

Marco Reggiani and Jessica Gagnon

Introduction

Scotland has historically been recognized for its commitment to social and scientific progress. Education has been central to shaping the nation's liberal and reformist identity, setting it apart from other nations within the UK and beyond. Scotland, for example, was the first nation of the UK to repeal in 2000 Section 28 (or Section 2A as it was known in Scotland) – a law that prohibited local authorities and schools from 'promoting the acceptability of homosexuality'. This legislative change, which was one of the early acts of the Scottish Parliament, marked a significant step towards addressing discrimination against LGBTQ+ individuals. More recently, in 2019, Scotland claimed to be the first nation in the world to support the development of LGBTQ+ inclusive education across the school curriculum – hoping to reduce bullying and help children thrive in more equitable, diverse and inclusive environments (Educational Institute of Scotland 2023).

Higher education institutions in Scotland have recently started to play an increasingly key role in promoting LGBTQ+ inclusion. By fostering welcoming environments, universities can ensure that queer staff and students feel safe, valued and supported – which is key to well-being, success and satisfaction. Inclusive policies and practices, as well as socially orientated research, can also influence society more broadly, for example by promoting better understanding and representation of queer people. Scottish universities have long been aware of this unique position, although their commitments to social justice have not always been demonstrated in practice. The renewed efforts in the sector to address barriers for queer and other marginalized people recognize not only that work still needs to be done but also that inclusion is beneficial for innovation – for example, by producing more resilient institutions that can tackle complex problems and ensure national and global prosperity.

In STEM (Science, Technology, Engineering and Mathematics) fields, addressing equity, diversity and inclusion (EDI) of LGBTQ+ individuals is critical to recruit and retain diverse talent. STEM disciplines have been historically characterized by lack of diversity – which has reproduced and reinforced hostility and bias against a number of marginalized groups, for example, queer people, disabled people and people of colour. Suggestions that groups do not belong in science or engineering as well as suggestions that meritocracy works or that complete objectivity is possible have hindered the initiatives that are required to remove disadvantages and create more inclusive research environments. Lack of visibility has further complicated addressing specific inequities that queer people might face by obscuring both the subtle and overt forms of discrimination and exclusion. In the last two decades, research has started to explore the experiences of LGBTQ+ people in STEM. Existing studies have highlighted how queer academics and students face significant and intersectional barriers in STEM including structural disadvantages, homophobia, transphobia and discrimination (Mattheis et al. 2019; Reggiani et al. 2024a, 2024b). Still, more research is needed to understand the experiences of underrepresented and historically excluded people in STEM, including a focus on the recruitment and retention of LGBTQ+ researchers.

As queer people and academics with expertise in both social sciences and STEM, through our research and advocacy work, we have actively contributed not only to a better understanding of the experiences of LGBTQ+ people in STEM but also to transforming higher education institutions, particularly in Scotland. Through the STEM Equals project,[1] for example, we co-founded and organized StrathPride, the LGBTQI+ Staff and Postgraduate Student Network at the University of Strathclyde. The network provides an opportunity to build a more diverse and inclusive university community and enhance the support and visibility of LGBTQ+ people. We organized events where LGBTQ+ students and academics in STEM could showcase their research and discuss their lived experiences. We advocated for more equitable policies and collaborated with the university leadership and other colleagues to make change happen. More recently, with two US-based colleagues, we completed the LGBTQual+[2] project to address issues of attrition and retention for LGBTQ+ in STEM in the UK and the United States. This ongoing work has started to reveal the ways different institutional cultures and the wider context shape the experiences of queer students and academics in STEM across the two countries.

While reflecting both on extant research and the work that has been done by higher education institutions to remove barriers for queer people in STEM, critical approaches are essential. Moreover, without robust evaluations of EDI policies, practices, interventions and programmes, there is a risk that these efforts might reinforce existing inequalities or overlook the nuanced experiences of LGBTQ+ individuals. This work is key to make sure that initiatives and approaches to address the inclusion of queer people in STEM and, more broadly, in higher education genuinely foster inclusivity rather than providing just the illusion of progress.

In this chapter, we employ intersectional and queer approaches to explore STEM university environments where the tension between the progressive ideals of Scottish higher education institutions and the lived experiences of LGBTQ+ individuals collide. Developed by Black feminism at the crossroads between activism and legal studies, intersectionality theory (Collins 2015; Crenshaw 1989[3]) provides a framework to understand, analyse and address overlapping systems of oppression and illuminate how they create unique experiences of oppression and privilege. Intersectionality theory embraces non-additive conceptions of inequities and, by applying an intersectional lens, this study acknowledges the multifaceted identities of LGBTQ+ individuals and the different ways in which they experience inclusion and exclusion in STEM fields. Queer theory challenges dominant and (hetero)normative patterns (Butler 1990; Halberstam 2020; Sedgwick 1990), providing critical lenses through which to examine not only the ways sexuality and gender are performed but also how institutional and professional cultures in STEM reproduce normativity. Intersectional and queer theories benefit from each other. Queer theory challenges essentialist identity constructions, while intersectionality theory connects these anti-essentialist approaches with critical analysis of the material consequences of oppression across social categories.

In this chapter we focus on the experiences of thirty-three participants across the STEM Equals and LGBTQual+ projects who were based in Scottish universities at the time of data collection. Overall, ten participants were academics and twenty-three were PhD students. Four identified as asexual, eight as bisexual, six as gay woman/lesbian, eleven as gay man, one as pansexual, three as queer, one as questioning and three preferred to self-describe – with participants able to select more than one category. Regarding gender, fifteen participants identified as women, fourteen as men and four as non-binary/genderqueer. Six participants identified as trans. Eighteen participants described themselves as white British, one as white Irish, one as white Gypsy or Irish Traveller, eleven as having other white backgrounds, two as Asian/Asian British and one preferred to self-describe. In terms of nationality, among participants in the STEM Equals project (n = 24), six identified as Scottish, six as English, three as British (without specifying any nation within the UK), six were EU nationals and six selected a nationality from non-EU countries.[4] In the LGBTQual+ project, demographic information about nationality was not collected. According to information around ethnicity and focus groups conversations, among participants based in Scottish universities (n = 9), five identified as individuals who were from non-British backgrounds. Twelve participants identified as disabled or reported to have a disability or a long-term condition. Eleven participants self-identified as working class, seventeen as middle class, one preferred to self-describe and four declined to indicate their social class identity.

During focus groups and interviews, we prompted participants to discuss their social identities, challenges and issues of intersectional oppression and the support they have encountered in their academic journeys. This allows for an in-depth, nuanced and reflexive thematic analysis of participants' lived experiences. In this chapter, we employ the terms LGBTQ+ people and queer people interchangeably to describe a wide range of sexual and gender identities in an inclusive and intersectional way. We use the expression 'people of colour', but we also acknowledge that collective terms for underrepresented and marginalized groups risk homogenizing the experiences of racism and prejudice (Sobande and hill 2022).

By employing these theoretical and methodological approaches, and with a focus on higher education in Scotland, this chapter explores the mechanisms that shape the experiences of LGBTQ+ individuals in STEM. In particular, we take a closer look at the ways STEM environments (re)shape queerness and the multiple, contingent ways participants negotiate systemic and interlocking oppressions and inclusion. We explore our participants' experiences of navigating their queer place in STEM as well as in Scottish space. We conclude by highlighting the ways queer academics and PhD students attempted to create what feels like home for their queer identities.

Without a map across hostile terrain

LGBTQ+ academics and students in STEM face hostile and unwelcoming environments, where heteronormative and cisnormative assumptions are deeply ingrained. Invisibility, lack of representation and marginalization can lead to feelings of isolation and a decreased sense of belonging (Mattheis et al. 2019; Reggiani et al. 2024a, 2024b). Queer academics and students in STEM are also faced with a lack of opportunities, mentorship and support, and research highlights that this complex web of challenges can harm career progression. It is within this environment, across often hostile terrain, that our LGBTQ+ participants find themselves trying to find their place both as queer people and as scientists and engineers.

To address EDI for queer academics in STEM, Scottish universities have started to introduce a combination of support networks and community-led initiatives. This action has often been spearheaded by both a few funded projects and by the work of committed individuals and groups. More broadly, this work can be framed within the activities implemented in Scottish higher education institutions to create inclusive curricula, come to terms with the legacy of slavery and colonialism and educate staff and students about bias and discrimination. Scotland has made headlines for LGBTQ+ inclusion compared with other UK nations, as evidenced by being the first of the UK nations to overturn Section 28 in 2000 and, more recently, being named the 'best country in Europe for LGBTI legal equality' in both 2015 and 2016.

As a result of Scotland's progressive efforts around inclusivity for queer people, the country has cultivated a reputation for learning and working environments that are perceived, in some cases, as more welcoming, supportive and affirming. For example, Gavin (white British, trans man, asexual/bisexual), a disabled PhD student, shared:

> When it came to applying for PhDs – I mean, 'cause I'm trans for context – because of [different policies and the political landscape] I refrained from applying anywhere south of the border. Stuck to Scotland. I just thought it's not worth the risk, you know what I mean. I understand completely [that this] kind of cut me off from a lot of opportunities and a lot of things I'd actually really wanted to do. And places I'd wanted to go. But I wasn't willing to [take the] risk.

While Gavin deemed that Scotland was currently a safer place for trans people than the rest of the UK, it was painful for him to accept that his safety and well-being came at the cost of losing professional opportunities and chances. Moreover, it is worth noting that good institutional practices (for example around name change processes or support for gender-affirming healthcare) are by no means a consistent or universal standard across Scottish universities. Some have cultivated a reputation for being welcoming and supportive of the needs of queer and other marginalized staff and students. By comparison, other institutions have enabled more toxic work and research cultures to thrive. For example, when discussing his previous experience in a Russell Group university in Scotland, Matthew (white British, gay, man), a Scottish PhD student from a working-class background, found the environment extremely conservative – something that he associated with a small cohort of fellow students and the fact that most academics were 'old white men'. In comparison, the university where he decided to pursue his doctorate felt much more inclusive thanks to the presence of affirming supervisors, a wider research group and more welcoming academic climates in his department.

Many participants' accounts resonated with our own stories as queer, international researchers who moved to Scotland initially for precarious, fixed term research contracts, a decision with strong implications for both our personal and professional journeys. We recognize that, though we have navigated oppressions related to some of our identities, we have also benefitted from white privilege, which impacted our experiences as new residents of Scotland. In Glasgow, we found opportunities to create community, establish new connections and participate in the queer life of the city. At the university, we supported each other, found space to thrive despite the precarity of neoliberal academia and strategized with LGBTQ+ colleagues and allies to create space for progress towards greater inclusion and equity.

However, even in environments that have been mostly welcoming, we have had to contend with both subtle and overt issues of oppression. For example, when we received bigoted and hateful comments and emails because of our identities and because of our equity focused research, there are no clear mechanisms by which we might seek support, highlighting that organizations, including universities and research funders, have not fully considered the risks and challenges marginalized researchers are likely to face, especially if they undertake EDI research. Our work highlighted that discrimination and exclusion are still widespread in Scotland and higher education – which was expected but that, at times, made us question our ability to move forward while protecting our well-being.

By employing intersectional lenses, the experiences of queer academics and students in STEM can be compared with those of other marginalized groups (e.g. people of colour, women, disabled people or working-class people). This reveals patterns of systemic exclusion and bias that pervade STEM professional cultures and institutions that have been shaped by Western, white, male and heteronormative epistemologies. Decades of research have shown, for example, that women face systematic biases, along with discrimination and exclusion that have an impact on their career trajectories and well-being. People of colour face systemic racism – which intersects with other forms of social oppression to determine unique experiences of marginalization. Disabled and working-class academics and students in STEM also suffer inequities and barriers to inclusion. Yet, when compared to other social identities less work has been done to understand and address the experiences of and the barriers against queer people in STEM. This is due, in part, to a lack of demographic data, which contributes to render queer identities invisible and makes it difficult to compare and identify specific factors that affect their career trajectories. On the other hand, far fewer resources have been allocated by universities and funding bodies to address LGBTQ+ inclusion – despite recently published commitments institutions have made to create equitable opportunities and research environments.

The few initiatives aimed at supporting queer students and academics in STEM have typically centred on visibility. Examples include creating and sharing profiles of queer scientists and engineers or celebrating LGBTQ+ communities during LGBTQ+ History Month or Pride Month. These efforts are based on the idea that increased visibility is essential to providing role models, fostering a sense of belonging, challenging stereotypes and cultivating more inclusive and innovative environments. Nevertheless, it is critical to recognize that these initiatives often adopt an additive approach to diversity and lack intersectionality. More broadly, they fail to address the complex, situated and historical structures that determine oppression for both queer and other marginalized individuals in STEM and higher education institutions. This limits the impact of visibility campaigns. At best, they represent an important step to shift the conversation and create momentum for change. However, without awareness of systemic challenges that exist both in higher education and the wider society, these efforts might inadvertently put additional pressure and risk on queer scientists – as seen, for example, in the bullying, harassment and threats of violence that some LGBTQ+ scientists have faced on social media.

EDI work is fraught with contradictions. One of the key challenges is represented by the complexities of reforming institutions that are still characterized by systemic barriers and cultural resistance to social justice. This makes it difficult to translate commitments to action and secure investments that are sustained over time. Moreover, intersectional approaches and attentiveness to diversity within queer communities mean that one-size-fits-all approaches are limited and ineffective; policies must be crafted to address the specific needs and concerns of different groups, for example, transgender and non-binary individuals. Institutional inertia ends up shifting the onus of creating inclusion from senior leadership to marginalized individuals who are often in precarious and/or early career roles. This work, which is usually unacknowledged and unrewarded, ends up further marginalizing queer academics and students – who are then more likely to face attrition.

The positivist epistemologies of science, deeply rooted heterocentric norms, systemic biases and the historical lack of diversity complicate the work of making STEM disciplines more inclusive for queer people. The emphasis on objectivity and meritocracy that exist in STEM can obscure systemic oppression against queer individuals and can lead to undervaluing or undermining efforts to address diversity and inclusion. The lack of role models and mentors, particularly in senior positions, makes it difficult for queer people to see themselves progressing in their STEM careers. In addition, queer academics and students might encounter resistance from individuals and groups who are either unaware of or actively opposed to LGBTQ+ inclusion. As a result, often the emphasis of inclusion strategies is focused on individuals from excluded groups changing themselves or doing the work to 'fit in' rather than changing the working and research cultures that create the exclusions they experience. Therefore, even well-intentioned initiatives and colleagues might reproduce hetero- and homonormative ideas of queerness rather than challenging the norms that create oppression and exclusion and promoting cultural shifts that are needed to actively and radically welcome different perspectives, social identities and experiences.

Despite these challenges, LGBTQ+ individuals in STEM in Scotland continue to demonstrate resilience and agency, and there are encouraging signals that some positive change is happening. On the one hand, research into the experiences of queer people in STEM has expanded and awareness is increasing among institutions, funders and learned societies about the importance of addressing issues of LGBTQ+ inclusion. On the other hand, there has been an increase in initiatives led by queer communities in STEM. This includes, for example, annual conferences, dedicated networks, small-scale funding opportunities and scholarships to promote both queer science and queer people in science. Yet, grassroots activities often lack the resources to be sustainable over time or tackle the complexities of queer inclusion in STEM, particularly when it comes to addressing intersectional and compounded oppression.

Navigating queer identities in STEM environments

As a consequence of persistent exclusion, all of our participants faced the dilemma of negotiating their queer identities in sometimes (or often) hostile STEM environments. This included, for example, negotiating visibility or how they performed their gender identity. Navigating (in)visibility can be both challenging and affirming, and it determines unfair emotional labour for LGBTQ+ individuals (Reggiani et al. 2024a). Negotiating queer identities in STEM is further complicated by the ways academics and students' perceptions of their gender and sexuality interact with their professional STEM identities and the different norms and expectations found in learning and work environments.

Participants shared that it took time to consider whether it was safe to be visible, often wondering if it was ok to come out in this place or to this individual or team. They wondered about the consequences for professional progression and what colleagues might think. Queer academics and students faced such thoughts on a daily basis, sometimes for months, and every time they moved to a different institution or started working with a new line manager or supervisor. In fact, for LGBTQ+ people, coming out and being visible are not one-off events but rather repeated actions. Moreover, identities are fluid and contextual – thus participants might change the way they identify over time, for example, around their gender, sexuality and disability, which further complicates the work to navigate intersectional oppression.

Concerns were reinforced whenever participants experienced subtle or outright exclusionary behaviours – which appear to still be pervasive even in institutions that have formal policies and mechanisms in place to address prejudiced statements or actions, including homophobia and transphobia. Vee (white British, non-binary/genderqueer, queer), a PhD student in science who moved from England to Scotland to pursue their research, shared some exclusionary behaviour they had faced:

> [Sometimes] not feeling welcome within the department can come from comments made from other researchers. I've had comments on my pin badges and from the lad who started his PhD at the same time as me: 'There are too many of those flags. It's all too confusing and I don't get it' … To my face, he uses no pronouns

at all when talking about me. When I'm out of earshot he will use binary she/her pronouns and I've been told that this is what he's doing. I don't know if there are any allies in the department, so there's no one I can go to saying 'Am I being ridiculous about this, or is this something I need to raise with my supervisor?'

This casual and everyday discrimination not only impacted Vee's well-being but it was also detrimental to their sense of belonging in the department, particularly given they did not know other visible queer individuals or allies.

On the contrary, positive experiences contribute to affirm identities and ease fears. Roberta (white, woman, lesbian), PhD student in engineering who relocated to Scotland from another European country, and Thomas (white British, gay, man), a PhD student in science, discussed the empowering impact of rainbow lanyards and other items used to identify as members of LGBTQ+ communities or their allies:

> Roberta: One of my supervisors had some rainbow stuff [in] his office ... It was just nice to talk to him about [myself] and laugh together. It made us closer somehow because it's like something personal, but still nice to share. I think seeing more rainbows stuff in the [department] would make everything just better.
> Thomas: I really agree with what you said about having a visual cue to make it a safer space. For example, with [a] colleague that you don't know who is gay, that might be an indication that it is a safe environment for them to come out as well.

This discussion highlights that, in environments where invisibility has been historically the norm, even 'the smallest bit of visibility makes a huge difference' (Matthew, PhD student, white British, gay, man).

Queer women experienced the overlapping effects of homophobia and sexism, whereas ableism created additional barriers for queer disabled individuals. Queer working-class participants faced more financial burdens than their middle-class peers and encountered the class divide within academia. Whether they identified as working class or not, participants who behaved or performed their identities in ways that were stereotyped by others as 'working class' (for example, having an 'East End' Glaswegian accent) reported class-based overt and covert discriminations.

Among our participants, being from outside of Scotland and/or the UK[5] represented both a challenge and an opportunity. Moving to a different place might offer a renewed sense of freedom, an opportunity to authentically express one's identities or better access to resources for personal growth and safety. However, crossing borders also means leaving behind support networks and relocating to a place where there are different rules, cultures and norms that regulate queer identities and expressions, community belonging and academic life. Within our data, queer people of colour moving to Scotland, for example, had to contend with both homophobia and racism, as exemplified by the case of Sai (Asian, gay, man), a PhD student from Southeast Asia. While in Scotland he could be more open about his sexuality, he also frequently encountered racism in his day-to-day life, such as other students making casual racist remarks about his nationality or his cultural foods. In the society of students from his country – a space he had joined to find community and solidarity – he was confronted with homophobia:

> I joined the society and started feeling good and I was quite open about my sexuality. Then someone randomly came up to me … and they were like: 'Why are you gay? … You can get a woman.' I'm just like … that's so weird … it's inappropriate. I backed out of the conversation and I just left that event … After that, I distanced myself from the society and I quit completely after a few months.

Participants discussed that facing microaggressions, correcting misgendering, navigating (in)visibility and combating stereotypes diverted energies away from their research, learning and academic achievements. Moreover, the lack of support from colleagues and institutions can exacerbate feelings of isolation, making it harder for queer academics and students to thrive in STEM fields. We named this a 'Slippery Slope to Discrimination', to illustrate the systemic challenges faced by women and LGBTQ+ people in STEM, oppression is dynamic and inequities can have a cumulative impact when individuals face multiple and escalating exclusions (Reggiani et al. 2024b).

Our research challenges the idea that higher education, Scotland and STEM subjects are necessarily progressive spaces. Rather, our research reveals fractures between political and public commitments to EDI and the lived experiences of queer people – particularly those who are multiply-marginalized. LGBTQ+ academics and students in Scotland continue to face barriers to inclusion, and being visibly or openly queer in STEM can mean many costs, including emotional labour, loss of opportunities, discrimination and exclusion. To create space for transformation and lasting inclusion, institutions, including universities and governments, must be more accountable for funding the staffing and robust action required to address both systemic and intersectional oppressions. Only then will queer individuals be able to feel at home and thrive in STEM subjects and in Scotland.

Finding or creating home: Queer spaces in STEM

By reflecting on their experiences, participants suggested that, too often, the work undertaken by institutions to foster equity and inclusivity for LGBTQ+ people, including specifically within STEM, is still surface-level and insufficient, not leading to long-lasting, far-reaching transformational institutional change. As a result, some participants discussed taking proactive steps and actively finding ways to build welcoming queer spaces where they could feel at home.

One of the strategies employed to create more visibly inclusive STEM departments and laboratories was role modelling. In becoming a role model, participants were possibly motivated by the desire to connect with other queer individuals and demonstrate to them that it was possible to have a career in STEM. For academics in particular, role modelling included being open about their identities with colleagues and students, participating in initiatives for visibility or displaying and wearing recognizable symbols (e.g. rainbow lanyards, rings, pride flags). Diego (white, gay, man), an academic in engineering, relocated to Scotland from a different European country. Diego found that the professional culture in his department was 'primitive', particularly around issues of gender and sexuality. However, he was keen to contribute to creating a more inclusive and welcoming academic community:

> For me, helping to educate the next generation of engineers is something that's very important. I am starting to think that I would like to take some action, for example regarding visibility of [the] LGBT community ... [As an academic] I thought that I could be like a role model for some of the students. I think that, you know, my experience could be useful for somebody.

As exemplified by Diego's story, participants felt that by becoming role models for queer colleagues and students they could not only provide much-needed representation but also contribute to inclusivity more broadly.

Another strategy employed by both academics and students to foster a sense of community was joining and contributing to LGBTQ+ networks at their institutions or in their fields. By joining networks, participants could meet other queer people and find space to advocate for LGBTQ+ inclusion. In STEM-dedicated networks and events, they could also share their research achievements, find collaborators and discuss specific issues of discrimination.

For the most part, participants had positive experiences when engaging with initiatives to create more inclusive STEM spaces for LGBTQ+ people. Many noted that dedicated staff and student networks helped to foster more welcoming STEM environments, which in turn improved their academic and professional experiences by making them feel less alone. However, those more directly involved with organizing networks and support for LGBTQ+ communities recognize that, while beneficial to improve academic cultures, these efforts were usually not meaningfully recognized by universities and might end up creating additional and unsustainable workloads.

When reflecting on the importance of finding and creating spaces for queer people, participants focused their attention on both higher education institutions and the broader context in which they were located. Some mentioned, for example, the benefits of living in cities like Glasgow where they could find community, relationships and activities. This is the case of Guido (Mediterranean,[6] non-binary/genderqueer, pansexual), a PhD student:

> I come from a [a different country in Europe and a very small town]. So that's not the most open-minded [place], and also [at] the time I was closeted ... I'd say that I wouldn't have accepted myself if it wasn't for Glasgow ... I honestly chose Glasgow because ... it seemed like the most open and diverse city in Scotland.

Being used to moving across institutions, cities and, sometimes, countries, others used online tools to maintain connections with peers and friends. By experimenting with different ways to connect and create a sense of home for themselves, participants became quite sophisticated in constructing support networks. Olivia (white British, woman, asexual), a disabled PhD student, described that after moving to Scotland from England she was quick to integrate new networks into existing relationships.

> I've already effectively built my support network here on the models of what I've had in the past ... [At the University] Disability support-wise, I have a mentor I see weekly and I just know who I can check in with if I need to. Community-wise, just friends, teammates, that sort of thing. I do a few extracurriculars and at least two of them have quite a lot of LGBT people ... Online, I have a group of friends I've known for [years] ... We're across five different time zones. I'm still very much in touch with them.

Olivia's experience demonstrates the ways that intersecting social identities can play a role in shaping support networks. While queer groups and communities might provide a space to find support on issues of gender and sexuality, they might not be fully inclusive spaces for queer disabled people, queer people of colour and/or working-class queer people. Therefore, some participants discussed searching for support and solidarity elsewhere. Those who had stronger networks outside academia usually found community and affirmation through external connections. In contrast, academics and students without local external networks – for example, those who recently moved to Scotland – often felt a greater need to engage in institutional initiatives that foster inclusivity and support within their academic environments. These differences highlight the varied and intersectional experiences of LGBTQ+ people in STEM and emphasize the importance of examining context holistically when it comes to exploring and addressing issues of belonging and well-being.

These examples paint a complex picture of queer belonging in higher education and STEM in Scotland. By reflecting on their experiences, participants recognized that universities can and should do better to provide support and remove barriers for all LGBTQ+ academics and students, both in STEM and beyond. They highlighted, for example, the need to provide better and more effective training around intersecting issues faced by queer people and other oppressed groups. More broadly, participants called for greater institutional accountability and urged for bold, transformative changes to make STEM and higher education truly welcoming and just.

Conclusion

In this chapter, we explored the experiences of LGBTQ+ academics and PhD students in STEM working in Scottish higher education institutions through the lenses of intersectional and queer approaches. Findings highlight that, in STEM fields historically characterized by a lack of diversity and inclusion, significant challenges remain for queer people. Nevertheless, LGBTQ+ academics and students continue to find ways to create their own queer spaces and networks of support – even in fields and institutions where systemic barriers, hostility and exclusion persist. Trying to find one's place across hostile terrains, navigating queer and STEM identities, finding community and creating a sense of home are complex, non-linear and sometimes labour-intensive processes. Our institutions should be shouldering more of the burden of that labour to enable students and staff from underrepresented and historically excluded identities, including queer people, to thrive.

Queer academics and PhD students participating in our research recognized Scotland's efforts to position itself as a progressive and liberal nation. Similarly, they appreciated the work that some Scottish universities have put in place to remove barriers and promote equity for LGBTQ+ communities. More inclusive climates have had a positive impact on the well-being and sense of belonging of some participants. However, our findings suggest that universities are not necessarily progressive and that inclusivity is by no means the standard. Although our research was focused on LGBTQ+ people in STEM, participants' accounts suggest that a similar conclusion can be applied, more broadly, to LGBTQ+ rights and inclusion in Scotland – which challenges and nuances ideas about the special, or exceptional, place of 'progressive' nations like Scotland.

While progress has been made, more needs to be done to create authentic inclusion in Scottish higher education. Research and sustained investments are needed to remove barriers for queer people, so that universities can become places where everybody can thrive and be their authentic selves without fear of repercussion. These efforts should be guided by intersectional and queer approaches, paying attention to marginalized and underrepresented individuals within LGBTQ+ communities.

Rather than making queer academics and students 'fit in' institutions that (re)produce systemic oppression and privilege, the experience of our participants suggests that is possible to imagine different (and queer) futures in higher education. New forms of community and solidarity are possible. This would require, however, removing not only barriers to inclusion for LGBTQ+ communities but also reimagining more broadly the role and the functioning of universities. Against the multiple and complex challenges faced by Scottish higher education institutions, we would like to recommend a shift towards more sustainable, equitable and inclusive research and learning environments.

Notes

1. The STEM Equals project was funded by the EPSRC, the Engineering and Physical Sciences Research Council. Data were collected in 2019 and 2020.
2. The LGBTQual+ project was funded by the Royal Society of Chemistry and the Science and Innovation Network. Data were collected in 2024.
3. We intentionally cite Crenshaw's first naming of intersectionality in 1989 to make clear that intersectionality is not a new term that's become a popular fad, but rather a term and theory with a 35+-year history.
4. Participants could select more than one nationality, if that applied.
5. In total, seventeen participants identified as being from outside or being born outside of Scotland or the UK.
6. Instead of employing a category derived from the UK census to identify their ethnicity/race, the participant chose to self-describe.

References

Butler, J. *Gender Trouble: Feminism and the Subversion of Identity*. London: Routledge, 1990.
Collins, P. H. 'Intersectionality's Definitional Dilemmas'. *Annual Review of Sociology* 41, no. 1 (2015): 1–20.
Crenshaw, K. 'Demarginalizing the Intersection of Race and Sex'. *University of Chicago Legal Forum* 1989, no. 1 (1989): 138–67.
Educational Institute of Scotland. Taking Pride in Teaching. The Power of Inclusive Education. Edinburgh: EIS, 2023.
Halberstam, J. *The Queer Art of Failure*. Durham, NC: Duke University Press, 2020.
Mattheis, A., Arellano, D. C.-R. D. and Yoder, J. B. 'A Model of Queer STEM Identity in the Workplace'. *Journal of Homosexuality* 67, no. 13 (2019): 1839–63.
Reggiani, M., Gagnon, J. D. and Lunn, R. J. 'A Holistic Understanding of Inclusion in STEM: Systemic Challenges and Support for Women and LGBT+ Academics and PhD Students'. Science Education (2024b): 1–33.
Reggiani, M., Gagnon, J. D. and Lunn, R. J. 'LGBT+ Academics' and PhD Students' Experiences of Visibility in STEM: More Than Raising the Rainbow Flag'. *Higher Education* 87 (2024a): 1–19.
Sedgwick, E. K. *Epistemology of the Closet*. Oakland: University of California Press, 1990.
Sobande, F. and hill, l. *Black Oot Here: Black Lives in Scotland*. London: Bloomsbury, 2022.

25

Disabled queer student experiences of Scottish higher education

Jack McKinlay

The claim of Scotland being 'world leading' across a wide range of areas – politically and socially – is a recurring one. This claim intertwines with the narrative of Scotland as a 'wee' but 'different' place – a nation that positions itself as separate from England and distinct on the global stage. A parallel 'different' narrative exists within universities: progressive, inclusive and welcoming to a diverse array of students. Universities often position themselves as exceptional or elite institutions, alongside public commitments to equality, diversity and inclusion (EDI). These commitments are frequently showcased through polished statements, awards and the marketing of EDI 'achievements' (Dawson 2023). Commitments to diversity are widely expressed across Scotland's universities, but the extent to which they are realized can vary. Universities in larger cities can have greater material resources at their disposal, while those in smaller, more rural areas may face different challenges. The universities my participants attend reflect this diversity, spanning Russell Group universities, known for their prestige, global rankings, competitive entry requirements and research funding (e.g. University of Glasgow, University of Edinburgh); post-92 universities, which gained university status following the Further and Higher Education Act 1992, emphasizing applied learning, vocational education and widening participation (e.g. Glasgow Caledonian University, Queen Margaret University, University of the West of Scotland); technological focus universities, which focus on STEM, vocational education and industry partnerships (e.g. Heriot-Watt University, University of Strathclyde); and smaller regional institutions (e.g. University of Highlands and Islands). Although Scottish universities champion themselves as 'different' or 'leading' in diversity drives (e.g. LGBT Charter), policies and public narratives can fail to reflect experiences of students who embody multiple positions, with their experiences not always fitting within academic spaces (Falconer and Taylor 2017).

This chapter centres the experiences of disabled queer students as they navigate Scottish universities. Their stories, shaped by intersecting inequalities, provide a lens through which to look differently at universities. I grapple with the complexities and nuances of experiences as layered, messy and multifaceted, reflecting university and student experiences, as well as broader theoretical discussions around queer-crip data, identities and positions (McRuer 2006; Guyan 2022). Queer research often focuses on the 'normative' LGBTQ+ subject (Taylor 2023) – typically young, white, gay, middle-class men – and within universities, diversity is often celebrated in ways that cater to and are shaped by these 'normative' subjects, particularly those within elite institutions. This narrow framing of queer lives reinforces exclusionary norms, as well as overlooks queer experiences beyond this narrative. I have met and interviewed people who sit against and challenge this 'go-to', dominant queer narrative. I have a range of participants whose sexual and gender identities may not always receive 'queer' attention. Additionally, the traditional narrative of university attendance tends to focus on the young, full-time undergraduate student, attending physical institutions. Queer disabled students have a diverse range of experiences across time and place, often reflecting a queer-crip temporality.[1] Some have attended university, left and later returned to complete a different degree; others have been 'pushed' off the physical campus and onto virtual platforms; and some have paused or altered their academic experiences due to health challenges. My sample includes participants from various degree programmes and university types across varying rankings in Scotland, with most studying in the urban central belt cities of Glasgow and Edinburgh. The sample includes both undergraduate (UG) and postgraduate (PG) students with diverse disabilities such as autism, ADHD, dyslexia, diabetes, chronic pain, fatigue, mobility issues, arthritis, depression and anxiety. This chapter invites readers to engage with the question: *who* and *what* is allowed into university and what this means for a 'progressive', 'inclusive' Scotland?

Here, there and penguins

My interest in disabled queer research is a personal one. As a gay disabled man, my educational experience – through primary and secondary school and then into college and university – has played a role. My parents observed my struggle with words from an early age, and after some time, I was later diagnosed with dyslexia at eight years old. Dyslexia was explained to me as a 'learning difficulty' making reading and spelling more challenging. At the time, I didn't know anyone else with dyslexia. I internalized this 'difficultly' as something to keep quiet about, to which being dyslexic became a felt difference. I was then taken out of classes for extra help on my reading and spelling. 'Why do you get taken out of class?' I would be asked by my peers. 'Just to do some reading' I would respond, trying not to make it seem unusual. This feeling of difference was felt greater when I was in the lowest reading and maths group in primary school. I saw the 'smart' kids were all together, reading books that had smaller lettering and more pages per chapter. My reading books had larger lettering, pictures in them and less pages per chapter. I became hyper-aware of hierarchies, particularly as my primary school years progressed. The 'smart' kids would go to another classroom for maths class. I remained in my seat. The 'smart' kids would fly through their reading books. I would stay with the same book for weeks on end. I felt and observed these differences each day. However, my love for learning persisted, and secondary school would be better, surly? I arrived at secondary school and started in a mid-level English class and, to my surprise, a top-level math class.

For a brief moment I felt like I had 'made it'. But after one week and a single test, I was moved to the lowest math group. I, once again, felt and observed these hierarchies. My parents reached out to the school raising concerns about the lack of disability accommodations with the head of the department dismissing these – 'It's maths – there isn't much reading, so he should've been fine'. My mother's fury was palpable. I was devastated by the demotion. When I got home that day, my mum told me, 'You've got two choices: bury your head in the sand and accept it, or work hard.' Those words have stayed with me.

I struggled to make friends in my early years of secondary school. Often, I would float between different social groups or spend my break times in a computer room. It wasn't until I was in fourth year of secondary school that I found a group who I'm still friends with to this day. Noticing my early years of social difficulties, my parents explored an autism diagnosis. It wasn't until after I was diagnosed that I found out my mum would phone my pastoral care teacher numerous times asking for her support in getting me assessed. She often refused and said 'Jack has loads of friends'. After many years, and a lot of push-back, I was diagnosed with autism at sixteen years old. Despite living with dyslexia for many years and becoming more aware of disabilities more generally, I still kept this to myself.

Teachers were aware of my disabilities as I'm sure it was on my educational record. I often wonder *if* and *how* this would have changed their views of me as a 'capable' or 'good' student. I was often told, implicitly and explicitly, that I would struggle to get my exams, and that university – the place over there – wasn't somewhere for someone like me – a disabled person. As a PhD student now reflecting on my past history as I write this, I recognize how far I've come. I'm at that 'somewhere' place I was told wasn't for me. I'm over there now. That said, university remains a peculiar experience, and one that is steeped in doubt and imposter feelings. During an imposter workshop in my first year of PhD life, I was asked to identify my 'imposter animal'. I chose a penguin. My reason – I plod along, and if I fall into the water then (hopefully) I swim. This image has stayed with me, prompting questions about other penguins in academia (Addison et al. 2022): Where are they? How has university life been for them? What are their experiences? As I've progressed in my PhD experience, I've encountered a few fellow penguins among queer disabled students – who are drawn to the bright lights of university.

A bright light

Anticipations of the 'student experience' begin long before enrolment, and for disabled queer students, university often symbolizes hope and opportunity, a space for self-discovery, identity exploration and escaping home-life constraints:

> You grow up knowing that something is different [with you], struggle with making friends during school, and then come to the big bright city and university and think things will be very different. (Bethany, twenty-eight, female, bisexual, she/her, white British, PG)

Bethany touches on topics of identity, belonging and a search for change, suggesting a past–present–future journey marked by a sense of difference and isolation from an early age. Yet, Bethany believed university would bring acceptance, representing hope, optimism and the expectation of transformation. This anticipation of gain was also spoken about by others, including Dan:

> One of the teachers that spoke to me, he was a modern studies teacher, and after I failed one of my prelims he was like 'look, you can always fry burgers, but you can't always go to uni, this is the year you really should put your head down and get your exams, because I believe you can do this'. (Dan, twenty-three, trans man, pansexual, he/him, white European, PG)

Dan highlights university as a 'bright light' symbolizing opportunity, achievement and self-fulfilment. His teacher's belief in his potential marks a pivotal moment, with university as a gateway to a brighter future for Dan. The teacher's comment about 'frying burgers' implies a classed fixity, where university could offer him a chance for class mobility, personal transformation and a promising future. This creates a choice for Dan: go for what seems inevitable or strive towards the 'bright light'. The teacher's encouragement becomes a catalyst for him to pursue higher education, symbolizing not just a place but a state of mind, where hard work and self-belief leads to a better future, be it materially or emotionally.

For some disabled queer participants university allows an escape from their original homes under parental or guardianship care, where they can embrace aspects of their identities that were restricted or unrealizable. Scotland is often known for its LGBTQ+ rights and progression, and arguably Scottish universities have also taken on work of being inclusive to queer students. Katie and Dorothy reflect on this sexual escapism:

> I was like 'well, I get the freedom to explore my sexuality a bit more, maybe drink', so I was really excited with the prospect of having my freedom … yeah moving from home I was able to explore my sexuality and I thought 'great, I'll join the society, that will help me explore and I'll feel a part of something' … I got a chance to finally be able to date people and have sex. I hadn't had proper sex until I went to uni. (Katie, twenty-three, female, lesbian, she/her, mixed race, UG)

> When you go to university there is a hope that you are going to meet all these new people and figure out yourself, and that life is going to be so different and wonderful. You just go on your own journey during university and you're more comfortable with who you are … it's easier when you go to uni to do all that, and to become more comfortable with yourself. And then maybe the sort of higher you go in uni then it just gets even better. (Dorothy, fifty-eight, female, lesbian, she/her, white Scottish, PG)

For both Katie and Dorothy, university represented more than academic opportunity – it was a chance to explore their sexuality, allowing them to live on their own terms, away from familial constraints. Many participants saw university as a space that not only allowed but also actively supported queer identities, standing in stark contrast to home environments where such exploration was restricted or discouraged. Leaving home was not just about education; it was a step toward personal liberation – university was an escape from heterosexuality and a path towards queerness.

Despite the difference in years, and the difference in university LGBTQ+ inclusion policies between Katie's current undergraduate attendance and Dorothy's past one, university has been a place where exploring sexuality felt more accessible. Dorothy's experience underscores the enduring role of universities in fostering queer self-exploration, while Katie's more recent perspective reinforces this continuity. Hence, both accounts express a similar sentiment; universities have been, and continue to be, spaces of opportunity for queer self-discovery and have been and still remain 'big places' in the 'wee place' of Scotland, offering vital spaces for queers, both past, present and, potentially, future.

While policy frameworks have progressed, the lived experiences of many queer disabled students suggest that deeper structural changes are still needed to feel included beyond initial access. The UK Equality Act 2010 recognizes both disability and sexuality as independent protected characteristics, obligating universities to uphold these protections. However, in practice, these identities can collide with institutional structures failing to consider both. As a result, queer disabled students can find themselves caught between policies that address one aspect of their identity but not the complexities of both. Despite institutional commitments to inclusivity, university frameworks can struggle to integrate intersectional experiences, leaving students questioning whether they are 'allowed here'.

Am I allowed here?

Getting through the doors of university was exciting, and for some unexpected. Yet, after time spent on campus, in classrooms and navigating social spaces (or struggling to do so), a lingering question emerged: is this really a place for me? Many participants carried this uncertainty, as the structures and expectations of university life signalled that they didn't 'fit', leading them to attribute this to their embodied identities. Doubts about whether they had made the right choice in attending, or whether they should continue, remained persistent. Feelings of being unsupported – sometimes materially, other times emotionally – shaped their university experience, leaving many questioning their place:

> I was just like 'well, I'm obviously not smart enough or good enough to be here. I'm not out, I've got these health conditions right now I'm going through, I'm working class, I'm a carer', so there was just these things that were going on, and I didn't fit the mould of what a uni student should be. (Caroline, thirty-seven, female, lesbian, she/her, white Scottish, PG)

Caroline's reflection highlights the deep sense of exclusion she feels within academia, rooted within, what she felt as her intersectional issues. Caroline's health, working-class background, caregiving responsibilities and not being openly queer compounded her sense of inadequacy within university, as these factors clashed with the ideal 'mould' of a university student. This mould – defined by straightness, youth, health, financial stability and a singular focus on academic achievements and ability unimpeded by external responsibilities and identities – excludes those whose lived realities deviate from these ideals.

Not all Scottish universities reinforce this mould in the same way. While Russell Group universities may reflect 'traditional' academic ideals, post-92 and technological universities focus on widening participation and flexibility for non-normative students. The introduction of part-time study, mature student support and caregiving recognition are some ways universities have challenged exclusion. However, Caroline, who attended both Russell Group and post-92 universities, felt the weight of these expectations even in more inclusive institutions, raising questions about how effectively universities challenge these norms in practice. Caroline's experience shows that institutional structures and dominant student cultures can still implicitly favour idealized or 'typical' students, regardless of university type. Blaming oneself as not 'fitting' was also conveyed:

> It was just really hard to feel like I was welcomed and wanted at uni, because at times you feel like a burden to them ... It's not even that I wasn't accepted, I was definitely the problem student. (River, twenty-five, non-binary, queer, she/they, white Scottish, UG)

River's quote conveys a deep sense of alienation and self-blame, reflecting a pervasive feeling of not belonging and the emotional labour required for them to exist in spaces that may overlook their identities. River discussed frequently encountering systems that are not designed with them in mind (e.g. gender-neutral bathroom facilities, inaccessible campus layout), leading to situations where accommodations or support feel like impositions and that they were 'the problem' – being tolerated rather than valued, accommodated rather than embraced. This reflects systemic barriers and unspoken expectations that marginalize those who don't fit with able-bodied, heterocisnormativity or able norms. Due to the inaccessible campus layout, River had to leave the physical university and move to online learning, isolating them from the wider student population, thus creating a sense of otherness, both physically and emotionally.

Caroline and River's experiences highlight how university environments can leave students feeling like burdens rather than valued members of the academic community. This sense of exclusion is not just personal but structural, shaped by how universities position disability and sexuality within their frameworks of support. While LGBTQ+ student societies exist to foster community, disability services often operate through a 'fixing' framework, where support is treated as an adjustment rather than an integral part of university life. This distinction could reflect broader institutional attitudes – queerness as something students must create for themselves, while disability is treated as a problem to be managed by institutionally employed staff members – both of which shape students' experiences of belonging and exclusion.

Caroline and River's accounts challenge normative frameworks that define who is seen as a 'legitimate' or 'good' student. Their experiences underscore how universities can, at times, fail disabled queer students, leaving them to question their place within these institutions. Their narratives encapsulate the emotional toll of navigating spaces that frame difference as difficulty. Erika further elaborates on this struggle:

> There is always going to be that expectation to act and perform in certain ways at uni. And you may always be looked at different because of who you are. (Erika, forty, female, pansexual, she/they, white British, PG)

Erika highlights the sense of conformity that she faces at university and the pressure she feels to play a role of herself to in navigating a normative university environment. Often times this meant not only deciding whether to 'come out', but also *who* to tell, *when* to tell and *why* to tell. In this way, the university environment demands not only an academic performance of writing well and critical comprehension, but also the performance of identity, creating an additional layer of emotional labour. Such performativity can lead to a sense of disconnection, as vital aspects of one's identity are sidelined to navigate and survive – raising questions about whether universities, as part of Scotland's evolving civic democratic landscape, offer spaces of inclusion or perpetuate barriers. KQ, studying at an urban university, felt his queerness was more accepted in Scotland compared to China. In contrast, Phoebe, attending a rural university, noted that her queerness felt less visible or affirmed after moving away from an urban city:

> Initially, I was in closet. I never came out to anyone … I enjoy the freedom and the LGBT rights in Scotland. We don't have that in China. Yeah, before I came to Scotland I wasn't confident about my gay identity, and I had no pride of being gay … Being in Scotland is so good for that … But here [Scotland] I can be free. I can be me. I am allowed to. And people don't care. People here [Scotland] want people to be happy. (KQ, thirty-three, male, gay, he/him, PG)

> Being from Glasgow and being around the gay scene, people dress differently, whereas at the uni it is very much leggings and a hoodie or shorts and a hoodie if you're a guy. Yeah, just a very heteronormative place to be, everyone merged as one. So like it was very much like you have to be straight-passing … I feel totally at home in Glasgow, and then you move to uni and life just got a bit slower. (Phoebe, twenty-two, female, bisexual/queer, she/they, UG)

KQ and Phoebe illustrate the nuanced ways in which location intersects with their experiences of queerness. KQ spoke highly of both Scotland and his Scottish university as playing a key role of his queer identity, reflecting on Scotland's ongoing reputation as a progressive space for LGBTQ+ rights. He contrasts the freedom and acceptance he feels in Scotland with the restrictions he faced in China. Terms like 'freedom' reflect his belief of Scotland's legal and societal progressiveness, offering a sense of validation and permission to 'be me', aligning with Scotland's image as a safe haven for LGBTQ+ individuals.

KQ's experience underscores the complexities of place-based identity, as the freedom he experiences in Scotland, or more specifically the central belt of Scotland, can contrast sharply with the experiences in more rural areas of Scotland where queerness may not be as visible as urban areas. Phoebe highlights the contrast between the more vibrant and diverse LGBTQ+ scene in urban cities and the more homogenous, heteronormative atmosphere at the rural university. She compares the way people dress in Glasgow's gay scene compared with the heteronormative culture at university, where 'leggings and a hoodie' are the standard. This stark difference underscores the tension Phoebe feels between the freedom to express and feel her queerness in the urban versus the rural.

Disabled queer identities are felt multiply and variously on Scottish campuses. Students often face a pressure to conform, leading to feelings of alienation and questioning whether they truly belong in university spaces. Erika's phrase 'certain ways' highlights a recurring theme in this subheading: disabled queer participants often feel unwelcome because they do not fit the traditional mould of a university student. However, many participants also reflected on the opportunity to create spaces where they could shape their own mould – both for themselves and others – as a way of 'fixing' their university experience.

Can we fix it?

Participants have described university as a space of optimism and potential freedom, yet also of exclusion. In feeling out of place, participants spoke of the weight of changing their experience. They felt that university structures were not supporting them, and thus had to do this themselves ('it was me that had to change the experience' – Caroline). While most felt it was on them to change the experience and create their own inclusive spaces, Ben spoke of some actions their university was taking:

> We [student representatives] sat down and they [university management] went 'what are the biggest issues facing trans and non-binary people in [university name], and what can we do?' And then that produced a massive action list that me and the director of student services review pretty much every 3 or 4 weeks ... queerness really is respected from staff and students in general, like I say we had a round table talk with the president of the uni. (Ben, twenty-one, non-binary, bisexual, he/they, white British, UG)

The structured round table meetings involving student representatives and high-level university staff demonstrate an institutional effort to listen and act on the concerns of trans and non-binary students. The involvement of both students and university decision-makers reflects the potential for high-level collaboration and discussion between staff and students in creating a queer(er) university environment. The reference to 'queerness really is respected' indicates that respect is embedded not just in policy but also reflected in the actions of university management, where queerness is 'on the agenda'. However, this structured, visible initiative raises questions about how replicable this model is across other Scottish universities and whether it reflects a broader institutional culture. Ben, as a student representative, knows these conversations are happening primarily because of their position, whereas other students who are not student representatives may be unaware of these initiatives and conversations. Yet, recognizing these successes, we can learn to create a more inclusive 'wee place' in Scottish universities – where the diversity of students is not only acknowledged but actively supported.

While the above structured roundtable meetings demonstrate a high-level institutional commitment to inclusivity, Timothy argued that change often comes from within the student community, where belonging and affirmation can counter the marginalization faced by trans and non-binary individuals.

> I feel like university is made in the people, the people that are around you, the friends that you've made. That's really where university comes from. I feel very lucky that I've been able to have friends that are totally comfortable with me being autistic and asexual. It's just a really nice feeling. (Timothy, twenty-two, non-binary, asexual queer, he/they, white Scottish, UG)

Timothy's reflection highlights how social connections shaped university life and affirmed their disabled queer identity, challenging the view of higher education as solely academic or institutional. They state, 'university is made in the people' – reflecting the 'People Make Glasgow' phrase – emphasizing the friendships made are central in university. For Timothy, these relationships define the university experience, framing it as a social rather than solely intellectual space. The acceptance of their autistic and asexual identities by friends provides essential emotional support, enhancing their well-being and sense of inclusion alongside academic growth. Timothy's experience also underscores that inclusion depends not just on EDI policies but on social environments that embrace diverse identities. By describing themself as 'very lucky' to have a supportive community, Timothy acknowledges that such acceptance is not universal, and thus reflects broader inequities in experiences. Their narrative demonstrates that belonging at university is often forged through interpersonal relationships, not institutional structures or policies, and highlights the importance of fostering peer networks. Many participants described joining student-led societies or networks to foster peer networks. However, Ashwin and Samantha shared that despite the 'welcome-to-all' ethos often promoted by these groups, attending these events felt uncomfortable and challenging to navigate:

> I think it is very white, and so being a person of colour and you go along hoping to see and find a community of LGBT people of colour and that wasn't there was difficult and sad for me to see that. So like that impacted my mood of like 'oh, where are my friends?' (Ashwin, forty-three, queer, gay, he/they, South Asian, PG)
>
> It took me a while to like just be engaged with them. I think for at least for LGBT society what took me a while was gauging how white it is. Umm. I think that

that was like a huge kind of barrier for me and for my friends as well. (Samantha, twenty-one, female, queer, she/her, Chinese, UG)

Although most Scottish universities now market themselves as 'international' and position themselves as 'big places' on the world stage – Glasgow's 'World Changers Welcome' campaign being one such example – Ashwin and Samantha's experience of navigating student-led societies was narrower. Universities frequently deploy narratives of global, international diversity, yet these institutions remain shaped by a predominantly white Scottish cultural landscape, with limited racial diversity (Mahn 2019).

Scotland's progressive national identity is often positioned in contrast to England, with narratives of acceptance and inclusivity distinguishing it from Westminster politics. Yet, institutional diversity work can sometimes prioritize performative optics over meaningful structural change. This tension is evident in the whiteness that permeates LGBTQ+ spaces: while commitment to inclusion is publicly proclaimed, racial exclusions persist. The disillusionment experienced by Ashwin and Samantha reflects broader concerns about racism in Scottish higher education. Despite universities' public championing of equality, diversity and inclusion, the lived experiences reveal that whiteness remains deeply embedded in both the cultural and structural fabric of these institutions. Whiteness, as Ashwin and Samantha make clear, is not merely about numerical dominance, but also about who is not in the space with them. While universities may celebrate diversity, institutional whiteness continues to shape student social experience, including in my own interactions with participants as a white, Scottish man.

What now?

In this chapter, I shared the understandings of disabled queer students at Scottish universities. Their experiences, marked by a spectrum of emotions – hope, optimism, worry, self-doubt and blame – highlight complex the emotional and social journeys within university. University represents more than just academic achievement; it is a space for self-discovery, community and escape from limiting environments. For many, these opportunities feel unattainable elsewhere, reinforcing the idea that university is symbolically a 'big place' in the 'wee place' of Scotland.

Students at Scottish universities embody a diverse range of identities and positions that defy the static, normative view of the 'typical' student. As institutions claim to foster equality, diversity and inclusion, they have the potential to contribute to a more equal society. However, if dominant narratives continue to obscure the complexities of queer disabled student identities and experiences, universities risk reinforcing, rather than dismantling, structural and intersecting inequalities. The experiences of my participants reflect broader systemic issues within Scottish universities, reminding us that these challenges must be addressed by universities in order to create spaces where students are valued for both their academic abilities and their diverse identities.

Encouragingly, examples of different queer-inclusive practices exist across Scottish universities. Ben's participation in a trans and non-binary roundtable discussion with both students and university management demonstrates meaningful dialogue and institutional responsiveness. Similarly, the keynote presence of Emma Roddick MSP at the Queer and the Cost of Living Crisis seminar series, as someone out about 'queer' and 'disabled' experience, reflects consolidated recognition of queer issues both in and beyond the campus. My enduring quandary is about who feels they can engage with these opportunities and conversations. Students, particularly those in prominent positions within student-led groups, may find these conversations more accessible and may likely be invited to participate. For others, these initiatives and conversations may feel out of reach, for example, those who are not yet 'out', not a part of university union groups, or who have risks associated with increased visibility. Conversations and opportunities need to be widely promoted to ensure broader participation, contributing to Scotland's civic democracy.

Yet inclusion is not simply about representation; it is also about how students experience and navigate university life. I hope to have highlighted how aspects like belonging and acceptance – often assumed to be easily attainable at university – can be complex. Much like the buzzword 'inclusion', 'belonging' is often used without fully understanding its complexities. It is frequently reduced to mere assimilation into the dominant, normative culture of the university, marginalizing those who do not fit into predefined student moulds. Such moulds are largely designed for those able to navigate university structures and who become even more 'included'. In this context, ideals of a 'good' student and the values attributed to ability are exalted, even as universities promote civic-minded ideals of community and inclusivity. This creates a paradox where disabled queer students can be both included and at odds with the framing of higher education diversity. The presence of EDI awards and charters, while suggestive of commitment, can be self-serving and perpetuate bad practices, raising important questions about their true purpose and the communities they serve (Mahn 2019; Addison et al. 2022; Dawson 2023). While these accolades may reflect institutional claims of inclusivity, they do not always align with the lived realities of students whose experiences do not fit the homogeneous university culture. Moving forward, institutions must recognize that simply being physically present on campus does not equate to inclusion. It is crucial for institutions to consider qualitative experiences rather than relying solely on meeting the standards set by awards and legislation or using quantitative student experience surveys that attempt to fit experiences neatly into a tick-box.

For Scottish society, these issues matter as achieving inclusion and belonging within universities align with the country's values of civic equality, progression and acceptance. However, this is not simply a question of university policies; it is also about resources and external structural factors. The challenges of inclusion and belonging can be limited by broader university and government constraints, meaning that the push for more inclusive practices must also consider how external factors, such as government/university (under)funding, shape what is possible within Scottish higher education institutions. Ultimately, this chapter contributes to the growing conversation around queer disabled students' experiences in Scottish higher education, highlighting the challenges and possibilities for creating more inclusive and supportive spaces.

Note

1. Queer-crip time challenges normative, linear, ableist and heteronormative understandings of time, such as life milestones (e.g. marriage, reproduction, retirement). It emphasizes alternative ways of experiencing time, shaped by disabled queer lives and desires and highlights how time and life trajectories are shaped by ableist, cisheteronormative assumptions (Halberstam 2005).

References

Addison, M., Breeze, M. and Taylor, Y. (eds). *The Palgrave Handbook of Imposter Syndrome in Higher Education*. Cham: Palgrave Macmillan, 2022.

Dawson, L. 'Beyond Box Ticking and Buzzwords: A Queer, Working-Class, Anti-racist, Anti-ableist Sharing in UK Academia'. In Y. Taylor, M. Brim and C. Mahn (eds), *Queer Precarities in and out of Higher Education*, 1st ed., pp. 97–116. London: Bloomsbury Academic, 2023.

Falconer, E. and Taylor, Y. 'Negotiating Queer and Religious Identities in Higher Education: Queering "Progression" in the "University Experience"'. *British Journal of Sociology of Education* 38, no. 6 (2017): 782–97. https://doi.org/10.1080/01425692.2016.1182008.

Guyan, K. *Queer Data*. London: Bloomsbury Academic, 2022.

Halberstam, J. *In a Queer Time and Place: Transgender Bodies, Subcultural Lives*. New York: New York University Press, 2005.

Mahn, C. 'Black Scottish Writing and the Fiction of Diversity'. In M. Breeze, Y. Taylor and C. Costa (eds), *Time and Space in the Neoliberal University: Futures and Fractures in Higher Education*, pp. 119–41. Cham: Palgrave, 2019.

McRuer, R. *Crip Theory: Cultural Signs of Queerness and Disability*. New York: New York University Press, 2006.

Taylor, Y. *Working Class Queers: Time, Place and Politics*. London: Pluto Press, 2023.

26

NOHOMO in the classroom: Queer ideas through and beyond Scottish classrooms

Dan Brown

It was embarrassing and uncomfortable, but I ate and left no crumbs. (Primary 7 boy, Edinburgh)

One of the first times I felt sickly aware of my queerness was one afternoon at my auntie's house while playing with my cousins. I had just recently watched the film *Yours, Mines & Ours*, a 2005 Nickelodeon film starring Dennis Quad, Rene Ruso, Miranda Cosgrove and Drake Bell. In the film Drake Bell's character is an artist, and wears a metal chain on his waist with sharpies attached so as to always be ready to create a new piece of artwork. Drake Bell's character was of course my favourite (for obvious reasons now), and so young ten-year-old Dan wanted to emulate this by finding a metal chain and attaching some mini sharpies to it. I spent the day chuffed with my new look, feeling like I was really embodying Drake Bell from the film, until my Mum caught me running up the stairs – 'What is that you're wearing?' she said and so I explained, 'Well get it off, do you know what you look like?' she replied. I obviously had no idea what she was referring to, so I answered as naive as a ten-year-old does – 'No?' She laughed and was looking at my auntie for reassurance at this point, 'It's what gay people wear, gay people wear chains on their jeans like that!' The idea of dressing 'gay' had never been placed on me until that moment. I was always aware that performing anything remotely feminine would always welcome name-calling and the fear of being called gay, so I never dared do that, but I was so confused how something as simple as having a belt full of sharpies made me gay. Drake Bell wore it in the film and he isn't gay? I just couldn't get my head around this fact at all I have been thinking about this moment from my growing up a lot during the process of making my own work 'NOHOMO'[1] a piece of dance performance for young audiences exploring the patriarchal constraints placed upon young queer working-class people and how we deal with the shame and internalized homophobia that comes from those experiences. The story I just shared is one of the earliest memories I have of feeling shame in regards to my queerness – perhaps because at this point I was becoming more self-aware that my sexuality maybe wasn't the norm. I think it is really easy to read the above story and feel a certain way about my Mum's parenting, don't worry I have gone through all of this myself. It's easy to go after the person, and yes it wasn't great, but we have to look at the wider context and social conditioning of how someone could react like this and that is what I aim to do with NOHOMO. In this chapter I am going to be talking about the development process of NOHOMO from its initial inception, to the research and development periods within primary and secondary schools in Scotland and finally finishing with the future life of the work. I am writing this chapter with the knowledge that my lived experiences are that of a white cisgender Scottish man and that I am aware that my lived experience is not the same as other marginalized working-class queers.

The Blackburn mentality

My whole upbringing has been spent in Blackburn, West Lothian, a small town based between Glasgow and Edinburgh. The town is mostly known for its most famous export, 'Britain's Got Talent' star Susan Boyle. For the first six years of my life I lived with my Mum in a rented upstairs four-in-a-block apartment. My birth father chose not to be part of my life and so my Mum became a single mother with one income from the age of twenty-five in 1995. When growing up, Blackburn was rated among the 10 per cent most deprived areas in Scotland according to the Scottish Index of Multiple Deprivation (SMID 2012), now according to the 2020 report it has fallen into the 5 per cent most deprived areas (SMID 2020).

Growing up in Blackburn meant growing up in very close proximity to violence and deprivation. There weren't – and still aren't – a lot of safe spaces for young people to go to for after school activities. Instead, we would share the streets with a lot of the Blackburn young team (gangs), where a lot of young boys would be swooped up under peer pressure to join said groups in order to survive, and if you didn't you would be a target. Luckily for me, I had friends who inhabited the protected space and so were able to vouch for my 'soundness' and I could be safe. A lot of the violence came from a heavy helping of sectarianism, a subject that I hadn't experienced until my Dad (my step-dad) came into my life when I was six. My room became Rangers-themed, I was taken to Ibrox for a stadium tour for my tenth birthday, I would collect the SPFL (Scottish Premier Football League) sticker album – I transformed from a young boy with a bowl cut into a shaved head, Rangers Football Club jersey-wearing Sid from 'Toy Story' look alike.

As well as all of the above external material changes, my growing up was also changing in terms of expectations that were placed on me. Toxic masculine expectations punctuated my teenage years: the expectation and demand of having to play football, the expectation and demand of having a girlfriend, the expectation and demand to not be effeminate in any shape or form. Growing up became filtered through this lens, and any deviation of this was met with revolt much like the anecdote about Drake Bell at the start of this chapter. I had to learn pretty quickly that in order to survive through living in Blackburn and going into high school was to fit into this expectation of identity.

In the 2017 BBC Three series *Queer Britain* (BBC 2017), a short series that explored queer topics in Britain from body image to racism in the queer dating scene, we meet John, a queer person from West Lothian who had previously lived in Blackburn before having to move into sheltered accommodation due to homophobic and violent attacks against him. In a segment during the show John and the presenter Riyadh Khalef visit his old house in Blackburn, the very same street I grew up on for the first six years of my life. He talks about how during his time living in Blackburn he had bricks and stones thrown against his windows and fireworks sent through his door. As they talk about this they are interrupted by a member of the community shouting 'faggot bastard' at John, to which John describes as 'The Blackburn Mentality'.

This 'Blackburn Mentality' is how I've come to describe living and growing up in Blackburn. It's the small town mentality, a community with a lack of diversity or even exposure to said diversity, and so small-minded ideals are passed down from one generation to the other, creating intergenerational community trauma. That is how I perceived my lived experience growing up in this small town. By the time I got to high school, supported by friends, I came out at the age of fifteen. I came out by sending a text to my Mum as I played video games upstairs, she thought it was a joke at first until I started to ball my eyes out. We had a chat in the living room, their main concern being how bad the bullying was going to get – it seemed that 'The Blackburn Mentality' had finally come for their son.

However, that never happened. Instead, I had a large group of friends, we would be together every weekend, go round to each other's houses and be with each other every break and lunch time – it was brilliant not a hiccup! When I came out to one of my straight male friends over MSN Messenger he said, 'That's fine you can hang out with us still because you don't look or act gay' – a win! Phew! When we went round to his parents' house, 'Don't mention the fact you're gay, my dad and my brother hate gay people' – okay? On reflection, it seemed that my acceptance from the straight males of the group was because I didn't 'act' or 'look' gay. Thank god my Mum told me to take off that stupid chain.

I took that advice head on and covered myself in head-to-toe Adidas tracksuits, I never wore anything bold and was judgmental of the other gay boy in the year below who would wear his Louis Vuitton scarf everyday to school – at least I'm not that gay! All of this to survive the 'Blackburn Mentality' rooted in patriarchy, propped up by sectarianism and dished out by generation after generation of the Blackburn community. Of course, I am aware that this isn't just exclusive to working-class communities – middle-class communities are also perpetrators of this behaviour – and not all working-class peoples' experiences are all the same. I am just using this analogy as to make sense of my own lived experience. As queer people in small towns, we learn very quickly that in order to live comfortably we must pass to survive. 'Like the Terminator, we learn to scan new environments for potential threats. Can we be ourselves? Do we have to tone down our mannerisms? Can we mention our partners? Is the bus safe for us? Can I come out in this new Job?' (Todd 2018, 44). Such questions run through our minds all the time even if we are only returning home for a visit.

NOHOMO 2020

After school I studied my Higher National Diploma in Acting at Edinburgh College (2013–15) and, later, my BA in Contemporary Performance Practice at The Royal

Conservatoire of Scotland (RCS, 2016–20). With a desperate need to remove myself from the 'Blackburn Mentality' I strived to get myself into the big cities, Edinburgh and Glasgow. In my final year of study at RCS I began making my degree show. During the course of the last four years of study I was focussed on exploring 'person' as a midpoint between playing a character and performing as yourself: 'One plays a role, then, to get out of one-self, to locate a form for one's thoughts and feelings' (Landy 1993, 39). As a vehicle to mediate autobiography in performance. My practice is rooted in autobiographical work and relating the micro to the macro, sharing lived experiences that audiences may recognize themselves within, 'Stories have an inspirational, educational and consciousness – raising potential and might then have real effects on the future lives or life-courses of their witnesses' (Heddon 2008, 34). Stories are inherently part of autobiography, and it is this ability of sharing one's autobiography to have an effect on an audience that I am particularly drawn to in the use of autobiographical performance.

Over the course of my final year I created a one-hour piece of performance called NOHOMO exploring my own autobiography growing up queer and my struggles with internalized homophobia and shame as a result of this. I utilized space and the Sci-Fi genre as a thematic tool to tell this story, placing myself in persona as 'Spaceman' covering myself head to toe in an astronaut uniform which masked myself from the audience in order for me to feel more comfortable performing my own autobiography, but also as metaphor for the masking of my queerness over my growing up as I have mentioned above.

The work was structured together by three video logs that would interrupt the performance to play on the projector screen behind me. In the video logs I would deliver text that referred to my autobiography growing up and moments in my journey such as the story I mentioned above about friends at school. The work was also heavily influenced by Joseph Campbell's *The Hero's Journey* to unpack masculinity and the expectations of young men, using the Sci-Fi genre and archetypes within those films to explore this further.

Unfortunately, on 15 March 2020, the day before I was due to premiere the work, we got the news that the performance was cancelled as a result of the growing situation around Covid-19. The performance was never presented and an audience never got to see it. Part of me was absolutely devastated but another part was relieved, relieved because I was extremely anxious about presenting it, especially to family members who were planning to come along. The work didn't feel safe for me to perform, it still felt extremely exposing, even though I had planned to mediate as much of myself from the subject matter through persona – there is only so far sticking a giant astronaut helmet over your head can take you. Over the course of the lockdown, I had a lot of time to reflect back on what worked and what didn't work. Would I ever get to perform NOHOMO again? Did I even want to present NOHOMO again?

Charting a new voyage

Graduating into a pandemic after studying an arts degree doesn't seem to be the best situation to find oneself and yet there I was. Floating aimlessly in the depths of overthinking and despair, would the arts recover? Would there be any more arts? What was going to happen to the world next? I think, like a lot of us, I was doing an extreme amount of doomscrolling over this time. Doomscrolling is 'the activity of spending a lot of time looking at your phone or computer and reading bad or negative news stories' (Cambridge Dictionary 2024). Consuming endless amounts of negativity all in order to stay connected. Over the course of the pandemic we were beginning to see a shift in the media and politics on LGBTQ+ issues: fears of drag queens reading stories to children, trans issues becoming a political football, and LGBTQ+ education in schools being called into question. It felt that we were going backwards in the move for equality for the LGBTQ+ community.

In 2022, LGBT Youth Scotland (2022) released a report: *Life in Scotland for LGBT Young People 2022*. They highlighted that there had been a reduction in the percentage of participants that rated Scotland to be a good place to be LGBT, decreasing from 81 per cent in 2017 to 65 per cent in 2022. They also reported that only 10 per cent of participants rated their experience of school for LGBT people as 'good' (Stonewall 2022). In response to this information and as a result of all the doomscrolling I had been doing, I began thinking about reimagining NOHOMO as a dance piece for young audiences. Alongside making performance, I work in socially engaged practices, mainly with young people in and outside of schools. I work as a collaborator with other companies – most regularly with 21Common and National Theatre of Scotland (NTS) who I have been working with since 2020. During this time I have made a film with learning disabled adults, worked as lead artist on 21Common's Disruptive Pedagogy within Glasgow and acted as video designer and a performer in 'Thank U, Next', part of the current NTS season (2023–4), touring across schools in Scotland. I am inspired by working with young people; they are unapologetic, rich learners and always changing. Within this context, my practice seeks to interrogate what 'work for young audiences' means when their world is more complex than ever before. What type of performance can we co-author? What type of performance is available to a young audience? What does risk mean? What does it mean to truly meet their experiences of the world? How can I forge new dawns for children's theatre in Scotland?

Launchpad 2023

In March 2023 I applied to Imaginate's Launchpad programme. Launchpad is a programme for early career artists who are interested in making theatre and dance for young audiences to have a space for research and development within the sector, from Imaginate, an organization in Scotland that is focussed on bringing theatre and dance to children and young people. I applied with my reimagining of NOHOMO as a dance piece for young audiences, with the aim of creating a scratch performance in October 2023, and as part of the creating process I would go into schools and run workshops with young people aged 12–14 years to get a grasp on their understanding of LGBTQ+ issues, the language that they are using to talk about said topics and their general viewpoints as young people ready to lead the next generation. It felt extremely important that if I was to make a show for young people, I had to make it with them – as they are the experts.

Over the course of my development time with Imaginate, I was able to run two workshop sessions with young people at a high school in Edinburgh – located within a working-class area according to SMID. This pairing came through one of the teachers at the school being involved with Imaginate and was keen to have us in the room. We worked with S1 in the morning (around ages 11–12) and then S2 (12–13) and S3 (13–14) in the afternoon. The workshop was delivered by dance dramaturg on NOHOMO artist Emma Lewis-Jones, facilitator Sally Charlton and myself – all of us queer. We opened the workshop with general introductions to us as facilitators and a short brief about the show and why we were there. I had imagined when writing the plan for the workshop that I would introduce that the idea for the show came from my own lived experiences of being an out queer person in a small working-class town. In a conversation with Emma and Sally on the train before we pulled into Edinburgh, we spoke about how this could potentially be very exposing for me and also the potential result of the young people censoring their answers if we had named ourselves as queer in the room. We decided not to out ourselves.

We first asked the class to create a list of ten positive and negative words to describe the LGBTQ+ community. We asked them to be bold and brave with their answers, swearing was allowed, homophobic language was allowed, but not to be directed towards other young people in the room. I believe that not naming ourselves as queer in the space helped the task as the young people did not refrain from the language that we were looking to interrogate. The show is called NOHOMO, a popular phrase used by people to make it clear that their actions are not gay in any way shape or form a phrase popularized during my own teenage years, so it was important for me to understand the language young people were using today. The most popular positive words were 'Happy' and 'Confident' the most popular negative words were 'Gaybo' and 'Zesty' with 'Faggot' in a close by second – still as popular as ever it seems.

The next task was a spectrum of difference, a task that involves the facilitator speaking out loud a variety of statements to the group, with one end of the room signalling highly agree and the other end of the room being highly disagree, the middle being not sure and in-between, the participants are allowed to place themselves anywhere on this spectrum, that is, a little bit towards highly agreed meaning they are still not 100 per cent sure. This task was completed by all three classes that we worked with on this day. We gave the cohorts statements that were rooted in stereotypes, generalized sweeping statements that were not authentic to the life of the LGBTQ+ community; we wanted the statements to be what you may hear online or in the school playground.

This exercise gave way to excellent discussion from all three groups. What we noted from group 1, the younger group of the three, was that some of their responses were stereotypically more homophobic. They also backed up a lot of their points with reference to survival skills. One young person in group 1 responded to the statement 'Gay men are masculine' by saying 'you lose your survival traits when you become more feminine'. Another responded to the statement 'Being masculine is good' by saying 'without men we'd have no babies'. It interested and shocked us how rooted the young people were in traditional gender stereotypes, however the older pupils rejected the task entirely questioning the use of the stereotyped statements, calling the statements out for their binary assumptions and in short dismantling the whole task – it's a facilitators worse nightmare when your task falls apart but what we found from it was a lot of resilience and hope. At the end of the task one young person in the older group said 'every question has been a stereotype, that's why we've stayed in the centre', another, 'the only problem with both masculinity and femininity is when they are taken to extremes', another, 'It's an over-sexualized stereotype that gay men are feminine or play the role of a hetero woman.' We left the session focussed on how we could combat the views of the younger group that we found were more aligned with the 'Blackburn Mentality'.

In our second session I wanted to work with the group on facts and statistics. We spent a lot of time in the previous session asking for their thoughts and opinions and I wanted to challenge some of their rebuttals with numbers. I adapted the spectrum of difference task by simplifying it to true or false, no in-between or unsure, the statements had to be either or because we were working with statistics. The statistics and numbers came from Stonewall's LGBTQ+ Facts and Figures part of their website (Stonewall 2022): some of the statements the young people found to be the most shocking include: 7/10 football fans have seen/heard homophobia in the crowd; 35 per cent LGBTQ+ staff hide at workplace; half of LGBTQ+ people suffer from depression; one-third of LGBTQ+ people participate in faith activity. The highest number of students were shocked at the fact in relation to faith based LGBTQ+ people. In response to our first fact 'Half of LGBT people (52 per cent) said they have experienced depression in the last year', one young person in the false tick box section asked 'Isn't pride about happiness?'

This question from this young person really brought to mind the weaponization and dehumanization of queer people in the media – the amount of mind numbing 'debates' on 'Good Morning Britain' around LGBTQ+ rights springs to mind. Queer people are painted with a stereotypical brush of rainbow joy and happiness, when it suits, yet within our community there is still a lot of hurt and suffering. Without queer education throughout schools, we continue to allow young people's queer content to be primarily shaped through what they find on their phones, and that makes me feel a little less hopeful.

With the older groups we worked to create masculine and feminine movements based on stereotypes of hyper masculine and hyper feminine movements, that is, a limp wrist or tensing bicep muscles, as performance material that I could take into the rehearsal studio with me to create a basis for the dance element of NOHOMO. What we found was a real discomfort in performing opposite traditional gender roles or gender in general with a few young people opting to sit out. One young person said, 'the movements we performed were not what you'd usually see these people do' in reference to creating movements based on gender, and another young boy said in response to performing feminine movements 'my brain just said DON'T DO IT'. Again, it seems although there is a greater understanding of the complexity of gender within the older groups there was still a large discomfort of playing into those for a short hour. Of course this is due to a plethora of reasons: high school social dynamics, hormones, embarrassment, boredom. But it does bring to question, what is the best way to break down those structures that hold discomfort and embarrassment to push through and discuss the above topics?

When creating the above workshops, we were fully aware that there would have been young people in the class, out or not, who would have found some of the conversation points extremely difficult to hear – perhaps especially from their peers. A teacher spoke to us at the end of the session to say that they were queer themselves and found it hard to listen to what was being said. We made sure that in all our workshops we let the young people know of websites they could go to in order to seek help if anything felt overwhelming for them in the room and that their teachers were also available to talk through anything if necessary.

At the October 2023 performance sharing of NOHOMO, we invited the S3 group of young people from a local high school to come along and watch the twenty minutes of performance I had made from my time with them. After a week of research and development in Dance Base in Edinburgh with Emma and costume designer Alison Brown, I had put together three small snippets that came from our time in school. At a feedback session after the session the young people were able to recognize the themes and topics of the show, everything seemed to click into place around why we had been running the workshops after they watched the show. Their learning was clicking together like a jigsaw puzzle, one piece was connecting to the next to create a full picture. They were also able to recognize some of their own movements that they had created as part of the workshops in the performance, which made them feel a real sense of purpose and understanding of why we had asked them to push themselves through their discomfort in order to make moments of performance.

Edinburgh International Children's Festival 2024

At the beginning of 2024 I was asked if I wanted to present a further work in progress (WIP) of NOHOMO to delegates at the Edinburgh International Children's Festival (EICF) 2024. With this opportunity came the offer of more research and development time – especially within schools. When I presented the work at the last event to a room full of peers in the industry and in education, one teacher mentioned that they thought the work would be brilliant for their pupils in Primary 6–7 (9–11 years old). With this feedback, I set out to run workshops in primary schools this time around as well as working with the older groups back at the previous high school.

With the primary school workshops I wanted to embed them more into the fiction of the world, drawing on Dorothy Heathcote's practice of Process Drama (Bolton and Heathcote 1995) by using drama and fiction to explore a topic or themes. This time we were based in another Edinburgh school, in a new area that wasn't working class with their P7 class.[2] I was joined by Sally again as another facilitator on the workshops. We had three sessions with this group of young people and so we created a three-part structure: (1) Introduction and visits to gendered planets, (2) Visit to a 'Gay' planet and (3) Utopia planets for Spaceman. Here we named the planet as a 'Gay' planet as we wanted to be specific to the journey of the Spaceman within the performance to make it clear for the young people.

In our first session Sally opened the workshop as I stood outside in costume awaiting my entrance. I walked in as Spaceman, moving slowly and not talking, only interacting through gesture movements – this immediately captured their attention and imagination. Later I took off the helmet and introduced myself as Dan, the artist making this work about Spaceman, again we did not refer to our queerness or my own autobiography. We told the group that in the show Spaceman has left earth because earth has been cruel to him because of his sexuality and so now he is lost in space trying desperately to find a place where he can call home and be accepted.

We led the group onto a task where we landed on a masculine planet, we asked the group what the name of this planet was and after a healthy democratic vote we voted on Venton. This planet, the group decided, was heavily protected by the largest army in the universe and had its own crypto currency. Notably, the majority of the girls in the group voiced their discomfort in being on that planet. We then created a movement piece that a masculine planet might present, similar to the task done with the high school group the year before, with one young girl responding, 'It felt like breaking the universe because it felt wrong / awkward.'

The next week we touched down on a 'feminine' planet, described only as this to the young people, and found that the young boys in the group were not particularly happy about this. It created a sort of male-versus-female dynamic but nothing that was malicious as the group was very respectful to each other and it was reiterated that all had value in being in a place that made them feel comfortable. A young boy reflected after presenting a movement piece on the feminine planet: 'It was embarrassing and uncomfortable, but I ate and left no crumbs.' Next, we touched down on the 'gay' planet. I put gay in commas this way because you're right, what exactly is a 'gay' planet? We're definitely on one now and it is always useful to unpack terms, meanings and stereotypes within the world of NOHOMO. We voted again on the name of the planet before me and Sally revealed what type of planet it was, and we voted on calling it ZiZiZoZa. We adapted the spectrum of difference tasks, asking the group to vote on laws that we could potentially pass on 'ZiZiZoZa':

- Gay men don't play / like Football
- Gay men and women are not allowed to get married
- Gay men are feminine
- Gay women are masculine
- Gay men and women cannot be parents
- Gay women dress like boys / wear baggy clothes
- Gay men must have a limp wrist at all times
- Gay women must have short hair
- Gay men aren't strong / have muscles
- Gay men and women should keep their sexuality a secret

This group was extremely articulate in preceding activities and so we wanted to challenge them with this task to have a deeper discussion on the matter. They were all extremely kind and understanding, with excellent knowledge and understanding of queer issues, with real lived experiences such as a teacher who had adopted a child with his husband. This experience reminds me about the beginning of my chapter with regards to my Mum and her lack of exposure to queerness and being stuck in the 'Blackburn Mentality'. If my Mum had this type of education growing up, then I believe my growing up would be different. If we foster young people to go into the world with love and compassion, then that is what they are going to give and get in return. At the end of the session, we had a short check out with any questions or feelings people had with regards to the day's session, one young person put up their hand and ask:

'Is this your show?'
'Yes'
'Are you Spaceman?'
'Yes, I'm Spaceman, I'm playing Spaceman'

She smiled with a knowing smile as she asked the question and nodded at my response as if to say 'I knew it', me and Sally also smiled to each other, a quiet moment of acknowledgment for us all.

In our final session we explored a Utopia for Spaceman, where would he end up? We discussed as a group that none of the planets we visited suited, they were all too stereotypical and didn't feel quite right. I asked them to respond to Carl Sagan's 'Pale Blue Dot' text, a reflective text about earth that had informed the beginning of NOHOMO back in 2019. They thought about how Spaceman might be considering planet earth from such a faraway distance at the edge of the galaxy. Here are some short responses:

A place where we thrive, where we live, somewhere we can think, somewhere we can watch the sun rise, just to set again. A speck of life, in this vast universe. This is our home, we must keep it alive while we can, because if we don't, this place can't be the little planet it's supposed to be. It's like if you have a baby, you want to cherish it and give it all your love. We must do the same for our planet. Don't wake up and think 'Oh I will never fit in'. Do you want to know something? Everyone fits in on our little, but big, pale blue dot.

I am looking back at my distant planet. It is my home but I do not belong. This is my home. This is my home? Is this my home? My home is space, this is where I belong. But deep inside I'll know where my home is, Earth. It might be dirty and wet and green but it's where I belong, where everyone belongs no matter if you're gay or lesbian or trans or bisexual. If you're black or white or you're something in between. Earth is my home, earth is my home. Earth is HOME!

Such responses reframed the work for me, I had always thought of Spaceman finding a new planet, it hadn't even occurred to me that he would even think to go home but it just made complete sense. In our week of research and development to prepare for the sharing, Emma and myself came into the rehearsal room energized by the work that Sally and I had done at Edinburgh. It felt that a new viewpoint and lease of life was given to us after working with this specific group of young people and I guess that is the beauty of it. I came into the rehearsal process with the idea of using a black hole as a metaphor for coming out, this terrifying, dark entity that if we go through, we have no idea what life is like on the other side – and I wonder if this sounds familiar to readers. What we soon realized was that the black hole in this story is a positive message, framed through the lens of the young people from Edinburgh. We looked at this stage of development with more hope. We named the evil spaceship that Spaceman is stuck on as 'Venton' as if sent away to learn masculine ideals and we named the black hole as 'ZiZiZoZa' the beautiful destruction that we need to send ourselves through to become who we really are on the outside.

NOHOMO in the classroom and beyond

The sharing at the EICF went extremely well and we were able to share our research and the work with an audience who all seemed excited about the future of the work. Spaceman has even made an appearance at The Merchant City Children's Festival as a walkabout character for a day. The aim with NOHOMO is to finally finish making the show and then create a pack of engagement workshops that we can go into schools with, as well as school groups coming along to see a performance of NOHOMO at a local theatre. It is important for the work and for our team that when we do tour the work that we are reaching out to the most vulnerable areas in Scotland like Blackburn, so we can break down the small town mentalities all across the country and foster a generation of young people who want to work through the embarrassment and discomfort and to ultimately engage in their world and communities with love and compassion.

Notes

1. NOHOMO was the original working title for the show. During the course of developing the work the show has changed names and is yet to be finalised.
2. We took this opportunity as we wanted to explore the workshops with primary school children, but it is my intention that for future workshops I would aim to work with primary schools in deprived areas of Scotland.

References

BBC. 'Out on the Streets | Queer Britain – Episode 3', 2017. www.youtube.com/watch?v=CDNA6Of7j7g. Accessed 24 August 2024.

Bolton, G. M. and Heathcote, D. *Drama for Learning: Dorothy Heathcote's Mantle of the Expert Approach to Education*. Dimensions of Drama Series. Cambridge: Heinemann Drama, 1995.

Cambridge Dictionary. 'Doomscrolling', 2024. https://dictionary.cambridge.org/dictionary/english/doomscrolling. Accessed 24 August 2024.

Heddon, D. *Autobiography and Performance*. Basingstoke: Palgrave Macmillan, 2008.

Landy, R. *Persona and Performance*. New York: Guilford Press, 1993.

LGBT Youth Scotland. 'Life in Scotland for LGBT Young People in 2022', 2022. https://lgbtyouth.org.uk/life-in-scotland-for-lgbt-young-people-in-2022/. Accessed 24 August 2024.

SIMD (Scottish Index of Multiple Deprivation). 2012. https://simd.scot/#/simd2012/BTTTFTT/8/-4.0158/55.9049/. Accessed 24 August 2024.
SIMD (Scottish Index of Multiple Deprivation). 2020. https://simd.scot/#/simd2020/BTTTFTT/8.946666666666667/-4.0158/55.9049/. Accessed 24 August 2024.
Stonewall. 'LGBTQ+ Facts and Figures', 2022. ww.stonewall.org.uk/cy/lgbtq-facts-and-figures. Accessed 24 August 2024.
Todd, M. *Straight Jacket*. London: Bantam Press, 2018.
Yours, Mines and Ours (2005) [Film]. Directed by Raja Gosnell. USA: Paramount Pictures.

Index

activism 14, 26–34, 96, 113, 173, 184, 213, 215, 227, 261, 264, 271, 276–7, 279, 282–283, 292
Adele Patrick 4, 13–15, 18
archives 196, 222–8, 234–5, 241
austerity 6, 5, 88

Black Scottish 5, 141–50, 189–98, 275–90
Brexit 41, 44, 79–82, 83–8, 90

census 3, 16, 25, 46, 51–61, 82, 84, 91, 129, 162, 288, 302
citizenship 5–7, 65–8, 80–5, 90, 134, 143, 177
class 3, 5, 7, 8, 10, 11, 13–14, 17, 31, 41, 52, 65–7, 72–73, 80–87, 91, 100–3, 122, 130, 135, 137–8, 156, 165, 178–80, 183, 184, 189, 199, 219, 220, 223, 279, 293, 295, 298, 301, 306, 308–9, 317–18, 324
colonialism/postcolonialism 15, 70, 73, 88, 133, 178, 217, 276–9, 285
countryside/Rural 2, 4, 36, 83, 91, 111, 120–1, 153–63, 179
COVID-19 6, 14, 71, 83, 110, 112, 216, 218, 222, 225, 241–2, 264, 266, 320
Creative Scotland 11

devolution 12, 88, 106, 107, 227, 280
diaspora 4, 178
digital culture 4, 17, 121, 215, 217, 222, 225, 247–59
disability 17, 25, 31, 52, 56, 60, 71, 88, 101, 293, 297, 305–15

Edwin Morgan 237–45, 247–8, 251, 253
Ely Percy 10, 11, 14, 15
Emma Roddick 2, 4, 6, 7, 8, 315
Equality Act (2010), UK 6, 7, 18, 27, 32, 34, 40, 43, 45–8, 59, 173, 176, 309
equality, diversity and inclusion (EDI) 6, 94, 305, 314

Equality Network 4, 7, 15, 26, 29, 34, 120, 234, 267
European Union (see Brexit) 84

feminism 14, 16, 39, 49, 51, 60, 72, 93, 96, 107, 110, 162, 179, 182, 185, 191

Gender Recognition Act 34, 35, 68, 95, 114, 162, 176, 261
Glasgow Women's Library 12, 18, 189, 197, 219, 227, 231

hate crimes 1, 7, 25–37, 42, 43, 86, 88, 106, 173–4
higher education 133, 275–315
highlands 3, 11, 157, 217, 225, 230, 305
homonationalism 15, 80, 84
housing/homelessness 8, 12, 65–66, 74, 132, 135, 137, 138, 156, 158

inclusive education 4, 8, 41, 88, 96, 129, 291
intersectionality 8, 51, 60, 109, 216–17, 292–3, 296, 302

Jackie Kay 144, 242, 245, 275–84

Maud Sulter 189–98
menstruation 93–103
migration 153–209
museums 225–35
music 69–70, 74, 105, 122, 192, 231, 249, 280, 282, 284

New Glasgow Boys 13
New Scots 11–12, 129–39, 177, 279

Patrick Harvie 4, 7, 8, 9
pride 9, 68, 70, 72–4, 87, 102, 113–14, 119–23, 127, 154, 162, 180–1, 225, 227–32, 292, 296, 299, 311, 323

provincialism 79–81

racism 12, 15, 28, 49, 61, 67–68, 80, 82, 90–1, 106, 114, 126–30, 135, 139, 177, 181, 190, 194, 217, 275–87, 293, 295, 298, 314, 318
referendum 6, 80, 94–5, 103, 131, 134–5, 139, 162, 280, 288
revolution 16, 65–75

Scots 4, 10, 14, 24, 190, 252, 255, 278, 285
ScotsGay 10
Scottish Trans Alliance 4
Scottish Independence (see Referendum) 79, 87, 88, 280
Section 28/2a 7, 8, 10, 40, 44, 73, 118, 129, 153–4, 161, 214, 291, 294
sexism 11, 12, 16, 80, 159, 298
South Asian 82, 89–90, 177–87, 199–288, 313

STEM 291–303
Sue John 4, 13, 15
Supreme Court Ruling, UK 7, 18, 27, 29, 32, 47, 106–7

teaching 31, 214–15, 276, 279–80, 284, 287, 317–28
Time for Inclusive Education (TIE) Campaign 4, 41
Tim Hopkins 7

Westminster 7, 40–1, 45, 48, 74, 80, 88, 105–6, 130, 137, 161, 215, 314
whiteness 73, 80–3, 90, 106, 111, 148, 186, 217, 221, 275, 276, 286–7, 314
Women in Profile 13

youth 26, 44, 86, 120, 138, 157–8, 160, 183, 216, 226, 231, 233–5, 275, 310, 321

zines 95, 242, 255